The gardener plucks fruits and flowers, but does not harm the trees; the bee sucks the honey but does not damage the flowers. In the same way the king should collect his taxes but should not cause any suffering to his subjects. One who kills the goat at best gets one meal; one who feeds it well can get milk for several years—**Kautilya in *Arthashastra***

Just as the sun extracts water from the reservoirs and gives it back in the form of showers, so does the ruler extract tax from his subjects and gives it back to them in the form of prosperity—**Kalidasa in *Raghuvansa***

We are aware that the landscape has changed significantly with implementation of GST. In every sense, this has been a monumental reform. Centre and States coming together and agreeing to pool in their sovereign power of taxation for common good of the country was unprecedented. 17 taxes and 13 cesses became one tax. Multitude of rates instantly became four. Almost all commodities saw rate reduction. Tens of returns were replaced by one. Taxpayer's interface with tax departments got reduced. Border checks got eliminated. Goods started moving freely across states, which saved time and energy. A truck started doing two trips in the same time in which it was doing one. Thus, dream of *one nation, one tax, one market* was realised.

—Speech of Union Finance Minister Nirmala Sitharaman
While Presenting 2019-20 Budget (Final)
to the Parliament on July 5, 2019

GST and
Micro, Small and Medium Enterprises (MSMEs) in India

(GST Law as on July 1, 2019)

M.M. Sury

New Century Publications
New Delhi, India

New Century Publications,
4800/24, Bharat Ram Road,
Ansari Road, Daryaganj,
New Delhi – 110 002 (India)

Tel.: 011-2324 7798, 4358 7398, 4101 7798
E-mail: info@newcenturypublications.com

www.newcenturypublications.com

Editorial office:
LG–7, Aakarshan Bhawan
4754-57/23, Ansari Road, Daryaganj,
New Delhi – 110 002

Tel.: 011-4356 0919

First Published: **2019**

ISBN: **978-81-7708-494-8**

Published by New Century Publications and printed at Milan Enterprises, New Delhi

Designs: Patch Creative Unit, New Delhi

PRINTED IN INDIA

About the Book

After missing several deadlines and overcoming almost a decade of political differences, Goods and Services Tax (GST) in India was finally rolled out on July 1, 2017. Undoubtedly, GST represents the biggest tax reform in the fiscal history of India.

The pre-GST system of indirect taxes was marked by multiplicity of taxes and rates at the Central and State levels which resulted in a complex tax structure ridden with hidden costs for trade and industry.

In sharp contrast to the earlier system, GST is an all-India unified, uniform and harmonized indirect tax system. The old system was mainly manual and opaque while the new system is technology-based and hence transparent.

GST subsumed a profusion of Central and State indirect taxes to create a single unified market. In all, 8 Central and 9 State taxes/duties were abolished to pave way for the introduction of GST.

The new tax is contributing to make India a seamless national market, boosting trade and industry and, in turn, economic growth. Common tax bases and common tax rates—across goods and services and across States and between Centre and States—are facilitating administration and improved compliance while also rendering manageable the collection of taxes on inter-State supply of goods and services.

Though a game-changing fiscal innovation, GST is a complex and evolving phenomenon. It is by no means easy, particularly for the non-experts, to understand its riddles and cobwebs.

The present work is an attempt to explain various aspects of GST in simple, lucid and non-technical language. It would be helpful for a cross-section of readers including teachers and students of economics, commerce, law, public administration, business management, and chartered accountancy. It will also serve the needs of legislators, business executives, policy analysts, entrepreneurs and investors, and others interested in understanding the basics of GST.

The book contains 41 chapters organized into 8 parts.

Part I, consisting of 5 chapters, provides conceptual clarity as regards taxation of goods and services and describes the pre-GST indirect tax system of India.

Part II, comprising 5 chapters, records the efforts of the Empowered Committee (EC) of State Finance Ministers in preparing the road map for the implementation of GST; enactment of the Constitution (One Hundred and First Amendment) Act, 2016; establishment, meetings and decisions of Goods and Services Tax Council (GST Council) up to the Thirty-fifth Meeting held on June 21, 2019; enactment of Central and State legislations for the roll out of GST; and the current Constitutional provisions pertaining to distribution of taxation powers between the Centre and the States.

Part III, containing 6 chapters, deals with the meaning and salient features of GST; components of GST; concept of supply and the levy of GST; input tax credit (ITC); exclusions, exemptions, threshold limits of turnover, negative list and composition scheme; and rate structure of GST.

Part IV, consisting of 4 chapters, spells out the provisions of GST law pertaining to certain special entities/sectors, viz. casual and non-resident taxable persons, charitable and religious trusts, real estate sector, services of goods transport agencies (GTAs) and electronic way bill (e-way bill) system.

Part V, comprising 5 chapters, is devoted to implementation, administration and technological infrastructure of GST. The topics in this part include registration, tax invoice, accounts and records, returns, GST payments, tax deduction at source (TDS), tax collection at source (TCS), reverse charge mechanism (RCM), refunds, assessment, scrutiny, audit, advance ruling, appeals, offences and penalties, anti-profiteering provisions, technological infrastructure and institutional set-up for GST.

Part VI, containing 7 chapters, examines the impact of GST on various macro economic aggregates and sectors of the Indian economy, namely gross domestic product (GDP), employment, industry and trade, prices, exports and imports, government revenues, and fiscal federalism.

Part VII, consisting of 7 chapters, is exclusively devoted to the interaction between GST and micro, small and medium enterprises (MSMEs). It covers importance of MSMEs, exempted and nil-rated goods and services, threshold levels of turnover for goods and services, composition levy scheme, soft tax rate policy and simplified compliance procedures for MSMEs, and sector-specific concessions/reliefs for MSMEs.

Part VIII has 2 chapters, one dealing with current challenges facing GST (including fraudulent transactions) and the other discussing the future of GST.

Bibliography and index also form part of the book.

About the Author

M.M. Sury received his B.A. (Hons.), M.A., and Ph.D. degrees in economics from the University of Delhi. He taught economics in the same University for 42 years. Specialising in fiscal economics, he has published extensively on the Indian fiscal system in recognised national and international journals, including *Small Industry Bulletin for Asia and the Pacific* (United Nations, Bangkok), *Bulletin for International Fiscal Documentation* (International Fiscal Association, Amsterdam), *Asian-Pacific Tax and Investment Bulletin* (Singapore), *Journal of the Indian School of Political Economy* (Pune), *Indian Economic Journal* (Bombay), and *Margin* (New Delhi). He was a Visiting Fellow at the International Bureau of Fiscal Documentation, Amsterdam (May 1989), a Fellow at the Indian Institute of Advanced Study, Shimla (1991-92) and a Visiting Fellow in the Department of Law and Management, University of Mauritius, Mauritius (September-October, 2000). He was Economic Adviser, First Delhi State Finance Commission (1996-97).

Contents

About the Book .... vii-viii
About the Author viii
Preface .... xviii-xx
Abbreviations/Acronyms Related to GST .... xxi-xxii
Unit and Currency Conversion Table xxiii

Part I: Taxation of Goods and Services in India Prior to the Introduction of GST

1. Taxation of Goods and Services: Theoretical Settings **1-17**
1.1 Tax Policy and Tax Bases
1.2 Determinants of Tax Yield
1.3 Objectives of Tax Policy
1.4 Direct versus Indirect Taxes
1.5 Specific versus Ad Valorem Duties
1.6 Operating Costs of a Tax
1.7 Excise Duties
1.8 Taxation of Services
1.9 Customs Duties
1.10 Sales Tax
1.11 Value Added Tax (VAT)
1.12 Incidence of Taxation

2. Union Excise Duties, Modified Value Added Tax (MODVAT) and Central Value Added Tax (CENVAT) **18-37**
2.1 Constitutional Provisions Regarding Union Excise Duties
2.2 Various Types of Excise Duties
2.3 Different Procedures to Collect Excises
2.4 New Excise Tariff Nomenclature
2.5 Administration of Excise Taxation
2.6 Revenue Significance of Excise Duties
2.7 Commodity Coverage
2.8 Excise Tariff Structure
2.9 Multiplicity of Excise Tariff
2.10 Simplification of Excise Tariff
2.11 Excises on Inputs and the Introduction of Modified Value Added Tax (MODVAT) and Central Value Added Tax (CENVAT)
2.12 Exemptions and Concessions

3. Taxation of Services by the Central Government **38-41**
3.1 Constitutional Provisions
3.2 Introduction and Widening of Service Tax
3.3 Service Tax: A Critique

4. State Level Sales Tax/Value Added Tax (VAT) **42-52**
4.1 Intra-State Sales Tax
4.2 Replacement of Sales Tax by Value Added Tax (VAT)
4.3 Central Sales Tax (CST) on Inter-State Sales

5. Problems Created by Multiple Taxation of Goods and States' Exclusion from Taxing Services **53-58**
5.1 Multiplicity of Taxes and Rates
5.2 Complexity of Administration and Compliance
5.3 Tax Cascading
5.4 States' Exclusion from Taxing Services

Part II: Early Thoughts, Preparations for GST and Current Constitutional Provisions Pertaining to Taxes

6. Empowered Committee (EC) of State Finance Ministers and the Road Map for GST **59-74**
6.1 The Genesis
6.2 Role of the Empowered Committee (EC) of State Finance Ministers
6.3 Summary of Recommendations of the First Discussion Paper (FDP)
6.4 Model GST Design Advocated by Thirteenth Finance Commission (XIII-FC)
6.5 Fourteenth Finance Commission (XIV-FC) on GST
6.6 Issues and Problems in Designing GST

7. Enactment of Constitution (One Hundred and First Amendment) Act, 2016 **75-85**
7.1 Constitution (One Hundred and Fifteenth Amendment) Bill, 2011
7.2 Constitution (One Hundred and Twenty-second Amendment) Bill, 2014
7.3 Constitution (One Hundred and First Amendment) Act, 2016: Main Features
7.4 Taxes Subsumed under GST
7.5 Phasing out of Central Sales Tax (CST)
7.6 Abolition of Cesses

8. Establishment, Meetings and Decisions of Goods and Services Tax Council (GST Council) **86-115**
8.1 GST Council: Constitutional Provisions
8.2 Guiding Principle and Decision-making at GST Council
8.3 Functions of GST Council
8.4 Meetings and Decisions of GST Council Prior to the Introduction of GST
8.5 Meetings and Decisions of GST Council after the Introduction of GST
8.6 Summary of Decisions Taken by GST Council in Various Meetings

9. Enactment of Central and State Legislations for Implementation of GST **116-121**
9.1 Central Legislations
9.2 State Legislations
9.3 GST in Budget Speeches of the Finance Ministers
9.4 Chronology of Events that Led to the Introduction of GST

10. Current Constitutional Provisions Pertaining to Distribution of Taxation Powers between the Centre and the States **122-138**
10.1 Distribution of Taxation Powers
10.2 Special Provisions with Respect to Goods and Services Tax
10.3 Restrictions on the Taxation Powers of the States
10.4 Exemption of Property of the Union from State Taxation
10.5 Exemption of Property and Income of a State from Union Taxation
10.6 Sharing of Central Taxes
10.7 Surcharges on Certain Duties and Taxes for the Purposes of the Union (Article 271)
10.8 Duties Levied by the Union but Collected and Appropriated by the States (Article 268)
10.9 Taxes Levied and Collected by the Union but Assigned to the States (Article 269)
10.10 Levy and Collection of Goods and Services Tax in the Course of Inter-State Trade or Commerce (Article 269A)
10.11 Goods and Services Tax Council (GST Council) (Article 279A)
10.12 Taxes and Duties in List I (Union List) of the Seventh Schedule not being Levied at Present
10.13 Taxation Powers to Local Governments
10.14 Powers of District Councils to Levy Taxes in Tribal Areas
10.15 Freedom as to Payment of Taxes for Promotion of any Particular Religion
10.16 Rationale for Constitutional Arrangements

10.17 Definitions
10.18 Summary of Constitutional Provisions Pertaining to Taxes

Part III: Basics of GST

11. Meaning and Salient Features of GST **139-148**
11.1 What is GST?
11.2 Salient Features of GST

12. Components of GST **149-157**
12.1 Central Goods and Services Tax (CGST)
12.2 State Goods and Services Tax (SGST)
12.3 Union Territory Goods and Services Tax (UT-GST)
12.4 Integrated Goods and Services Tax (IGST)
12.5 Compensation Cess
12.6 Rationale for Different Categories of GST

13. Concept of Supply and Levy of GST **158-173**
13.1 Supply is the Taxable Event in GST
13.2 Scope of Supply
13.3 Different Kinds of Supply
13.4 Location of Supplier and Place of Supply
13.5 Point of Levy and Time of Supply
13.6 Value of Taxable Supply
13.7 Stock Transfers

14. Input Tax Credit (ITC) **174-190**
14.1 What is Input?
14.2 Input Tax
14.3 Input Tax Credit (ITC)
14.4 Eligibility and Conditions for Availing ITC
14.5 Non-availability of ITC in Certain Cases
14.6 Apportionment of ITC
14.7 Input Tax Credit for Capital Goods
14.8 Input Service Distributor (ISD)
14.9 ITC in Case of Inverted Duty Structure (IDC)
14.10 ITC on Job Work
14.11 ITC on Transfer of Business
14.12 Prescribed Order of Cross Utilization of ITC
14.13 Invoice Matching for ITC
14.14 Hypothetical Numerical Examples to Explain the Working of CGST, SGST, IGST and ITC

14.15 What is the Rationale for ITC?

15. Exclusions, Exemptions, Threshold Limits of Turnover, Negative List, and Composition Levy Scheme **191-194**
15.1 Scope of GST
15.2 Goods outside the Purview of GST (Exclusions)
15.3 Goods within the Purview of GST but Currently Kept in Abeyance
15.4 Goods and Services Exempted from GST
15.5 Goods and Services Supplied by Businesses within Prescribed Threshold Limits of Aggregate Turnover
15.6 Activities or Transactions which Are Treated Neither as a Supply of Goods nor a Supply of Services
15.7 Composition Levy Scheme

16. Rate Structure of GST **195-208**
16.1 Determination of the Revenue Neutral Rate (RNR)
16.2 GST Council Decisions on Rate Structure
16.3 Rate Structure of GST on Goods
16.4 Rate Structure of GST on Services
16.5 Downward Revision of Rates in the Twenty-third Meeting of the GST Council
16.6 Downward Revision of Rates in the Twenty-eighth Meeting of the GST Council
16.7 Downward Rate Revision by Thirty-first Meeting of the GST Council
16.8 Dual Rate on Lotteries
16.9 GST Rate on Electronic Vehicles (EVs)

Part IV: GST on Certain Special Entities/Sectors

17. GST on Casual and Non-resident Taxable Persons **209-213**
17.1 GST on Casual Taxable Persons
17.2 GST on Non-resident Taxable Person

18. GST on Charitable and Religious Trusts **214-217**
18.1 Conditions for GST Exemption
18.2 Nature of Exemptions
18.3 GST on Management of Educational Institutions by Charitable Trusts
18.4 GST on Hospital Managed by Charitable Trusts
18.5 Other Cases

19. GST on Real Estate Sector 218-220
19.1 GST on Real Estate Transactions Prior to the Decisions of Thirty-third Meeting of the GST Council
19.2 Decisions Taken at the Thirty-third Meeting of GST Council
19.3 Decisions Taken at the Thirty-fourth Meeting of GST Council

20. Services of Goods Transport Agencies (GTAs) and Electronic Way Bill (E-way Bill) System 221-226
20.1 Services of Goods Transport Agencies (GTAs)
20.2 Electronic Way Bill [E-Way Bill (EWB)]

Part V: Implementation, Administration and Technological Infrastructure of GST

21. Registration, Tax Invoice, Accounts and Records, and Returns 227-239
21.1 Registration for GST
21.2 Tax Invoice, Credit and Debit Notes
21.3 Accounts and Records
21.4 Filing of Returns
21.5 Compliance Controversy

22. GST Payments, Tax Deduction at Source (TDS), Tax Collection at Source (TCS), Reverse Charge Mechanism (RCM) and Refunds 240-254
22.1 GST Payments
22.2 Tax Deduction at Source (TDS)
22.3 Tax Collection at Source (TCS)
22.4 Reverse Charge Mechanism (RCM)
22.5 Refunds

23. Assessment, Scrutiny, Audit, Advance Ruling, Appeals, and Offences and Penalties 255-261
23.1 Assessment of Tax Payable
23.2 Scrutiny of Returns
23.3 Audit of Registered Persons
23.4 Inspection, Search, Seizure and Arrest
23.5 Demands and Recovery (and Limitation Period)
23.6 Advance Ruling
23.7 Appeals and Revisions (Dispute Resolution Mechanism)
23.8 Offences and Penalties

24. Anti-profiteering Provisions 262-268
24.1 Consumer Protection in India

24.2 CGST Act, 2017 on Anti-profiteering
24.3 Institutional Mechanism for Anti-profiteering

25. Technological Infrastructure and Institutional Set-up for GST 269-274
25.1 Goods and Services Tax Network (GSTN)
25.2 Ministry of Finance
25.3 National Academy of Customs, Excise and Narcotics (NACEN)
25.4 Serious Frauds Investigation Office (SFIO)

Part VI: Impact of GST on the Indian Economy

26. GST: An All-India Unified, Uniform and Harmonized Indirect Tax System 275-280
26.1 From Fragmented to Unified Indirect Tax System
26.2 From Differing to Uniform Tax Practices
26.3 From Tax Rivalry to Tax Harmony

27. GST, Gross Domestic Product (GDP), Employment Generation and Formalization of the Economy 281-284
27.1 GST and GDP Growth
27.2 GST and Employment Generation
27.3 GST and Formalization of the Economy
27.4 GST and Black Money

28. GST, Industry and Trade 285-288
28.1 Unified, Uniform and Harmonized Indirect Tax System
28.2 One-country, One-tax, and One-market
28.3 Absence of Tax Cascading
28.4 Hassles-free Movement of Goods
28.5 Easy Compliance
28.6 Reduced Interface between Taxpayer and Tax Collector

29. GST and Prices 289-292
29.1 Why Prices Have Not Increased Post-GST?
29.2 Pre- and Post-GST Indirect Tax Burden
29.3 Relief in Overall Tax Burden

30. GST, Exports and Imports 293-300
30.1 GST and Exports
30.2 GST and Imports

31. GST and Government Revenues 301-303
31.1 Reduction in Operating Costs
31.2 Controls on Leakages and Revenue Efficiency
31.3 Abolition of Central Cesses
31.4 Inclusion of Services in the Tax Base
31.5 States' Share in IGST on Imports
31.6 Compensation Provisions

32. GST and the Changed Landscape of Fiscal Federalism in India 304-310
32.1 From Mutually Exclusive to Concurrent Powers of Taxation
32.2 Compensation to States for the Loss of Revenue Due to GST Implementation
32.3 Constitutional Provisions and the Law for Compensation to States
32.4 GST Compensation Cess
32.5 GST and Co-operative Federalism
32.6 Enhanced Need for Co-operative Federalism in the 21st Century

Part VII: GST-MSMEs Interface

33. Why Are MSMEs Important in the Indian Economy? 311-319
33.1 Estimated Number of MSMEs
33.2 Share of MSMEs in Gross Domestic Product (GDP)
33.3 Estimated Employment in MSMEs
33.4 Social Face of MSMEs
33.5 Advantages of MSMEs
33.6 Nature of MSMEs
33.7 GST and the Ministry of MSMEs

34. Goods and Services Exempted from GST 320-322
34.1 Constitutional and Legal Provisions
34.2 Classification of Exemptions
34.3 Kinds of Exemptions

35. Goods and Services Supplied by Businesses within Prescribed Threshold Limits of Aggregate Turnover 323-325
35.1 Purpose of Threshold Limit of Aggregate Turnover:
35.2 Methodology to Compute Aggregate Turnover
35.3 Provisions Prior to April 1, 2019
35.4 Provisions Effective April 1, 2019
35.5 To Be or Not to Be

36. Composition Levy Scheme for MSMEs 326-332
36.1 What is Composition Scheme under GST?
36.2 Who Can Opt for Composition Scheme?
36.3 Persons Not Eligible for Composition Scheme
36.4 Conditions for Availing Composition Scheme
36.5 How to Opt for Composition Scheme?
36.6 How to Withdraw from Composition Scheme?
36.7 Tax Payment under Composition Scheme
36.8 Returns, Accounts and Records under Composition Scheme
36.9 Advantages and Disadvantages of Composition Scheme

37. Soft Tax Rate Policy for MSMEs 333-334
37.1 Soft Tax Rate Policy in Relation to Goods
37.2 Soft Tax Rate Policy in Relation to Services

38. Simplified Compliance Procedures for MSMEs 335-336
38.1 Simplified Return Filing
38.2 GST on Advances Received
38.3 Other Trade-friendly Measures for MSMEs

39. Sector-specific Concessions and Reliefs 337-338
39.1 Handicrafts
39.2 Textiles

Part VIII: A Critical Review of GST

40. Challenges and Issues Facing GST 339-345
40.1 Fraudulent Transactions
40.2 Need for Strong IT Infrastructure
40.3 Public Outreach and Knowledge Sharing
40.4 Progressivity of GST
40.5 Dispute Resolution Mechanism
40.6 Fiscal Autonomy of States

41. GST: An Incomplete Journey 346-352
41.1 Alcoholic Liquors
41.2 Petroleum Products
41.3 Tobacco and Tobacco Products
41.4 Electricity Duty
41.5 Taxes on Entertainments and Amusements

Bibliography 353-356
Index 357-362

Preface

The basic objective of tax reforms in any country should be to establish a tax system that is economically efficient, distributionally acceptable, and simple to administer. GST is India's most ambitious and remarkable indirect tax reform. Its objective is to levy a single uniform tax across India on all goods and services. Levy of GST—encompassing both goods and services—by the Centre and the States simultaneously in a large and complex federal system is perhaps unprecedented in global tax history.

Prior to enactment of the Constitution (One Hundred and First Amendment) Act, 2016, taxation powers between the Centre and the States were clearly demarcated in the Constitution of India with no overlaps between their respective domains. In other words, there were no concurrent powers of taxation (or joint occupancy of tax fields) by the two levels of government. The absence of joint occupancy of tax fields successfully minimised double taxation, tax rivalry between the Centre and the States, and duplicate tax administration.

Broadly speaking, the important sources of indirect tax revenue for the Centre were customs duty, excise duty (except on alcoholic liquors) and service tax. States collected the major part of their indirect tax revenue from tax on sales and purchases, excise duty on alcoholic liquors, octroi or entry tax, electricity duty and taxes on luxuries, entertainments and amusements.

In the case of inter-State sales, the Centre had the power to levy Central Sales Tax (CST), though the tax was collected and retained entirely by the originating States.

In fact, taxes with inter-State base and those in the case of which all-India uniformity in rates was desirable—to facilitate industry and trade—were vested in the Central Government. Taxes which were location-specific and related to subjects of local consumption were with the States.

In the pre-GST arrangements, the indirect tax system of India suffered from various disabilities like multiplicity of taxes and rates, complexity of administration and compliance and tax cascading (*tax-on-tax*).

The Constitution (One Hundred and First Amendment) Act, 2016 inserted Article 246A in the constitution which now confers concurrent powers to both Parliament and State Legislatures to make laws with respect to goods and services tax (GST). The dual GST imposes tax on the same taxable event—supply of goods and services—simultaneously by the Centre and the States. Both the Centre and the States are empowered to levy GST across the value chain from the stage of manufacturing to consumption. The credit of GST paid on inputs at every stage of value addition is available for the discharge of GST liability on the output, thereby ensuring that GST is charged only on the value addition component at each stage. This mechanism has ensured that there is no *tax-on-tax* on goods and services.

By amalgamating a large number of Central and State taxes into a single tax and allowing set-off of prior-stage taxes, GST has mitigated the ill effects of *cascading* or *pyramiding* and paved the way for a common national market. Introduction of GST would make India's products competitive in the domestic and international markets. GST is not merely a tax reform. It is also a reform that would revolutionize the way business is conducted in India.

Since major Central and State indirect taxes have got subsumed under GST, the multiplicity of taxes has been substantially reduced which, in turn, is expected to decrease the operating costs of the indirect tax system. With GST in place, the burden of Central sales tax (CST) has also been removed. The uniformity in tax rates and procedures across the country will go a long way in reducing compliance costs.

The Government of Prime Minister Shri Narendra Modi has placed a great deal of emphasis on controlling black money. This has been reflected in a series of measures taken recently. These measures can be significantly complemented by GST which has an in-built self-policing feature, and hence more effective in reducing corruption and rent-seeking. The complementary role of GST in curbing black money has at least two aspects. The first relates to the self-policing incentive inherent in GST. To claim input tax credit, each dealer has an incentive to request documentation from the dealer behind him in the value-added/tax chain. Provided the chain is not broken through wide ranging exemptions, especially on intermediate goods, this self-policing feature of GST can work very powerfully. Secondly, GST has a dual monitoring structure—one by the States and one by the Centre. Hence, there is greater probability of evasion being detected. Even if one tax authority overlooks and/or fails to detect evasion, there is the possibility that the other overseeing authority will catch the offender.

Introduction of GST from July 1, 2017 has concurrently empowered the Centre and the States to levy and collect the new tax. The assignment of concurrent jurisdiction to the Centre and the States for the levy of GST requires an institutional mechanism to ensure that decisions related to the structure, design and operation of GST are taken jointly by the two tiers of the government. Goods and Services Tax Council (GST Council) is the unique institutional mechanism for this purpose with constitutional force.

The introduction of GST has marked a clear departure from the scheme of distribution of taxation powers between the Centre and the States as was envisaged in the Constitution of India. GST has charted out a new course for fiscal federalism in India, focusing on co-operation between the Centre and States in deciding tax rates on various goods and services. Signifying the spirit of co-operative federalism, GST is a historic and game-changing tax reform. The introduction of GST has changed the landscape of fiscal federalism in India.

It is noteworthy that States are constitutionally entitled to full compensation for any shortfall in revenues on account of implementation of GST. The compensation formula entails a secular revenue growth of 14 percent for tax revenue of States (with 2015-16 as the base year) over the 5 years of the compensation period.

GST has been an initiative that has commanded broad consensus across the political spectrum. It has also been a model of co-operative federalism in practice with the Centre and States coming together as partners in embracing growth and employment-enhancing reforms. It was a long-awaited reform and its implementation has validated expectations of important government actions and effective political will to modernize the economy.

MSMEs sector has emerged as a highly vibrant and dynamic sector of the Indian economy over the years. It contributes significantly in the economic and social development of the country by fostering entrepreneurship and generating employment opportunities at comparatively lower capital cost than large industries. MSMEs are complementary to large industries as ancillary units and this sector contributes significantly in the inclusive industrial development of the country. MSMEs also help in industrialization of rural and backward areas, thereby reducing regional imbalances, and assuring more equitable distribution of national income and wealth.

In view of the crucial role of MSMEs in employment generation and development of the economy, it is imperative for the Government to make it easier for this sector to do business and comply with rules and regulations in force. In recognition of the same, relief to this sector in GST laws has been a priority area for the tax authorities. In fact, MSMEs sector is the pampered child of GST. Small manufacturers, traders and service providers have been given special consideration under the GST regime.

In short, GST has left behind an inefficient, complicated and fragmented indirect tax system. Signifying the spirit of co-operative federalism, GST is a historic and game-changing tax reform. Domestically, it will help improve governance, strengthen tax institutions, facilitate *Make in India* by *Making one India*, and impart buoyancy to the tax base. GST requires a very high level of compliance. The age of hand-written ledgers, account books, balance sheets and manual record-keeping is gone. Everything is now online—from tax payment to filing of returns and to claiming of refunds. Moreover, IT-based tax information has to be updated regularly.

The present narrative on GST and MSMEs in India is basically descriptive in nature with analytical and normative comments at some places. The work draws, in good measure, on the information furnished by various Ministries/Departments of the Government of India and other organizations, notably the publications and websites of the following: Ministry of Finance; Ministry of Micro, Small and Medium Enterprises; Ministry of Law and Justice; Central Board of Indirect Taxes and Customs (CBIC); Goods and Services Tax Council (GST Council); Reserve Bank of India (RBI) and NITI Aayog. Use of material provided by these sources is gratefully acknowledged.

New Delhi **M.M. Sury**
2019

Abbreviations/Acronyms Related to GST

AA	Adjudicating Authority
AB	Authorized Bank
AT	Aggregate Turnover
B2B	Business-to-business
B2C	Business-to-consumer
BCD	Basic Customs Duty
BV	Business Vertical
CBEC	Central Board of Excise and Customs
CBIC	Central Board of Indirect Taxes and Customs
CCI	Competition Commission of India
CCPC	Central Consumer Protection Council
CEIB	Central Economic Intelligence Bureau
CENVAT	Central Value Added Tax
CGST	Central Goods and Services Tax
CGST Act	Central Goods and Services Tax Act, 2017
CGST Rules	Central Goods and Services Tax (CGST) Rules, 2017
CST	Central Sales Tax
CVD	Countervailing Duty
DTA	Domestic Tariff Area
EC	Empowered Committee
EIC	Economic Intelligence Council
E-Way Bill	Electronic Way Bill
EWB	Electronic Way Bill
FC	Finance Commission
FDI	Foreign Direct Investment
FDP	First Discussion Paper
FIU	Financial Intelligence Unit
FRBM Act	Fiscal Responsibility and Budget Management Act
GST	Goods and Services Tax
GST Council	Goods and Services Tax Council
GSTN	Goods and Services Tax Network
GTAs	Goods Transport Agencies
HSN	Harmonised System Nomenclature
IGST	Integrated Goods and Services Tax
IGST Act	Integrated Goods and Services Tax Act, 2017
IGST Rules	Integrated Goods and Services Tax Rules, 2017
IP	Intellectual Property
IRDA	Insurance Regulatory and Development Authority
ITC	Input Tax Credit
LPG	Liquefied Petroleum Gas

MGL	Model GST Law
MIS	Management Information System
MODVAT	Modified Value Added Tax
MoF	Ministry of Finance
MSP	Managed Service Provider
NACEN	National Academy of Customs, Excise and Narcotics
NCAER	National Council of Applied Economic Research
NEFT	National Electronic Funds Transfer
NSDL	National Securities Depository Limited
NSTEDB	National Science and Technology Entrepreneurship Development Board
PAN	Permanent Account Number
PDS	Public Distribution System
RBI	Reserve Bank of India
RTGS	Real Time Gross Settlement
SAD	Special Additional Duty
SDI	Skill Development Initiative
SEBI	Securities and Exchange Board of India
SEZs	Special Economic Zones
SFIO	Serious Frauds Investigation Office
SGST	State Goods and Services Tax
TCS	Tax Collection at Source
TDS	Tax Deduction at Source
UT	Union Territory
UT-GST	Union Territory Goods and Services Tax
UT-GST Act	Union Territory Goods and Services Tax Act, 2017
UT-GST Rules	Union Territory Goods and Services Tax Rules, 2017
VAS	Value Added Services
VAT	Value Added Tax
VGF	Viability Gap Funding
WCO	World Customs Organization
WTO	World Trade Organization

Unit and Currency Conversion Table

Unit Conversion

1 lakh	= 0.1 million
10 lakh	= 1.0 million
1 crore	= 10.0 million
100 crore	= 1.0 billion

Currency Conversion

The unit of currency in India is Indian Rupee, symbolized as ₹. As per reference rate of Reserve Bank of India (RBI) for **July 3, 2019**:

US$ 1	= 68.87
UK£ 1	= 86.60
Euro (€) 1	= 77.72
Japanese Yen (¥) 100	= 64.00

Fiscal Year

Fiscal year in India runs from April 1 to March 31 of the following year

Pre- and Post-metric Systems of Currency and Measures in India

Metric system of currency in India was introduced from April 1, 1957

In the Pre-metric system, one Rupee was = 16 annas and one anna was = 4 paise

In the Post-metric system,

One Rupee = 100 paise

One mile = 1.6 kilometres

One yard = 0.9144 metre

One acre = 0.4046 hectare

Part I
Taxation of Goods and Services in India Prior to the Introduction of GST

1

Taxation of Goods and Services: Theoretical Settings

Taxes are as old as civilizations. Taxes are imposed so that a government may perform its traditional functions (defence, and maintenance of law and order), undertake welfare and developmental activities, and make provision for public goods to satisfy collective needs of the people. It has also to pay for its own administration. It needs financial resources for these purposes and taxation is one method of transferring money from private to public hands. Taxation is necessary because what the government gives it must first take away.

1.1 Tax Policy and Tax Bases

A tax is a compulsory payment made to general government without any direct *quid pro quo*. General government includes central, state, and local governments. Tax payments are compulsory and the benefits provided by government to taxpayers are neither direct nor proportional to such payments. Every tax is made up of two elements: a base, i.e. the object to be taxed and a rate structure, indicating how the base is to be taxed.

Ultimately, all taxes are imposed by politicians helped by bureaucrats. Tax policy pertains to: (a) level of taxation, i.e. tax-GDP ratio, (b) composition of tax revenue, and (c) use of tax incentives.

Tax policy is an important determinant of the investment climate in a country. Rates of direct taxes determine the incentives to work, save and invest, while the level and structure of indirect taxes influence the aggregate demand and thus the scale of operations on the one hand and relative prices of different goods and services on the other.

The base of a tax is the legal description of the object which is taxed. Tax bases, or what eminent fiscal expert Richard Musgrave calls *tax handles*, are numerous but the common ones are listed in Table 1.1. Broadening the tax base means application of a tax to a larger portion of the object already being taxed. Erosion of the tax base means narrowing of the tax base through special exemptions and concessions. A good tax base is one which can easily be measured and monitored. Thus, a realized capital gain is a good base for taxation as compared to an accrued capital gain.

It is the availability of tax bases that determines the nature of tax system in a country. Furthermore, it is the nature of the tax base that determines the final resting place of the burden of a tax. To quote Richard Musgrave, "Apart from the level and distribution of income, the availability of *tax handles* is related to the economic structure of the country. Thus, the administration of an income tax is much more difficult where employment is in small establishments. Profits taxation is not feasible until accounting practices attain minimal standards, and it is difficult if firms are small and unstable. Product taxes cannot be imposed at the retail level if retail establishments are small and impermanent. Effective land taxation is difficult where food is home-consumed, the agricultural sector is largely non-monetized, and land surveys are inadequate in providing proper valuations. On the other hand, taxation is simplified in a highly open economy where imports and exports pass through major ports and thus can be readily established by tax authorities". [1]

Table 1.1: Common Bases for Taxation

Tax/Duty	Base
Excise duty	Value (in case of ad valorem duty) and quantity (in case of specific duty).
Sales tax	Sales of business.
Customs duty	Crossing of goods over national frontiers.
Inter-state sales tax	Crossing of goods over boundaries of states within a country.
Octroi/terminal taxes	Crossing of goods over boundaries of local areas within a state.
Income tax	Income earned by an assessee during an accounting year.
Gift tax	Value of gifts made by an assessee during an accounting year.

A closed economy will have no customs revenue and an agricultural economy with small business establishments cannot operate corporation tax. The relative importance of various tax bases differs in different countries and it may change in a country over a period of time. In this context, Harley Hinrichs in his book *General Theory of Tax Structure Change during Economic Development* has mentioned the following five stages through which tax structure has changed historically as economies have developed.

- **First Stage:** A traditional society relies primarily on traditional direct taxes like taxes on land, livestock, water rights etc.
- **Second Stage:** Society breaks away from old ways and indirect taxes become more important, especially external indirect taxes (i.e. taxes on foreign trade).
- **Third Stage:** Traditional direct taxes decline relative to national income and governmental revenues.
- **Fourth Stage:** Domestic commodity production increases and internal indirect taxes (excise duties and sales taxes) grow rapidly to replace customs duties.
- **Fifth Stage:** Economy gains maturity and modern direct taxes like personal income and corporate profit taxes become dominant.

1.2 Determinants of Tax Yield

Amount of money collected from a tax or a tax system is called tax yield. If the cost of collecting a tax is deducted from the gross tax yield, the resultant amount is net tax yield.

Tax yield is determined by a host of factors, the following of which are more important:

1. Coverage of the tax.
2. Exemptions/concessions.

3. Rate structure.
4. Degree of tax compliance.
5. Penal provisions.
6. Administrative efficiency.

There can be other factors also, specific to particular taxes. For example, the yield from excise duties also depends upon industrial progress and the general health of the economy. Similarly, revenue from customs duties is affected by factors like import policy, availability of foreign exchange, and international trade climate.

1.3 Objectives of Tax Policy

Why are taxes imposed? They are imposed for a variety of reasons. Tax policy has a number of functions to perform and objectives to satisfy.

Apart from its traditional functions (defence, and maintenance of law and order), a modern government undertakes welfare and developmental activities and makes provision for public goods to satisfy collective needs of the people. It has also to pay for its own administration. It needs financial resources for these purposes and taxation is one method of transferring money from private to public hands.

Taxation is a potent instrument to shape and influence the socio-economic policies of a country. It is, of course, difficult to formulate a set of universally acceptable goals of tax policy because: (a) different countries are in different stages of economic development, (b) objectives of economic policy differ in these countries, (c) priorities of economic policy are different and (d) objectives and priorities of economic policy continually change with the changing economic, social, and political milieu.

Though the concept of an ideal tax system for a country is linked with the peculiar characteristics of its economy yet tax policy is usually assigned the following four functions in the stated order in a typical developing economy:

1.3.1 Resource Mobilization: The first and foremost objective of tax policy in a country is to raise resources for public authorities for administration and development. Taxes are the main instrument for transferring resources from private to public use. By designing an appropriate tax structure, resources can be raised from those who are holding them idly or squandering them on luxury consumption.

1.3.2 Resource Allocation: Scarcity of real resources in developing countries calls for their optimum utilisation. Since the composition of investment is an important determinant of growth rate of the economy, public policy must discourage the flow of resources to *low priority* areas so that they could be diverted to *vital* sectors of the economy. By imposing high tax rates on luxuries and other low priority items (such as motor cars, air conditioners, and jewellery), the government can discourage the consumption and production of such items, ensuring in the process release of resources for high priority sectors. Conversely, production of necessities of life and employment-oriented industries can be encouraged by offering tax concessions or even subsidies.

1.3.3 Distributive Justice: Distributive justice or economic justice is an important function of tax policy. Economic justice relates largely to distribution of tax burden and benefits of public expenditure. It is a component of the broader concept of social justice which encompasses, besides distributive justice, such questions as treatment of women and children, and racial and religious tolerance in a society.

1.3.4 Stabilization: Initial developmental efforts are generally marked by inflationary tendencies in an economy. Inflation, if uncontrolled, may thwart all development plans and bring misery to the poor. A reasonable degree of price stability should be a primary concern of a government's tax policy.

1.4 Direct versus Indirect Taxes

A direct tax is one the ultimate burden of which falls on the person on whom it is levied. In other words, it is a tax that cannot be shifted from the original payer to someone else. It is contrasted with indirect tax which can readily be shifted to ultimate consumers of the commodity or service taxed.

John Stuart Mill, the celebrated British economist of the 19th century, distinguished between direct and indirect taxes as follows, "A direct tax is one which is demanded from the very person who, it is intended or desired, should pay it. Indirect taxes are those which are demanded from one person in the expectation and intention that he shall indemnify himself at the expense of another". [2]

Direct taxes, like income tax, though administratively inconvenient, are preferred because they: (a) can be related to ability-to-pay, (b) satisfy the principle of certainty, and (c) create civic consciousness.

An indirect tax is one which can be shifted from the original payer to the ultimate consumer of the commodity or service taxed. Import duties, excise levies, and sales taxes are generally regarded as indirect taxes. Thus, an excise duty on cigarettes, levied on producers, is usually passed on to the consumers in the form of higher prices.

Indirect taxes (also called hidden taxes) are convenient to collect but lack equity attribute. They do not allow considerations for the personal circumstances of taxpayers as do direct taxes. It is not possible to grant exemptions or allow deductions or to have a progressive rate schedule. Indirect taxes are borne in relation to the consumption expenditure which constitutes a higher percentage of income for lower income groups than for persons in higher income brackets. It is true that incidence of indirect taxes depends mainly on two factors:

1. Selection of commodities for taxation.
2. Rate of tax on selected commodities

It is desirable that luxuries and comforts are chosen for heavy taxation with necessities of life either exempted or moderately taxed. However, in poor countries the demand for luxury items is limited apart from being price elastic. Conversely, the demand for necessities is vast and price inelastic, obliging tax authorities to extend the tax net to daily needs. This has a tendency to fuel inflation.

It is almost universally accepted that indirect taxes are inferior to direct taxes in terms of equity attribute. The distribution of indirect tax burden is often, though not always, regressive and even the poorest of the poor are made to contribute to public exchequer. The chief advantage of indirect taxes is that they are convenient to collect.

The distinction between direct and indirect taxes is nebulous. The definitions of these two types of taxes have been a subject of long-drawn debate in public finance literature.

Income tax, property tax, and payroll tax are generally considered direct taxes, although many economists believe that it is possible to pass on these taxes under certain circumstances. Corporate income tax, a supposedly direct tax, is known to be shifted to consumers in many countries. [3]

Thus, demarcation between direct and indirect taxes is ambiguous because of conflicting empirical evidence of tax incidence studies. Direct taxes can be shifted under certain circumstances while taxes on commodities may stick on the producers finally. [4]

1.5 Specific versus *Ad Valorem* Taxes

This classification is relevant in the case of taxes/duties on commodities. Customs duties, excise levies, and sales taxes on commodities may take specific or *ad valorem* form.

A specific or volumetric duty represents a fixed amount of tax on a unit of the physical quantity of the product.

Specific duty is generally preferred for commodities the classifications and sub-classifications of which are not numerous, i.e. the commodity is a standardised one, e.g. sugar. A specific duty is easy to apply besides having the political and psychological advantages of obscuring the actual ratio of the tax to the selling price. It is, however, price-neutral in the sense that price changes, if any, in the commodity do not affect the revenue yield. Specific duty is quality-neutral also unless differential rates are prescribed with reference to the quality of the product.

There can be many variants of the specific form of duty. If a flat amount per unit of a commodity is levied irrespective of the price range, it is a simple specific duty. It may be simple specific with initial exemption. However, if the flat amount per unit changes with the price range of the commodity, it becomes a graduated specific duty.

An *ad valorem* (according to value) duty is imposed as a fixed percentage of the price of the product taxed. This form of duty is preferred when a commodity has many classifications and sub-classifications, e.g. textiles.

An *ad valorem* duty is responsive to price changes and thus ensures an undiminished proportion of taxes in national income. The main problem in applying *ad valorem* rate is the determination of the tax base, i.e. valuation of production.

An *ad valorem* duty may be a simple one, a duty collected as a fixed proportion of the price irrespective of the price range. As a variant of this, the commodity in question may be completely exempted till the price reaches a pre-determined maximum level. When different duty rates apply to different price brackets of a commodity, it becomes a graduated or bracketed *ad valorem* duty. So long as the price remains within a single bracket, the rate of the duty remains the same. Generally, commodities in higher price brackets bear a higher duty rate and vice versa.

Sometimes, both specific and *ad valorem* duties are levied on a single item. This pattern is called specific-cum-ad valorem duty or compound duty.

1.6 Operating Costs of a Tax

These are made up of administrative costs plus compliance costs of a tax.

1.6.1 Administrative Costs: These are costs incurred by public authorities in administering a tax. These costs (also called expense ratio) include wages of tax officials and expenditures on stores and supplies for running tax administration. They are interpreted in terms of cost-yield ratio which means cost of collection expressed as a proportion of tax revenue. A lower cost-yield ratio is considered indicative of the efficiency of tax administration. Unusually high cost-yield ratio is a drag on the public exchequer. Thus, cost-yield ratios may be used to evaluate administration of competing taxes.

The concept of cost-yield ratio suffers from various limitations and therefore needs to be used carefully as an index of tax efficiency. The ratio depends upon the nature of a tax. Generally, cost of collecting direct taxes is high as compared to indirect taxes. The ratio is also affected by the nature of tax administration. If separate administration is used for each tax, the scope for scale economies is greatly reduced. Conversely, if a single administration deals with a variety of taxes of similar nature (e.g. all direct taxes), cost-yield ratio may fall due to scale economies.

Cost-yield ratio is also influenced by the nature of an economy. The ratio is generally high in developing countries which are in the process of evolving their tax systems. Widespread illiteracy and lack of accounting practices make assessment procedures extremely difficult in these countries.

Equity considerations may demand a tax system which is poor in terms of cost-effectiveness. Thus, there may be a conflict between cost-effectiveness and equity. Pointing out another limitation, G.K. Shaw has observed, "The cost-yield ratio provides a purely static insight into the efficiency of a given tax which may be misleading in terms of the potential dynamic evolution of the tax. Thus, for example, a tax in its infancy may have high costs associated with the establishment of the appropriate administration and collection machinery and yet its future prognosis may be favourable if it is progressively based or confronts income elastic demand conditions". [5]

It is noteworthy that reduction in cost of collection which leads to ineffective enforcement and hence tax evasion, is false economy. Similarly, employment of incompetent and/or inadequate staff can result in harassment of taxpayers and multiplying appeals and hence increased cost of compliance. Properly understood, the principle of economy requires lowest possible costs consistent with effective administration and existing level of facilities to taxpayers. While interpreting cost-yield ratio, account should also be taken of compliance costs which may differ from tax to tax.

1.6.2 Compliance Costs: Compliance costs refer to costs incurred by taxpayers and/or third parties in complying with a tax, over and above the tax payment made to public authorities. The third party compliance costs are those incurred by firms in discharging their legal responsibility as tax collectors, e.g. deducting income tax from salaries and passing it on to the tax authorities.

The following three types of compliance costs may be distinguished:

- **Money Costs:** These include payment for legal advice, fees to accountants or to valuers for valuation of property (for purposes of death duties, wealth tax etc.), cost of postage, telephone calls, travelling, books, and in some cases litigation.

- **Time Costs:** These include time taken to consult tax advisers, complete tax returns, and to travel to tax offices.
- **Psychic Costs:** These refer to the worries and anxieties associated with tax payment. [6]

1.7 Excise Duties

Excise duties are imposed by a government on commodities produced or manufactured domestically. They are also known as production taxes. They are collected from the producers of excisable goods.

Exemptions and concessions are an integral part of the excise system. Excise preferences and reliefs are given to promote a wide spectrum of socio-economic objectives. If used judiciously, such tax preferences can become an effective tool of economic change on desired lines. Thus, exemptions and concessions are necessary to ensure progressivity in the structure of commodity taxation.

1.7.1 Golden Rules of Excise Taxation: The Indian Fiscal Commission, 1921-22, enunciated the following five golden rules of excise taxation, which with necessary modifications seem to be relevant to this day.

1. Excise duties should ordinarily be confined to industries which are concentrated in large factories or small areas.
2. They may properly be imposed for the purpose of checking the consumption of injurious articles and especially on luxuries coming under this category.
3. Otherwise they should be imposed for revenue purpose only.
4. While permissible on commodities of general consumption, they should not press too heavily on poorer classes.
5. When an industry requires protection, any further necessary taxation on its products may, if the other conditions are fulfilled, take the form of excise duty *plus* an additional import duty. The latter should fully countervail the former and may be pitched at a higher price. [7]

1.8 Taxation of Services

Service sector is very wide in its range. It includes, *inter alia*, health care, education, social security, leasing, entertainment, credit rating agencies, telecommunications, transport, publicity and advertising, insurance, banking, legal and financial services.

From equity point of view, services should be taxed in the same way as goods. Taxation of goods and exclusion of services distorts the relative prices of goods vis-à-vis services, encouraging artificially the demand for services. In the process, the allocation of resources is also distorted. If tax is imposed on goods and not on services, a relatively high rate of tax would be required on goods to generate a given amount of revenue. If tax is imposed both on goods and services, a moderate tax rate can yield the given revenue. Administratively, taxation of both goods and services is desirable because it would reduce disputes pertaining to distinction between goods and services.

Like goods, services can also be classified into two broad categories: essential services (e.g. health and education) and luxury services (e.g. entertainment and tourism). The rationale for exemption/lenient tax treatment of essential services is the same as for essential goods. Similarly, luxury services should be taxed at a high rate like luxury goods.

1.9 Customs Duties

These are duties on the import and export of goods levied by a national government. They become payable when the goods cross the customs boundaries of the nation. Hence, they are also called border taxes.

Customs duties are probably the most ancient form of taxation. They are as old as international trade itself. Just as domestic production flows provide the base for excise taxation so also international trade flows are the basis for customs duties. These duties are levied either on specific basis (i.e. as a stated amount per unit of weight, volume etc.) or on *ad valorem* basis (i.e. as a percentage of the value of goods imported or exported). Customs duties can be classified into two categories: import duties, and export duties.

1.9.1 Import Duties: Goods imported into a country are chargeable to a duty. The duty may be a percentage of the value of the goods (i.e. ad valorem rate) or at a specific rate. Import duties are usually levied with ad valorem rates and their base is determined by the domestic value of the imported goods calculated at the official exchange rate.

Apart from the revenue function, import duties provide a protective barrier for domestic industries. There are two main purposes of import duties: (a) to raise revenue for the government (revenue tariff) and (b) to discourage imports in order to protect a nation's domestic industry (protective tariff) or to correct disequilibrium (deficit) in its balance of payments. Other measures to protect indigenous industries from foreign competition are import licensing, import quotas, and outright import ban.

A. Countervailing Duties: These are duties in addition to the normal import duties levied on goods imported into a country. The rate of countervailing duty is generally equal to the excise duty imposed on like items produced domestically. The argument is that normal import duty represents the desirable degree of protection to internally produced goods which are not subject to excise duty. When excise duty is levied or the rate of an existing one is increased, a corresponding enhancement in import duty is required to preserve the accepted degree of protection.

B. Anti-dumping Duties: Dumping is a practice of selling goods in a foreign country at a price below their domestic selling price, after allowing for differences due to transportation expenses, tariffs, and other cost justifications. Many governments view the activity as an unfair competitive practice and frequently expose those engaged in dumping to the imposition of an anti-dumping duty. It is imposed to discourage dumping. The tariff rate is usually the difference between the normal selling price and the dumping price.

1.9.2 Export Duties: Export duties are imposed on export values expressed in domestic currency. Export duties can become an important source of revenue when a country enjoys monopoly or near-monopoly in certain products in the international market. Thus, when there is considerable disparity between the domestic and international prices of certain goods, levy of export duties is justified to mop up a part of the profits of exporters. Export duty on an item is levied after considering such factors as domestic production, likely exportable surpluses, demand for the item in the foreign markets, changes in exchange rates, and prices prevailing in the international market.

1.10 Sales Tax

Sales tax is normally an *ad valorem* levy imposed on the seller with reference to the transaction of sale. On the basis of the stage of collection, sales tax is classified into: (a) multi-point sales tax, and (b) single-point sales tax.

1.10.1 Multi-point Sales Tax: As a multi-point levy, sales tax may be applied at two or more stages of production and distribution and becomes akin to a turnover tax applicable at each transaction of purchase and sale. Multi-stage sales tax is politically expedient. A given amount of revenue can be raised at a lower rate of taxation which also reduces the temptation for tax evasion.

The chief demerit of multi-point sales tax is its encouragement to vertical integration of production and distribution processes. Thus, it discriminates against non-integrated firms. Producers of finished products prefer to produce their own materials and components, and this tendency harms the interest of independent suppliers, particularly small ones. Furthermore, multi-point sales tax discriminates against those goods, and their consumers, which have to pass through numerous transactions. In view of these disadvantages, John Due has opined, "On administrative as well as economic and equity grounds the objections to the multi-stage form are so great as to suggest its complete rejection, regardless of circumstances". [8]

1.10.2 Single-point Sales Tax: A single-point sales tax applies to one stage, either at the manufacturing, or the wholesale, or the retail level. At the manufacturing level, sales tax applies to the sale by manufacturer of finished product and is similar to excise duty. At the wholesale level, the tax applies to the last wholesale transaction, i.e. purchase by retailer. The retail sales tax applies to the final sale which means sale to the consumer.

The main advantage of single-point sales tax is that it does not discriminate against non-integrated firms as does multi-point sales tax. It, thus, discourages vertical integration and promotes horizontal integration. As regards the stage of its imposition, the retail stage is considered the most satisfactory due to the following reasons.

1. Sales tax at the retail stage is collected when final sale to the consumer takes place. Thus, it avoids what economists call the *cascading* or *pyramiding* effect of a tax. The contention is that middlemen apply fixed percentage mark-ups to purchase prices and if the purchase price include taxes (as is the case if sales tax is imposed at manufacturer's, or wholesaler's level), the mark-ups will be applicable to the tax component of the purchase prices as well, a situation which must be avoided in the interest of the consumers.
2. A given revenue can be realised by applying a lower tax rate at the retail stage as compared to other stages because the margins of all middlemen are included at the final

stage of sale, meaning thereby the enlargement of the tax base at the retail stage.

3. The desired change in the ratio of tax to consumer expenditure can be achieved more effectively in case of retail-stage sales tax. This will be difficult at *other stages* because the margins of dealers on various goods, besides being applied to the tax component of the purchase prices, may differ significantly.
4. Sales tax at the retail stage can be shown separately from the price and thus made known to the purchaser, increasing tax consciousness among the taxpayers.
5. Expected changes in the rates of retail sales tax do not lead to changes in inventory position of the firms. Anticipated changes in the rates of sales tax at *other stages* may influence inventory decisions of the firms causing dislocation in trade circles.

However, retail-stage sales tax has its own problems, the chief being the large number of taxpayers in the form of small shopkeepers and scattered retail outlets. In developing countries, the problem of tax administration is more acute in view of widespread illiteracy, lack of monetisation, and poor accounting practices. From administrative viewpoint, this form of taxation is costlier and cumbersome, offering ample scope for tax evasion and corruption.

Sales tax at manufacturing or wholesale stage is administratively preferable because the number of taxpayers is small and readily identifiable. However, the problem of *cascading* will reappear. In fact, the farther we move from the retail level, the more serious the problem of *cascading* becomes. In short, the problem boils down to a trade-off between economic rationale and administrative efficiency. The relative weightage to competing objectives depends on political judgement and the economic circumstances under which the sales tax system has to operate.

1.11 Value Added Tax (VAT)

VAT, a fiscal innovation of early 1950s, has claimed world-wide attention as more and more countries are adopting it in varying degrees to reform their systems of commodity taxation.

1.11.1 Meaning and Measurement of Value Added: To understand the meaning of value added tax, it is necessary first to explain the term *value added* as used in economics.

Under the simple commodity production system of the olden days, goods were produced locally and in most cases, for local consumption. Normally, the producer him-self was the seller of his products. In contrast, modern system of production is highly complex involving acute division of labour, large-scale production, and a wide market for the output. The final product as handed down to the consumer does not represent the efforts of one production unit but a host of independent manufacturers, big and small. Firms buy raw materials, components, capital goods from each other and sell their products through a chain of dealers, wholesalers, and retailers. The value of the final product as it reaches the customer represents the reward of the services of various factors of production rendered at different stages in the chain of production and distribution. The final value is the sum total of values added at different stages.

The value added at a particular stage is measured through two alternative approaches: (a) subtraction method and (b) additive method.

Both these approaches are based on the identity that total sale proceeds of a firm from its output during a given period are equal to the cost of inputs, wages, rent, interest, depreciation, and profits. Under the subtraction method, value added is measured by deducting value of inputs from the value of output (O-I). If the cost of inputs is deducted from total proceeds, the remainder represents the sum of factor incomes plus depreciation. Alternatively, additive method adds together various types of factor incomes generated, and depreciation. In practice, subtraction method is considered more workable and therefore widely relied upon.

1.11.2 Meaning and Computation of VAT: VAT is a multi-point tax with set off for tax paid on purchases. It is collected in instalments at each transaction in the production-distribution system. It does not have cascading effect due to the system of deduction or credit mechanism.

It is a tax on consumption. The final and total burden of the tax is fully and exclusively borne by the domestic consumer of goods and services. It being a tax on domestic consumption, no VAT is charged on goods exported. It is an alternative mechanism of collection of tax. Value added tax is, therefore, a multi-stage sales tax levied as a proportion of the value added, i.e. sales minus purchases, which is equivalent to wages plus profits.

Value added tax is levied on the sellers of goods and services based on value added by their respective units. The base for VAT is determined by value added at a particular stage of production or distribution. In other words, inputs of a firm are not taxed. At each point, the firm is reimbursed the tax which it has already paid at the time of purchasing the inputs. Thus, there is no cascading effect. Meaning of VAT becomes clearer when it is juxtaposed against conventional turnover tax (excise duty, sales tax) which falls on the total value of the product at each stage of production chain and is called a cascade type tax.

As already noted, subtraction method is popular one to measure value added and hence to compute VAT. There are two ways to compute VAT according to subtraction method. Under the first method, called the sales less purchases or accounts procedure, the rate of tax is multiplied by the difference of output and inputs, t (O - I). Under the second method, called the tax credit or invoice procedure, the product of the rate of tax and input is deducted from the product of the rate of tax and output, t (O) - t (I). [9] The latter is more common in practice. The VAT liability of a seller under it is equal to the tax arising from its total sales minus a credit for the tax paid by it on its purchases. The seller charges full tax from his buyer but pays to the government the difference between the tax charged and the one already paid on his (seller's) inputs.

The VAT required to be shown on any given invoice is not the seller's VAT liability with respect to that sale but which he can collect from buyer. In fact, the VAT liability is determined only at the end of the taxable period when he takes into account all of his purchases from other taxpayers. It is important to note that the ultimate burden of VAT rests on the consumer. In this connection the Indian Indirect Taxation Enquiry Committee, 1978, observed, "Since the value of a product increases as it goes through successive stages of processing or production, the tax passed on to the successive buyers keeps increasing. The final buyer, i.e. the consumer, cannot pass the tax, nor can he claim tax credit, since he is not a taxable person under VAT. The intention is that the full tax on the product, though collected in instalments from producers at different stages, should be borne by the final buyer". [10]

One distinct advantage of the invoice method is its self-enforcing characteristic because tax credit for a firm is subject to the proof of its having paid the tax to its supplier. This feature of the VAT is particularly emphasised in countries where tax compliance is rather poor.

1.11.3 Treatment of Depreciation under VAT: There are three ways to treat the cost of capital goods whose use in the production process is spread over time.

1. Since value added is defined as output minus input, it is necessary to clarify whether input includes depreciation of capital goods. One interpretation is that it does, i.e. depreciation (also called capital consumption) is excluded from the value added so that value added reflects the sum of wages, interest, rent, and profits. This is called the *income variant approach* under which the base for taxation is *net value added* by each producer. The *net value added* is defined as gross receipts minus purchases of intermediate goods and depreciation. This corresponds to the concept of net national product in national accounting.
2. The second approach is to exclude the cost of capital goods from value added instead of granting allowance for depreciation over the life of capital goods, and is called the *consumption variant approach.* Value added is now defined as gross receipts minus purchase of intermediate products and capital expenditure on machinery etc. Since producers are allowed to deduct their capital expenditures, the base for taxation is restricted to the value of production of consumer goods only.
3. Lastly, it is possible that the cost of capital goods is not allowed to be excluded when they are initially purchased and no allowance is made for depreciation when they are used in production. Value added equals gross receipts minus the cost of purchasing intermediate goods. In other words, it is the sum of wages, rent, interest, profits, and depreciation. This may be called the *gross product variant* and is the most comprehensive form of VAT. It corresponds to gross national product concept of social accounting.

The consumption variant approach permits a firm to deduct purchases of capital goods (i.e. gross investment) while income variant concept allows it to deduct depreciation only. In this sense, the base for VAT is bigger under the income variant than under the consumption variant by the amount of net investment (gross investment minus depreciation). In brief,

Income variant = Gross receipts – Costs of intermediate goods – Depreciation.

Consumption variant = Gross receipts – Costs of intermediate goods – Costs of capital goods.

Gross product variant = Gross receipts – Cost of intermediate goods.

1.11.4 Benefits and Limitations of VAT: VAT is a multi-stage tax levied on all stages of production and distribution of a commodity. It is collected in instalments on the basis of value added at each stage of production and distribution of a commodity. It is a comprehensive levy covering almost all production and distribution in its fold. It is different from excise duties which, in many cases, are selective in nature.

Under VAT, each input is taxed only once. Since an input is taxed only once, VAT avoids cascading which is the chief disadvantage of the traditional system of excise and sales taxation. Excise duties, and multi-point sales taxes levied on gross output tax the same input repeatedly as goods pass along different stages of production. [11] This type of taxation encourages vertical integration of industries, a tendency harmful to the growth of small-scale sector.

Since the cumulative effect of input taxation is absent under VAT, the cost of production increases by the amount of tax itself. Thus, by preventing unnecessary cost escalation, VAT promotes competitiveness of domestic Industries in the world market and thereby generates favourable effects on exports.

Among the various limitations of VAT, the following are more common. VAT is levied on ad valorem basis and does not admit of physical output as the basis for tax liability determination. Excise duties may be imposed on ad valorem or specific or ad valorem-cum-specific basis, or even in the form of a compounded levy.

Ideally, VAT should be imposed at a uniform rate at all stages of production and distribution so that tax credit claims can be made easily. Excise duties, as also sales taxes, are imposed at different rates depending upon the nature of the commodity taxed.

VAT is more suitable under a unitary form of government, i.e. under a single tax authority for commodity taxation. In a federation where different tiers of government enjoy overlapping commodity taxation powers, VAT is difficult to operate due to tax rivalry and lack of coordination among federal and provincial governments.

A VAT regime is theoretically meant for a unified market in which the VAT levied can always be set off against taxes already paid, irrespective of the state-wise location of the manufacturing or trading entities.

1.11.5 Rate Structure under VAT: In its ideal form VAT should be imposed at a uniform rate or at the maximum 2-3 rates. The higher the number of rates, the more complicated the operation of VAT. To quote, "Experience has shown that the introduction of several rates complicates the administration of VAT considerably. The complication arises from the fact that the taxpayer is forced to maintain separate records in order to match inputs and parts of outputs that may be taxed at different rates. The difficulties are said to be particularly felt by multi-product firms. The easiest form of VAT to administer would be one with a single rate. For various socio-economic reasons, however, governments which have adopted VAT have found it necessary to introduce more than one rate, but the number of rates has to be strictly limited". [12]

VAT generally discriminates between necessities, comforts, and luxuries in a big way. Many necessities are either exempt or bear a very low rate of tax. Contrarily, luxuries are subject to a high rate of taxation. The underlying philosophy of this approach is that direct taxes in themselves cannot lessen economic inequalities and some degree of progression and differentiation has to be there to achieve the objective. VAT tends to be regressive if there is uniformity or limited number of rates.

1.12 Incidence of Taxation

Incidence in economics refers to the distributional effects of a fiscal measure. Thus, tax incidence means *who bears the burden of taxes?* More specifically, incidence of taxation refers to the final resting place of tax burden as against the impact which means the first place where a tax is imposed. The incidence of a tax is on the person who ultimately pays it, i.e. who cannot shift it any further.

Due to economic transactions, a tax percolates through many parts of the economy and the burden of it can be shifted, forward or backward, by the original taxpayer to other entities.

When taxes are imposed, disposable real incomes of the people get reduced. Real incomes may be reduced either because there is reduction in disposable money income (direct taxes) or because the prices of products purchased are enhanced (indirect taxes). To use the Musgravian formula [13], the disposable real income (DRY) of a household may be defined as

$$DRY = \frac{E - Ty}{P + Ts} = \frac{DY}{GP}$$

where E is earning, Ty is income tax, P is the price (at factor cost) of products bought, and Ts is the sales tax (or some other commodity tax) addition thereto. DY is disposable or after-tax money income, and GP is the gross (or market) price.

Changes in Ty operate on the earnings (as producers) side of the household account. Changes in Ts operate on the expenditure (as consumers) side of the account. Thus, an increase in income tax lowers DRY via an increase in Ty and hence a fall in DY. An increase in sales tax lowers DRY via an increase in Ts and hence in GP. It is clear now how disposable real income of a household is subject to both direct and indirect tax effects. The total incidence of a tax system on an individual is equal to the sum of tax burden borne by him as a producer and as a consumer.

For every rupee raised as tax, there is a corresponding reduction in the disposable real income of someone or another. Reduction in one's disposable real income is taken to be equivalent to the tax realisation by the government. Incidence analysis pertains to tracking down individuals or households whose real incomes are truncated when taxes are imposed. Incidence analysis deals with the diffusion of tax burden among different economic classes in a country.

Endnotes

1. Richard Musgrave and Peggy Musgrave, *Public Finance in Theory and Practice*, New York: McGraw-Hill Book Company, 1989, p. 595.
2. *Collected Works of John Stuart Mill,* University of Toronto Press, 1965, Volume III, Book V, Chapter 3, p. 825.
3. For United States, see M. Krzyzaniak and R.A. Musgrave, *The Shifting of the Corporation*

Income Tax, Baltimore: John Hopkins University Press, 1963; For India, see G.S. Laumas, 'The Shifting of Corporation Income Tax: A Study with Reference to Indian Corporations', *Public Finance*, Volume 21, No. 4, 1966, pp. 462-473.

4. For a detailed discussion on the distinction between direct and indirect taxes, see: (i) Ursula K. Hicks, "The Terminology of Tax analysis", in *Readings in the Economics of Taxation*, The American Economic Association, London: George Allen and Unwin Ltd., 1959, pp. 214-216; (ii) D. Walker, "Direct versus Indirect Taxes", in *Public Finance*, edited by D.W. Houghton, England: Penguin Books Ltd., 1972, pp. 349-375.
5. G.K. Shaw, "Leading Issues of Tax Policy in Developing Countries: The Economic Problems", in Alan Peacock and Francesco Forte (eds.), *The Political Economy of Taxation*, Basil Blackwell, Oxford, 1981, p. 153.
6. For details, see Cedric Sandford, "Economic Aspects of Compliance Costs", in Alan Peacock and Francesco Forte (eds.), *The Political Economy of Taxation*, Basil Blackwell, Oxford, 1981, pp. 163-173.
7. Government of India, *Report of the Indian Fiscal Commission* (Chairman: Ibrahim Rahimatoola), 1921-22, p. 87.
8. John F. Due, *The Problems of Tax Administration in Latin America*, Baltimore: The John Hopkins Press, 1959, p. 417.
9. Let output be ₹ 500, input ₹ 400, and VAT 10 percent. Then, t (0-I) = 1/10 (500-400) = ₹ 10, and t(0) - t(I) = 1/10 (500) - 1/10 (400) = ₹ 10.
10. Government of India, Ministry of Finance, *Report of the Indirect Taxation Enquiry Committee* (Chairman: L.K. Jha), Part II, 1978, p. 283.
11. It can be argued that double taxation of commodities can be avoided if excise duties are restricted to only final consumer goods. To compensate for the loss of revenue, rates of duty on final goods may be appropriately raised upwards.

    Several difficulties arise in adopting this approach. For one, certain goods are capable of being used as intermediate goods and also as final consumer goods as, for example, tyres and tubes. If tyres and tubes are exempted from tax, there is discrimination in favour of consumers who use them as replacement items. If these goods are subject to taxation, there is possibility of their being taxed again at the retail sales tax level, causing cascading effect. Therefore, it is not always possible to replace input taxation by tax on final output. Taxation of inputs is unavoidable and in a sense part and parcel of the indirect tax system. However, the harmful effects of this necessary evil can be lessened if appropriate methods are devised to allow refund wherever it is deemed necessary to do so. Value added tax is one such device whose scope (i.e., at what stage or how many stages) may be altered depending upon local conditions.

    Furthermore, it is administratively easier to tax inputs rather than final goods produced with those inputs. It is convenient to tax aluminium than articles made of aluminium or cotton yarn than cotton fabrics.
12. *Report of the Indirect Taxation Enquiry Committee*, *op. cit.*, p. 289.
13. Richard Musgrave and Peggy Musgrave, *Public Finance in Theory and Practice* (New York: McGraw-Hill Book Company, 1989), p. 240.

2

Union Excise Duties, Modified Value Added Tax (MODVAT) and Central Value Added Tax (CENVAT)

Prior to their subsumation under the GST, excise duties were an important source of indirect tax revenue for the Central Government. They were levied on a wide range of products of the industrial sector of the economy. However, the excise system was leaky (riddled with extensive exemptions) and characterized by multiplicity of specific and ad valorem rates.

2.1 Constitutional Provisions Regarding Union Excise Duties

By virtue of powers vested in it under Entry 84 of List I (Union List) in the Seventh Schedule of the Constitution, the Central Government was authorised to impose, "duties of excise on tobacco and other goods manufactured or produced in India except: (a) alcoholic liquors for human consumption, (b) opium, Indian-hemp and other narcotic drugs and narcotics, but including medicinal and toilet preparations containing alcohol or any substance included in sub-paragraph (b) of this entry". [1, 2]

To pave the way for GST, Section 17 of the Constitution (One Hundred and First Amendment) Act, 2016 substituted the following entry for the old Entry 84:

"84. Duties of excise on the following goods manufactured or produced in India, namely: (a) petroleum crude; (b) high speed diesel; (c) motor spirit (commonly known as petrol); (d) natural gas; (e) aviation turbine fuel; and (f) tobacco and tobacco products". (Table 2.1)

Table 2.1: Entry 84 of List I (Union List) in the Seventh Schedule of the Constitution

Before Constitution (One Hundred and First Amendment) Act, 2016	After Constitution (One Hundred and First Amendment) Act, 2016
Duties of excise on tobacco and other goods manufactured or produced in India except: (a) alcoholic liquors for human consumption; (b) opium, Indian hemp and other narcotic drugs and narcotics, but including medicinal and toilet preparations containing alcohol or any substance, included in sub-paragraph (b) of this entry.	Duties of excise on the following goods manufactured or produced in India, namely: (a) petroleum crude; (b) high speed diesel; (c) motor spirit (commonly known as petrol); (d) natural gas; (e) aviation turbine fuel; and (f) tobacco and tobacco products.

Petroleum and petroleum products have been constitutionally included as *goods* under GST. However, it has also been provided that petroleum and petroleum products shall not be subject to the levy of GST till notified at a future date on the recommendation of the GST Council. The present taxes levied by the Centre and the States on petroleum and petroleum products—excise duty/CENVAT by the Centre and sales tax/VAT by the States—will continue to be levied in the interim period. The five petroleum products which have been kept in abeyance for the purpose of GST are the following: (a) petroleum crude, (b) motor spirit (petrol), (c) high speed diesel, (d) natural gas, and (e) aviation turbine fuel.

Tobacco and tobacco products are subject to GST. In addition, the Centre has the power to levy Central excise duty on these products.

It is noteworthy that GST Council is entrusted to make recommendations to the Union and the States on taxes, cesses and surcharges levied by the Union, the States and the local bodies which may be subsumed in the goods and services tax [(Article 279A (4)(a)].

Apart from allocating taxation powers, the Constitution also provides for the sharing of certain taxes between the Centre and the States. Prior to the Constitution (Eightieth Amendment) Act, 2000, excise duties belonged to the category of taxes which *may* be divided between the Centre and the States (Article 272) and the subject matter of this division fell within the purview of the Finance Commission [Article 280(3)(a)]. In other words, the sharing of excise duties was permissive and therefore the States did not enjoy a constitutional right to claim a share out of the revenues from Central excises. However, successive Finance Commissions took the view that permissive sharing, contemplated under Article 272 was not only justified but even necessary in view of the growing financial needs of the States. Therefore, ever since April 1, 1952, the States got a share of the proceeds of Central excises. The Tenth Finance Commission fixed this share at 47.5 percent for the quinquennium 1995-2000. However, the Constitution (Eightieth Amendment) Act, 2000 substituted a new Article for Article 270 under which States were given a percentage share of all Central taxes and duties. However, the surcharge levied for purposes of the Union under Article 271 was excluded from the divisible pool. Moreover, Article 272 of the Constitution was omitted by the same amendment.

Pre-GST system of Union excise duties is explained in the rest of this chapter.

2.2 Various Types of Excise Duties

In accordance with the provisions of the Constitution, various types of excise duties and cesses were imposed by the Union Government on commodities covered by the Central Excise Act, 1944 and other Acts. Before they were subsumed under GST, the important duties in operation were the following.

2.2.1 Basic Excise Duty: Levied under Section 3 of the Central Excise Act, 1944, this was the main duty commonly known as basic excise duty. This duty was fixed with reference to the value, weight, volume, unit, length or area of the excisable goods. These details were given in the Schedule of the Central Excise Tariff Act, 1985.

2.2.2 Additional Duties in Lieu of Sales Tax: These duties were imposed under the Additional Duties of Excise (Goods of Special Importance) Act, 1957, which provided for the levy and collection of additional duties on sugar, tobacco, cotton fabrics, rayon or artificial silk fabrics and woollen fabrics produced or manufactured in India. These duties were in addition to the duties payable under the Central Excises and Salt Act, 1944, and replaced, by agreement with State Governments, the sales tax levied by them on these commodities. The net proceeds from additional excise duties were distributed among the States in accordance with the principles of distribution formulated and the recommendations made by the Finance Commissions from time to time.

2.2.3 Cesses: These were levied under separate enactments on certain commodities and the revenue was earmarked for specific purposes. For example, handloom cess was levied on fabrics to raise funds for developing *khadi* and other handloom industries and for promoting the sale of *khadi* and other handloom cloth. Cesses were also levied under various Acts on tea, jute, indigenous crude oil, paper, sugar, *bidis*, automobiles, vegetable oils, and television sets.

The Central Excise Act, 1944, was the main enactment under which duties were levied on different commodities. Under Section 37 of this Act, a set of rules known as the Central Excise Rules, 1944 were framed to implement the provisions of the Act. Another set of rules under the same section dealt exclusively with the valuation of the excisable commodities and was known as Central Excise (Valuation) Rules, 1975. The Act and the Rules were amended from time to time. Broadly speaking, the Act embodied the substantive law, and the Rules contained both substantive law and procedural matters.

Although the Central Government was empowered to levy duties on agricultural products also, it refrained to do so in view of the administrative difficulties involved. Therefore, the excise system remained confined mostly to the products of the industrial sector with the notable exceptions of tea and coffee.

2.3 Different Procedures to Collect Excises

Central excise duties were assessed and collected through a vast network of offices scattered all over the country. There were various procedures to assess and collect excise duties.

2.3.1 Physical Control System: This procedure, based on personal verification of production by excise officers, was the chief procedure to realise excise duties till it was replaced by a new system called self-removal procedure from June 1, 1968. Under the physical control method, excise control was exercised by the officers of the Excise Department who were posted at the factory to keep watch over the operations in the various departments of the factory to prevent illegal disposal of the manufactured articles. The physical control procedure was based on personal verification of production, storage, and clearance of excisable goods.

The manufacturers, however, were unhappy with this direct interference in the manufacturing process. Therefore, ever since Independence in 1947 they had been demanding abolition of the physical control scheme and its replacement by a system based on audited accounts. The Taxation Enquiry Commission, 1953-54, favoured the retention of the physical control system. It observed, "It seems to us reasonable for the

Government to ensure that for the period intervening between production and clearance the goods should be kept in a proper place and under adequate supervision. The procedure followed in India in this regard is also practically the same as that obtaining elsewhere. Physical supervision is considered to be necessary in such cases in almost every country". [3]

The organised sector, however, continued to build up pressure for the replacement of the physical control system and ultimately the self-removal procedure was introduced with effect from June 1, 1968. A few commodities were still subject to the physical control system including sugar, chewing tobacco, and matches.

2.3.2 Self-Removal Procedure (SRP): Under this liberal system, introduced in place of the physical control system, an assessee was allowed to take clearances on his own assessment of the duty liability without prior permission of physical checks by excise officers. This procedure was applicable to most of the commodities under the excise net. An assessee was, however, required to get his classification list approved by the excise authorities before effecting any removal. In the classification list the assessee detailed the description of the goods produced so that they could be categorised in terms of the rate of duty applicable to them.

In the case of *ad valorem* duties, the assessee was further required to submit a price list showing the prices charged along with discounts and deductions, if any. In essence, the SRP was a record-based system of duty collection relying on mutual trust and belief. Unfortunately, heavy evasion of excise duty took place under this scheme. Excise evasion under this liberal scheme was generally resorted to by following such malpractices as incorrect accounting of goods, undervaluation of goods, and flouting the conditions subject to which any goods could be exempted from duty.

2.3.3 Compounded Levy Scheme: This was another procedure for the benefit of small-scale sector and for administrative convenience. Levying of excise duties on small-scale sector was a major problem of the excise system. In many cases, small-scale sector accounted for a significant portion of the output of an industry and it became necessary to subject it to excise taxation. However, the procedures adopted for collection of excise from big firms were often found expensive and time-consuming when applied to small firms. This necessitated the adoption of special procedures suitable for small-scale sector.

Under the compounded levy scheme introduced in 1954, a lump sum payment was made on the basis of some installations, e.g. the number of looms in case of textile units. Once the compounded levy was paid, the producer became free from all excise formalities except to maintain a record of looms in operation. The scheme was applicable to small units producing *khandasari* and cotton fabrics produced on power looms. This system afforded considerable advantages to the small producers because they were saved from the cumbersome normal excise procedures and also by the fact that the fiscal burden under compounded levy was generally lower than the burden under normal procedures.

2.4 New Excise Tariff Nomenclature

The year 1986 was a landmark in the evolution of excise taxation in India. In that year a new internationally accepted harmonised system of commodity classification was introduced in place of the then existing antiquated system introduced by the British. The history of excise tariff classification dates back to the year 1944 when the Central Excises and Salt Act, 1944 was passed, consolidating separate enactments for different goods. This Act of 1944 covered 11 tariff items which were arranged in alphabetical order.

In 1960, the tariff items, the number of which had soared to 30, were rearranged in accordance with the sections of the Standard International Trade Classification (SITC). By 1986, the excise tariff schedule covered 137 tariff items and if account is taken of the sub-items, the number was well over 355 main classifications. The description of tariff commodities was based on the definitions of the Indian Standard Institution, and the descriptions and explanatory notes of the Customs Co-operation Council Nomenclature (CCCN). The domestic trade parlance was also relied upon.

On September 22, 1984, the Government set up a Technical Study Group to undertake a comprehensive review of the then existing tariff nomenclature. The Group drafted a comprehensive and elaborate tariff nomenclature broadly patterned on Harmonised System Nomenclature (HSN), fully corresponding up to 2-digit level (i.e. Chapter level) in respect of 82 of the effective 96 chapters in the HSN. It also suggested that the new tariff should be provided for by a separate Act to be called the Central Excise Tariff Act in place of the then existing system of tariff being governed by the First Schedule of the Central Excises and Salt Act, 1944.

The recommendation of the Technical Study Group as regards the new tariff nomenclature was accepted by the Government and a new Central Excise Tariff Act, 1985, was passed for the purpose. The excise tariff based on the internationally accepted harmonised commodity description and coding system came into effect from February 28, 1986, ushering a new era in excise taxation. The Schedule of the Central Excise Tariff Act, 1985, described the excisable commodities and the rate of duty leviable on them. The new tariff was spread over 91 chapters and covered around 700 four-digit headings and 1,400 six-digit headings.

2.5 Administration of Excise Taxation

There was an elaborate administrative machinery for the collection of excise duties. At the apex level was the Central Board of Excise and Customs (CBEC)—a statutory Board forming part of the Department of Revenue in the Ministry of Finance. The Board, consisting of a chairman and five members, was responsible for the proper collection of customs and Central excise duties, and framing and implementation of related fiscal policies under the control and direction of the Union Finance Minister.

Under CBEC, there were 34 Commissionerates of Central excise at the field level, entrusted with the task of collecting Central excise duties. Each of the Commissionerates was headed by a Commissioner of Central Excise who was aided by a number of Additional Commissioners and Deputy Commissioners. A group of Commissionerates was headed by a Chief Commissioner.

For administrative convenience, each Commissionerate was divided into a number of divisions, each such division headed by an Assistant Commissioner. A division was further sub-divided into a number of ranges. Each range was headed by a Superintendent of Central Excise who, in turn, was assisted by a number of Inspectors.

In fact, the range was the basic unit in the administrative set up responsible for the proper assessment of Central excise duties and generation of the statistical information relating to revenue collection. The range was the primary unit which was in contact with the assessees and tried to ensure that the laws and procedures were properly followed by the production units.

To ensure that the goods were properly classified, assessable value correctly determined, and the duties correctly paid, each Commissionerate had an internal audit wing which was headed by an Additional Commissioner directly responsible to the Commissioner of Central Excise. The internal audit was in addition to the statutory audit conducted by the Comptroller and Auditor-General of India.

Each Commissionerate had an anti-evasion wing headed by an Additional Commissioner directly responsible to the Commissioner of Central Excise. The anti-evasion wing made checks on the basis of intelligence and information to ensure that duties were properly paid and there was no evasion of duties or leakage of revenue. In some Commissionerates, there was a separate Commissioner to look after the judicial and adjudication work. There were Commissioners who attended to appeals against orders passed by officers lower in rank to them.

Moreover, a number of supportive organisations under the CBEC undertook work of a specialised nature. Thus, there was the Directorate of Inspection headed by a Chief Commissioner which undertook the inspection of Central excise formations. The Directorate of Anti-Evasion had the responsibility to ensure all-India co-ordination of anti-evasion work. The National Academy of Customs, Excise and Narcotics was entrusted with the task of training officers. The Directorate of Publicity and Public Relations was responsible for printing and publicity. The Directorate of Statistics and Intelligence was responsible for compiling and updating statistical information.

2.6 Revenue Significance of Excise Duties

In the post-Independence period, the relative share of excise duties in Central Government's tax collections had increased precipitously. In 1950-51, excise duties accounted for a modest 16.8 percent of the total Central tax collections: ₹ 68 crore out of ₹ 404 crore. Within a span of 20 years, the proportionate share shot up to 54.9 percent in 1970-71. It declined to 49.3 percent in 1980-81 and further down to 42.6 percent in 1990-91. It stood at 36.3 percent in 2000-01 and 17.4 percent in 2010-11. It was estimated at 19.5 percent in the budget for 2016-17 (Table 2.2). A Government document noted the following reasons for this downward trend, "The buoyancy of excise has suffered because of a variety of factors including numerous exemptions and concessions which have given rise to substantial administrative and legal complexities. Recent years have witnessed an unprecedented increase in litigation". [4]

Table 2.2: Trends in the Relative Revenue Significance of Union Excise Duties in Gross Tax Revenues* of the Central Government: Selected Years

(₹ crore)

Central taxes	1950-51	1960-61	1970-71	1980-81	1990-91	2000-01	2010-11	2016-17#
A+B Gross tax revenues	404 (100.0)	888 (100.0)	3,206 (100.0)	13,179 (100.0)	57,576 (100.0)	1,88,603 (100.0)	7,93,072 (100.0)	16,30,888 (100.0)
A. Direct Taxes	174 (43.1)	290 (32.6)	870 (27.1)	3,004 (22.8)	11,025 (19.1)	68,306 (36.2)	4,45,962 (56.2)	8,47,097 (51.9)
B. Indirect taxes of which	229 (56.7)	599 (67.5)	2,337 (72.9)	10,175 (77.2)	46,552 (80.9)	1,20,297 (63.8)	3,47,110 (43.8)	7,83,791 (48.1)
Union excise duties	68 (16.8)	414 (46.6)	1,759 (54.9)	6,500 (49.3)	24,514 (42.6)	68,526 (36.3)	1,38,299 (17.4)	3,18,670 (19.5)

* Before transferring States' share in Central taxes.
# Budget estimates.
Figures in parentheses are corresponding percentages of gross tax revenues.
Sources: Government of India, Ministry of Finance, *Explanatory Memorandum on the Budget of the Central Government* (various years); *Receipts Budget* (various years); and *Budget at a Glance*, 2016-17.

Although excise duties were imposed on a large number of commodities, a substantial proportion of revenue was derived from a limited number of items. These high revenue yielding commodities included iron and steel, motor spirit, tyres and tubes, cigarettes, cement, plastics and refined diesel oil. It is noteworthy that many of the high revenue yielding items were commodities of mass consumption and therefore the burden of excise duties fell on all sections of society.

2.7 Commodity Coverage

As already noted, excise taxation in India was fairly selective in terms of commodity coverage during the pre-Independence period. However, the need for resources required for planned economic development made it necessary to rely on excise taxation for additional funds. This was particularly so in view of the extremely narrow base for direct taxation and the dwindling relative revenue significance of customs duties owing to euphoria for import restrictions and substitution. The scope for extension of excise coverage improved considerably as development efforts were intensified for the production of industrial goods that enjoyed a relatively large and stable domestic market.

The Taxation Enquiry Commission (TEC), 1953-54, after having studied the then existing excise system, made important recommendations in terms of commodity coverage. It recommended the extension of excise coverage to sewing machines, vegetable oils, woollen textiles, biscuits, paper, dry batteries, electric lamps, aerated waters, electric fans, glass and glassware, paints and varnishes, and ceramics. In the opinion of the TEC these industries had developed sufficiently as a result of protection and it was necessary to impose excises on them to raise the much needed revenue for financing development programmes.

Consequent upon the recommendations of the TEC, the history of excise taxation in India since 1954 was one of increasing commodity coverage. Cement, footwear, rayon or artificial silk fabrics, and soap were added to the excise system in 1954. In 1955, excise duties were imposed on paints and varnishes, paper, woollen fabrics, electric batteries, electric light bulbs, and electric fans. In 1956, the excise net was extended to vegetable non-essential oils, rayon or synthetic fibres and yarn, and motor cars.

With the start of production of diesel oil and other fuel oils at the new refineries in Bombay, excise duty was imposed on a variety of petroleum products for the first time in 1956. These included refined diesel oil, diesel oil, and furnace oil. In 1959, excise duties were imposed on asphalt, bitumen, and tar.

The early 1960s witnessed another big expansion in the coverage of excise taxation in India. In 1960, eleven additional goods were subjected to excise duties including aluminium, pig iron, silk fabrics, and motor vehicles. In 1962, the number of additional products brought under the excise system was sixteen and included, *inter alia*, soda ash, caustic soda, cosmetics and toilet preparations, glass and glassware, copper and copper alloys etc. In 1962, ten more products including gases, rubber products, plywood, jute manufactures, and iron and steel products were covered under the excise net.

In 1968, duties were imposed on radio-parts, steel furniture, leather cloth, and chocolates. The biggest expansion was witnessed in 1971 when 25 additional products including linoleum, ready-made garments, vacuum flasks, and pressure cookers were brought under the excise net. The process of covering more and more items under the excise system reached its pinnacle when Tariff Item No. 68 was introduced in 1975. Tariff Item No. 68 was a catch-all item which encompassed all goods not elsewhere specified in the excise tariff. This residual tariff item was abolished with the introduction of a harmonised system of commodity classification introduced from February 28, 1986. The large assortment of commodities under this head got scattered under proper heads in the new nomenclature of excise tariff.

The Tax Reforms Committee (Chairman: Raja Chelliah), 1991, identified many items which were outside the excise net but which could be considered for levying excise duty. Some of the identified items were butter and cheese, skimmed milk powder, spices, fertilisers, feature films, wood pulp, umbrellas, bicycles, toys and sports goods, buttons, and vacuum flasks.

2.8 Excise Tariff Structure

Once the commodities for excise taxation were identified, the next step was to formulate a tariff structure for various commodities.

2.8.1 Statutory versus Effective Rates: Rates of excise duty approved by the Parliament were termed as statutory or tariff rates. However, the Government enjoyed the power to exempt, by notification, any excisable goods from the whole or any part of duty leviable on such goods. In exercise of this power, the Government determined and notified from time-to-time the effective rates of duty. The rationale for granting such powers to the executive was that during the period intervening two consecutive budgets, necessary adjustments might have to be made to regulate exports, consumption, and prices of different commodities. However, the delegation of this power to the executive led to frequent changes in excise rates, creating an unsettling atmosphere for trade and industry and problems for the administration.

Moreover, since the notifications were technically not rules, there was no obligation to place them on the table of the House. Consequently, the Parliament did not always have the information on the variations made in the rates approved by it. The determination of the operative or effective rates of duty by executive decisions led to abridgement of Parliamentary control over the excise system.

Under the Central Excise Tariff Act, 1985, the Government was empowered to enhance the rates of duty specified in the Schedule of the Act through notifications. The increase of duty was subject to certain limits and such powers were exercised only in emergent circumstances. The notifications bringing into force such increases were subject to approval by the Parliament. The said limits were: (a) in case where the rate of duty immediately before the issue of notification is nil, a rate of duty not exceeding 50 percent *ad valorem* may be specified, and (b) in any other case, the increase in the rate of duty shall not be more than twice the rate of duty in force immediately before the issue of notification.

2.8.2 Specific versus *Ad Valorem* Duties [5]: In the early days of the excise system of independent India, the emphasis was on specific rates due to administrative reasons. However, the emphasis shifted to *ad valorem* rates when the economy started experiencing frequent spells of inflation. The 1970s saw a big shift from specific rates of duty to *ad valorem* rates. While introducing the change in the 1969-70 budget, the Finance Minister observed, "...*ad valorem* duties are more rational than specific duties whose incidence declines during periods of rising prices and increases when prices fall. *Ad valorem* duties can also act as a spur to reduction in costs and prices". [6] He converted the then existing specific rates into *ad valorem* rates on cement, vegetable products, electric fans, lighting tubes and bulbs, soaps, soda, and sodium silicate. The change of duties on paper and cotton fabrics into *ad valorem* tax was effected in 1976 and on paints, varnishes, radios, and tape recorders in 1977.

However, beginning with the 1980s, the tendency to shift to *ad valorem* rates was not only halted but reversed in view of an unprecedented spurt in litigation which mainly pertained to disputes over classification and valuation of goods for purposes of excise levies. As a measure to combat tax avoidance and evasion, the basis of duty was changed from *ad valorem* to *ad valorem*-cum-specific rate or specific rate on a number of commodities. Important commodities where the shift took place (with year of change given in brackets) were: flat glass, aluminium metal (1982), paper, aerated waters, motor cars, cigarettes, sugar (1983), paper boards, tyres for buses and trucks (1984), gases, tubes and flaps of tyres, and colour television sets (1985).

The Technical Study Group on Central Excise Tariff, 1985, made estimates of the relative revenue significance of various forms of excise duty. The share of specific duties (including the specific component of *ad valorem*-cum-specific duties) was estimated at

₹ 8,242.91 crore or 66.7 percent of the total estimated excise revenue of ₹ 12,361.35 crore for the year 1985-86. The rest of the revenue was attributable to *ad valorem* duties. Broadly speaking, specific duties accounted for two-thirds of the revenue and the *ad valorem* duties for the remaining one-third. [7]

The balance further tilted in favour of specific duties as the policy of conversion from *ad valorem* rates to specific rates continued right up to 1990-91. In this connection, the Tax Reforms Committee (Chairman: Raja Chelliah), 1991, observed, "As a result of this gradual shift to more and more specific rates over the years, the share of revenue from specific-rated items has increased from a level of about 46 percent of the total revenue in 1981-82 to 65 percent in 1986-87 and has currently (presumably 1990-91) reached a level of about 70 percent". [8] The Committee examined the advantages and disadvantages of *ad valorem* and specific rates of duty and concluded, "the advantages of having *ad valorem* duties far outweigh the administrative benefits derived by switching over to specific duties. In a system of comprehensive taxation with a wide coverage of MODVAT, it would be necessary to have by and large only *ad valorem* duties in order to ensure a rational system of taxation". [9] Following the recommendations of the Committee, a modest switch over to *ad valorem* rates was made in the 1992-93 Budget.

At the time of its subsumation under GST, excise duty was levied at specific rates on cigarettes, coffee, tea, sugar, beverages, mineral fuels, mineral oils, silk, man-made staple fibres, and iron and steel. *Ad valorem* rates of duty predominated for commodities including organic chemicals, pharmaceutical products, leather, footwear, ceramic products, tools and implements, machinery and mechanical appliances, electrical machinery and equipment, and miscellaneous manufactured articles. A few commodities, viz. cotton fabrics, paper and paper boards, were subject to *ad valorem*-cum-specific rates of duty.

2.9 Multiplicity of Excise Tariff

The excise rate structure was provided by the Schedule of the Central Excise Tariff Act, 1985, which included goods ranging from toys to nuclear reactors. The Schedule was divided into 20 sections covering 96 chapters. Goods falling under each chapter were divided and sub-divided into numerous headings and sub-headings. The statutory rate of duty applicable in respect of each item was shown against the appropriate commodity heading/sub-heading. These statutory rates were modified, if necessary, by Government notifications to determine effective rates of duty.

Prior to tax reforms initiated in 1991, excise taxation in India was an interesting example of the multitude of rates which were subject to frequent revisions. Numerous considerations contributed to the complexity of excise rates. The labyrinthine intricacies of the tariff often led to confusion and litigation amongst the taxpayers and revenue authorities.

Commodities such as sewing machines, water coolers, and bicycles, though on the tariff list, were completely exempt from the payment of duty. However, a host of other commodities were subject to a wide amplitude of excise rates. The rate of duty on necessities of life like food products (cheese, butter, vegetable oils), pharmaceutical products, and footwear ranged from 10 to 15 percent *ad valorem*. Rates of excise duty on semi-luxuries like washing machines, tape recorders, refrigerators, and colour televisions ranged from 25 percent to 40 percent *ad valorem*. Luxury items like cosmetics and air-conditioners suffered a high rate of duty ranging from 100 to 110 percent.

Most capital goods, classified under chapter 84 of excise tariff, were subject to duty ranging from 15 to 20 percent *ad* valorem. Some important items under this category were machine tools, cranes, agricultural machinery, textile machinery, printing machinery, calculating machines, automatic data processing machines, and other office machines.

Tobacco items were conspicuous by high rates of duty. Successive upward revision of excise duty on cigarettes was a notable feature of tobacco tariff in India. Upward revision of excise duty on cigarettes was almost an annual feature. No surprise that the commodity earned such nicknames as *annual hardy, old faithful* etc.

Broadly speaking, necessities of life were either exempt or paid a low rate of duty, semi-luxuries were moderately taxed, and luxuries and tobacco products stood out distinctly as high-rated tariff items. Capital goods were subject to a relatively low rate of duty.

2.9.1 Committee on Rationalisation and Simplification of Tax Structure (Chairman: S. Bhoothalingam), 1968: This Committee recommended, *inter alia*, a general excise duty at the rate of 10 percent *ad valorem* on all manufactured products. [10] However, this recommendation was not accepted by the Government.

2.9.2 Indirect Taxation Enquiry Committee (Chairman: L.K. Jha), 1978: This Committee also considered the problem of multiplicity of rates. It recommended a set of four excise rates. The Committee observed, "Instead of a pattern of which some product groups are very heavily taxed while others have remained either totally exempt or have been taxed at very low rates, the attempt should be to tax all consumer products, including those now falling under Tariff Item No. 68, at rates of 10, 20, 30 or 40 percent (cumulative), though some exceptional products may need to be taxed at lower or higher rates on special consideration". [11]

By suggesting a 10 to 40 percent range, the Committee virtually favoured a ceiling on excise rates. The Government disfavoured any drastic regrouping of the then existing rates. In his 1979-80 budget speech the Finance Minister observed, "A major restructuring of the excise tariff has to be ruled out in view of the need for resources and on other pragmatic considerations. Also, there is reason to apprehend that a major departure from the present pattern of excise taxation may upset the balance between different sectors of production". [12]

2.9.3 Technical Study Group on Excise Tariff (Chairman: J. Dutta), 1985: The Study Group favoured a drastic reduction in the number of duty rates to simply duty collection and compliance. The group recommended a band of five duty rates: middle rate, two rates below it and two above. Besides this, it also suggested a *zero rate* category. The middle rate (M) was defined to represent overall average incidence of excise duties. The two rates below this middle rate (L1 and L2) were suggested for adoption for inputs and important items of real mass consumption. The two rates in the upper scale (H1 and H2) could be applied to a few inputs, consumer durables and items consumed largely by the rich. The *zero rate* was recommended for products which deserved exceptional treatment on economic or social or administrative considerations.

The Group attempted only a broad and vague exercise of rate levels in terms of middle, below the middle, and above the middle rates of duty without specifying, even on a tentative basis, the duty rates in numerical terms. By leaving the actual fixation of rates to fiscal authorities, the Group left the exercise wide open.

2.9.4 Task Force on Indirect Taxes (Chairman: Vijay Kelkar), 2002: The Task Force recommended the following excise duty structure (Table 2.3).

Table 2.3: Central Excise Duty Structure Recommended by the Task Force on Indirect Taxes

Rate (percent)	Description of the commodity
0	Life-saving drugs and equipments, security items, food items, necessities and the like, and agricultural products.
6	Processed food products and matches.
14	Standard rate for all items not mentioned against other rates.
20	Motor vehicles, air-conditioners and aerated water.
Separate rates for tobacco products and their substitutes (like pan masala)	

Source: Government of India, Ministry of Finance and Company Affairs, *Report of the Task Force on Indirect Taxes*, December 2002, p. 181.

2.10 Simplification of Excise Tariff

2.10.1 Triple Rate Excise Structure: Multiple rates of commodity taxes were long considered a weakness of the indirect tax system of India. Admitting the problems created by the multiplicity of rates, the Finance Minister in his 1999-2000 budget speech observed, "The multiple rates of indirect tax are generally recognised to be a major source of misclassification, tax evasion and avoidance and cumbersome litigation. The multiplicity also encourages inefficient allocation of resources. Over a 100 countries in the world now enjoy the benefits of a value added tax (VAT) with very small number of rates in each case". [13]

Thus, in a landmark move, the Finance Minister announced in his 1999-2000 budget a triple rate excise structure. In other words, the then existing 11 major ad valorem rates were reduced to 3, viz. a central rate of 16 percent, a merit rate of 8 percent and a demerit rate of 24 percent. This was done by: (a) merging the existing rates of 5 percent, 10 percent and 12 percent into the existing 8 percent rate, (b) creating a new rate of 16 percent by merging the existing 13 percent, 15 percent and 18 percent rates into it, and (c) fixing a new rate of 24 percent in substitution of the existing rate of 25 percent. The initiative of the Finance Minister to rationalise the rate structure of excise system was widely appreciated.

2.11 Excises on Inputs and the Introduction of Modified Value Added Tax (MODVAT) and Central Value Added Tax (CENVAT)

One perennial problem of the Indian excise system was the taxation of inputs (raw materials, components, and other intermediates) and the resulting cascading effect on the prices of final products. Prior to the Second Five Year Plan (1956-61), excise coverage was limited to consumer goods with the notable exception of steel ingots. However, the need for additional resources for successive Plans necessitated extension of the excise net to capital goods and raw materials. Various inputs like internal combustion engines, aluminium, cotton yarn, woollen yarn, fertilisers, chemicals, were brought within the excise ambit. The disadvantages of input excises are well-known. [14] However, levies on inputs formed an integral part of the excise system in India for reasons of sheer administrative convenience.

2.11.1 Pre-MODVAT Arrangements: Prior to 1986, excise duty was levied on both inputs used and the output produced. This meant that an amount paid as tax on the input was subject to taxation again at the output level (with limited set offs). This was applicable to each intermediate good in the manufacturing process. This *tax on tax* led to cascading of taxes. This problem was sought to be addressed by the VAT regime under which tax paid on the inputs was deducted from the tax payable on the output. Similarly, sales tax also had a cascading effect through the distribution chain.

Prior to the introduction of MODVAT in 1986, there were provisions in the Central Excises and Salt Rules, 1944, under which certain inputs were exempted from taxation to minimise the cumulative effect of excise levies. Thus, Rule 56-A of the said Rules, introduced in 1962, allowed the manufacturers of certain notified finished excisable goods to bring excise-paid components (for example compressors for refrigerators) to take credit for the said duty in the Proforma Credit Account to get adjustment of duty on the final excisable good.

The Indirect Taxation Enquiry Committee (Chairman: L.K. Jha), 1978, which made an in-depth study of the cascading effect of input excises, recommended a wider extension of Rule 56-A to products falling under different tariff items. The same Committee recommended also the introduction of value added tax (VAT) at the manufacturing stage, called MANVAT, to tackle the problem of cascading effect of excise taxation.

The Long Term Fiscal Policy Statement (December 1985) also envisaged the extension of the Proforma Credit Scheme and observed, "The basic approach will be to move towards an extension of the present system of proforma credit to all excisable commodities with the exception of a few like petroleum, tobacco, and textile products. This programme would amount to a modified system of VAT or MODVAT for short. The programme will be implemented in a phased manner over a period of years, taking due account of the revenue implications, the need to revise administrative procedures and the lessons from experience gained in the early stages of the reform". [15]

In pursuance of the proposal made in the Long Term Fiscal Policy Statement, the Government introduced MODVAT with effect from March 1, 1986. It was introduced for a selected number of commodities and in a step-by-step manner for all commodities in terms of CENVAT in 2002-03.

2.11.2 MODVAT Scheme: Features and advantages of MODVAT scheme were as under.

MODVAT scheme provided for instant and complete reimbursement of excise duty and additional duty of customs (countervailing duty) paid on the components and raw materials when used in the manufacture of the final products. Articles which were not used as inputs in the manufacturing process were not eligible for credit under this scheme.

Initially, the MODVAT scheme covered 38 chapters of the schedule to the Central Excise Tariff Act, 1985. These chapters pertained to the products of chemical and allied industries, paints and packaging materials, plastics, glass and glassware, rubber products, base metals and articles of base metals, machinery and mechanical appliances including electrical equipment, motor vehicles, and certain miscellaneous manufactured products. In 1987, the scheme was extended to all the remaining chapters (except those relating to textiles, tobacco, and the petroleum sector). The extension covered food products, mineral products, leather and travel goods, footwear, paper and paper-board, wood and cork products, asbestos cement products, and precious metals. As long as the inputs and the final products were covered by the specified chapters, credit of duty on inputs was available. In 1994, MODVAT scheme was extended to tobacco, fibres, yarn and fabrics, and petroleum products (excluding motor spirit and high speed diesel oil) used as input.

MODVAT scheme was further expanded and rationalised in the sense that all inputs (excepting motor spirit and high speed diesel oil) and all capital goods were included in the eligible list of MODVAT scheme. However, the availability of MODVAT credit on capital goods was spread over a period of 2 years.

A. Features: The features of the MODVAT scheme were as follows:

1. The credit under MODVAT was available to a manufacturer of a final product only if the final product was dutiable. Where the final product manufactured by a manufacturer was exempt from excise duty then no credit of the duty paid on the inputs was available. Credit was allowed only after the evidence of payment of duty was received by the excise department.
2. Where the same input was used for different finished products, some of which were not dutiable, the credit of duty was allowed only for that part attributable to inputs which were used for the manufacture of dutiable finished products.
3. Credit of the duty paid on the inputs under the MODVAT scheme could be utilised for payment of duty on the final products in which the inputs were used.
4. Under the MODVAT scheme, credit of duty was not restricted to raw materials and components only but covered all specified inputs which were used in the manufacture of final products.
5. Machines, plant, equipments, apparatus, tools or appliances used in the manufacture of the final products were not covered by the term *inputs* for the purpose of MODVAT benefits.
6. Under the MODVAT scheme, inputs could be either procured from outside or manufactured within the factory. In either case, the duty credit was available to the extent of duty actually paid.

The Government had made it clear in its Long Term Fiscal Policy Statement (1985) that the proposed MODVAT scheme was to be broadly revenue-neutral. Thus, along with the introduction of MODVAT which considerably reduced the cost of final products, the rates of duty on final products were suitably revised upwards by the Finance Act, 1986, to retain the collection of excise duties at the earlier level. This was justified on grounds of resource mobilisation for the Five Year Plans.

B. Advantages: MODVAT scheme had the following advantages:

1. It aimed at making excise levies transparent so that the effective rate of taxation on a particular commodity could be known. This information was helpful in undertaking meaningful studies of excise incidence. The results of these studies could be used to control excise burden on different commodities to ensure the desired degree of progressivity in the excise levies.
2. It sought to avoid cascading effects associated with a traditional turnover tax. In particular, it worked as a cost-saving device through the availability of instant credit of the duties paid on the inputs and the consequent reduction of the interest costs.
3. MODVAT scheme improved the competitive strength of the small-scale sector by allowing credit of duty which could be in excess of the duty actually paid on the inputs made by the small-scale units.
4. MODVAT scheme encouraged indigenisation because full set off was available when indigenous inputs were used. However, no credit of basic and auxiliary customs duties was permissible on imported materials and components. Although MODVAT scheme provided for set off of countervailing duty [16], this element of import duty was not very significant in comparison with other elements of import duty, viz. basic and auxiliary duties. As the scope of MODVAT was widened, the process of indigenisation gathered momentum.
5. MODVAT scheme was designed to encourage exports by making them more competitive in the international market. Since MODVAT allowed set off through different stages of production, the final duty became clear on final goods which could be exported without payment of duty under bond. The payment of duty drawback was swifter in view of the transparency of excise duty.
6. MODVAT checked excise evasion because credit of input duty could not be claimed unless actual production was declared to the excise authorities.
7. MODVAT scheme also helped to reduce the number of disputes—arising on account of classifications requiring lower or higher rates of duty—because the duty element on a large number of components became irrelevant for manufacturers in view of set off. Previously, a selective set off triggered disputes as regards the eligibility of an input for set off. The introduction of Harmonised System Nomenclature in 1986 further reduced the scope for ambiguities.

Some experts felt that MODVAT was old wine in a new bottle because the facility under it was practically the same as was available under Rule 56-A as mentioned above. In other words, MODVAT scheme was only an extension and liberalisation of the proforma credit facility already in operation. Though some degree of similarity did exist, the two schemes could not be termed identical. Rule 56-A scheme was restrictive and had several procedural formalities, e.g. a manufacturer had to intimate the Excise

Department about the arrival of input materials for verification by the excise officials. Moreover, it was applicable on a commodity-to-commodity basis and involved discretion in taking decisions. MODVAT scheme was more comprehensive and rule-based and therefore curtailed the discretionary powers of the Excise Department. MODVAT credit on inputs could be availed on the basis of a duplicate copy of the invoice.

The Tax Reforms Committee (Chairman: Raja Chelliah), 1991, examined, *inter alia,* the scope of extending the MODVAT scheme and observed, "there is no alternative to gradually transforming the present excise tax system, consisting of two parts, namely: (a) MODVAT, and (b) excise on gross value basis with no set off for some sectors, into a genuine VAT at the manufacturing level. Manufacturing and such a VAT should include also the 'manufacture' of services although some services may be exempted on practical considerations". [17]

2.11.3 Introduction of CENVAT: As already noted, in his 1999-2000 budget, the Finance Minister had introduced three ad valorem rates of basic excise duty, namely 8 percent, 16 percent and 24 percent. Furthering the reform of excise taxation, the 2000-01 budget introduced a single rate CENVAT by converging the three ad valorem rates to a single rate of 16 percent. The 8 percent excise rate was abolished and most of the items under it were moved to 16 percent rate. Similarly, items that were mainly in the nature of raw materials or intermediates were moved from the 24 percent rate to 16 percent CENVAT. However, in addition to the 16 percent CENVAT rate, three rates of special excise, viz. 8 percent, 16 percent, and 24 percent were introduced. While the CENVAT rate was modvatable, the special excise duties were not, i.e. users could not avail of MODVAT credit of these duties. Some of the commodities on which special excise duties applied included white cement, glazed tiles, cosmetics, air conditioners, aerated water and chewing tobacco. Since these commodities were not in the nature of inputs therefore they were not modvatable.

The standard rate of excise duty (CENVAT) was brought down to 8 percent after two successive reductions in December 2008 and February 2009. It was increased to 10 percent in the Budget for 2010-11. It was further increased to 12 percent in the Budget for 2012-13 and remained the same for the financial year 2013-14 and 2014-15.

Undoubtedly, the Government provided a stable excise system to create confidence among the entrepreneurs, particularly the prospective ones, so that they could plan their investment and production without the Damocles sword of excise changes hanging over their heads. The application of CENVAT at fewer rates and the new system of CENVAT credits resulted in fewer classification disputes, reduced tax cascading, and greater neutrality of the tax. It was also hoped that CENVAT would encourage the State Governments to implement their agreed programme for converting their sales tax into VAT by April 1, 2001.

However, CENVAT was levied on goods manufactured or produced in India. This gave rise to definitional issues as to what constituted manufacturing, and valuation issues for determining the value on which the tax was to be levied. While these concepts had evolved through judicial rulings, it was recognized that limiting the tax to the point of manufacturing was a severe impediment to an efficient and neutral application of tax. Manufacturing itself formed a narrow base.

Moreover, the effective burden of tax became dependent on the supply chain, i.e. the taxable value at the point of manufacturing relative to the value added beyond this point. It was for this reason that virtually all countries had abandoned this form of taxation and replaced it by multi-point taxation system extending to the retail level.

The starting base for the CENVAT was narrow, and was further eroded by a variety of area-specific, and conditional and unconditional exemptions.

Under the Constitution, the Central Government was empowered to impose excise duty on goods produced or manufactured. It had no power to carry forward the tax up to the retail stage. Thus, CENVAT was a kind of VAT at the manufacturing stage. In any case, it paved the way for a national VAT.

2.12 Exemptions and Concessions

2.12.1 Rationale: As in other countries, exemptions and concessions were an integral part of the excise system. Excise preferences and reliefs were given to promote a wide spectrum of socio-economic objectives. Exemptions/concessions were justified on following grounds:

1. Exemptions/concessions ensured progressivity in the structure of commodity taxation.
2. They induced entrepreneurs to undertake activities which they would have otherwise shrunk, e.g. adopting labour-intensive techniques of production.
3. They were designed to promote enterprises deemed *vital* by society (though it is controversial as to which activities are *vital* and require governmental support).
4. Exemptions/concessions provided the desired flexibility to the tax system to deal with changing market situation. They were used as a corrective mechanism to stabilise demand, production, and profits of different industries.
5. Due to continuous diversification of the economy and inflation, markets for various commodities had not remained stable in India after Independence. Because of the changing market conditions, the levels of profit in different industries had also been fluctuating and on balance had shown a rising trend. Excise rates, it was argued, should be modified upward to mop up excess profits and downward to boost sluggish demand for idle-capacity industries.
6. Exemptions were sometimes granted on administrative considerations. The duty on unmanufactured tobacco was abolished in 1979 mainly on account of the administrative difficulty of assessing and collecting duty from a large number of growers, and curers. Similarly, exemption of smaller of the small industries was also due to administrative problems. Agricultural products were also exempt owing to the same reason.

2.12.2 General Exemptions: There were various general exemptions which purported to serve a wide variety of socio-economic objectives. Thus, goods of the following description were exempt from the whole of the duty of excise leviable thereon.

1. All excisable goods, produced in a technical, educational and research institute during the course of imparting technical training of an academic or vocational nature.
2. All excisable goods donated for the welfare of defence personnel.
3. All excisable goods donated to the National Defence Fund or to the Ministry of Defence.
4. Excisable goods, supplied as stores for consumption on board a vessel of the Indian navy.
5. All excisable goods sent abroad as exhibits in any international trade fair or exhibition.

Apart from these general exemptions, excise tariff was extensively used to serve a host of other objectives including export promotion, industrial development, and mopping up a part of high profits earned by certain industries.

2.12.3 Labour-intensive Technology: Excise exemptions and concessions were particularly important in promoting labour-intensive technology and small-scale industries. Central excise law contained provisions the sole objective of which was employment generation. Products of a number of industries were exempt from excise duty if they were manufactured without the aid of power. Duty differentials were used to discourage mechanisation in certain industries.

Similarly, concessions were available to the handloom sector of the textile industry. Processed *khadi* cloth woven on handloom wholly from hand spun cotton yarn or in admixture with similar silk and/or woollen yarn enjoyed full exemption since 1969. Cotton fabrics manufactured on handlooms and processed by a factory owned by a registered handloom co-operative society enjoyed full exemption from duty.

The Expert Committee on Tax Measures to Promote Employment (Chairman: V.M. Dandekar), 1980, made estimates of the annual cost of protecting or subsidising employment through concessions in excise duties. It found that the annual cost of protecting or subsidising employment through concessions in excise duties was ₹ 523 per full-time worker in the handloom industry, ₹ 881 in *khandasari*, and ₹ 2,669 in the cottage sector of the match industry. [18]

2.12.4 Concessions to Small Industries: In line with Government's policy of encouraging small-scale industries, a wide range of concessions and exemptions from excise duty was available to small producers to enable them to stand in competition with large-scale manufacturers. Also, relatively simple and concessional procedures were followed for the assessment and collection of excises from the small-scale sector. As a part of the Comprehensive Policy Package on SSI and Tiny Sector announced by the Prime Minister on August 30, 2000, the excise exemption limit for SSI was raised from ₹ 50 lakh to ₹ 1 crore with effect from September 1, 2000.

As regards duty exemption for the small-scale sector, the Task Force on Indirect Taxes (Chairman: Vijay Kelkar), 2002 recommended as under:

- Duty exemption should be extended to only small units with a turnover of ₹ 50 lakh.
- Duty exemption limit for the larger SSI units should be gradually brought down to ₹ 50 lakh as per the following time frame: from ₹ 100 lakh to ₹ 75 lakh by the year 2004-05 and from ₹ 75 lakh to ₹ 50 lakh by the year 2005-06.

2.12.5 Problems Created by Exemptions/Concessions: These were as follows:

1. Excise concessions narrowed the tax base and therefore adversely affected government revenues.
2. Excise concessions interfered with the designing of the excise system and led to complexities in the excise law which, in turn, led to tax evasion and litigation.
3. They also obscured the evaluation of excise system, particularly from equity angle.
4. Excise concession to a particular industry led to a chain reaction (i.e. similar demands by other industries), causing unsettling effects on producers, consumers, and the administration.
5. Exemptions/concessions were often the result of persistent representations and pressure tactics by industry and trade than any economic justification.
6. It was not always possible to segregate the effects of duty reduction on production, costs, prices, and consumption because duty concessions operated in conjunction with other non-tax policy measures to affect the production process.

2.12.6 Misuse of Concessions: Though preferential treatment to small units and labour-intensive methods of production was desirable, the misuse of these concessions created doubts as regards the ultimate beneficiaries of such facilities. Concerned about the misuse of excise concessions, the Finance Minister in his 2001-2002 budget speech announced the withdrawal of exemption on certain items and observed, "Products of SSI are exempt from excise duty up to ₹ 1 crore. This exemption is intended to provide fiscal support to the genuinely small producers. I propose to withdraw this exemption in respect of the following items, in which misuse of the exemption is more than likely: (a) cotton yarn, (b) ball or roller bearings, and (c) arms and ammunition for private use". [19]

It was well-established that certain products—particularly footwear, domestic electrical appliances, electronic goods, and wires and cables—were purchased on a fairly large scale by established concerns from the exempted sector and marketed in the brand names of such concerns. However, under a scheme introduced in 1986, a small-scale manufacturer of excisable goods was allowed to clear his goods with the brand name of another manufacturer and was eligible for exemption for such clearances. Clearly, the small producers depended heavily on private marketing organisations to sell their products and this dependence needed to be reduced by strengthening and building up co-operatives and other officially sponsored marketing organisations to market the products of small sector.

Endnotes

1. Excise duties on liquor and other narcotics are imposed by the State Governments under provisions of Entry 51 of List II (State List) in the Seventh Schedule.
2. Duties of excise on medicinal and toilet preparations containing alcohol were levied by the Centre under Article 268 but they were collected and appropriated by the States within which they were leviable. These were levied by the Centre to ensure uniformity in their rate throughout the country. Section 6 of the Constitution (One Hundred and First Amendment) Act, 2016 abolished the duties of excise on medicinal and toilet preparations.
3. Government of India, Ministry of Finance, *Report of the Taxation Enquiry Commission,* (Chairman: John Matthai), 1953-54, Vol. II, p. 323.
4. Government of India, *Long Term Fiscal Policy*, 1985, p. 25.

5. For conceptual clarifications regarding specific and ad valorem duties, see section 1.5 of chapter 1 of this book.
6. Government of India, Ministry of Finance, *Speeches of Union Finance Ministers, 1947-48 to 1984-85*, p. 313.
7. Government of India, Ministry of Finance, *Report of the Technical Study Group on Central Excise Tariff*, Part I, 1985, Table 6, p. 7.
8. Government of India, Ministry of Finance, *Interim Report of the Tax Reforms Committee,* (Chairman: Raja Chelliah), 1991, p. 113.
9. Ibid., p.114.
10. Government of India, Ministry of Finance, *Final Report on Rationalisation and Simplification of Tax Structure,* (Chairman: S. Bhoothalingam), 1968, p. 8.
11. Government of India, Ministry of Finance, *Report of the Indirect Taxation Enquiry Committee,* (Chairman: L.K. Jha), Part II, 1978, p. 174.
12. *Speeches of Union Finance Ministers,* op. cit., p. 459.
13. Government of India, Ministry of Finance, *Budget Speech of the Finance Minister*, 1999-2000, Part B, p. 21.
14. Excises on inputs enhance costs and profits and therefore increase the prices of goods much more than the amount of excise collected. The cost of production increases because producers and middlemen require larger amounts of working capital to maintain the necessary stocks of inputs. Prices of finished products tend to reflect taxes imposed on inputs used. If the middlemen apply fixed percentage mark ups to purchase prices as their profit and if the purchase prices include taxes, the mark ups will be applicable to the tax component of the purchase price as well. In other words, increase in the price of the manufactures is in excess of the excise revenue accruing from input taxes.

    Further still, excises on inputs may promote vertical integration in an industry, a trend which is harmful to the growth of small-scale sector. Lastly, input excises impose an inequitable burden on different economic classes by not discriminating between essential and non-essential uses of a product. For example, an excise on aluminium hits indiscriminately the use of the product for decoration purpose as well as for making utensils (generally used by the poor).

    Notwithstanding the various disadvantages of input excises, governments in many countries impose duties on inputs due to administrative convenience. Many items of inputs are the end-product of one manufacturer but merely a component for another (e.g. tyres and tubes) and are also used as replacement items. Exemption of such items will be discrimination in favour of replacement consumption and certain commodities (say motor cars) may be sold with avoidable components and accessories stripped off. Moreover, provisions can be made in tax laws to minimise the cascading effects of input excises.
15. *Long Term Fiscal Policy,* op. cit., p. 38.
16. It is an element of import duty equivalent to excise duty on domestically produced goods.
17. Government of India, Ministry of Finance, *Final Report of the Tax Reforms Committee,* (Chairman: Raja Chelliah), Part I, 1992, p. 36.
18. Government of India, Ministry of Finance, *Report of the Expert Committee on Tax Measures to Promote Employment* (Chairman: V.M. Dandekar), 1980, pp. 91, 113 and 117.
19. Government of India, Ministry of Finance, *Budget Speech of the Finance Minister, 2001-2002, Part B*, p. 27.

3

Taxation of Services by the Central Government

From equity point of view, services should be taxed in the same way as goods. Taxation of goods and exclusion of services distorts the relative prices of goods vis-à-vis services, encouraging artificially the demand for services. In the process, the allocation of resources is also distorted. If tax is imposed on goods and not on services, a relatively high rate of tax would be required on goods to generate a given amount of revenue. If tax is imposed both on goods and services, a moderate tax rate can yield the given revenue. Administratively, taxation of both goods and services is desirable because it would reduce disputes pertaining to distinction between goods and services.

Service sector is very wide in its range. It includes, *inter alia*, healthcare, education, social security, leasing, entertainment, credit rating agencies, telecommunications, transport, publicity and advertising, insurance, banking, legal and financial services.

Till 1994, Indian tax system traditionally relied on commodity taxation for generating revenue for the Central and State Governments. The two major commodity taxes of the Central Government were excise duties and customs duties while at the level of the States, sales tax/VAT was the main commodity tax. Tax revenue from the agricultural sector being negligible, the industrial sector continued to constitute the only principal tax base till the mid-1990s. The extension of excise duties to more and more commodities of the industrial/manufacturing sector reached a saturation point in due course of time.

The composition of national income in India had changed steadily over the years. While the share of agriculture and allied activities in the gross domestic product (GDP) had declined, that of the tertiary sector had increased. The expansion of services sector was conducive for employment generation and improved quality of life. The compositional shift of GDP in favour of the services sector, was in line with the development experience of a number of countries. It is well-known that as an economy develops, the shares of industrial and service sectors in GDP increase at the cost of the agricultural sector.

Despite the fact that the services sector had shown substantial buoyancy , it remained outside the tax net till 1994. This pattern of tax structure development in India was contrary to the experience of most other countries where taxation of commodities and services grew hand in hand. In this connection, the Finance Minister, in his 1994-95 Budget Speech to Parliament, observed, "There is no sound reason for exempting services from taxation when goods are taxed and many countries treat goods and services alike for tax purpose". [1]

Tax Reforms Committee (TRC) [Chairman: Raja Chelliah], 1991 also recommended imposition of tax on certain select services, viz. advertising, non-life insurance and telephone services and services of stock brokers.

Thus, in order to impart buoyancy to government revenues and to provide consistency and equity in the tax structure via-a-via the composition of income, a modest effort was made in the 1994-95 budget when a 5 percent tax was imposed on telephone and non-life insurance services and services of stock brokers with effect from July 1, 1994.

The introduction of service tax ushered in a major structural change in the system of indirect taxes in the form of a wider tax base and facilitated the process of rationalization of excise duties, resulting in lower tax burden on productive sectors. Over the years, the number of services subject to service tax increased and so also the rate leviable on them.

3.1 Constitutional Provisions

The Central Government had no specific powers to tax services when it introduced service tax on select services from July 1, 1994. It was done under its residual powers of taxation vide Entry 97 of List I (Union List) in the Seventh Schedule of the constitution. The tax extended to the whole of India except the State of Jammu and Kashmir. The service tax being an indirect tax, its administrative control was vested with the Central Board of Excise and Customs (CBEC). The sharing of the revenue from service tax was on the basis of the recommendations of the Finance Commission, as applicable to other central taxes.

However, the Constitution (Eighty-eighth Amendment) Act, 2003 put service tax in List I (Union List) of the Seventh Schedule by inserting Entry 92C in that List. Furthermore, this amendment inserted a new Article 268A which provided for service tax to be levied by the Union and collected and appropriated by the Union and the States. The new Article was as follows:

268A. "(1) Taxes on services shall be levied by the Government of India and such tax shall be collected and appropriated by the Government of India and the States in the manner provided in clause (2).

(2) The proceeds in any financial year of any such tax levied in accordance with the provisions of clause (1) shall be:

(a) collected by the Government of India and the States;

(b) appropriated by the Government of India and the States;

in accordance with such principles of collection and appropriation as may be formulated by Parliament by law".

Thus, Article 268A specified that the principles of collection and appropriation of taxes on services will be determined by Parliament. In other words, the revenue from taxation of services was excluded from the purview of the Finance Commission.

In this connection, the Twelfth Finance Commission remarked, "With service taxes having been excluded from the ambit of the recommendations of the finance commission, the idea of an overall shareable pool of central taxes appears to be in the process of being reversed. While service taxes are likely to prove highly buoyant in the near future, these will not be subjected to sharing with the states under the Constitution, although other statutory arrangements can be made, which can include sharing as well as assignment. It may be noted that hitherto items under Articles 268 and 269 were subjects that were generally of inter-state nature with limited revenue importance. These were wholly assigned to the states. In this context, it needs to be stressed that any legislation passed by Parliament with respect to appropriation of service tax proceeds must take care to ensure that the revenue accruing to the states through any proposed changes should not be less than the share that would accrue to them, had the entire service tax proceeds been part of the shareable pool". [2]

It is noteworthy that the above mentioned provisions (Entry 92C and Article 268A) of Constitution (Eighty-eighth Amendment) Act, 2003 were never brought into force. In other words, these provisions were never notified. Hence, tax on services continued to be levied under the residuary entry, i.e. Entry 97 of List I (Union List) in the Seventh Schedule of the constitution These two items (Entry 92C and Article 268A) were omitted by the Constitution (One Hundred and First Amendment) Act, 2016 to pave way for the introduction of Goods and Services Tax (GST) which was finally rolled out on July 1, 2017.

Apart from the Centre, the States also had powers to tax certain services specified in clause (29A) of Article 366 of the Constitution. This sort of division of taxing powers created a grey zone which led to confusion and legal disputes. This problem was solved with the implementation of GST.

3.2 Introduction and Widening of Service Tax

In view of the need for additional resources, rising contribution of service sector to GDP and the recommendations of Tax Reforms Committee, 1991, a modest effort was made in the 1994-95 budget when a 5 percent tax was imposed on telephone and non-life insurance services and services of stock brokers with effect from July 1, 1994. The coverage of service tax was extended to advertising, courier and radio paging services from November 1, 1996.

In his 1997-98 budget speech, the Finance Minister maintained that services are products as much as manufactured goods and hence both must bear taxes. With these considerations in view he extended the service tax to the services provided by the following: transporters of goods by road, consulting engineers, custom houses, steamer and clearing and forwarding agents, air travel agents, tour operators and car rental agencies, outdoor caterers, *pandal* contractors and *mandap* keepers, and manpower recruitment agencies.

In the 1998-99 budget, service tax on the transportation of goods by road, outdoor caterers, and *pandal* contractors was abolished. However, its net was extended to services provided by architects, interior decorators, management consultants, chartered accountants, cost accountants, company secretaries, private security services, real estate agents and real estate consultants, market research agencies, credit rating agencies, underwriting agencies, and slaughter houses using mechanised means for large animals.

Acknowledging the potential of service tax, Government expanded its coverage from time-to-time. However, keeping in view the social objectives of state policy, the Government refrained from taxing services in the field of health and education. [3]

For the financial year 2016-17, the standard rate of service tax was 14 percent. In addition, Swachh Bharat Cess @ 0.5 percent was also leviable. From June 1, 2016, Krishi Kalyan Cess @ 0.5 percent was also leviable.

3.3 Service Tax: A Critique

The expanding base of service tax provided a promising source of revenue, but there were some caveats which had to be kept in mind. First, the scope for expanding the service tax net to more and more services got narrower as the net was widened. The contribution of the expanding net, therefore, reduced over time. Second, the preponderance of small service providers below the taxable limit of turnover constrained the scope of revenue mobilization beyond a certain level.

The introduction of the service tax was a mixed blessing. While it broadened the tax base, its structure was complex. The tax was levied on specified services, classified into one hundred odd different categories. This approach spawned many disputes about the scope of each category. Unlike goods, services are malleable, and can and are often packaged into composite bundles that include taxable as well as non-taxable elements. Also, there is no standardized nomenclature for services, such as the Harmonised System Nomenclature (HSN) for goods.

Furthermore, there was a complicated rate structure. Although there was one statutory rate, in practice there were 10 other rates because of the so-called *abatement* which amounted to fixing a rate different from the standard rate and not allowing further input tax credits. Abatement was necessitated, in some part, because of uncertainty in the base, and specifically being unable to distinguish *goods* from *services*. Further, there was incomplete provision of input tax crediting for goods, and incomplete cross-crediting between goods and services. Added to this was the Central sales tax (CST) which was levied on the sale or purchase of goods in the course of inter-State trade.

The key problem with the service tax was the basic approach of levying it on specified services, each of which generated an extensive debate as to what was included in the base. Ideally, the tax base should be defined to include all services, with a limited list of exclusions (the so-called negative list). The Government was reluctant to adopt this approach for the fear that it could bring into the tax net many services that are politically sensitive. [4]

Service tax was abolished by Section 17 of Constitution (One Hundred and First Amendment) Act, 2016 to pave way for the introduction of GST.

Endnotes

1. Government of India, Ministry of Finance, *Budget Speech of the Finance Minister, 1994-95, Part B*, p. 24.
2. Report of the Twelfth Finance Commission (2005-10), November 2004, pp. 15-16.
3. In the case of excise and sales tax also, commodities such as medicines and books were either exempt or taxed at very low rates.
4. As late as from July 1, 2012, the concept of taxation on services was changed from a Positive List of services to a Negative List regime. This changed the taxation system of services from tax on the specified services to tax being levied on all services, other than those mentioned in the Negative List or which were exempted by a notification.

4

State Level Sales Tax/Value Added Tax (VAT)

Prior to the introduction of GST, taxation of goods by the States was characterized by a base (sales) that extended all the way to the retail stage. Lists of exemptions, rates of taxation, compounding schemes and rules and regulations varied across States. It was a nightmare for a business entity doing business in more than one State.

By virtue of powers vested in them under Entry 54 of List II (State List) in the Seventh Schedule of the Constitution, the states were authorised to impose, "taxes on the sale or purchase of goods other than newspapers, subject to the provisions of Entry 92A of List I".

To pave the way for GST, Section 17 of the Constitution (One Hundred and First Amendment) Act, 2016 substituted the following entry for the old Entry 54:

"54. Taxes on the sale of petroleum crude, high speed diesel, motor spirit (commonly known as petrol), natural gas, aviation turbine fuel and alcoholic liquor for human consumption, but not including sale in the course of inter-State trade or commerce or sale in the course of international trade or commerce of such goods". (Table 4.1)

Table 4.1: Entry 54 of List II (State List) in the Seventh Schedule of the Constitution

Before Constitution (One Hundred and First Amendment) Act, 2016	After Constitution (One Hundred and First Amendment) Act, 2016
Taxes on the sale or purchase of goods other than newspapers, subject to the provisions of Entry 92A of List I.	Taxes on the sale of petroleum crude, high speed diesel, motor spirit (commonly known as petrol), natural gas, aviation turbine fuel and alcoholic liquor for human consumption, but not including sale in the course of inter-State trade or commerce or sale in the course of international trade or commerce of such goods.

Petroleum and petroleum products have been constitutionally included as *goods* under GST. However, it has also been provided that petroleum and petroleum products shall not be subject to the levy of GST till notified at a future date on the recommendation of the GST Council. The present taxes levied by the Centre and the States on petroleum and petroleum products—excise duty/CENVAT by the Centre and sales tax/VAT by the States—will continue to be levied in the interim period. The five petroleum products which have been kept in abeyance for the purpose of GST are the following: (a) petroleum crude, (b) motor spirit (petrol), (c) high speed diesel, (d) natural gas, and (e) aviation turbine fuel.

It is noteworthy that GST Council is entrusted to make recommendations to the Union and the States on taxes, cesses and surcharges levied by the Union, the States and the local bodies which may be subsumed in the goods and services tax [(Article 279A (4)(a)].

Pre-GST system of sales tax/VAT is explained in the rest of this chapter.

4.1 Intra-State Sales Tax

As already noted, under Entry 54 of List II (State List) in the Seventh Schedule of the Constitution, the States were given the power to levy "a tax on sale or purchases of goods other than newspapers". Enjoying this Constitutional right, different State Governments levied sales tax on a wide range of commodities at different rates with diverse procedures and rules for its collection. The Central Government also entered the field in so far as it prescribes the ceiling rate of sales tax on goods in inter-State trade. In the case of three important commodities, viz. textiles, sugar, and tobacco, additional duties of excise were imposed in lieu of sales tax, the proceeds of which were distributed among the States.

Different States adopted different variants of the sales tax due to a number of reasons including administrative convenience, ad hoc measures to increase tax revenues, and to attract enterprise in their respective areas. Sales tax in a State could take the form of a single point, double-point and/or multi-point levy. However, single-point was the main type of sales tax imposed on most commodities in all States. In most States, a significant part of sales tax revenue originated from first-point levy, i.e. at the manufacturer's level. Some States also levied surcharges on sales tax as an ad hoc measure to augment their resources.

The rate structure of sales tax was further complicated in view of different lists of exemptions/concessions, numerous nominal rate categories, and different administrative procedures in each of the States. These variations caused disparities in the effective rate of sales tax on similar commodities in different States. Agricultural commodities like cereals and pulses were either exempted or subjected to low rate of sales tax, ranging from 2 to 3 percent. For most commodities, the rate of single-point levy varied between 4 to 8 percent. However, in the case of luxury items (like motor cars and refrigerators), the rate could go up to even 15 percent in some States. The rate of multi-point levy hovered around 4 percent.

4.1.1 Revenue Significance of Sales Tax: An outstanding development in the sphere of State finances after Independence in 1947 was the precipitous growth in the relative revenue significance of sales tax levied under Entry 54 of List II (State List) in the Seventh Schedule of the Constitution. It grew considerably in depth and coverage, and formed the mainstay of States' tax revenue. It was levied not only on consumer goods but also on raw materials and capital goods. In 1950-51, the relative share of sales tax was 26.1 percent: ₹ 58 crore out of a total collection of ₹ 222 crore from States' taxes. Recording a precipitous growth in relative revenue significance, sales tax was estimated to contribute 62.0 percent to States' own tax revenues in the 2015-16 budgets of the State Governments (Table 4.2). It is noteworthy that sales tax was replaced by State-VAT—sales tax with set-off provisions. Haryana was the first state to replace its sales tax by VAT on April 1, 2003. Other States followed suit. State-VAT, in turn, has been subsumed under GST.

Table 4.2: Trends in the Relative Revenue Significance of Sales Tax in Total Revenue from States' Own Taxes: Selected Years

(₹ crore)

State taxes	1950-51	1960-61	1970-71	1980-81	1990-91	2000-01	2010-11	2015-16
A+B Revenue from States' own taxes	222 (100.0)	455 (100.0)	1,546 (100.0)	6,665 (100.0)	30,145 (100.0)	1,16,717 (100.0)	4,78,594 (100.0)	9,69,594 (100.0)
A. Direct taxes	55 (24.7)	110 (24.2)	140 (9.1)	271 (4.1)	1,230 (4.1)	3,457 (2.9)	12,307 (2.6)	21,774 (2.2)
B. Indirect taxes of which	167 (75.3)	345 (75.8)	1,406 (90.9)	6,394 (95.9)	28,915 (95.9)	1,13,260 (97.1)	4,66,287 (97.4)	9,47,820 (97.8)
1. Sales tax	**58 (26.1)**	**158 (34.7)**	**755 (48.8)**	**3,887 (58.3)**	**16,476 (54.6)**	**68,386 (58.6)**	**2,90,682 (60.7)**	**6,00,851 (62.0)**

2015-16 Budget estimates

Figures in parentheses indicate corresponding percentages of the total revenue from States' own taxes.

Sources: Reserve Bank of India, *Report on Currency and Finance,* Volume II, (various years); and Government of India, Ministry of Finance, *Indian Public Finance Statistics, 2015-2016,* Tables 1.7 and 3.2 (excerpted).

4.1.2 Problems Created by Sales Tax: Perhaps no other tax impinged on so large a number of interests as sales tax. Firstly, it impacted the consumers who ultimately bore its burden. Next, there were the dealers from whom it was collected, and in many cases the producers also came in its ambit in case it was levied at the manufacturer's level. Then there were the State Governments, always anxious to extend its scope and retain their hold on it. Furthermore, the Central Government decided the rate of sales tax on goods of special importance in inter-State trade. Consequently, the operation of sales tax created a host of problems which may be summarised as follows.

1. Sales tax was a levy on commodities which, in most cases, were also subject to excise duties. As excise duty and sales tax were levied by different layers of Government, it became difficult to determine judiciously the impact of these levies on production, investment, and the consumers. No attempt to rationalise commodity tax system could succeed if the Centre and States acted independently without co-ordination among themselves.
2. A closely related problem was the taxation of inputs and capital goods, by the Central and State Governments, through excise duties and sales tax respectively. Apart from generating cascading effect, sales tax on inputs benefited comparatively richer States at the cost of poorer States. To quote, "The (sales) taxation of inputs also means that its burden falls on consumers outside the State. While procedures exist for refund of excise duties on a product when it is exported outside the country, the sales tax paid on inputs is not rebated. In consequence, the more developed States which have attained high levels of agricultural or industrial production are able to

derive additional resources, by taxing consumers in other States, while the resource mobilisation capacity of the less developed States, which have to depend on most of their needs being met by imports from other States, is weakened". [1] This reverse flow of funds was further strengthened by the frequent hikes in the rate of Central sales tax (CST).

Originally at 1 percent, CST rate steadily increased to 4 percent, thereby imposing undue burden on the importing States and defeating, in the process, the very objective of Central Sales Tax Act of 1956.

To tackle the problem of cascading effect associated with the taxation of intermediate goods, reforms at the Central level provided instant credit of excise duty paid on inputs under the modified value added tax (MODVAT) scheme. Although State laws did provide relief through exemptions in regards to sales tax when inputs are sold to manufacturers, such concessions were limited and lacked uniformity. This lacuna in the sales tax system hindered reform of indirect tax system in India.

3. In order to attract trade and industry to their respective areas, some States indulged in a kind of *rate war* (competitive reductions in sales tax rates). It is true that some States lacked infrastructural facilities and to compensate for that sales tax concessions came handy to attract industries, but this shortcut eroded the resource-base of the States, so vital for the development of infrastructure which alone could guarantee their speedy development on permanent footing.
4. Differential rates of sales tax on the same set of commodities in different States often led to uneconomic diversion of trade as well as production centres. It was not uncommon for people of one State making purchases in other States to avoid or reduce sales tax liability. Apparently, purchases from lower tax States to those where rates were higher were beneficial so long as the cost of transporting goods was lower than the tax differential. Purchase of truck chassis in Daman (a Union Territory levying a low rate of 3 percent) by the residents of a far off State of Jammu and Kashmir was a popular case in point.

   Similarly, rate differentials caused flight of capital and enterprise from high to low tax rate States thereby distorting natural selection of production centres based on geographical advantages, leading to unnecessary transportation of raw materials and finished goods and hence cost escalations. Such a misallocation of resources undermined economic efficiency and thereby retarded developmental efforts.
5. Sales tax had another disadvantage in that it discouraged horizontal integration and on the contrary encouraged vertical integration in industries. Firms tried to produce their own components in order to avoid sales tax. This tendency harmed the growth of ancillary units which were mainly in the small-scale sector.
6. Different types of sales tax (multi-point, double-point, and single point) with varying procedures and rules in different States caused difficulties for the traders, particularly small ones, leading to harassment, corruption, and litigation.

4.2 Replacement of Sales Tax by Value Added Tax (VAT)

The replacement of the state sales taxes by VAT in 2005 marked a significant step forward in the reform of domestic trade taxes in India. Implemented by the Empowered Committee of State Finance Ministers (Chairman: Asim Dasgupta) [2], it addressed the distortions and complexities associated with the levy of tax at the first point of sale under the erstwhile system and resulted in a major simplification of the rate structure and broadening of the tax base. The consensus reached among the States for uniformity in the VAT rates brought an end to the harmful tax competition among them. It also lessened the cascading of tax.

In mid-1990s, most states had agreed to phase out the incentive-related exemptions and implement floor rates of sales tax. As part of the nation wide efforts to redesign commodity taxation and the implementation of CENVAT at the level of the Centre, many States modified their sales tax regimes to launch a state level VAT under the scheme prepared by the Empowered Committee of State Finance Ministers for this purpose.

4.2.1 Minimum Rate Agreement among States, 1989: As already noted, some States had been indulging in a sort of *rate-war* to attract trade and industry to their respective regions. To avoid this unhealthy competition, the Chief Ministers agreed, at their conference in New Delhi on February 9-10, 1989, that all the States would adopt the minimum floor level rates as recommended by the Committee of Sales Tax Commissioners in its report of 1984 in respect of 29 identified items. The Chief Secretaries of northern States (Punjab, Haryana, Himachal Pradesh, Rajasthan, Delhi, and Uttar Pradesh) had recommended in May 1994 that there should not only be a uniform rate of sales tax but the slabs of this tax be reduced in these States.

In this connection the Tax Reforms Committee, 1991, observed, "As regards sales tax, the Committee is of the view that this tax could be converted into a form of State VAT within the manufacturing sector. There may be no need for levying sales tax at more than two rates since the distributional and other non-revenue objectives could be left to be performed by the Central taxes which apply uniformly throughout the country". [3]

4.2.2 State Finance Ministers' Conference, 1994: The State Finance Ministers' Conference held in New Delhi on May 27, 1994 failed to arrive at a consensus on the replacement of indirect taxes at the State level by a value added tax. The matter was deferred indefinitely by appointing a ten-member Committee of State Finance Ministers to go into this and related questions.

4.2.3 Preliminary Discussion on State-level VAT, 1995: The first preliminary discussion on State-level VAT took place in a meeting of Chief Ministers convened by Dr. Manmohan Singh, the then Union Finance Minister in 1995. In this meeting, the basic issues on VAT were discussed in general terms and this was followed up by periodic interactions of State Finance Ministers.

4.2.4 Chief Ministers Conference, 1999: In a significant meeting of all the Chief Ministers, convened on November 16, 1999 by Shri Yashwant Sinha, the then Union Finance Minister, two important decisions, among others, were taken. First, before the introduction of State-level VAT, the unhealthy sales tax *rate war* among the States must end, and sales tax rates would need to be harmonised by implementing uniform floor rates of sales tax for different categories of commodities with effect from January 1, 2000. Secondly, on the basis of achievement of the first objective, steps would be taken by the States for introduction of State-level VAT after adequate preparation. For implementing these decisions, a Standing Committee of State Finance Ministers was formed which was then made an Empowered Committee of State Finance Ministers.

4.2.5 Report of Empowered Committee, 2001: The Empowered Committee met regularly. All the decisions were taken on the basis of consensus. On the strength of these repeated discussions and collective efforts, involving the Ministers and the concerned officials, it was possible within a period of about a year and a half to achieve nearly 98 percent success in the first objective, namely harmonisation of sales tax structure through implementation of uniform floor rates of sales tax.

After reaching this stage, steps were initiated for systematic preparation for introduction of State level VAT. Again, in order to avoid any unhealthy competition among the States which might lead to distortions in manufacturing and trade, attempts were made from the very beginning to harmonise the VAT design in the States, keeping also in view the distinctive features of each State and the need for federal flexibility. This was done by the States collectively agreeing, through discussions in the Empowered Committee, to certain common points of convergence regarding VAT, and allowing at the same time certain flexibility to accommodate the local characteristics of the States.

Along with these measures, steps were taken for necessary training, computerization and interaction with trade and industry. While these preparatory steps were taken, the Empowered Committee got a significant support from Shri P. Chidambaram, the then Union Finance Minister, when he responded positively in providing Central financial support to the States in the event of loss of revenue in transitional years of implementation of VAT.

The Empowered Committee, through its deliberations over the years, finalised a design of VAT to be adopted by the States. The model design sought to retain the essential features of VAT, while at the same time, providing a measure of flexibility to the States, to enable them to meet their local requirements. The main features of the VAT design finalised by the Empowered Committee were the following:

1. Rates of VAT on various commodities were to be uniform for all the States/UTs. There were 2 basic rates of 4 percent and 12.5 percent, besides an exempt category and a special rate of 1 percent for a few selected items. The items of basic necessities were put in the zero-rate bracket or the exempted schedule. Gold, silver and precious stones were put in the 1 percent schedule. There was also a category with 20 percent floor rate of tax, but the commodities listed in this schedule were not eligible for input tax rebate/set off. This category covered items like motor spirit (petrol), diesel, aviation turbine fuel, and liquor.
2. Model VAT design made provision for eliminating the multiplicity of taxes. In fact, all the State taxes on purchase or sale of goods (excluding entry tax in lieu of octroi) were required to be subsumed in VAT.

3. Provision was made for allowing input tax credit, which was the basic feature of VAT. However, since the VAT being implemented was intra-State VAT only and did not cover inter-State sale transactions, input tax credit was not made available on inter-State purchases.
4. There were provisions to make the system more business-friendly. For instance, there was provision for self-assessment by the dealers. Similarly, there was provision of a threshold limit for registration of dealers in terms of annual turnover of ₹ 5 lakh. Dealers with turnover lower than this threshold limit were not required to obtain registration under VAT and were exempt from payment of VAT. There was also provision for composition of tax liability up to annual turnover limit of ₹ 50 lakh.
5. Regarding the industrial incentives, the States were allowed to continue with the existing incentives, without breaking the VAT chain. However, no fresh sales tax/VAT-based incentives were permitted.
6. Exports were zero-rated, with credit given for all taxes on inputs/purchases related to such exports.

It was emphasised that the States must think in terms of economic development of the country as a whole and encourage the free flow of trade and commerce in the economy.

At a Conference of Chief Ministers and Finance Ministers of various States held on July 5, 2001 in New Delhi, the Report of the Empowered Committee of State Finance Ministers on VAT (Chairman: Asim Kumar Dasgupta), was accepted and adopted for the introduction of VAT with effect from April 1, 2002. The VAT design recommended by the Empowered Committee was geared to achieve the following objectives:

1. Eliminate the cascading burden of taxation by setting off the tax paid on inputs against that on output.
2. Reduce distortions in the economy caused by double taxation.
3. End market fragmentation with a uniform regime of taxation followed in all the States.
4. Ensure one category of tax-exempted commodities for all the States.
5. Ensure two VAT rates: a uniform 4 percent for all States on goods of basic necessities and a uniform floor rate of 10 percent for other commodities (except a few items such as bullion and liquor).
6. Ensure uniform set of procedures for VAT assessment to be followed by all the States, including the use of permanent account number (PAN) as a common business identifier.
7. Ensure that States implemented uniform floor rates of sales tax by July-end 2001, failing which faulting States could be penalised by discontinuing Central Government assistance.

In view of the apprehensions expressed by a large number of States about possible revenue losses in the initial years of introduction of VAT, an assurance was given to the States that the Government of India would compensate the States to the extent of 100 percent of revenue loss in the first year (2002-03), 75 percent of the loss in the second year (2003-04) and 50 percent of the loss in the third year (2005-06). A Committee of

State Finance Secretaries was appointed to evolve clear and measurable criteria for judging revenue loss, if any, due to the introduction of VAT.

4.2.6 Agreement of January 23, 2002: At the Conference of State Finance Ministers held on January 23, 2002 a final decision was taken that all States and Union Territories would introduce VAT from April 2003. This position was reiterated by all States at the Conference of State Chief Ministers held on October 18, 2002. Empowered Committee of State Finance Ministers endorsed the suggestion that every State Legislation on VAT should have a minimum set of common features. Accordingly, a model VAT Bill was circulated to all the States.

4.2.7 Meeting of State Finance Ministers, 2003: Again, at a meeting of the Finance Ministers of all States/Union Territories on January 17, 2003, States and Union Territories again reiterated their firm commitment to introduce VAT from April 1, 2003. It was decided that the VAT legislations of all States and UTs would have common provisions in respect of all important matters and that a simple VAT legislation with maximum convergence would be implemented. It was also agreed that along with the introduction of VAT, the origin-based Central sales tax (CST) would be phased out. It was also agreed that the Additional Duties of Excise (Goods of Special Importance) Act would be suitably amended to empower States to levy sales tax/VAT on sugar, textiles and tobacco with a ceiling rate of 4 percent. This would be done without affecting the existing levy of Additional Duties of Excise on these items by the Union Government.

The Empowered Committee of State Finance Ministers agreed upon the following sequence of steps to ensure introduction of VAT in place of retail sales tax system in States.

1. Passing of VAT legislation and framing of rules and regulations.
2. Computerisation of dealers who would fall within the ambit of VAT.
3. Training of tax officials, traders and consumer associations.
4. Publicity for consumers.
5. Implementation of VAT, assigning VAT identification numbers to tax payers.
6. Implementing transitional measures for introduction of VAT.

4.2.8 Agreement of June 2004: At a meeting of the State Finance Ministers with the Union Finance Minister on June 18, 2004, it was decided that all States would introduce a uniform VAT from April 1, 2005. The proposed VAT would replace the taxes levied by different States like sales tax and octroi. Coinciding with the introduction of VAT, the Central Government would bring down the Central sales tax (CST) rate from 4 percent to 2 percent. The CST would be phased out in 2006-07. It was also decided that traders with an annual turnover up to ₹ 5 lakh would be exempt from VAT. This decision was aimed at ending traders' opposition to VAT. It may be recalled that States had missed at least five deadlines for the introduction of VAT, mainly due to resistance from trading community.

As a consequence of all these steps, the States started implementing VAT beginning April 1, 2005. After overcoming the initial difficulties, all the States and Union Territories were able to implement VAT. The Empowered Committee monitored closely the process of implementation of State-level VAT.

4.2.9 Role of the Central Government: Introduction of State VAT was an important reform measure at the State level. The State VAT replaced the earlier sales tax systems of the States. VAT, being a 'tax on sale or purchase of goods within a State' was a State Subject by virtue of Entry 54 of List II (State List) of the Seventh Schedule of the Constitution of India. Since sales tax/VAT was a State subject, the Central Government played the role of a facilitator for successful implementation of VAT. Some of the steps taken by the Central Government in this regard were as follows:

1. A package for payment of compensation to States for any revenue loss on account of introduction of VAT was implemented.
2. Financial support under Mission Mode Project (MMP) was provided to States/UTs in order to enable them to take up computerization of their tax departments.
3. A separate project for computerization of tax administration of Himachal Pradesh and Jammu and Kashmir was sanctioned.
4. 50 percent funding was provided to the Empowered Committee of State Finance Ministers for implementation of the TINXSYS Project for tracking of inter-State transactions.

4.2.10 Shortcomings of State VAT: Complexities under the State VAT related primarily to classification of goods to different tax rate schedules. Theoretically, one might expect that the lower tax rates would be applied to basic necessities that are consumed largely by the poor. This was not the case under the State VAT. The lowest rate of 1 percent applied to precious metals and jewellery, and related products—unacceptable from the distributional perspective. The middle rate of 4 percent applied to selected basic necessities and also a range of industrial inputs and IT products. In fact, basic necessities fell into three categories—exempted from tax, taxable at 4 percent, and taxable at the standard rate of 12.5 percent. The classification was arbitrary, with no well-accepted theoretical underpinning. Whatever the political merits of this approach, it was not conducive to lower compliance costs. Most retailers found it difficult to determine the tax rate applicable to a given item without referring to the legislative schedules. Consumers were even less aware of the tax applicable to various items. This gave rise to leakages and rent-seeking.

Another source of complexity under the State VAT was determining whether a particular transaction constituted a sale of goods or not. This problem was most acute in the case of software products and intangibles such as the right to distribute/exhibit movies or time slots for broadcasting advertisements.

The issue of cascading taxation was partly addressed when all the states adopted the concept of VAT for state sales tax. Several central and state taxes were excluded from VAT. Sectors such as real estate, oil and gas production etc. were exempt from VAT. Further, goods and services were taxed differently, thereby making the taxation of products complex.

Broadly speaking, the experience of implementing VAT was quite encouraging. The new system was received well by all the stakeholders, and the transition was quite smooth with the Empowered Committee (EC) constantly reviewing the progress of implementation. The EC advised the States to constantly interact with trade and industry to remove their apprehensions, if any, and to ensure that the benefits of VAT due to input tax credit and reduction in tax rates (wherever applicable) were passed on to the consumers.

Introduction of VAT in the States was a more challenging exercise in a federal country like India, where each State, in terms of constitutional provision, is sovereign in levying and collecting State taxes. In the sales tax regime (before the introduction of VAT), apart from the problem of multiple taxation and burden of adverse cascading effect of taxes, there was also no harmony in the rates of sales tax on different commodities among the States. Not only were the rates of sales tax numerous (often more than ten in several States), and different from one another for the same commodity in different States, but there was also an unhealthy competition among the States in terms of sales tax rates—so-called *rate war*—often resulting in revenue loss.

It is in this background that attempts were made by the States to introduce a harmonious VAT in the States, keeping at the same time in mind the issue of sovereignty of the States regarding the State tax matters.

4.3 Central Sales Tax (CST) on Inter-State Sales

Consequent upon the Constitution (Sixth Amendment) Act, 1956, the Central Sales Tax (CST) Act, 1956 was enacted which came into force on January 5, 1957. The following three main objectives of the CST Act were stated in the Preamble:

1. To formulate principles for determining when a sale or purchase of goods takes place in the course of inter-State trade or in the course of import into or export from India.
2. To provide for the levy, collection, and distribution of taxes on sale of goods in the course of inter-State trade or commerce.
3. To declare certain goods to be of special importance in inter-State trade and specify the restrictions to which State laws imposing taxes on the sale and purchase of such goods of special importance shall be subject.

The regulations contained in the CST Act provided, *inter alia*, for a degree of uniformity by prescribing a maximum rate of sales tax on certain goods considered important for the whole country. According to Section 3 of the CST Act, a sale or purchase of goods was deemed to take place in the course of inter-State trade if it: (a) occasions the movement of goods from one State to another, or (b) is effected by a transfer of documents of title to the goods during their movement from one State to another.

Section 14 of the Act declared certain goods to be of special importance in inter-State trade and commerce. These were coal, cereals, cotton, cotton yarn, cotton fabrics, crude oil, hides and skins, iron and steel, jute, oilseeds, pulses, rayon and artificial silk fabrics, sugar, tobacco, woollen fabrics. The list of *declared goods* originally covered by the Act in 1956 was expanded twice, once in 1957 to include textiles, sugar, and tobacco, and again in 1976 to include cereals (like wheat, paddy, rice etc.), crude oil, and pulses.

Section 15 of the Act laid down the rate structure. The rates were different depending upon the classes of goods and the status of the person to whom the goods were sold. Thus, goods were either *declared goods* (goods of special importance) or *non-*

declared goods while a person was either a registered or a non-registered dealer. Based on these classifications, the rates of sales tax were prescribed by the Central Government though the tax was administered (i.e. assessed, collected and appropriated) by the State Governments by virtue of the powers delegated to them by the Central Government under Article 258(1) of Constitution.

CST was a state-level tax, applied to inter-state sales of goods, based on the origin principle. The tax law (including the base, rates, and the procedures) was enacted by Parliament, but the entire revenue accruing under the levy of CST was collected and kept by the State in which the sale originated. The Act excluded taxation of imports and exports. It was a perfect example of absolute harmonization, with the States enjoying the risks and rewards of ownership of the tax.

CST was subsumed under GST when the latter came into force on July 1, 2017.

Endnotes

1. Government of India, Ministry of Finance, *Report of the Indirect Taxation Enquiry Committee,* (Chairman: L.K. Jha), 1977, Part I, p. 50.
2. See endnote 5 of chapter 6 of this book for a note on Empowered Committee.
3. Government of India, Ministry of Finance, *Tax Reforms Committee-Final Report*, Part I, (Chairman: Raja Chelliah), August 1992, p. 174.

5

Problems Created by Multiple Taxation of Goods and States' Exclusion from Taxing Services

Prior to the implementation of GST, indirect tax system of India was inefficient, complicated and fragmented. For example, State level sales tax/VAT was a levy on commodities which, in most cases, were also subject to excise duties imposed by the Centre. As excise duty and sales tax were levied by different layers of Government, it became difficult to determine judiciously the impact of these levies on production, investment, and the consumers. Since the Centre and States acted independently without co-ordination among themselves, there was hardly any possibility to rationalize commodity tax system successfully.

5.1 Multiplicity of Taxes and Rates

The multiplicity of taxes at the Central and State levels resulted in a complex indirect tax structure in the country that was ridden with hidden costs for the trade and industry. There was no uniformity of tax rates and structure across States.

Differential rates of sales tax on the same set of commodities in different States often led to uneconomic diversion of trade as well as production centres. It was not uncommon for people of one State making purchases in other States to avoid or reduce sales tax liability. In order to attract trade and industry to their respective areas, some States indulged in a kind of *rate war* (competitive reductions in sales tax rates).

Likewise, rate differentials caused flight of capital and enterprise from high to low tax rate States thereby distorting natural selection of production centres based on geographical advantages, leading to unnecessary transportation of raw materials and finished goods and hence cost escalations.

It is noteworthy that GST has subsumed under it 17 indirect taxes (8 Central and 9 State taxes). GST is a single tax on the supply of goods or services or both, right from the manufacturer to the consumer. Credits of input taxes paid at each stage are available in the subsequent stage of value addition, which makes GST essentially a tax only on value addition at each stage.

5.2 Complexity of Administration and Compliance

In spite of the improvements made in the tax design and administration, the systems at both the Central and State levels remained complex. Their administration left a lot to be desired. There were often disputes and court challenges, and the process for resolution of disputes was slow and expensive. At the same time, the systems suffered from substantial compliance gaps, except in the highly organized sectors of the economy.

There were several factors contributing to this unsatisfactory state of affairs. The most significant cause of complexity was the existence of exemptions and multiple rates, and the irrational structure of the levies. These deficiencies were the most glaring in the case of the CENVAT and the service tax.

Compounding the structural or design deficiencies of each of the taxes was the poor or archaic infrastructure for their administration. Taxpayer services were virtually non-existent or grossly inadequate under both Central and State administrations. Many of the administrative processes were still manual, not benefiting from the efficiencies of automation. All this not only increased the costs of compliance, but also undermined revenue collection.

5.3 Tax Cascading

Tax cascading was the most serious flaw of the pre-GST indirect tax system. There was a burden of *tax-on-tax* in the erstwhile system of Central excise duties and States' sales taxes. It increased the cost of production and put Indian suppliers at a competitive disadvantage in the international markets. It created a bias in favour of imports, which did not bear the hidden burden of taxes on production inputs. It also detracted from a neutral application of tax to competing products. Although the statutory rate was uniform, the effective tax rate (i.e. statutory rate on finished products and the implicit or hidden tax on production inputs) varied from product to product depending on the magnitude of the hidden tax on inputs used in their production and distribution. The intended impact of government policy towards sectors or households was negated by the indirect or hidden taxation in a cascading system of taxes.

There was a burden of multiple taxation in the form of Central excise duty and the States' sales tax systems. Before any commodity was produced, inputs were first taxed, and then after the commodity got produced with input tax load, output was taxed again. This was causing burden of multiple taxation (i.e. *tax-on-tax*) with a cascading effect. Moreover, in the sales tax structure, there was also a system of multi-point sales taxation at subsequent levels of distributive trade, thus aggravating the cascading effect further.

Tax cascading occurred under both the Central and State taxes. The most significant contributing factor to tax cascading was the partial coverage of Central and State taxes. Oil and gas production, mining, agriculture, wholesale and retail trade, real estate construction, and a range of services remained outside the ambit of excise duties and the service tax levied by the Centre. The exempt sectors were not allowed to claim any credit for the excise duties or the service tax paid on their inputs.

Similarly, under the States' sales tax, no credits were allowed for the inputs of the exempt sectors, which included the entire service sector, real estate sector, agriculture, oil and gas production and mining.

No credit of excise duty and service tax paid at the stage of manufacture was available to the traders while paying the State level sales tax, and vice-versa. Further, no credit of State taxes paid in one State could be availed in other States. Hence, the prices of goods and services got artificially inflated to the extent of this *tax-on-tax*.

Another major contributing factor to tax cascading was the Central sales tax (CST) on inter-state sales, collected by the originating state and for which no credit was allowed by any level of government.

The introduction of Central VAT (CENVAT) did remove the cascading burden of taxes to a good extent by providing a mechanism of set-offs for tax paid on inputs and services up to the stage of production, and was an improvement over the pre-CENVAT Central excise regime. Similarly, the introduction of VAT by the States removed the cascading effect by giving set-off for tax paid on inputs as well as tax paid on previous purchases and again was an improvement over the previous sales tax regime.

However, both the CENVAT and the State VAT had certain deficiencies. CENVAT was deficient because it did not extend to include the chain of value additions in the distributive trade below the stage of production. Further, it did not include several Central taxes (such as additional excise duties, additional customs duties, surcharges etc.) in its overall framework. Hence, the benefits of a comprehensive input tax set-offs were not available to manufacturers/dealers under CENVAT.

Likewise, in the State-level VAT scheme, CENVAT load on the goods was not removed and the cascading effect of that part of tax burden had remained unrelieved. Moreover, there were several taxes in the States (such as luxury tax, entertainment tax, etc.) which had not been subsumed under the VAT. In addition, although the burden of Central sales tax (CST) on inter-State movement of goods had been lessened with reduction of CST rate from 4 percent to 2 percent, this burden had also not been fully phased out.

In any case, CENVAT and State VAT were much better than the system that prevailed earlier. Notable among the improvements made were the following:

1. Rationalization of the CENVAT rates by reducing their multiplicity and replacing many of the specific rates by ad valorem rates based on the maximum retail price (MRP) of the products.
2. Introduction of the service tax by the Centre, and a substantial expansion of its base over the years.
3. Replacement of the single-point state sales taxes by the VAT in all of the States and Union Territories.
4. Reduction in the Central sales tax (CST) rate to 2 percent, from 4 percent, as part of a complete phase out of the tax.

These changes yielded significant dividends in economic efficiency of the tax system, ease of compliance, and growth in revenues.

With the introduction of GST, a continuous chain of set-off from the original producer's point and service provider's point up to the retailer's level has been established, eliminating the burden of all *cascading* or *pyramiding* effects of an indirect tax system. This is the essence of GST. GST taxes only the final consumer. Hence the cascading of taxes (*tax-on-tax*) is avoided and production costs are cut down.

GST has taken under its wings a profusion of indirect taxes of the Centre and the States. It has integrated taxes on goods and services for set-off relief. Further, it has also captured certain value additions in the distributive trade. There is now a continuous chain of set-offs which would eliminate the burden of all cascading effects.

By amalgamating a large number of Central and State taxes into a single tax and allowing set-off of prior-stage taxes, GST has mitigated the ill effects of cascading and pave the way for a common national market. A system of seamless tax credits throughout the value-chain, and across boundaries of States, has ensured that there is minimal cascading of taxes. This would reduce hidden costs of doing business.

Complete and comprehensive input tax set-off and phasing out of CST would reduce the cost of locally manufactured goods and services. These may lead to lowering of tax burden on an average dealer in industry and trade. This will increase the competitiveness of Indian goods and services in the international market and give boost to Indian exports.

5.4 States' Exclusion from Taxing Services

During the pre-GST system, States were precluded from taxing services. This arrangement posed difficulties in taxation of goods supplied as part of a composite works contract involving a supply of both goods and services, and under leasing contracts, which entailed a transfer of the right to use goods without any transfer of their ownership. While these problems were addressed by amending the Constitution to bring such transactions within the ambit of the State taxation [1], services per se remained outside the scope of state taxation powers. This limitation was unsatisfactory from two perspectives.

First, the advancements in information technology and digitization have blurred the distinction between goods and services. Under Indian jurisprudence, goods are defined to include intangibles, e.g. copyright, and software, bringing them within the purview of state taxation. However, intangibles are often supplied under arrangements which have the appearance of a service contract. For example, software upgrades (which are goods) can be supplied as part of a contract for software repair and maintenance services. Software development contracts could take the character of contracts for manufacturing and sale of software goods or for rendering software development services, depending on the roles and responsibilities of the parties. The so-called value added services (VAS) provided as part of telecommunication services include supplies some of which could be considered goods. An on-line subscription to newspapers could be viewed as a service, but online purchase and download of a magazine or a book could constitute a purchase of goods. This blurring also clouds the application of tax to transactions relating to tangible property. For example, disputes have arisen whether leasing of equipment without transfer of possession and control to the lessee would be taxable as a service or as a deemed sale of goods.

The traditional distinctions between goods and services found in the Indian Constitution have become archaic. In markets today, goods, services, and other types of supplies are being packaged as composite bundles and offered for sale to consumers under a variety of supply-chain arrangements. Under the pre-GST division of taxation powers, neither the Centre nor the States could apply the tax to such bundles in a seamless manner. Each could tax only parts of the bundle, creating the possibility of gaps or overlaps in taxation.

The second major concern with the exclusion of services from the state taxation powers was its negative impact on the buoyancy of State tax revenues. With the growth in per capita incomes, services account for a growing fraction of the total consumer basket, which the states could not tax. With no powers to levy tax on incomes or the fastest growing components of consumer expenditures, the States had to rely almost exclusively on compliance improvements or rate increases for any buoyancy in their *own-source revenues*.

Despite a certain degree of success, there were still certain shortcomings in the structure of VAT both at the Central and at the State level. The shortcoming in CENVAT of the Centre lied in non-inclusion of several Central taxes in the overall framework of CENVAT, such as additional customs duty, surcharges etc., and thus keeping the benefits of comprehensive input tax and service tax set-off out of reach for manufacturers/dealers. Moreover, no step was taken to capture the value-added chain in the distribution trade below the manufacturing level in the scheme of CENVAT.

In the State-level VAT structure there were also certain shortcomings. There were several taxes in the nature of indirect tax on goods and services—such as luxury tax, entertainment tax etc.—and not yet subsumed in the VAT.

The design of the CENVAT and state VAT was dictated by the constraints imposed by the constitution, which allowed neither the Centre nor the States to levy taxes on a comprehensive base of all goods and services and at all points in their supply chain. The Centre was constrained from levying the tax on goods beyond the point of manufacturing, and the States in extending the tax to services. This division of tax powers made both the CENVAT and the state VAT partial in nature and contributed to their inefficiency and complexity.

In short, pre-GST indirect tax system of India was mired in multi-layered taxes levied by the Central and State Governments at different stages of the supply chain. It suffered from the following drawbacks:

1. Multiplicity of taxes and tax rates.
2. Complexity of administration and compliance.
3. Tax cascading.
4. States' exclusion from taxing services.

GST has subsumed a profusion of Central and State indirect taxes to create a single unified market. It is slated to make India a seamless national market, boosting trade and industry and hence growth rate.

GST is a tax on goods and services with comprehensive and continuous chain of set-off benefits from the producer's point and service provider's point up to the retailer's level. It is essentially a tax only on value addition at each stage, and a supplier at each stage is permitted to set-off, through a tax credit mechanism, the GST paid on the purchase of goods and services. The final consumer only bears the GST charged by the last dealer in the supply chain.

Endnote

1. Section 4 of the Constitution (Forty-sixth Amendment) Act, 1982, inserted the following clause 29A in Article 366 of the Constitution to deem a tax on the following six items to be a tax on the sale or purchase of goods.

[(29A). "tax on the sale or purchase of goods" includes:

(a) a tax on the transfer, otherwise than in pursuance of a contract, of property in any goods for cash, deferred payment or other valuable consideration;

(b) a tax on the transfer of property in goods (whether as goods or in some other form) involved in the execution of a works contract;

(c) a tax on the delivery of goods on hire-purchase or any system of payment by instalments;

(d) a tax on the transfer of the right to use any goods for any purpose (whether or not for a specified period) for cash, deferred payment or other valuable consideration;

(e) a tax on the supply of goods by any unincorporated association or body of persons to a member thereof for cash, deferred payment or other valuable consideration; and

(f) a tax on the supply, by way of or as part of any service or in any other manner whatsoever, of goods, being food or any other article for human consumption or any drink (whether or not intoxicating), where such supply or service, is for cash, deferred payment or other valuable consideration, and such transfer, delivery or supply of any goods shall be deemed to be a sale of those goods by the person making the transfer, delivery or supply and a purchase of those goods by the person to whom such transfer, delivery or supply is made].

Part II

Early Thoughts, Preparations for GST and Current Constitutional Provisions Pertaining to Taxes

6

Empowered Committee (EC) of State Finance Ministers and the Road Map for GST

After an arduous journey of 12 years—beginning with the mention of Goods and Services Tax (GST) by the Finance Minister Shri P. Chidambaram in his budget speech for 2005-06 on February 28, 2005—GST finally became operative on July 1, 2017. The historic tax reform saw various ups and downs during this period.

6.1 The Genesis

GST was first recommended by the Task Force on Implementation of the Fiscal Responsibility and Budget Management Act, 2003 (Chairman: Vijay Kelkar). The Report of the Task Force observed, "The introduction of the GST at both Central and State levels should be accompanied by the withdrawal of all cascading taxes such as octroi, Central Sales Tax, state level sales taxes, entry tax, stamp duties, telecom license fees, turnover taxes, tax on consumption or sale of electricity, taxes on transportation of goods and passengers etc. This removal of inefficient and distortionary taxes would constitute a major milestone for reforms in Indian public finance.

The Central Excise Act and the taxation of services by the Finance Act, 1994, will be subsumed under the central goods and services tax. This should be implemented through a legislation which may be named Indian Goods and Services Act. The States will need to simultaneously introduce corresponding legislation for taxation of goods and services which will subsume their existing State-level cascading taxes. Under this proposed *grand bargain*, the States obtain revenues from taxation of services, and from access to GST on imports. More importantly, India would obtain the full efficiencies of a single national VAT, while retaining a federal structure". [1]

The idea of moving towards the GST was first mooted by the then Union Finance Minister Shri P. Chidambaram in his budget speech for 2005-06 on February 28, 2005. He observed, "In the medium to long-term, it is my goal that the entire production-distribution chain should be covered by a national VAT, or even better, a goods and services tax, encompassing both the Centre and the States". [2] Reiterating the desirability of switching over to GST, he remarked in his budget speech for 2006-07, "It is my sense that there is a large consensus that the country should move towards a national level Goods and Services Tax (GST) that should be shared between the Centre and the States. I propose that we set April 1, 2010 as the date for introducing GST. World over, goods and services attract the same rate of tax. That is the foundation of a GST. People must get used to the idea of a GST". [3, 4]

6.2 Role of the Empowered Committee (EC) of State Finance Ministers

While declaring its intention to introduce GST from April 1, 2010, the Central Government had indicated that the Empowered Committee (EC) of State Finance Ministers [5] would work with the Central Government to prepare a road map for the introduction of GST. Hence, EC—which had formulated the design of State level VAT—prepared a report on a Model and Road Map for GST. Pursuant to this, on May 10, 2007, EC set up a Joint Working Group consisting of representatives of the EC and the Government of India.

This Joint Working Group got itself divided into three Sub-Groups and had several rounds of internal discussions as well as interaction with experts and representatives of Chambers of Commerce and Industry. On the basis of these discussions and interaction, the Sub-Groups submitted their reports which were then integrated and consolidated into the report of Joint Working Group (November 19, 2007).

6.2.1 Model and Road Map for GST: This report was discussed in detail in the meeting of the EC on November 28, 2007, and the States were also requested to communicate their observations on the report in writing. On the basis of these discussions in the EC and the written observations, certain modifications were considered necessary and were discussed with the representatives of the Department of Revenue, Ministry of Finance, Government of India. With the modifications duly made, a final version of the views of EC resulted in the preparation of *A Model and Road Map for Goods and Service Tax in India* (April 30, 2008). The model and road map, while recommending that a dual GST be put in place, also provided preliminary views on the Central and State taxes to be subsumed within the GST.

The *model* detailed the operational issues which needed to be addressed, including the number of rates, exemptions and exclusions from GST, as well as the treatment of inter-state transactions.

The *road map* outlined the legal and administrative steps which needed to be taken in order to comply with the April 1, 2010 deadline.

These views of EC were then sent to the Government of India, and the comments of Government of India were received on December 12, 2008. These comments were duly considered by the EC (December 16, 2008), and it was decided that a Committee of Principal Secretaries/Secretaries of Finance/Taxation and Commissioners of Trade Taxes of the States should be set up to consider these comments, and submit their views.

The Committee held detailed deliberations on January 5-6, 2009, and submitted its recommendations to the Empowered Committee. The Empowered Committee considered these recommendations in its meeting held on January 21, 2009 and accepted them in-principle.

6.2.2 First Discussion Paper on GST: As a follow-up of this in-principle acceptance, a Working Group consisting of the concerned officials of the State Governments was formed who, in association with senior representatives of Government of India, submitted their recommendations in detail on the structure of GST.

After taking into account a detailed view on the recommendations of the Working

Group of officials and other related matters, EC released the *First Discussion Paper on Goods and Services Tax in India* (November 10, 2009, for discussion with industry, trade, agriculture and people at large. The comments of Government of India on the proposed design of GST were sent to the Empowered Committee in January 2010. A joint group of officers was constituted to prepare draft Constitutional Bill, Central GST legislation, model State GST legislation and rules required to introduce GST. To operationalize the GST, the Constitution (One Hundred and Fifteenth Amendment) Bill was introduced in the Lok Sabha in March 2011 to enable Parliament and State Legislatures to make laws for levying GST on every transaction of supply of goods or services or both. Some goods, namely crude petroleum, diesel, petrol, aviation turbine fuel, natural gas and alcohol were not to come under the purview of the GST.

The Discussion Paper was divided into 4 sections. Section 1 gave a brief reference to the process of introduction of VAT by the Centre and the States and also indicated the precise points where there was a need for further improvement. This section also showed how GST could bring about this improvement. With this as the background and justification for GST, section 2 then described the process of preparation for GST. Thereafter, section 3 presented in detail the comprehensive structure of the GST model. For illustrating this GST model further, there was in the end an annexure on frequently asked questions and answers.

6.3 Summary of Recommendations of the First Discussion Paper (FDP)

6.3.1 Goods and Services Tax Model for India: FDP took note of the significant administrative issues involved in designing an effective GST model in a federal system with the objective of having an overall harmonious structure of rates. Together with this, it emphasized the need for upholding the powers of Central and State Governments in their taxation matters. Further, it underlined the need to propose a model that would be easily implementable, while being generally acceptable to stakeholders.

A dual GST structure with defined functions and responsibilities of the Centre and the States was recommended. An appropriate mechanism that would be binding on both the Centre and the States would be worked out whereby the harmonious rate structure along with the need for further modification could be upheld, if necessary with a collectively agreed constitutional amendment.

Salient features of the model recommended by FDP were as follows:

1. GST should have two components—one levied by the Centre (referred to as Central GST), and the other levied by the States (referred to as State GST). Rates for Central GST and State GST would be prescribed appropriately, reflecting revenue considerations and acceptability. This dual GST model would be implemented through multiple statutes (one for CGST and SGST statute for every State). However, the basic features of law such as chargeability, definition of taxable event and taxable person, measure of levy including valuation provisions, basis of classification etc. would be uniform across these statutes as far as practicable.
2. Central GST and the State GST would be applicable to all transactions of goods and

services made for a consideration except the exempted goods and services, goods which remain outside the purview of GST and the transactions which are below the prescribed threshold limits.

3. Central GST and State GST are to be paid to the accounts of the Centre and the States separately. It would have to be ensured that account-heads for all services and goods would have indication whether it relates to Central GST or State GST (with identification of the State to whom the tax is to be credited).
4. Since the Central GST and State GST are to be treated separately, taxes paid against the Central GST shall be allowed to be taken as input tax credit (ITC) for the Central GST and could be utilized only against the payment of Central GST. The same principle would be applicable for the State GST. A taxpayer or exporter would have to maintain separate details in books of account for utilization or refund of credit. Further, the rules for taking and utilization of credit for the Central GST and the State GST would be aligned.
5. Cross utilization of ITC between the Central GST and the State GST would not be allowed except in the case of inter-State supply of goods and services under the IGST mode.
6. Ideally, the problem related to credit accumulation on account of refund of GST should be avoided by both the Centre and the States except in the cases such as exports, purchase of capital goods, input tax at higher rate than output tax etc. where, again refund/adjustment should be completed in a time bound manner.
7. To the extent feasible, uniform procedure for collection of both Central GST and State GST should be prescribed in the respective legislation for Central GST and State GST.
8. Administration of the Central GST to the Centre and for State GST to the States was recommended. This would imply that the Centre and the States would have concurrent jurisdiction for the entire value chain and for all taxpayers on the basis of thresholds for goods and services prescribed for the States and the Centre.
9. FDP noted that existing threshold prescribed in different State VAT Acts—below which VAT was not applicable—varied from State to State. A uniform State GST threshold across States was desirable and, therefore, it was recommended that a threshold of gross annual turnover of ₹ 10 lakh—both for goods and services for all the States and Union Territories—may be adopted with adequate compensation for the States (particularly, the States in North-Eastern Region and Special Category States) where lower threshold had prevailed in the VAT regime. Keeping in view the interest of small traders and small-scale industries and to avoid dual control, the threshold for Central GST for goods may be kept at ₹ 1.5 crore and the threshold for Central GST for services may also be appropriately high.
10. Composition/compounding scheme for the purpose of GST should have an upper ceiling on gross annual turnover and a floor tax rate with respect to gross annual turnover. In particular, there should be a compounding cut-off at ₹ 50 lakh of gross annual turn over and a floor rate of 0.5 percent across the States. The scheme should

also allow option for GST registration for dealers with turnover below the compounding cut-off.

11. Taxpayer would need to submit periodical returns, in common format as far as possible, to both the Central GST authority and to the concerned State GST authorities.
12. Each taxpayer would be allotted a PAN-linked taxpayer identification number with a total of 13/15 digits. This would bring the GST PAN-linked system in line with the prevailing PAN-based system for Income tax, facilitating data exchange and taxpayer compliance.
13. Keeping in mind the need of tax payer's convenience, functions such as assessment, enforcement, scrutiny and audit would be undertaken by the authority which is collecting the tax, with information sharing between the Centre and the States.

6.3.2 Subsumation of Central and State Taxes under GST: The various Central, State and Local levies were examined to identify their possibility of being subsumed under GST. While identifying these levies, the following principles were kept in mind:

1. Taxes or levies to be subsumed should be primarily in the nature of indirect taxes, either on the supply of goods or on the supply of services.
2. Taxes or levies to be subsumed should be part of the transaction chain which commences with import/manufacture/production of goods or provision of services at one end and the consumption of goods and services at the other.
3. Subsumation should result in free flow of tax credit in intra and inter-State levels.
4. Taxes, levies and fees that are not specifically related to supply of goods and services should not be subsumed under GST.
5. Revenue fairness for both the Union and the States individually would need to be attempted.

On application of the above principles, FDP recommended that the following Central taxes should be, to begin with, subsumed under the GST:

1. Central excise duty.
2. Additional excise duties.
3. Excise duty levied under the Medicinal and Toiletries Preparation Act.
4. Service tax.
5. Additional customs duty, commonly known as countervailing duty (CVD).
6. Special additional duty (SAD) of customs.
7. Surcharges.
8. Cesses.

Following State taxes and levies, to begin with, were recommended for subsumation under GST:

1. VAT/sales tax.
2. Entertainment tax (unless it is levied by the local bodies).
3. Luxury tax.
4. Taxes on lottery, betting and gambling.
5. State cesses and surcharges in so far as they relate to supply of goods and services.

6. Entry tax not in lieu of octroi.

6.3.3 Purchase Tax: Some of the States were getting substantial revenue from purchase tax and, therefore, they were not in favour of its subsumation under GST while majority of the States were of the view that no such exemptions should be given. The difficulties of the foodgrains producing States and certain other States were appreciated as substantial revenue was being earned by them from purchase tax and it was, therefore, felt that in case purchase tax had to be subsumed then adequate and continuing compensation should be provided to such States. This issue was discussed in consultation with the Government of India.

6.3.4 Tax on Items Containing Alcohol: Alcoholic beverages would be kept out of the purview of GST. Sales tax/VAT can be continued to be levied on alcoholic beverages as per the existing practice. In case it has been made VATable by some States, there is no objection to that. Excise duty, which is presently being levied by the States may not be also affected.

6.3.5 Tax on Tobacco Products: Tobacco products would be subjected to GST with ITC. Centre may be allowed to levy excise duty on tobacco products over and above GST without ITC.

6.3.6 Tax on Petroleum Products: As regards petroleum products, it was decided that the basket of petroleum products, i.e. crude, motor spirit (including ATF) and HSD would be kept outside GST as is the prevailing practice in India. Sales tax could continue to be levied by the States on these products with prevailing floor rate. Similarly, Centre could also continue its levies. A final view whether natural gas should be kept outside the GST would be taken after further deliberations.

6.3.7 Inter-State Transactions of Goods and Services: IGST model for taxation of inter-State transaction of goods and services would be adopted. The scope of IGST Model is that Centre would levy IGST which would be CGST plus SGST on all inter-State transactions of taxable goods and services with appropriate provision for consignment or stock transfer of goods and services. The inter-State seller would pay IGST on value addition after adjusting available credit of IGST, CGST, and SGST on his purchases. The Exporting State would transfer to the Centre the credit of SGST used in payment of IGST. The Importing dealer would claim credit of IGST while discharging his output tax liability in his own State. The Centre would transfer to the importing State the credit of IGST used in payment of SGST. The relevant information would also be submitted to the Central Agency which would act as a clearing house mechanism, verify the claims and inform the respective governments to transfer the funds.

6.3.8 GST Rate Structure: FDP suggested a two-rate structure—a lower rate for necessary items and goods of basic importance and a standard rate for goods in general. It also recommended a special rate for precious metals and a list of exempted items. For upholding of special needs of each State as well as a balanced approach to federal flexibility, and also for facilitating the introduction of GST, it was discussed whether the exempted list under VAT regime including goods of local importance be retained in the exempted list under State GST in the initial years. It was also deliberated whether the

Government of India may adopt, to begin with, a similar approach towards exempted list under the CGST.

The States were of the view that for CGST relating to goods, the Government of India may also have a two rate structure, with conformity in the levels of rate under the SGST. For taxation of services, there may be a single rate for both CGST and SGST. The exact value of the SGST and CGST rates, including the rate for services, would be made known duly in course of appropriate legislative actions.

6.3.9 Zero Rating of Exports: Exports would be zero-rated. Similar benefits may be given to special economic zones (SEZs). However, such benefits would only be allowed to the processing zones of the SEZs. No benefit to the sales from an SEZ to domestic tariff area (DTA) should be allowed.

6.3.10 GST on Imports: The GST will be levied on imports with necessary Constitutional Amendments. Both CGST and SGST should be levied on import of goods and services into the country. The incidence of tax would follow the destination principle and the tax revenue in case of SGST would accrue to the State where the imported goods and services are consumed. Full and complete set-off would be available on the GST paid on import on goods and services.

6.3.11 Special Industrial Area Scheme: After the introduction of GST, the tax exemptions, remissions etc. related to industrial incentives should be converted, if at all needed, into cash refund schemes after collection of tax, so that the GST scheme on the basis of a continuous chain of set-offs is not disturbed. Regarding Special Industrial Area Schemes, it was clarified that such exemptions, remissions etc. would continue up to legitimate expiry time both for the Centre and the States. Any new exemption, remission etc. or continuation of earlier exemption, remission etc. would not be allowed. In such cases, the Central and the State Governments could provide reimbursement after collecting GST.

6.3.12 Compensation during Implementation of GST: Despite the sincere attempts made by the Empowered Committee on the determination of GST rate structure, revenue neutral rates, it was difficult to estimate accurately as to how much the States would gain from service taxes and how much they would lose on account of removal of cascading effect, payment of input tax credit and phasing out of CST. In view of this, it would be essential to provide adequately for compensation for loss that might emerge during the process of implementation of GST for the next 5 years. The payment of this compensation will need to be ensured in terms of special grants to be released to the States duly in every month on the basis of neutrally monitored mechanism.

6.4 Model GST Design Advocated by Thirteenth Finance Commission (XIII-FC)

XIII-FC was required to consider 'the impact of the proposed implementation of Goods and Services Tax...including its impact on the country's foreign trade', while formulating its recommendations.

Given the large positive economic and fiscal externalities of the GST reform, putting in place an incentive structure to motivate all stakeholders to design and implement such a model GST was, therefore, a prime concern of XIII-FC. A number of State Governments and industry associations communicated to FC-XIII their concerns on the design and implementation of GST.

XIII-FC—which submitted its report in December 2009 for the period 2010-15—outlined the design and modalities of a model GST law. Such a model GST would not distinguish between goods and services. It should be levied at a single positive rate on all goods and services. Exports should be zero-rated. Tax compliance costs should be low and tax credits should be available seamlessly across tax jurisdictions. The other design and operational modalities of a model GST advocated by XIII-FC are outlined below.

6.4.1 Taxes to be Subsumed: For the GST to be purely consumption-based, all related indirect taxes and cesses should be subsumed into it. Thus, the Central GST portion would subsume the following taxes:

1. Central excise duties and additional excise duties.
2. Service tax.
3. Additional customs duty (countervailing duty).
4. All surcharges and cesses

State GST portion would subsume the following taxes:

1. Value added tax (VAT).
2. Central sales tax (CST).
3. Entry tax, whether in lieu of octroi or otherwise.
4. Luxury tax.
5. Taxes on lottery, betting and gambling.
6. Entertainment tax.
7. Purchase tax.
8. State excise duties.
9. Stamp duty.
10. Taxes on vehicles.
11. Tax on goods and passengers.
12. Taxes and duties on electricity.
13. All state cesses and surcharges.

6.4.2 Special Provisions for Certain Goods: The taxation of petroleum products and natural gas would be rationalised by including them in the tax base. High speed diesel, motor spirit and aviation turbine fuel could be charged GST and an additional levy by both the Central and State Governments. No input credit would be available against either Central GST or State GST on the additional levy. A similar treatment would be provided to alcohol and tobacco. Such an arrangement would ensure protection of existing revenues while taking care of environmental concerns.

6.4.3 Exemptions: No exemptions should be allowed other than a common list applicable to all states as well as the Centre, which should only comprise: (a) unprocessed food items, (b) public services provided by all governments excluding railways, communications, and public sector enterprises, (c) service transactions between an employer and employee and (d) health and education services.

A threshold of ₹ 10 lakh and a composition limit of ₹ 40 lakh have been agreed upon by the Empowered Committee for State GST in the first discussion draft. It is desirable that these limits be applied to Central GST as well. Sales of goods of local importance will fall within these threshold limits, thus keeping them out of the ambit of GST.

6.4.4 Treatment of Inter-state Sales: All transactions across tax jurisdictions should be free from tax. While exports will be zero-rated, inter-state transactions should be effectively zero-rated so as to ensure that the tax is collected by the consuming state consistent with the destination principle. Therefore, any model adopted must allow accurate determination and efficient transfer of input tax credit across tax jurisdictions. Further, the model should not impose any undue restrictions on tax credit set-off or increase in compliance costs.

6.4.5 GST on Imports: Imports from outside the country would be subject to GST on the destination principle. This will require that proof of consumption at a pre-determined destination state is provided. The procedure for collection and appropriation of this tax needs to be put in place. Rules for transferring this tax burden in the case of importers who sell to a consumer in a third state after the import is made, need to be clarified.

6.4.6 Operational Modalities: To reduce compliance costs and increase collection efficiency, all state GST laws should be harmonised. All stages of the taxation chain, from levy of the tax to its assessment, collection and appropriation, should be similar across states. This would involve similar rules across states, dealing not only with assessments, audit and refunds, but also with more basic issues like registration, filing of returns, treatment of transportation of goods etc.

6.4.7 Dispute Resolution and Advance Ruling Mechanism: An effective, efficient and uniform system for redressal of anomalies in the legislation should be put in place. This could be an independent and quasi-judicial authority with full powers to look into all disputes related to GST implementation, both at the Central and state levels. Such an authority could issue guidelines, administer and enforce agreement between states and the Centre, and between the states themselves. A common Advance Ruling Authority for both the Centre and the states should also be put in place.

6.4.8 Refunds: Prompt refunds form the core of an effective GST framework, especially as cross-utilisation of input tax credit across Central GST and State GST, is not envisaged. Delayed payment of refunds enhances the cost of dealer operations and reduces the efficiency of the tax system. The experience with refunds under the VAT regime is not reassuring, even though VAT laws in a number of states mandate payment of interest for delay. State Governments must adopt a more effective refund system. They could consider an electronic system where refunds are directly credited to the eligible dealer's bank account.

6.4.9 Disincentives for Non-compliance: Keeping in mind the experience under VAT it may become necessary to deter violations of agreement by visiting a penalty on non-complying states. XIII-FC recommended that state specific grants and the state's share of the GST incentive grant be withheld for the period during which a state is in violation of the agreement. If a state is in violation for only part of a year, its grant should be reduced to a proportionate extent.

6.4.10 Compensation/Incentive Grants: XIII-FC was aware that the tenor of the ongoing discussions on the GST model and implementation modalities did not include some of the major elements of the model GST. Any major deviation from the concept of the model GST would dilute its positive externalities, significantly reduce its benefits and reduce the incentive to switch over. To incentivise implementation of such a *grand bargain* between the centre and the states, XIII-FC recommended the sanction of a grant of ₹ 50,000 crore to be provided to all states in the aggregate, subject to the GST framework adopted being consistent with the *grand bargain*. XIII-FC recognized that while GST on the whole will be revenue neutral, there may be some winners and losers during the initial years of implementation. This grant will accommodate claims for compensation from the adversely affected states and balance will be distributed amongst states as per the devolution formula for sharing of Central tax revenues.

6.4.11 Modalities for Disbursing Compensation: States had requested that an objective compensation mechanism to support possible revenue losses after implementing GST be put in place. XIII-FC recommended the following:

1. Present Empowered Committee be transformed into a statutory Council of Finance Ministers with representation from the Centre and states. A GST Compensation Fund should be created under the administrative control of this Council.
2. Central Government shall transfer to the GST Compensation Fund amounts as indicated subject to prescribed conditionalities.
3. Amounts in the Fund should be used for compensating states for any revenue loss on account of adoption of the model GST and the *grand bargain* as indicated. The balance, if any, remaining on January 1, 2015, will be distributed amongst the states on the basis of the devolution formula used by XIII-FC for distributing resources in the divisible pool amongst states.
4. Amount be disbursed in quarterly instalments on the basis of the recommendations made by a three-member Compensation Committee comprising of the Secretary, Department of Revenue, Government of India; Secretary to the EC and chaired by an eminent person with experience in public finance. This person would be appointed by the Union Government.

6.5 Fourteenth Finance Commission (XIV-FC) on GST

There is merit in the universal application of GST in order to have a comprehensive base and, in the long run, all goods and services should be brought under the ambit of GST. In particular, exclusion of any goods from the ambit of GST through Constitutional guarantee is not desirable. This could lead to leakages of revenues due to disruption of tax credit chain and audit trails and would continue to have the problem of cascading. Further, the origin-based distortionary Central sales tax (CST) presently levied on inter-State sales of goods would have to be dispensed with once universalisation is achieved.

In the above context, the Commission recommended as under:

1. There are several challenges and many unresolved issues. In the absence of clarity on the design of GST and the final rate structure, XIV-FC expressed its inability to estimate revenue implications and quantify the amount of compensation in case of revenue loss to the States due to the introduction of GST.
2. The Union may have to initially bear an additional fiscal burden arising due to the GST compensation. This fiscal burden should be treated as an investment which is certain to yield substantial gains to the nation in the medium and long-run. GST compensation can be accommodated in the overall fiscal space available with the Union Government.
3. In the case of VAT, compensation was provided to the States for three years, at 100 percent in the first year, 75 percent in the second year and 50 percent in the third year. XIV-FC considered it appropriate to keep this precedent as the basis for compensation for GST also. However, given the scale of reform and the apprehensions of revenue uncertainty raised by the States, the revenue compensation should be for five years. It was suggested that 100 percent compensation be paid to the States in the first, second and third years, 75 percent compensation in the fourth year and 50 percent compensation in the fifth and final year.
4. XIV-FC recommended the creation of an autonomous and independent GST Compensation Fund through legislative actions in a manner that it gives reasonable comfort to States, while limiting the period of operation appropriately.

6.6 Issues and Problems in Designing GST

What were the thorny issues that required resolution and agreement before the Constitution could be amended to pave way for the introduction of GST? Implementing a tax reform of as vast as GST in a federal and diverse polity like India was by no means an easy task. It required the reconciliation of interests of various States with that of the Centre, revenue protection guarantee, dispute settlement mechanism and other clarities and assurances.

6.6.1 Origin-based versus Destination-based Taxation: An indirect tax can be either origin-based or destination-based. Origin-based tax (also called production tax) is levied where goods/services are produced. Destination-based tax (consumption tax) is levied where goods/services are consumed.

In the pre-GST era, when goods were sold within the State, then sales tax (later VAT) was levied, collected and appropriated by the concerned state. In case goods were sold in the course of inter-State trade, then Central Sales Tax (CST) was levied by Centre but the revenue was collected and appropriated by the exporting state (State of origin) where production or sale took place rather than the State where consumption happened (importing state).

The proposed GST was to be a consumption-based tax. IGST was to be levied by the Central Government on all inter-state transactions of taxable goods and services. IGST rate was to be broadly equal to CGST rate plus SGST rate. SGST component of IGST was to accrue to the importing State rather than the exporting state.

During the discussions to move to GST, many manufacturing States (Maharashtra, Tamil Nadu, Gujarat, Karnataka and others) expressed concerns over the loss of revenue on account of shift from origin-based to destination-based taxation. These States argued that they needed to collect at least some tax from inter-State sales in order to recover the cost of infrastructure and public services provided by them to the industries producing the goods which were consumed in other States. The counter view was that any value addition in a jurisdiction necessarily means extra income in the hands of the residents of that jurisdiction. Spending of this income on consumer goods expands the sales tax base of the producing State and hence contributes to its revenues. In fact, exporting state should be satisfied that goods produced by it are being consumed in other states. Enhanced production activities in the exporting state lead to more employment opportunities for its residents and profit earning by its entrepreneurs, apart from other benefits of higher production.

Nevertheless, to allay the fears of manufacturing states, it was decided to compensate states which may suffer revenue loss consequent upon the introduction of GST. To raise revenue for this purpose, compensation cess on the supply of certain goods (mainly luxury items) was decided upon.

Section 18 of the Constitutional (One Hundred First Amendment) Act, 2016 incorporated provisions for such compensation.

Goods and Services Tax (Compensation to States) Act, 2017 was enacted to levy compensation cess for providing compensation to the States for the loss of revenue arising on account of implementation of the goods and services tax.

For details, see chapter 32 of this book.

6.6.2 Rate Structure Determination: Considerable uncertainty prevailed as regards the revenue implications of the proposed GST. It was difficult to estimate accurately as to how much the States would gain by the inclusion of services in the GST. Similarly, it was difficult to estimate the loss of revenue on account of phasing out of CST. However, there was a broad consensus that the new tax should be revenue neutral. Hence, efforts were made in this connect and opinion of experts in the field was sought.

For details, see section 16.1 of chapter 16 of this book.

6.6.3 Alcohol and Petroleum Products: Alcohol for human consumption and petroleum products are major sources of revenue for the States. Since the States were uncertain about the impact of GST on their finances, they argued for the exclusion of these products from the ambit of GST. Hence, in the Constitution (One Hundred and Fifteenth Amendment) Bill, 2011, alcohol and five petroleum products—petroleum crude, high speed diesel, motor spirit (commonly known as petrol), natural gas and aviation turbine fuel)—were kept out of GST. However, this Bill lapsed with the dissolution of the 15th Lok Sabha on May 18, 2014.

In the Constitution (One Hundred and Twenty-second Amendment) Bill, 2014, only alcoholic liquor was kept outside GST and the above mentioned five petroleum products were proposed to be brought under GST from a date to be recommended by the GST Council. Thus, it was agreed to keep alcohol completely out of the purview of GST to ensure smooth transition to the new tax regime.

6.6.4 Compensation Guarantee: States were unsure about the financial consequences of the proposed GST. Many of them feared loss of revenue under the proposed GST. In view of these concerns, it was essential to provide adequately for compensation for loss that might emerge during the process of implementation of GST. The payment of this compensation was ensured in terms of special grants to be released to the States on the basis of neutrally-monitored mechanism. Section 18 of the Constitutional (One Hundred First Amendment) Act, 2016 incorporated provisions for such compensation.

In the very First Meeting of GST Council held on September 22-23, 2016, it was decided, inter alia, that Financial year 2015-16 would be the base year for compensating the States in case of any revenue loss to States following the implementation of GST.

6.6.5 Dispute Settlement Mechanism: A harmonized system of taxation like GST necessarily required compliance, by all stakeholders, with the decisions taken by the supreme body, which was later constituted as the GST council. However, the possibility of departure from the decision of such a body could not be ruled out. Any departure would affect other stakeholders and in such circumstances there was the need for a statutory body to which the affected party/parties could approach for dispute resolution. The nature of such dispute resolution body was a contentious issue in the deliberations for designing the proposed GST.

In the Constitution (One Hundred and Fifteenth Amendment) Bill, 2011, which lapsed with the dissolution of the 15th Lok Sabha, a Goods and Services Tax Dispute Settlement Authority was to be constituted. This body was judicial in nature and it was thought that its powers would override the supremacy of the Parliament and the State Legislatures. The Constitution (One Hundred and Twenty-second Amendment) Bill, 2014 departed from the lapsed GST Bill and proposed that the GST Council may decide about the modalities to resolve disputes arising out of its recommendation.

To sum up, a number of legal and administrative steps needed to be taken prior to the implementation of GST. These included consultation with stakeholders, amendments to the Constitution, enactment of new legislations at the level of Centre and the States, administrative reorganisation, staff training and conduct of awareness campaigns amongst stakeholders.

The Constitution did not envisage sharing of tax bases between the Centre and the States. Taxation powers were listed either in the State List or in the Central List of the Seventh Schedule, but not in the Concurrent List of the same Schedule. For the first time since the Constitution was enacted, a tax base under GST was proposed to be shared between the Centre and the States. It was, thus, necessary to put a firm arrangement in place for implementing the GST to prevent deviations from the agreed upon model by either the Centre or the States. It may be recalled that compliance of States with the previously agreed upon guidelines for VAT had not been very uniform. A number of States had deviated from the three-tier VAT rates. This experience underlined the need to put in place an enforcement mechanism. States were equally apprehensive that the

Centre may unilaterally raise tax rates without consulting them.

GST implementation brought several issues to the fore viz., determination of the revenue neutral rate, consensus on the divisible pool of resources, sharing the benefits of cesses, the administrative edifice and the technological platform. A dispute prevention mechanism was needed to facilitate a smooth transition to the GST. The evolution in central transfers and evolving fiscal federalism were to have a key bearing on the health of state finances over the medium term.

Endnotes

1. Government of India, Ministry of Finance, *Report of the Task Force on Implementation of the Fiscal Responsibility and Budget Management Act, 2003* (Chairman: Vijay Kelkar), July 16, 2004, p. 7.
2. Government of India, Ministry of Finance, *Budget Speech of the Finance Minister,* 2005-06, Part A, para 94.
3. Government of India, Ministry of Finance, *Budget Speech of the Finance Minister,* 2006-07, Part B, p. 26.
4. While presenting the budget for 2010-11 to the Parliament on February 26, 2010, Minister of Finance Shri Pranab Mukherjee, rescheduled the time limit for the implementation of GST and expressed the hope that GST, along with the Direct Tax Code (DTC), would be introduced from April 1, 2011.
5. Empowered Committee of State Finance Ministers (EC) was originally set up on July 17, 2000 by the Government of India with the State Finance Ministers of West Bengal, Karnataka, Madhya Pradesh, Maharashtra, Punjab, Uttar Pradesh, Gujarat, Delhi and Meghalaya as members with an objective to monitor the implementation of uniform floor rates of sales tax by States and Union territories, to monitor the phasing out of the sales-tax based incentive schemes, to decide milestones and methods of States to switch over to VAT and to monitor reforms in the Central Sales Tax system existing in the country. Subsequently, State Finance Ministers of Assam, Tamil Nadu, Jammu and Kashmir, Jharkhand and Rajasthan were also notified as the members of the Empowered Committee. On August 12, 2004, the Government of India decided to reconstitute the Empowered committee with State Finance/Taxation Ministers of all States as its members.

   The body was later registered as a Society under the Societies Registration Act (XXI of 1860). The registration certificate was issued on August 17, 2004. Presently, all the Ministers in-charge of Finance/Taxation of all State Governments and Union Territories with legislatures, Additional Secretary (Revenue), Government of India and Member Secretary, Empowered Committee are the members of the Empowered Committee. The Empowered Committee has its office in Delhi Sachivalaya, I.P. Estate, New Delhi where Government of NCT of Delhi has provided accommodation and other facilities. The Society has been receiving contribution from the State Government and Government of India to meet its administrative expenditure and undertake various other activities.

   Recently, in order to strengthen the EC, Thirteenth Finance Commission recommended that a grant of ₹ 30 crore be made to EC, so that they can pursue GST related research work and enhance capacities. Amount of ₹ 30 crore has accordingly been released to EC for creating a corpus of for this purpose.

7

Enactment of Constitution (One Hundred and First Amendment) Act, 2016

Why did the introduction of GST require amendments in the Constitution? The Indian Constitution demarcates the powers of taxation between the Central and State Governments. Prior to the enactment of Constitution (One Hundred and First Amendment) Act, 2016, the Centre had the power to tax goods up to the stage of manufacture and production. Similarly, the States had the power to tax sale and purchase of goods. The power to levy tax on services rested with the Centre exclusively. In other words, the Constitution did not provide for any concurrent taxing powers to the Centre and the States to tax goods and services.

However, for the purpose of introducing a unified goods and services tax across India, conferring of simultaneous powers on the Centre and the States to tax the complete supply chain from production to distribution, and both goods and services, was necessary. Moreover, the Constitution also did not empower the States to impose tax on imports. All these and other issues needed to be addressed through amendments in the Constitution.

7.1 Constitution (One Hundred and Fifteenth Amendment) Bill, 2011

On March 22, 2011, the Constitution (One Hundred and Fifteenth Amendment) Bill, 2011 was introduced in Parliament to enable the levy of GST. However, the Bill lapsed with the dissolution of the 15th Lok Sabha on May 18, 2014.

It is noteworthy that in the said Amendment Bill, alcohol for human consumption and five petroleum products, namely crude oil, petrol, diesel, aviation turbine fuel and natural gas, were kept out of GST.

However, in the Constitution (One Hundred and Twenty-second Amendment) Bill, 2014 (explained below), only alcohol for human consumption was kept outside GST and the above-mentioned five petroleum products were proposed to be brought under GST from a date to be recommended by the GST Council.

Thus, to ensure smooth transition and provide fiscal buffer to States, it was agreed to keep alcohol completely out of the ambit of GST.

The Central Government also retained its power to tax tobacco and tobacco products, though these are also under GST.

7.2 Constitution (One Hundred and Twenty-second Amendment) Bill, 2014

On December 19, 2014, the Constitution (One Hundred and Twenty-second Amendment) Bill, 2014 was introduced in the Lok Sabha to address various issues related to GST.

7.2.1 Main Features: The salient features of the Bill were as follows:

1. Conferring simultaneous power upon Parliament and the State Legislatures to make laws governing goods and services tax.
2. Subsuming of various Central indirect taxes and levies.
3. Subsuming of various indirect taxes and levies of State Governments.
4. Dispensing with the concept of *declared goods of special importance* under the Constitution.
5. Levy of integrated goods and services tax on inter-state transactions of goods and services.
6. GST to be levied on all goods and services, except alcoholic liquor for human consumption. Petroleum and petroleum products to be subject to the levy of GST on a later date notified on the recommendation of the GST Council.
7. Compensation to the states for loss of revenue arising on account of implementation of GST for a period of five years.
8. Creation of GST Council to examine issues relating to goods and services tax and make recommendations to the Union and the States on parameters like rates, taxes, cesses and surcharges to be subsumed, exemption list and threshold limits, model GST laws etc.

The Bill needed to be passed by a two-third majority in both Houses of Parliament and subsequent ratification by at least half of the State Legislatures.

The Bill was passed by the Lok Sabha on May 6, 2015. The Bill was referred to the Select Committee of Rajya Sabha on May 12, 2015. The Select Committee submitted its Report on the Bill on July 22, 2015. Rajya Sabha passed the Bill with 9 amendments on August 3, 2016. Lok Sabha passed the modified Bill on August 8, 2016 approving all the 9 amendments by the Rajya Sabha.

After getting approval of half of the States, [1] it was sent to the President for his assent which was given on September 8, 2016. The Constitution (One Hundred and Twenty-second Amendment) Bill, 2014 was notified as the Constitution (One Hundred and First Amendment) Act, 2016 with effect from September 16, 2016. It came into force from July 1, 2017.

The outer limit for GST rollout was mid-September 2017 given that the Constitution amendment provided a one-year window. In other words, due to constitutional compulsion, the GST had to be rolled out by September 16, 2017 as the existing indirect taxes would have come to an end, and it would not have been possible for either the Centre or the states to collect indirect taxes.

After passage of the Bill by both Houses of Parliament, ratification by State legislatures and receipt of assent by the President, the process of enactment was completed and the road to GST rollout was cleared.

7.3 Constitution (One Hundred and First Amendment) Act, 2016: Main Features

This amendment contained provisions which were necessary for the implementation of GST regime. It subsumed a number of indirect taxes, levied by the Central and State

Governments, under GST. The objective to bring about amendments in the Constitution was to confer power on Parliament and State legislatures to make laws for levying GST simultaneously on every transaction of supply of goods and services. The Amendment Act contained 20 sections.

7.3.1 Insertions of New Articles: Following insertions were made:

A. Article 246A: Special Provision with Respect to Goods and Services Tax: (a) The Legislature of every State, have power to make laws with respect to goods and services tax imposed by the Union or by such State. (b) Parliament has exclusive power to make laws with respect to goods and services tax where the supply of goods, or of services, or both takes place in the course of inter-State trade or commerce.

B. Article 269A: Levy and Collection of Goods and Services Tax in the Course of Inter-State Trade or Commerce: (a) Goods and services tax on supplies in the course of inter-State trade or commerce shall be levied and collected by the Government of India and such tax shall be apportioned between the Union and the States in the manner as may be provided by Parliament by law on the recommendations of the Goods and Services Tax Council. (b) The amount apportioned to a State shall not form part of the Consolidated Fund of India. [2]

In short, Article 269A was inserted to facilitate the levy of Integrated Goods and Services tax (IGST).

C. Article 279A: This Article provides for the constitution of a GST Council. The Union Cabinet in its meeting held on September 12, 2016 approved the setting-up of GST Council and its Secretariat. GST Council works on the basis of consensus. The guiding principle of GST Council is to ensure harmonization on different aspects of GST between the Centre and the States as well as among States. It has been provided in Article 279A that the GST Council, in its discharge of various functions, shall be guided by the need for a harmonized structure of GST and for the development of a harmonized national market for goods and services.

7.3.2 Omission of Article 268A: This Article dealing with service tax to be levied by the Central Government was deleted. Services are now taxed under GST.

7.3.3 Amendments of Existing Articles: These were as under:

A. Amendment of Article 248: The residuary power of legislation of Parliament under Article 248 is now subject to Article 246A.

B. Amendment of Article 249: Article 249 was amended so that if 2/3rd majority resolution is passed by Rajya Sabha, the Parliament will have power to make necessary laws with respect to GST in national interest.

C. Amendment of Article 250: Article 250 was amended so that Parliament will have powers to make laws related to GST during emergency period.

D. Amendment of Article 268: Article 268 was amended to omit excise duty on medicinal and toilet preparations.

E. Amendment of Article 269: Matters relating to sale or purchase of goods which now would be separately dealt with under Article 269A, were excluded from here.

F. Amendment of Article 270: This amendment provides that goods and services tax levied and collected by the Union shall also be distributed between the Union and the States.

G. Amendment of Article 271: This amendment puts restrictions on the power of the Parliament to levy surcharge on GST. In other words, it provides that goods and services on which GST is levied shall not be subject to any surcharge under Article 271.

H. Amendment of Article 286: Clause 3 of this Article relating to tax on certain specified goods with some restrictions was omitted.

I. Amendment of Article 366: The Amendment inserted the following new definitions in this Article.

12A. Definition of *goods and services tax.*

26A. Definition of *services.*

26B. Definition of *state.*

J. Amendment of Article 368: Article 279A (GST Council) also included in the list of Articles where approval of 50 percent of the State Legislatures required to amend the said Article.

7.3.4 Amendment of Sixth Schedule: This schedule relates to the provisions as to the Administration of Tribal Areas in the States of Assam, Meghalaya, Tripura and Mizoram. The Amendment gave power to levy taxes on entertainment and amusements to District Councils of these areas.

7.3.5 Amendment of Seventh Schedule:

A. Union List (List I): It was amended in the following manner:

1. Entry 84 earlier comprised duties of excise on tobacco and other goods manufactured or produced in India except: (a) alcoholic liquors for human consumption; (b) opium, Indian hemp and other narcotic drugs and narcotics, but including medicinal and toilet preparations containing alcohol or any substance, included in sub-paragraph (b) of this entry. After the amendment, it comprises duties of excise on the following goods manufactured or produced in India, namely: (a) petroleum crude; (b) high speed diesel; (c) motor spirit (commonly known as petrol); (d) natural gas; (e) aviation turbine fuel; and (f) tobacco and tobacco products.
2. Entry 92 (taxes on the sale or purchase of newspapers and on advertisements published therein) was omitted.
3. Entry 92-C (taxes on services) was omitted.

B. State List (List II): It was amended in the following manner:

1. Entry 52 (taxes on the entry of goods into a local area for consumption, use or sale therein) was omitted.
2. Entry 54 (taxes on the sale or purchase of goods other than newspapers, subject to the provisions of Entry 92-A of List I) was replaced by "taxes on the sale of petroleum crude, high speed diesel, motor spirit (commonly known as petrol), natural gas, aviation turbine fuel and alcoholic liquor for human consumption, but not including sale in the course of inter-State trade or commerce or sale in the course of international trade or commerce of such goods".
3. Entry 55 [taxes on advertisements other than advertisements published in the

newspapers (and advertisements broadcast by radio or television)] was omitted.

4. Entry 62 (taxes on luxuries, including taxes on entertainment, amusements, betting and gambling) was replaced by "taxes on entertainments and amusements to the extent levied and collected by a panchayat or a municipality or a regional council or a district council".

In short, some entries in the Seventh Schedule were modified/deleted to fall in line with the new GST regime.

Note: For a comparison of taxes within Union jurisdiction—as enumerated in List I (Union List) in the Seventh Schedule—before and after the enactment of Constitution (One Hundred and First Amendment) Act, 2016, see Table 10.1 of chapter 10 of this book. Similarly, for a comparison of taxes within State jurisdiction—as enumerated in List II (State List) in the Seventh Schedule—before and after the enactment of Constitution (One Hundred and First Amendment) Act, 2016, see Table 10.2 of chapter 10 of this book.

7.3.6 Compensation to States: Section 18 of the Constitution (One Hundred and First Amendment) Act, 2016 provided that Parliament shall, by law, on the recommendations of the GST Council provide for compensation to the States for loss of revenue arising on account of implementation of GST.

7.3.7 Transitional Provisions: Section 19 of the Constitution (One Hundred and First Amendment) Act, 2016 prescribed a timeframe of 1 year within which the subsuming of different indirect taxes under GST would take place and enable the competent legislatures to amend or repeal their existing laws to pave the way for the imposition of GST in the States.

7.3.8 Power of the President to Remove Difficulties: Section 20 of the Constitution (One Hundred and First Amendment) Act, 2016 provides the power to the President to remove any difficulty in giving effect to the provisions of the Constitution as amended by this Act within a period of three years.

Table 7.1 provides a summarized version of amendments in the Constitution made by the Constitution (One Hundred and First Amendment) Act, 2016.

Table 7.1: Summary of Amendments in the Constitution Made by the Constitution (One Hundred and First Amendment) Act, 2016

Provision	Section-wise brief description
Section 1	Short title and commencement
Section 2	Insertion of new Article 246A to provide for special provision with respect to goods and services tax. Concurrent power to both Parliament and State Legislatures to make laws with respect to taxation of goods and services.
Section 3	Amendment of Article 248. The residuary power of legislation of Parliament under Article 248 is now subject to Article 246A.

contd...

Section 4	Amendment of Article 249. If 2/3rd majority resolution is passed by Rajya Sabha, the Parliament will have power to make necessary laws with respect to GST in national interest.
Section 5	Amendment of Article 250. Parliament will have powers to make laws related to GST during emergency period.
Section 6	Amendment of Article 268 to omit excise duty on medicinal and toilet preparations.
Section 7	Omission of Article 268A which dealt with service tax levied by the Central Government.
Section 8	Amendment of Article 269. Matters relating to sale or purchase of goods which now would be separately dealt with under Article 269A, were excluded from here.
Section 9	Insertion of new Article 269A to facilitate the levy of Integrated Goods and Services tax (IGST).
Section 10	Amendment of Article 270 to provide that goods and services tax levied and collected by the Union shall also be distributed between the Union and the States.
Section 11	Amendment of Article 271 to put restrictions on the power of the Parliament to levy surcharge on GST.
Section 12	Insertion of new Article 279A for the constitution of a GST Council.
Section 13	Amendment of Article 286. Clause 3 of this Article relating to tax on certain specified goods with some restrictions was omitted.
Section 14	Amendment of Article 366 to insert definitions of: (a) *goods and services tax*, (b) *services* and (c) *state*.
Section 15	Amendment of Article 368. Article 279A (GST Council) also included in the list of Articles where approval of 50 percent of the State Legislatures required to amend the said Article.
Section 16	Amendment of Sixth Schedule to give power to levy taxes on entertainment and amusements to District Councils of specified areas.
Section 17	Amendment of Seventh Schedule. Some entries were modified/deleted to fall in line with the new GST regime.
Section 18	Mandatory compensation to States for loss of revenue arising on account of implementation of GST.
Section 19	Transitional provisions prescribing a timeframe of 1 year for switch over to GST.
Section 20	Power to the Present to remove any difficulty in giving effect to the provisions of the Constitution as amended by this Act within a period of three years.

For current constitutional provisions pertaining to distribution of taxation powers between the Centre and the States, see chapter 10 of this book.

7.4 Taxes Subsumed under GST

After the enactment of the Constitution (One Hundred and First Amendment) Act, 2016, 8 Central taxes and 9 State taxes were subsumed under GST.

7.4.1 Central Taxes Subsumed under GST: These were as under:

1. **Central Excise Duty:** All Union duties of excise were abolished except those on petroleum products and tobacco. [3]
2. **Duties of Excise (Medicinal and Toilet Preparations):** Duties on medicinal and toilet preparations were imposed under the Medicinal and Toilet Preparations (Excise Duties) Act, 1955. They included a range of medicinal items which were important from the viewpoint of public health policy. They had inter-State significance and therefore uniformity in regard to taxation was in larger national interest.
3. **Additional Duties of Excise (Goods of Special Importance):** These duties were imposed under the Additional Duties of Excise (Goods of Special Importance) Act, 1957 on sugar, tobacco, and textiles in lieu of sales tax. The net proceeds from additional excise duties were distributed among the States in accordance with the principles of distribution formulated and the recommendations made by the Finance Commissions from time to time.
4. **Additional Duties of Excise (Textiles and Textile Products):** The Additional Duties of Excise (Textiles and Textile Articles) Act, 1978 was enacted on December 6, 1978 with an intention to impose and collect extra excise duties on some textiles and textile products. The Act shall come into effect on October 4, 1978.
5. **Additional Duty of Customs [Commonly Known as Countervailing Duty (CVD)]:** Under Section 3(1) of the Customs Tariff Act, 1975, an additional duty on goods imported into the country was leviable. The rate of this duty was equal to the excise duty on like articles if produced or manufactured in India. CVD was meant to ensure that the level of protection provided by the basic import duty (under section 2 of the said Act) to domestic industry was not reduced.
6. **Special Additional Duty of Customs (SAD):** This duty, also known as special CVD, was levied under Section 3(5) of the Customs Tariff Act, 1975. It was equal to sales tax/VAT, local taxes or any other charge on a like article on its sale, purchase or transportation in India. Again, the purpose of SAD was to counter balance various state level taxes and provide level playing field to indigenous goods which had to bear these taxes/charges.
7. **Service Tax:** In view of the need for additional resources, rising contribution of service sector to GDP, service tax was introduced in India with effect from July 1, 1994 on a limited number of services. Its coverage was increased to more and more services from time to time. Service tax was abolished by Section 17 of Constitution (One Hundred and First Amendment) Act, 2016 to pave way for the introduction of GST. [4]
8. **Central Surcharges and Cesses Related to Supply of Goods and Services**

7.4.2 State Taxes Subsumed under GST: These are as under:

1. **State Sales Tax/VAT:** Under Entry 54 of List II (State List) in the Seventh Schedule of the Constitution, the States were given the power to levy "a tax on sale or

purchases of goods other than newspapers". Enjoying this Constitutional right, different State Governments levied sales tax on a wide range of commodities at different rates with diverse procedures and rules for its collection. Later on the States switched over to VAT. Sales tax was abolished (except on a few commodities) by Section 17 of Constitution (One Hundred and First Amendment) Act, 2016. [5]

2. **Central Sales Tax (CST):** CST was a state-level tax, applied to inter-state sales of goods, based on the origin principle. The tax law (including the base, rates, and the procedures) was enacted by Parliament, but the entire revenue accruing under levy of CST was collected and kept by the State in which the sale originated. The Act excluded taxation of imports and exports. [6]
3. **Purchase Tax:** It was a tax paid to the VAT department on purchase of goods from unregistered dealers. See also section 6.3.3 of chapter 6 of this book.
4. **Luxury Tax:** Luxury tax could mostly be seen in the usage bills of hotels, spas and specific resorts. Interestingly, this tax was chargeable on the room rented or the overall stay charges of the hotel, resort or spa, but not on the food and beverages served. The rate of luxury tax varied from state to state. Luxury tax for any state generally fell under the jurisdiction of the Commercial Taxes Department or the Excise Department. The duty of handling such taxes fell to different departments in different states but it was normally those institutions that also handled the imposition and collection of VAT, entertainment tax and service tax.
5. **Entry Tax (all forms):** Entry tax, an important source of revenue for local bodies, was a tax on the entry of goods into a local area from other areas for the purpose of consumption or sale. It was mentioned in Entry 52 of List II (State List) in the Seventh Schedule. Industry and trade circles had criticised the continuation of entry tax (octroi) and termed it as a retarding factor in the growth of business and commerce in the country. By obstructing the free movement of vehicles carrying goods, the levy of octroi caused delays and thus hampered industrial progress. Entry tax was abolished by Section 17 of the Constitution (One Hundred and First Amendment) Act, 2016.
6. **Entertainment and Amusement Tax (except when levied by the local bodies):** Under Entry 62 of List II (State List) in the Seventh Schedule of the Constitution, States were empowered to levy 'taxes on luxuries, including taxes on entertainment, amusements, betting and gambling'. In the changed scenario, taxes on entertainments and amusements can be levied and collected by panchayat etc. [7]
7. **Taxes on Advertisements.** These were imposed under Entry 55 of List II (State List) of the Seventh Schedule of the Constitution.
8. **Taxes on Lotteries, Betting and Gambling:** These were imposed under Entry 62 of List II (State List) of the Seventh Schedule of the Constitution.
9. **State Surcharges and Cesses Related to Supply of Goods and Services**

   Taxes such as stamp duty, toll tax, road tax, electricity duty etc. are not part of GST.

The GST Council shall make recommendations to the Union and States on the taxes, cesses and surcharges levied by the Union, the States and the local bodies which may in future be subsumed under GST.

7.5 Phasing out of Central Sales Tax (CST)

While making preparation for GST, it was also necessary to phase out the CST, because the latter did not carry any set-off relief and there was a distortion in the VAT regime due to export of tax from one State to other State.

The Empowered Committee accordingly took a decision to phase out CST on the understanding with the Centre that—since phasing out of CST would result in a loss of revenue to the States on a permanent basis—an appropriate mechanism to compensate the States for such loss would be worked out.

The rate of CST was successively reduced from 4 percent to 3 percent and 2 percent in 2007 and 2008 respectively. It was phased out with effect from the date of introduction of GST, i.e. July 1, 2017. CST, which was an origin-based tax, was inconsistent with GST which is a destination-based value added tax.

7.6 Abolition of Cesses

In its very first meeting held on September 22-23, 2016, GST Council decided to subsume all Central cesses under the GST (Table 7.2). A cess is a levy to raise funds for a particular purpose and not for the general revenues of the government.

Table 7.2: List of Cesses Abolished

S. No.	Nature of the cess	Date of abolition
1.	Education cess on taxable services	01.06.2015
2.	Secondary and higher education cess on taxable services	01.06.2015
3.	Mica Mines Labour Welfare Fund Act, 1946	21.05.2016
4.	Salt Cess Act, 1953	21.05.2016
5.	Merchant Shipping Act, 1958	21.05.2016
6.	Textile Committee Act, 1963	21.05.2016
7.	Limestone and Dolomite Mines Labour Welfare Funds Act, 1972	21.05.2016
8.	Tobacco Cess Act, 1975	21.05.2016
9.	Iron Ore Mines, Manganese Ore Mines and Chrome Ore Mines Labour Welfare Cess Act, 1976	21.05.2016
10.	Cine-workers Welfare Cess Act, 1981	21.05.2016
11.	Education cess on excisable goods	01.07.2017
12.	Secondary and higher education cess on excisable goods	01.07.2017
13.	Cess on cement	01.07.2017
14.	Cess on strawboard	01.07.2017
15.	Research and Development Cess	01.04.2017
16.	Cess on rubber (Rubber Act, 1947)	01.07.2017

contd...

17.	Cess on automobile [Industries (Development and Regulation) Act, 1951]	01.07.2017
18.	Cess on tea (Tea Act, 1953)	01.07.2017
19.	Cess on coal [Coal Mines (Conservation and Development) Act, 1974]	01.07.2017
20.	Cess on bidis (Bidi Workers' Welfare Cess Act, 1976)	01.07.2017
21.	Cess levied on water consumed by certain industries and by local authorities [Water (Prevention and Control of Pollution) Cess Act, 1977]	01.07.2017
22.	Cess on sugar (Sugar Cess Act, 1982, Sugar Development Fund Act, 1982)	01.07.2017
23.	Cess on jute goods manufactured or produced wholly or in part of jute (Jute Manufacturers Cess Act, 1983)	01.07.2017
24.	Clean energy cess (Finance Act, 2010)	01.07.2017
25.	Swachh Bharat Cess (Finance Act, 2015)	01.07.2017
26.	Infrastructure Cess and Krishi Kalyan Cess (Finance Act, 2016)	01.07.2017

Source: Government of India, Ministry of Finance, Department of Revenue, Central Board of Excise and Customs (CBEC) [since renamed as Central Board of Indirect Taxes and Customs (CBIC)] (website).

Endnotes

1. There are several Articles in the Constitution of India which define the financial relations between the Union and the States. A historic tax reform like GST involving huge interest of the State Governments was not possible without making suitable changes in the Constitution. These changes were carried out by the Constitution (One Hundred and First Amendment) Act, 2016.

   This Amendment marked the beginning of a constitutional experiment that would put India's federal character to test. The Constitution enumerates heads of legislation (including taxes) in the Seventh Schedule. Post-101st Amendment, most heads dealing with indirect taxation, which fell within the jurisdiction of the States, have been deleted and consolidated into a single tax head, namely GST under the newly added Article 246A. The legislative power to levy an integrated indirect tax system (GST) will be exercised in unison by the Centre and the States and the States inter se.

   To decide on matters related to GST, a GST Council has been provided for under the newly inserted Article 279A.

   It is noteworthy that amendment of the Constitution under Article 368 is a vast power of very wide import which permits the Parliament to effect changes to any portion of the Constitution. However, there are two checks imposed on this power. First is the judicially developed *basic structure doctrine* which is an Indian judicial principle that the Constitution of India has certain *basic* features that cannot be altered or destroyed through amendments by the Parliament. Key among these *basic features* are the fundamental rights granted to individuals by the constitution.

   Besides this, Article 368 itself contains a procedural check by entrenching certain provisions of the Constitution and requiring ratification from *not less than one-half of the States* in order to amend those provisions. These entrenched provisions deal with matters which have an effect on the federal structure and balance. The Seventh Schedule, comprising of heads of legislation, being an important feature of this structure and balance is also entrenched in Article 368. As the 101st Amendment deleted and altered certain heads of legislation under the Seventh Schedule, it had to be ratified by half of the States. Thus, the requirement of ratification constitutes an essential mechanism of maintaining the power balance under the federal system of India's Constitution.

2. GST on inter-State trade (called IGST) is collected by the Government of India and such tax is apportioned between the Union and the States. If proceeds of IGST are deposited in the Consolidated Fund of India, then every time there will be a need to pass an Appropriation Bill. Hence, apportionment of IGST takes place outside the Consolidated Fund of India. In fact, IGST is deposited into an IGST Account administered by the Central Government and is distributed between the Centre and the consuming State.
3. See Entry 84 in Table 10.1 of chapter 10 of this book. For a detailed discussion on Union excise duties before their abolition, see chapter 2 of this book.
4. For a detailed discussion on service tax before its abolition, see chapter 3 of this book.
5. See chapter 4 of this book for a detailed discussion on sales tax/VAT before its subsumation under GST.
6. For details, see section 4.3 of chapter 4 of this book.
7. See Entry 62 in Table 10.2 of chapter 10 of this book.

8

Establishment, Meetings and Decisions of Goods and Services Tax Council (GST Council)

GST Council is a joint forum of the Centre and the States created under Article 279A of the Constitution. [1] The recommendations made by the Council act as benchmark or guidance to Union as well as State Governments. Recommendations made by the GST Council take effect after changes are made in the relevant GST laws by the Parliament and the legislatures of the States and the Union Territories with legislature.

8.1 GST Council: Constitutional Provisions

The Constitution (One Hundred and Twenty-second Amendment) Bill, 2014, for introduction of Goods and Services Tax (GST) in the country, was accorded assent by the President on September 8, 2016, and the same was notified as the Constitution (One Hundred and First Amendment) Act, 2016.

As per Article 279A (1) of the amended Constitution, the GST Council was to be constituted by the President within 60 days of the commencement of Article 279A. The notification for bringing into force Article 279A with effect from September 12, 2016 was issued on September 10, 2016.

The Union Cabinet in its meeting held on September 12, 2016 approved the setting-up of GST Council and its Secretariat. The Cabinet, *inter alia*, took decisions for the following:

1. Creation of the GST Council as per Article 279A of the amended Constitution.
2. Creation of the GST Council Secretariat, with its office in New Delhi.
3. Appointment of the Secretary (Revenue) as the Ex-officio Secretary to the GST Council.
4. Inclusion of the Chairperson, Central Board of Excise and Customs (CBEC) [since renamed as Central Board of Indirect Taxes and Customs (CBIC)], as a permanent invitee (non-voting) to all proceedings of the GST Council.

The Cabinet also decided to provide adequate funds for meeting the recurring and non-recurring expenses of the GST Council Secretariat, the entire cost for which shall be borne by the Central Government. GST Council Secretariat shall be manned by officers taken on deputation from both the Central and State Governments.

GST Council is a joint forum of the Centre and the States. The Council consists of the following members:

1. Union Finance Minister—Chairperson.
2. Union Minister of State, in-charge of Revenue or Finance—Member.
3. Minister in-charge of finance or taxation or any other Minister nominated by each State Government—Members.

As per Article 279A (4), the Council will make recommendations to the Union and the

States on important issues related to GST, like the goods and services that may be subjected or exempted from GST, model GST laws, principles that govern place of supply, threshold limits, GST rates including the floor rates with bands, special rates for raising additional resources during natural calamities/disasters, special provisions for certain States etc.

8.2 Guiding Principle and Decision-making at GST Council

GST Council works on the basis of consensus. The guiding principle of GST Council is to ensure harmonization on different aspects of GST between the Centre and the States as well as among States. It has been provided in Article 279A that the GST Council, in its discharge of various functions, shall be guided by the need for a harmonized structure of GST and for the development of a harmonized national market for goods and services.

Article 279A of the Constitution provides that every decision of the GST Council shall be taken at a meeting by a majority of not less than 3/4th of the weighted votes of the Members present and voting, in accordance with the following principles:

1. The vote of the Central Government shall have a weightage of one-third of the total votes cast, and
2. The votes of all the State Governments taken together shall have a weightage of two-thirds of the total votes cast in that meeting.

One half of the total number of members of the GST Council shall constitute the quorum at its meetings.

The above arrangements are meant to protect the interests of each State and the Centre when the Council takes a decision and is in the spirit of co-operative federalism.

8.3 Functions of GST Council

GST Council is entrusted to make recommendations to the Union and the States on following matters pertaining to GST:

1. Taxes, cesses and surcharges levied by the Union, the States and the local bodies which may be subsumed in the goods and services tax.
2. Goods and services that may be subjected to, or exempted from the goods and services tax.
3. Model Goods and Services Tax Laws, principles of levy, apportionment of GST levied on supplies in the course of inter-State trade or commerce under Article 269A and the principles that govern the place of supply.
4. Threshold limit of turnover below which goods and services may be exempted from GST.
5. Rates (including floor rates with bands) of GST.
6. Any special rate or rates for a specified period, to raise additional resources during any natural calamity or disaster.
7. Special provision with respect to the States of Arunachal Pradesh, Assam, Jammu and Kashmir, Manipur, Meghalaya, Mizoram, Nagaland, Sikkim, Tripura, Himachal Pradesh and Uttarakhand.

8. Any other matter relating to GST as the Council may decide.

For more details regarding the powers and functions of GST Council, see section 10.11 of chapter 10 of this book.

8.4 Meetings and Decisions of GST Council Prior to the Introduction of GST

18 meetings of the GST Council were held before the roll out of GST on July 1, 2017. Decisions taken in these meetings are set out below.

8.4.1 First Meeting, September 22-23, 2016, New Delhi: The two-day inaugural meeting of the Council, consisting of Centre and State representatives, took the following decisions.

1. Businesses with an annual turnover of less than ₹ 20 lakh were exempted from GST.
2. The annual turnover limit was fixed at ₹ 10 lakh for the North-Eastern and hill States, which have been given a carve-out in the constitutional amendment that paved the way for GST.
3. State authorities would have jurisdiction over assessees with annual turnover of less than ₹ 1.5 crore. For those with turnover of over ₹ 1.5 crore, there would be cross examination by officers from either State or the Centre to avoid dual control.
4. Power for assessment of 11 lakh service tax assessees, who were currently assessed by the Centre, would remain with it. New assessees would be divided between the Centre and the States.
5. Financial year 2015-16 would be the base year for compensating the States in case of any revenue loss to States following the implementation of GST.
6. All cesses would be subsumed under the new tax.
7. A cross-empowerment model was agreed upon which would allow taxpayers to restrict their interaction to a single tax authority for Central GST, State GST and Integrated GST (IGST). Central GST and State GST are two components of a single GST levied on intra-state sales, while IGST applies to inter-State sales.
8. A consensus on composition scheme was arrived at and it was decided that traders with gross annual turnover cut-off of ₹ 50 lakh [2] can pay tax at specified rates which are lower that the GST rates. The composition scheme provides for an easier method of calculating tax liability and it allows option for GST registration for dealers with turnover below the compounding cut-off. The scheme was introduced to reduce the administration cost associated with collection of tax from small traders.

8.4.2 Second Meeting, September 30, 2016, New Delhi: The Council approved two agenda items. First, five sets of draft rules governing payments, refunds, returns, invoices, debt and credit notes were approved. These were finalised in anticipation of the GST legislations under which the final rules were to be notified. The second decision was with regard to the exemptions from various tax laws and taxes in place currently with which the Centre and States incentivise a variety of industries to invest.

8.4.3 Third Meeting, October 18-20, 2016, New Delhi: The third meeting of the GST Council, which ended a day ahead of schedule, failed to reach a decision on the GST rates. The Council discussed possible GST rates, including a four-slab structure of 6, 12, 18 and 26 percent with lower rates for essential items and highest band for luxury goods.

Centre proposed the imposition of a cess over and above the GST on ultra luxury and demerit goods such as big cars, aerated beverages and tobacco products. The Centre had proposed the cess as a means to fund compensation to States for tax revenue loss during the first five years of GST. However, most States objected to the proposal to levy an additional cess on demerit goods.

8.4.4 Fourth Meeting, November 3-4, 2016, New Delhi: The GST Council agreed on a four-slab GST rates of 5, 12, 18 and 28 percent on goods which it claimed would not be inflationary and yet protect revenues of Centre and State Governments. The broad objective was to maintain equivalence to the existing tax burden on various goods.

8.4.5 Fifth Meeting, December 2-3, 2016, New Delhi: In this two-day meeting of the GST Council consensus could not be reached on the issue of sharing of administrative powers between the Centre and the States. However, certain headway was made on finalization of the draft legislations, and the same were expected to be finalized in the next meeting of the Council. Due to the delay in building of consensus, GST implementation from April 1, 2017 became uncertain. The fifth meeting of the GST Council also deliberated on the impact of demonetisation on revenue.

8.4.6 Sixth Meeting, December 11-12, 2016, New Delhi: This two-day meeting was convened to sort out the vexed issue of *cross empowerment*, or dual control of assessees under the proposed pan-India indirect tax regime. The meeting was also expected to finalise three legislations—Central GST, Integrated GST and the Compensation Law—with the intent of placing these in Parliament during its ongoing Winter Session that ended on December 16, 2016. However, the deadlock continued on the issue of dual control between the Centre and the States in the December 11 meeting, and the December 12 meeting was cancelled.

8.4.7 Seventh Meeting, December 22-23, 2016, New Delhi: The GST Council in its seventh meeting decided to redraft the Compensation Bill to include *other receipts* apart from previously agreed cess on luxury and demerit goods as the source to fund compensation, with States voicing concerns about a likely decline in their revenues following the scrapping of high-denomination currency notes.

Even though the Council cleared most provisions of supporting draft Bills of compensation and Central GST (CGST), the Centre and the states failed to make a breakthrough over the vexed issue of division of control over tax assessees as it did not come up for discussion in the two-day long meeting. The pending issues of dual control and draft Integrated GST (IGST) Bill were left to be taken up in the next meeting.

8.4.8 Eighth Meeting, January 3-4, 2017, New Delhi: The issue of dual control remained unresolved. Some States raised a new issue of split in tax rate in the ratio of 60:40 between States and the Centre instead of equally dividing GST between the Centre and the States. Issues relating to administrative powers were left to be deliberated in the next meeting.

8.4.9 Ninth Meeting, January 16, 2017, New Delhi: The possibility of implementing GST by the targeted deadline of April 1, 2017, receded with the ninth meeting of the GST Council failing to agree on the contentious issue of administrative control of GST.

Eight earlier meetings of the Council had failed to resolve the deadlock between the Centre and the States on the issue of *cross empowerment*, or dual control of assessees, and who would exercise control over them.

The States wanted exclusive control on businesses with turnover below ₹ 1.5 crore (the existing threshold for central excise), including the service taxpayers.

Consensus was almost reached on the territorial control issue of levying GST on the high seas. The Centre's proposal to tax transactions that take place within 12 nautical miles from coastal state borders was opposed by several States, which feared loss of substantial revenue in this way.

8.4.10 Tenth Meeting, February 18, 2017, Udaipur: The tenth meeting of the GST Council managed to approve only one draft law pertaining to compensation to states, even as three crucial draft laws—Central GST (CGST), Integrated GST (IGST) and State GST (SGST)—got caught in a tussle between the States and the Centre. There were clashes between the Centre and the States over the drafting of minutes of the previous GST Council meeting, which held up the deliberations of the meeting. The dispute over the minutes related to the wordings over the division of new registrants, permission to States to tweak division of taxpayers after consultation with the Centre and referral of disputes relating to imports and exports to the Centre.

8.4.11 Eleventh Meeting, March 4, 2017, New Delhi: This meeting cleared the Central GST and Integrated GST Bills. It cleared the decks for the Central Government to take these two Bills to the Parliament for their passage.

The State GST and the UT-GST Bills were under the review of the Law Commission and were postponed to be taken up in the next meeting of the Council.

Small restaurants and *dhabas* became eligible for composition scheme and they would pay GST of 5 percent, to be shared equally between the Central and the State Governments.

8.4.12 Twelfth Meeting, March 16, 2017, New Delhi: The Council approved the Draft Bills for implementing GST in States and Union Territories (UTs). The UT-GST Draft Law was for the Union Territories of Chandigarh, Andaman and Nicobar Islands, Lakshadweep, Daman and Diu and Dadra and Nagar Haveli, which do not have legislative assemblies and thus not covered under the constitutional meaning of *state*.

The GST Council in its tenth meeting had approved a Draft Bill to compensate States for any revenue loss arising out of GST for a period of five years. In its eleventh meeting, it had cleared the Central GST (CGST) and Integrated GST (IGST) Bills.

Thus, the GST Council completed its formal approval to all the five legislations.

The GST Council also decided to levy cess on the following five categories of products to create a fund with a corpus of around ₹ 50,000 crore for meeting potential compensation liability.

1. *Pan masala*.
2. Chewing tobacco and cigarettes.

3. Luxury cars.
4. Aerated drinks and mineral water.
5. Coal and lignite.

The Council, however, kept the option of adding more items to the list later.

It also cleared a proposal to cap the cess on luxury cars and aerated drinks at 15 percent over the peak rate of 28 percent. However, the ceiling for the cess on *sin* goods would be much higher. It was said that for pan masala, the cap would be 135 percent. On tobacco and cigarettes, the cap would be 290 percent or ₹ 4,170 per 1,000 cigarette sticks. A call was yet to be taken on whether or not a cess would be imposed on *bidis*. The cess on coal and lignite (environment cess) would have an upper limit at ₹ 400 per tonne. The Council decided to levy cess on all cars and not only the luxury cars.

The actual cess on *demerit goods*, which would help create a corpus for compensating States for any loss of revenue from GST implementation in the first five years, may be lower than the approved caps as the Council kept a *little* headroom for future exigencies. For example, if a luxury car under pre-GST system suffered a total tax of 40 percent, then under the GST a 28 percent tax plus 12 percent cess (instead of 15 percent) may be levied to keep the tax incidence at the same level, leaving a headroom of 3 percent for future exigencies.

What the GST Council cleared was the ceiling. The exact levy was to be decided by it later. Table 8.1 shows the maximum rate of GST cess on various demerit goods decided by the Council in its twelfth meeting.

Table 8.1: Maximum Rate of GST Cess on Various Demerit Goods

Commodity	Maximum rate at which GST cess can be collected (percent)
Pan masala	135
Sweetened mineral and aerated water	15
Motor cars and vehicles (with the exception of motor vehicles for transportation of 10 or more people)	15
Tobacco products	₹ 4,170 per 1,000 sticks or 290 percent or a combination of both
Coal and lignite*	₹ 400 per tonne

*Environment cess (earlier known as clean energy cess).

The Council also cleared a proposal for the nil rate to be applied for goods and services going to special economic zones (SEZs). In other words, supplies made to SEZs would be zero-rated (a tax rate of zero) and considered as physical exports.

In the earlier draft, in case of procurement of supplies by SEZ, tax was to be paid and then refund claimed of such tax paid but as per the discussion in the Council meeting the same supplies were accepted as zero-rated.

It is noteworthy that GST regime has 9 sets of rules and regulations which form the basis of the implementation of GST. Out of the 9 sets of rules and regulations, the Council had already approved 5—registration, payment, invoices, returns and refund. The Council decided to finalize rules on the remaining four issues relating to composition scheme, valuation, input tax credit (ITC) and transitional provisions in the next (thirteenth) meeting on March 31, 2017.

8.4.13 Thirteenth Meeting, March 31, 2017, New Delhi: This meeting gave its tentative nod to four more sets of rules dealing with composition scheme, valuation, input tax credit (ITC), and transitional provisions. These sets of rules were left to be finalized after receiving industry feedback.

After this, the Council was left with the vexatious and time-consuming work of fitting the various goods and services into the four tax slabs.

8.4.14 Fourteenth Meeting, May 18-19, 2017, Srinagar (J&K): At this meeting, the Council agreed on a four-tier tax structure for services. The four slabs of 5 percent, 12 percent, 18 percent and 28 percent mirrored the GST rates on goods. The fitment of rates of goods was discussed during the Council meeting. The Council approved the rate structure on majority of the goods and services. In other words, the Council largely completed the exercise of fitment of various goods and services in different rate slabs.

8.4.15 Fifteenth Meeting, June 3, 2017, New Delhi: The main objective of the fifteenth meeting of the Council was to decide tax rates on certain remaining items which included gold, textiles and footwear.

The Council decided to tax gold, gems, and jewellery at 3 percent. A nominal rate of 0.25 percent was decided on rough diamond. GST on apparel below ₹ 1,000 was fixed at 5 percent. GST on all biscuits was fixed at 18 percent. GST on readymade garments was fixed at 12 percent and on yarn and fabric cotton at 5 percent. The Council decided to tax footwear priced below ₹ 500 at 5 percent and the rest at 18 percent. It decided to tax *bidis* at 28 percent without cess.

The Council decided to set up a committee to look into complaints regarding anti-profiteering clause.

All the States agreed to rollout GST from July 1, 2017.

8.4.16 Sixteenth Meeting, June 11, 2017, New Delhi: It may be recalled that the Council in its earlier meetings had decided a 4-slab GST rates of 5, 12, 18 and 28 percent for goods and services. It had fitted almost all goods and services into these 4 tax rates when it met in Srinagar on May 18-19, 2017 for its fourteenth meeting. GST rates for almost 1,211 goods and around 500 services were fixed.

However, representations were received from various stakeholders to reduce tax rates on a variety of items. Taking note of these representations, the Council lowered tax rates on 66 goods and services which included packaged food, insulin, school bags and movie tickets.

GST on cashew, *agarbattis* and insulin was reduced from 12 percent to 5 percent. It was reduced from 18 percent to 12 percent on packaged food, exercise books and cutlery. Similarly, it was reduced from 28 percent to 18 percent on plastic tarpaulin, school bags, computer printers and ball bearings. GST rate on children's colouring books was reduced from 12 percent to nil. Instead of a uniform rate of 28 percent on cinema tickets, it was made 28 percent on tickets above ₹ 100 and 18 percent for tickets up to ₹ 100.

The levy on job work for textiles, gems and jewellery, printing and leather was lowered from 18 percent to 5 percent.

The Council also widened the scope of a concessional tax payment scheme for small businesses and restaurants. It raised the turnover ceiling of ₹ 50 lakh to ₹ 75 lakh (subsequently raised to ₹ 1 crore in the twenty-second meeting held on October 6, 2017) per annum for businesses to take part in the GST composition scheme. The scheme allows traders, manufacturers and restaurant owners to pay presumptive tax at the rate of 1, 2, and 5 percent respectively. This would allow more small businesses to avail a hassle-free compliance regime. It is noteworthy that these segments are large job creators and hence a priority area for the Government. It may also be noted that service providers (except restaurants) are outside the ambit of this scheme.

While a lot of small businesses such as shopkeepers and small eateries are expected to opt for the scheme, manufacturers who supply to large buyers may be forced to be part of the GST chain.

The Centre and all the States (except West Bengal) decided to rollout GST from July 1, 2017.

Tax rate for lottery, rules for electronic way (e-way), bills to replace the challans and anti-profiteering rules were left to be decided in the subsequent meetings of the Council.

The Council decided to meet again on June 18, 2017 to take stock of the rollout preparedness and any new proposal from State Governments.

8.4.17 Seventeenth Meeting, June 18, 2017, New Delhi: The Council took the following decisions with respect to GST rates for services.

Accommodation in hotels, inns, guest houses, clubs, camp sites or other commercial places meant for residential or lodging purposes where room tariff is ₹ 2,500 and above but less than ₹ 7,500 per room per day shall attract GST rate of 18 percent with full ITC.

Accommodation in hotels including 5 star and above rated hotels, inns, guest houses, clubs, camp sites or other commercial places meant for residential or lodging purposes, where room rent is ₹ 7,500 and above per day per room shall attract GST rate of 28 percent with full ITC.

Supply of food/drinks in air-conditioned restaurant in 5-star or above rated hotels shall attract GST rate of 18 percent with full ITC.

It was decided that supply of lottery shall attract GST rates as under:

- Lottery run by State Governments: 12 percent of face value of lottery ticket.
- Lottery authorized by State Governments: 28 percent of face value of lottery ticket.

8.4.18 Eighteenth Meeting, June 30, 2017, New Delhi: This meeting of the Council was held hours before the final GST rollout on July 1, 2017. The Council reduced the tax on fertilizers from 12 percent to 5 percent. The decision was taken in view of apprehensions that the price of crop nutrient may increase following the implementation of GST. Another decision, which also brought relief to farmers, was to reduce the tax rate on exclusive parts of tractors from 28 percent to 18 percent. While issues relating to farmers were discussed, the meeting was originally called just to thank the Council members for helping in the implementation of GST.

8.5 Meetings and Decisions of GST Council after the Introduction of GST

17 meetings of the GST Council have been held post-GST so far. Decisions taken in these meetings are explained below.

8.5.1 Nineteenth Meeting, July 17, 2017, Through Video Conferencing: After the last Council meet on 30 June, 2017 it was decided that next meeting would take place on August 5, 2017. However, the date of the meeting was advanced as the Council wanted to take stock of the situation post-GST rollout and get a nation-wide report.

Thus, over two weeks into the GST regime, the all-powerful GST Council met on July 17, 2017 to take stock of the implementation of the new indirect tax. This was the first meeting of the Council since the launch of the GST on July 1, 2017. However, unlike the earlier meetings, when the Centre and the States used to sit across the table and decide on a plethora of issues, this time the interaction was through video conferencing.

Showing its ability to take quick decisions, the Council increased the fixed cess on cigarettes by 48 paise to 79 paise per stick (or ₹ 485 to ₹ 792 per thousand sticks). The move was aimed to prevent cigarette manufacturers to reap windfall arising out of an anomaly that had crept in during fixing the rates. It is noteworthy that this fixed cess is over and above the GST rate of 28 percent plus 5 percent ad valorem cess on the commodity in question.

8.5.2 Twentieth Meeting, August 5, 2017, New Delhi: The Council took several decisions including granting of in-principle approval to e-way bill provisions, implementing anti-profiteering measures, relaxation in GST rates for certain services, and fixing of liability on e-commerce operators in respect of small housekeeping services provided through them.

The Council gave in-principle approval to the e-way bill rules, which envisage a technology-driven tracking of movement of goods worth more than ₹ 50,000 and for sale beyond 10 kilometres distance. According to the provisions, there will be no check-posts and human interface would be minimized. Exempted goods have been kept out of the purview of the system.

The Council also gave approval to constitution of Standing Committee and State-level Screening Committees as provided in the provisions relating to anti-profiteering. It may be noted that anti-profiteering measures aim at ensuring passing of benefits of reduced rate of tax or increased availability of credits, under GST, to consumers.

The Council decided to cut the tax rate for job work throughout the textile chain and even for textile-related items (such as apparels, shawls, carpets) to 5 percent. Earlier, the GST for job works related to textile yarns, other than manmade fibres and textile fabrics, was 5 percent, while for manmade fibres, it was 18 percent. The move assumed significance as the rollout of GST from July 1, 2017 had met with several protests from the textiles sector that had demanded a cut in the tax rate on fabrics, which were brought in the tax net for the first time at the rate of 5 percent.

The rate for certain tractor parts was reduced to 18 percent from 28 percent. Tax rate on agricultural services of post-harvest and storage nature was reduced to 12 percent from the earlier rate of 18 percent.

The GST rate for government work contracts, for both Central and State Governments, was also cut to 12 percent with input tax credit from the earlier decided rate of 18 percent.

The Council in this meeting considered the issue that total tax incidence on motor vehicles post-GST had come down. Motor vehicles had become quite cheaper after the GST rollout on July 1, 2017. Under GST regime, cars attract the top tax rate of 28 percent. On top of this, a cess ranging from 1 percent to 15 percent was levied on them to create a corpus to compensate states for loss of revenue from GST implementation. The cess on SUVs and luxury cars was 15 percent. In other words, the total tax burden on such vehicles was 43 percent (28 percent plus 15 percent).

The Council recommended that the Central Government may move legislative amendments to increase the maximum ceiling of cess on motor vehicles to 25 percent from the existing 15 percent. The Council approved the proposal to hike cess on SUVs, mid-sized, large and luxury cars to 25 percent, from 15 percent.

This came after the Centre, along with several States, requested the Council to amend the existing cess on these vehicles as an *anomaly* has crept in while deciding the rates that needed rectification.

However, the decision on when to raise the actual cess leviable on the motor vehicles was deferred to be taken by the GST Council in due course.

Increase in the rate of maximum cess from 15 percent to 25 percent would increase the GST rate on these SUVs to 53 percent. This required amendment to the GST compensation law which was effected in due course.

The next meeting of the Council was fixed for September 9, 2017 in Hyderabad.

8.5.3 Twenty-first Meeting, September 9, 2017, Hyderabad: A registered person (whether migrated or new registrant), who could not opt for composition scheme, was given the option to avail composition scheme till September 30, 2017 and such registered person was permitted to avail the benefit of composition scheme with effect from October 1, 2017.

Previously, any person making inter-State taxable supplies was not eligible for threshold exemption of ₹ 20 lakh (₹ 10 lakh in special category states except J&K) and was liable for registration. It was decided to allow an exemption from registration to persons making inter-State taxable supplies of handicraft goods up to aggregate turnover of ₹ 20 lakh as long as the person has a permanent account number (PAN) and the goods move under the cover of an e-way bill, irrespective of the value of the consignment.

Similarly, a job worker making inter-State taxable supply of job work service was not eligible for threshold exemption of ₹ 20 lakh (₹ 10 lakh in special category states except J&K) and was liable for registration. It was decided to exempt those job workers from obtaining registration who are making inter-State taxable supply of job work service to a registered person as long as the goods move under the cover of an e-way bill, irrespective of the value of the consignment.

GST rate was reduced from 18 percent to 12 percent for services provided to the Government, a local authority or a governmental authority by way of construction, erection, commissioning, installation, completion, fitting out, repair, maintenance, renovation, or alteration of: (a) a civil structure or any other original works meant predominantly for use other than for commerce, industry, or any other business or profession, (b) a structure meant predominantly for use as an educational, a clinical or an art or cultural establishment and (c) a residential complex predominantly meant for self-use or the use of their employees or other persons like Members of Parliament/Members of State Legislatures, panchayats, municipalities and other local authorities.

To improve the ease of GST return filing, it was decided to set-up a committee to examine the IT challenges experienced by taxpayers in filing of GST returns. Further, the GST return due dates for certain types of returns were revised.

8.5.4 Twenty-second Meeting, October 6, 2017, New Delhi: In this meeting, various decisions and changes pertaining to composition scheme, GST return filing, reverse charge mechanism were announced which significantly benefited the micro, small and medium enterprises (MSMEs).

A. Threshold of Turnover for Composition Scheme: The composition scheme was made available to taxpayers having annual aggregate turnover of up to ₹ 1 crore as compared to the existing turnover of ₹ 75 lakh. This threshold of turnover for special category States, except Jammu and Kashmir (J&K) and Uttarakhand, was increased to ₹ 75 lakh from ₹ 50 lakh. The turnover threshold for J&K and Uttarakhand was decided to be ₹ 1 crore. The facility of availing composition scheme under the increased threshold was made available to both migrated and new taxpayers up to March 31, 2018. The option once exercised was made operational from the first day of the month immediately succeeding the month in which the option to avail the composition scheme was exercised. New entrants to this scheme were required to file the return in Form GSTR-4 only for that portion of the quarter from when the scheme became operational and allowed to file returns as normal taxpayers for the preceding tax period.

The increase in the turnover threshold made it possible for greater number of taxpayers to avail the benefit of easier compliance under the composition scheme and was, therefore, a welcome step from the viewpoint of micro, small and medium enterprises (MSMEs).

Earlier, persons who were otherwise eligible for composition scheme but were providing any exempt service (such as extending deposits to banks for which interest was being received) were being considered ineligible for the said scheme. It was decided that such persons who are otherwise eligible for availing the composition scheme and are providing any exempt service, shall be eligible for the composition scheme.

It was also decided to constitute a Group of Ministers (GoM) to examine measures to make the composition scheme more attractive.

B. GST Registration Requirement: Earlier, anyone making inter-State taxable supplies (selling goods or services from one state to another state), except inter-State job worker, was compulsorily required to register for GST, irrespective of turnover. It was decided to exempt those service providers whose annual aggregate turnover is less than ₹ 20 lakh (₹ 10 lakh in special category States except J&K) from obtaining registration even if they are making inter-State taxable supplies of services. This measure significantly reduced the compliance cost of small service providers.

It is important to note that only service providers have been provided this exception. Any person supplying goods will still be required to obtain GST registration mandatorily, if he undertakes inter-State sales.

C. Ease of Payment and Return Filing: Earlier, all regular taxpayers registered under GST were required to file 4 GST returns every month, namely GSTR-1, GSTR-2, GSTR-3 and GSTR-3B. Filing 4 GST returns a month and maintaining GST compliance was a major burden for small businesses that have limited resources. Hence, to reduce the compliance burden for small businesses and improve ease of doing business, a decision was taken to reduce the number of GST returns for small businesses. Thus, to facilitate the ease of payment and return filing for small and medium businesses with annual aggregate turnover up to ₹ 1.5 crore, it was decided that such taxpayers shall be required to file quarterly returns and pay taxes only on a quarterly basis instead of monthly basis. The registered buyers from such small taxpayers would be eligible to avail input tax credit (ITC) on a monthly basis, whether or not enrolled under the GST composition scheme.

D. Suspension of Reverse Charge Mechanism: Under reverse charge, registered taxpayers were required to pay GST when they purchased goods from an unregistered person, most times a micro or small business. Hence, many registered entities stopped transacting with micro and small businesses. The Council suspended reverse charge till March 31, 2018 so that it could be reviewed by a committee of experts.

Thus, registered taxpayers could purchase from unregistered persons without having to pay GST on reverse charge basis. This measure provided a major boost to micro, small and medium businesses.

E. GST on Advances Received: As per GST rules, whenever a taxable person receives advance, an *advance receipt voucher* must be issued and the GST on the advance received must be remitted to the Government. In case supply was later not provided and refund of advance was provided to the customer, then the supplier would have to claim refund.

The requirement to pay GST on advances received was proving to be burdensome for small dealers and manufacturers. In order to mitigate their inconvenience on this account, it was decided that taxpayers having annual aggregate turnover up to ₹ 1.5 crore shall not be required to pay GST at the time of receipt of advances on account of supply of goods. The GST on such supplies shall be payable only when the supply of goods is made.

F. Goods Transport Agencies (GTAs): GTAs were not willing to provide services to unregistered persons and were, in many cases, asking for GSTIN for transporting goods. In order to remove the hardship being faced by small unregistered businesses on this account, the services provided by a GTA to an unregistered person were made GST-exempt.

G. Tax Deduction at Source (TDS) and Tax Collection at Source (TCS): After assessing the readiness of the trade, industry and Government departments, it was decided that registration and operationalization of TDS and TCS provisions be postponed till March 31, 2018.

H. E-way Bill Implementation Postponed: As per e-way bill rules, any transportation of goods with a value of more than ₹ 50,000 would require an e-way bill. The e-way bill rules were earlier supposed to be implemented before December 2017. The GST Council decided to postpone the implementation of e-way bill provisions and rules to January 1, 2018.

I. Relief Package for Exporters: Mindful of the difficulties faced by exporters post-GST, leading to a decline in export performance and export competitiveness, the GST Council had set up in September 2017 a High Power Committee on Exports to recommend suitable strategies for helping this sector. This Committee had five senior Government functionaries from the Centre and an equal number from the States as members. After wide ranging discussions with major Export Promotion Councils and interacting with all stakeholders, the Committee presented its recommendations to the GST Council in this meeting.

The Council noted that the major difficulties constraining the export sector were on account of delays in refunds of IGST and input taxes on exports and working capital blockages as exporters have to upfront pay GST on inputs and capital goods for export production or for procuring goods for export.

The Council was unanimous that it is in the national interest to take all possible measures to support the exporting community, which earns valuable foreign exchange and provides significant employment especially in the small and medium sector.

Accordingly, the Council approved, inter alia, the following relief measures for exporters:

1. Merchant exporters were allowed to pay nominal GST of 0.1 percent for procuring goods from domestic suppliers for export.
2. Exporters were exempted from furnishing bond and bank guarantee when they clear goods for export.
3. Specified banks and public sector units (PSUs) were allowed to import gold without payment of IGST. This can then be supplied to exporters as per a scheme similar to advance authorization.
4. To restore the lost incentive on sale of duty credit scrips, the GST on sale-purchase of these scrips was reduced from 5 percent to 0 percent.
5. GST on bunker fuel was reduced to 5 percent for both coastal vessels and foreign going vessels to boost coastal shipping and improve India's competitiveness.

The Council expressed confidence that these measures would provide immediate relief to the export sector and enhance export competitiveness of India.

8.5.5 Twenty-third Meeting, November 10, 2017, Guwahati (Assam): Decisions were taken relating to changes in GST rates, ITC eligibility criteria, and exemptions and clarifications on levy of GST on services.

The Council decided to reduce tax rate on a wide range of mass use items from 28 percent to 18 percent. These items included, *inter alia*, chewing gums, detergents, chocolates, preparation for facial make-up, shaving and after-shave items, shampoo deodorants, washing powder, granite and marble.

In fact, the Government was facing intense heat from opposition-ruled States over keeping mass-used goods in the 28 percent bracket which was meant for luxury and demerit goods. About 227 items were under 28 percent rate category. The Council pruned this list to 50. In other words, the Council cut rates on 177 goods.

There was unanimity that in 28 percent category there should be only sin and demerit goods. Thus, the Council took a historic decision that in the 28 percent slab there will be only 50 items. Paints, cement, washing machines and air conditioners were retained in the 28 percent tax bracket.

5 percent GST without ITC was fixed for all stand-alone restaurants, irrespective of air-conditioned or otherwise. 5 percent GST without ITC was also fixed for food parcels (or takeaways). Restaurants in hotel premises having room tariff of less than ₹ 7,500 per unit per day would attract GST of 5 percent without ITC. Restaurants in hotel premises having room tariff of ₹ 7,500 and above per unit per day (even for a single room) would attract GST of 18 percent with full ITC. Outdoor catering would continue to be at 18 percent with full ITC.

The rate of GST on job work services in relation to manufacture of those handicraft goods in respect of which the casual taxable person has been exempted from obtaining registration, was reduced to 5 percent with full ITC.

Services by way of admission to *protected monuments* were made GST-exempt.

Exports of services to Nepal and Bhutan had already been exempted from GST. It was decided that such exporters would also be eligible for claiming input tax credit (ITC) in respect of goods or services used for effecting such exempt supply of services to Nepal and Bhutan.

8.5.6 Twenty-fourth Meting, December 16, 2017, Through Video Conferencing: This Meeting of the Council decided to make inter-State e-way bill compulsory from February 1, 2018. The system was to be ready by January 16, 2018. It was decided to introduce uniform system of e-way bill for inter-State as well as intra-State movement of goods across the country by June 1, 2018.

Till such time as the nation-wide e-way bill was ready, the States were authorized to continue with their own separate e-way bill systems. However, it was represented by the trade and transporters that this was causing undue hardship in the inter-State movement of goods.

Therefore, bringing in an all-India system of e-way bill became a necessity. The GST Council reviewed the progress of readiness of hardware and software required for the introduction of nationwide e-way bill system. After discussions with all the States, the following decisions were taken:

- The nationwide e-way bill system would be ready for roll out on a trial basis latest by January 16, 2018. Trade and transporters can start using this system on a voluntary basis from January 16, 2018.

- The rules for implementation of nationwide e-way bill system for inter-State movement of goods on a compulsory basis would be notified with effect from February 1, 2018. This will bring uniformity across the States for seamless inter-State movement of goods.
- While the system for both inter-State and intra-State e-way bill generation would be ready by January 16, 2018, the States may choose their own timings for implementation of e-way bill for intra-State movement of goods on any date before June 1, 2018.
- Uniform system of e-way bill for inter-State as well as intra-State movement would be implemented across the country from June 1, 2018.

8.5.7 Twenty-fifth Meeting, January 18, 2018, New Delhi: At this meeting, the GST Council declared yet another downward revision of GST rates on a number of goods and services. The Council decided to reduce tax rate on 29 items and 53 categories of services with effect from January 25, 2018.

GST rate on used (second-hand) medium and large cars and SUVs was reduced from 28 percent to 18 percent. The GST on used small cars and motor vehicles was reduced from 28 percent to 12 percent.

GST on bio-diesel, drinking water packed in 20-litre bottles, drip irrigation system, mechanical sprayer, bio-pesticides, sugar boiled confectionery etc. was brought down from 18 percent to 12 percent.

Tax on sales of liquefied petroleum gas (LPG) by private firms for domestic use and scientific equipment for satellite launch was reduced from 18 percent to 5 percent.

Tax on rice bran was reduced from 5 percent to 0 percent.

Tax rate on velvet fabric was reduced from 12 percent to 5 percent.

Tax on items like *mehendi* paste in cones, and tamarind kernel powder was slashed from 18 percent to 5 percent.

Tax rate on mining, drilling of natural gas was reduced to 12 percent.

Tax on diamonds and precious stones was reduced from 3 percent to 0.25 percent.

Cess on vehicles for ambulance was from 15 percent to 0 percent.

In the services segment, the Council decided to reduce taxes on transportation of crude, gas oil, gasoline, jet fuel and services relating to mining, exploration and drilling of oil and natural gas, among other things.

A large number of essential services were exempted from GST tax entirely. These included services like education admission, the conduct of examinations, entrance fees for entrance examinations and transportation of students up to higher secondary schools.

Tax on theme and water park tickets, go-carting and merry-go-rounds and ballet tickets was reduced from 28 percent to 18 percent.

The decision on inclusion of real estate in GST was deferred.

The Council approved a definition for handicrafts and designated 40 items as the handicrafts. The fitment committee was authorized to fix rates of these 40 handicraft items.

8.5.8 Twenty-sixth Meeting, March 10, 2018, New Delhi: It was decided to implement inter-state e-way bill from April 1, 2018. It was further decided to implement intra-state e-way bill from April 15, 2018 in a phased manner by categorizing the states into 4 lots.

Reverse charge mechanism (in case of supplies made by unregistered persons to registered persons) was delayed till July 1, 2018.

Tax deduction at source (TDS) and tax collection at source (TCS) applicability was postponed until June 30, 2018.

A committee was formed to look into the grievance redressal mechanism with respect to user's grievances surrounding the IT glitches on the GSTN.

8.5.9 Twenty-seventh Meeting, May 4, 2018, Through Video Conferencing: This meeting of the Council paved the way for single form GST return based on the recommendations of the Group of Ministers (GoM) on IT simplification. The GST return filing was made to happen only once every month compared to the three returns a month followed earlier. The Government claimed that the new system would become effective within a period of six months.

Besides this, the GST council also gave a green signal to making the GST Network a government entity as it was set to take over the 51 percent stake that was currently held by the private entities.

8.5.10 Twenty-eighth Meeting, July 21, 2018, New Delhi: The Council took decisions on issues relating to policy, law and procedures, including key recommendations on reduction in GST rates on a variety of goods and rationalisation of return filing system for small taxpayers. The Council recommended certain amendments to the CGST Act, 2017, IGST Act, 2017, UT-GST Act, 2017, and GST (Compensation to States) Act, 2017.

A. Tax Relief: The Council reduced GST rates on a variety of goods to provide relief to a cross-section of taxpayers.

GST Council took various decisions relating to exemptions, changes in GST rates, ITC eligibility criteria, rationalization of rates, relating to levy of GST on services.

B. Threshold Exemption: The threshold exemption limit for registration in the States of Assam, Arunachal Pradesh, Himachal Pradesh, Meghalaya, Sikkim and Uttarakhand was increased to ₹ 20 lakh from ₹ 10 lakh.

C. Composition Scheme: Upper limit of turnover for opting for composition scheme was decided to be raised from ₹ 1 crore to ₹ 1.5 crore.

Composition dealers were allowed to supply services (other than restaurant services), for up to a value not exceeding 10 percent of turnover in the preceding financial year, or ₹ 5 lakh, whichever is higher.

D. Reverse Charge Mechanism (RCM): The Council decided to apply GST on reverse charge basis on receipt of supplies from unregistered suppliers only on specified goods in case of certain notified classes of registered persons. RCM as such was suspended until September 2019.

E. Registration: Following decisions were taken:

- Taxpayers may opt for multiple registrations within a State/Union territory in respect of multiple places of business located within the same State/Union territory.
- Mandatory registration is required for only those e-commerce operators who are required to collect tax at source.
- Registration to remain temporarily suspended while cancellation of registration is under process, so that the taxpayer is relieved of continued compliance under the law.

F. No Supply (No Tax Payable) Transactions: Following transactions would be treated as No Supply (No Tax Payable) under Schedule III of the CGST Act, 2017.

- Supply of goods from a place in the non-taxable territory to another place in the non-taxable territory without such goods entering into India.
- Supply of warehoused goods to any person before clearance for home consumption.
- Supply of goods in case of high sea sales.

G. Scope of Input Tax Credit (ITC) Widened: ITC was made available in respect of the following:

- Most of the activities or transactions specified in Schedule III of the CGST Act, 2017.
- Motor vehicles for transportation of persons having seating capacity of more than thirteen (including driver), vessels and aircraft.
- Motor vehicles for transportation of money for or by a banking company or financial institution.
- Services of general insurance, repair and maintenance in respect of motor vehicles, vessels and aircraft on which credit is available.
- Goods or services which are obligatory for an employer to provide to its employees, under any law for the time being in force.

H. Simplified Returns: This meeting of the Council approved the new return formats and associated changes in law. It may be recalled that in the Twenty-seventh meeting held on May 4, 2018, the Council had approved the basic principles of GST return design and directed the law committee to finalize the return formats and changes in law. The formats and business processes approved in this (Twenty-eighth) meeting were in line with the basic principles with one major change, i.e. the option of filing quarterly return with monthly payment of tax in a simplified return format by the small taxpayers.

- All taxpayers excluding small taxpayers shall file one monthly return. The return is simple with two main tables. One for reporting outward supplies and one for availing input tax credit based on invoices uploaded by the supplier.
- NIL return filers (no purchase and no sale) shall be given facility to file return by sending SMS.
- The Council approved quarterly filing of return for the small taxpayers having turnover below ₹ 5 crore as an optional facility. Quarterly return shall be similar to main return with monthly payment facility but for two kinds of registered persons—

small traders making only B2C supply or making B2B + B2C supply. For such taxpayers, simplified returns have been designed (called *Sahaj* and *Sugam*). In these returns, details of information required to be filled is lesser than that in the regular return.

- The new return design provides facility for amendment of invoice and also other details filed in the return. Amendment shall be carried out by filing of a return called amendment return.

I. Other Decisions:

- Amount of pre-deposit payable for filing of appeal before the Appellate Authority and the Appellate Tribunal to be capped at ₹ 25 crore and ₹ 50 crore respectively.
- Commissioner to be empowered to extend the time limit for return of inputs and capital sent on job work, up to a period of 1 year and 2 years, respectively.
- Supply of services to qualify as exports, even if payment is received in Indian Rupees, where permitted by the RBI.
- Place of supply in case of job work of any treatment or process done on goods temporarily imported into India and then exported without putting them to any other use in India, to be outside India.
- A window for migration of tax payers on earlier indirect tax systems to GST was also opened till August 31, 2018, along with a simpler exit option for those who are no longer in business.

8.5.11 Twenty-ninth Meeting, August 4, 2018, New Delhi: The Council decided to set up a sub-committee, headed by Minister of State for Finance, to look into various issues and concerns of micro, small and medium enterprises (MSMEs). The issues related to law would be taken up by the law committee and issues related to rates would be taken up by the fitment committee. They would deliberate and submit their recommendations to the sub-committee.

The sub-committee would present its report to the Council for taking final decisions.

The GST Council also decided to experiment with a scheme to provide cash back for digital transactions. To promote compliance and collections, RuPay Debit and UPI-based transactions would get cash back of 20 percent for the GST paid, capped at ₹ 100. The Council decided to create software for this purpose.

GST rate cuts were put on hold for the time being in view of lower GST revenues.

8.5.12 Thirtieth Meeting, September 28, 2018, Through Video Conferencing: As per Article 279A [(clause 4, sub-clause (f)] of the Constitution, the GST Council is empowered to impose, "any special rate or rates for a specified period, to raise additional resources during any natural calamity or disaster".

The proposal of the State of Kerala for imposition of cess on SGST for rehabilitation and flood-affected works was discussed in this meeting of the Council. The Council decided to constitute a 7-member Group of Ministers (GoM) to examine the issue regarding modalities for revenue mobilization in case of natural calamities and disasters. [3]

The GoM was asked to submit its report by October 31, 2018.

Finance Secretary was asked to visit states in which there is shortfall of GST revenue and find out the reasons for that.

As regards cess for natural calamities, there is lot of confusion and controversy. Following points need clarification.

1. Whether the proposed cess would be state-specific or country-wide?
2. On what commodities it would be levied?
3. On which natural calamities it would be imposed?

If the natural calamity cess is levied only on SGST within Kerala, then for those businesses that purchase in Kerala for sales outside the state, the levy will get exported and it is still unclear how it will be refunded.

Also, there are concerns about consumers shifting from Kerala to neighbouring states of Tamil Nadu or Karnataka to buy goods, especially high-taxed goods like motor cars. Even 1 percent extra levy will incentivise consumers to opt for purchases outside Kerala.

It will be the same situation as was prevailing during pre-GST. Due to inter-state variations in the rates of VAT, prices of goods differed in different states, tempting residents of one state to make purchases in the other state. It led to uneconomic diversion of trade. A case in point was the purchase of motor cars. Haryana was a favourite destination for the residents of Delhi to buy cars because the rate of VAT on the product was lower as compared to Delhi. This is why some Delhi residents own cars with Haryana number plates. Purchase of truck chassis in Daman (a Union Territory levying a low rate of 3 percent VAT) by residents of a far-flung Jammu and Kashmir was another popular example in tax annals.

Similarly, rate differentials caused flight of capital and enterprise from high to low tax rate States thereby distorting natural selection of production centres based on geographical advantages. This led to unnecessary transportation of raw materials and finished goods and hence cost escalations. Such misallocation of resources undermined economic efficiency and thereby retarded developmental efforts.

After the introduction of GST from July 1, 2017, there is no incentive for residents of one state to make purchases in other states because GST rates on goods and services are uniform through out the country.

According to experts, a cess on SGST, as proposed by Kerala, will require tweaking of the whole returns software of the GSTN. GST is already a complicated tax. To make it more complex will be against the slogan of *Single tax, Simple tax* of the Government.

8.5.13 Thirty-first Meeting, December 22, 2018, New Delhi: In this meeting, various important decisions pertaining to GST rates and GST return filing and were taken.

A. Rate Reduction: In an exercise of GST rate cuts, 6 commodities were shifted from 28 percent to 18 percent rate category; 1 item from 28 percent to 5 percent; 3 items from 18 percent to 12 percent; 1 item from 18 percent to 5 percent; 3 items from 12 percent to 5 percent; 1 item from 12 percent to nil; and 2 items from 5 percent to nil rate category.

It was clarified that rate of 5 percent/18 percent is to be applied based on transaction value of footwear.

GST rate on cinema tickets above ₹ 100 was reduced from 28 percent to 18 percent and on cinema tickets up to ₹ 100 from 18 percent to 12 percent. GST rate on third-party insurance premium of goods-carrying vehicles was reduced from 18 percent to 12 percent.

B. Exemptions: Following exemptions were granted:

- Exemption from GST on supply of gold by nominated agencies to exporters of article of gold jewellery.
- Exemption from GST on proceeds received by Government from auction of gifts received by President, Prime Minister, Governor or Chief Minister of a State and public servants, the proceeds of which are used for public or charitable cause.
- Exemption from IGST/Compensation cess on vehicles imported for temporary purposes under the Customs Convention on the Temporary Importation of Private Road Vehicles.

The new return filing system shall be introduced on a trial basis from April 1, 2019 and on mandatory basis from July 1, 2019.

Changes made by CGST (Amendment) Act, 2018; IGST (Amendment) Act, 2018; UT-GST (Amendment) Act, 2018; and GST (Compensation to States) Amendment Act, 2018 and the corresponding changes in SGST Acts would be notified w.e.f. February 1, 2019.

8.5.14 Thirty-second Meeting, January 10, 2019, New Delhi: Important decisions were taken in this meeting with respect to threshold limits and composition scheme. Steps were also taken to provide compliance relief to small businesses.

A. Threshold Limits for Suppliers of Goods: The Council decided to provide two threshold limits for exemption from registration and payment of GST: ₹ 20 lakh and ₹ 40 lakh. Depending on their revenue consideration, States would have an option to decide, within a week, about one of the limits. This decision will now lead to various States having different threshold limits.

B. Threshold Limits for Service Providers: Service providers will continue to be required to register for GST once they cross a turnover of ₹ 20 lakh (₹ 10 lakh for Special Category States). Due to smaller businesses, the threshold is lower in Special Category States.

C. Composition Scheme: Three changes were recommended by the Council to give thrust to the composition scheme.

(a) Increase in Turnover Limit: The limit of annual turnover in the preceding financial year for availing composition scheme for goods was increased to ₹ 1.5 crore. Special Category States were asked to decide, within one week, about the limit in their respective States.

(b) Yearly Return: Persons enrolled under the composition scheme were earlier required to file return every quarter. They were allowed to file one annual return, but making quarterly payment of taxes due.

(c) Service Providers Also Eligible: Suppliers of services (or mixed suppliers) having an annual turnover in the preceding financial year up to ₹ 50 lakh were made eligible to enrol for the composition scheme. Such service providers would have to pay

GST at the rate of 6 percent (3 percent CGST + 3 percent SGST) of turnover. The said scheme shall be applicable to both service providers as well as suppliers of goods and services, who are not eligible for the presently available composition scheme for goods. They would be liable to file one annual return with quarterly payment of taxes (along with a simple declaration).

Above changes would be effective from April 1, 2019.

D. GST Cess: The Council approved the levy of cess on intra-State supply of goods and services in Kerala at a rate not of not more than 1 percent for a period not exceeding 2 years. This would be used as revenue mobilization measure for coping with devastation caused by floods in August 2018. GSTN and companies would need to modify their IT systems for incorporating this change. Moreover, this arrangement dilutes the slogan of One-Nation One-Tax.

E. Real Estate Sector and Lotteries: The Council decided to set up a 7-Member Group of Ministers to examine the proposal of giving a composition scheme to boost the residential segment of the real estate sector. A Group of Ministers shall be constituted to examine the GST Rate Structure on Lotteries.

8.5.15 Thirty-third Meeting, February 24, 2019, New Delhi: The Council was initially supposed to meet on February 20, 2019 via video conferencing but was later deferred to February 24, 2019 to meet in New Delhi, post refusal by some State Finance Ministers. The agenda of the meeting covered under-construction housing sector and private lottery distribution.

The Council decided a rate cut for the under-construction properties covering the residential segment as follows:

1. GST rate for non-affordable housing was reduced from 12 percent to 5 percent without ITC.
2. GST rate for affordable housing was slashed from 8 percent to 1 percent without the benefit of input tax credit (ITC).

No rate cuts were discussed for cement which is currently being charged a GST rate of 28 percent. Similarly, no decision was taken on lottery rate.

8.5.16 Thirty-fourth Meeting, March 19, 2019, via Video Conferencing: The meeting was convened to oversee and pass the circulars/notifications drafted by the rate fitment and legal committees on the rate cuts on housing announced in the Thirty-third Meeting held on February 24, 2019.

The meeting centred around the applicability of tax rates for under construction housing projects and the rules governing the transition from old rates to new rates for existing projects.

GST Council approved the transition plan for the implementation of the new tax structure for housing units.

8.5.17 Thirty-fifth Meeting, June 21, 2019, New Delhi: The Council extended the tenure of NAA by another 2 years to November 2021. It decided to introduce electronic invoicing (e-invoicing) in a phased manner for business-to business (B2B) transactions. It also made it mandatory for multiplexes to shift to an electronic ticketing (e-ticketing) system. These moves were aimed at curbing possible tax evasion.

The Council allowed the use of Aadhaar as proof for obtaining registration under GST.

The Council could not arrive at a decision on reducing GST on EVs. It, therefore, referred the proposal to cut GST rate on EVs from 12 percent to 5 percent and on electric chargers from 18 percent to 12 percent to the fitment committee.

8.6 Summary of Decisions Taken by GST Council in Various Meetings

GST Council was notified with effect from September 12, 2016. Including the first meeting of the Council on September 23, 2016, there have been 35 sessions so far on a range of issues including supporting legislations, GST rules, rates of taxes and fitment of a large number of goods and services into the four-tier structure of 5 percent, 12 percent, 18 percent and 28 percent.

Out of the 35 sessions so far, 18 took place before and 17 after the introduction of GST on July 1, 2017. All the decisions in the GST Council have been unanimous or through consensus. In other words, no occasion has arisen so far that required voting to decide any matter.

The major decisions taken in its various meetings are summarized in Table 8.2.

Table 8.2: Major Decisions Taken by GST Council in its Various Meetings

Prior to the Introduction of GST on July 1, 2017
First Meeting, September 22-23, 2016, New Delhi
• Businesses with an annual turnover of less than ₹ 20 lakh to be exempted from GST. • Threshold of annual turnover to be ₹ 10 lakh in the North-Eastern and hill States. • Financial year 2015-16 to be the base year for compensating the States in case of any revenue loss to States following the implementation of GST. • Under composition scheme traders with gross annual turnover cut-off of ₹ 50 lakh can pay tax at specified rates.
Second Meeting, September 30, 2016, New Delhi
• Five sets of draft rules governing payments, refunds, returns, invoices, debt and credit notes were approved. • Decisions were taken with regard to the exemptions from various tax laws and taxes in place currently with which the Centre and States incentivise a variety of industries to invest.
Third Meeting, October 18-20, 2016, New Delhi
• GST Council failed to reach a decision on the GST tax rates. The Council discussed possible GST rates, including a four-slab structure of 6, 12, 18 and 26 percent with lower rates for essential items and highest band for luxury goods. • Centre proposed the imposition of a cess over and above the GST on ultra luxury and demerit goods such as big cars, aerated beverages and tobacco products. • Centre proposed the cess as a means to fund compensation to States for tax revenue loss during the first five years of GST.

• Most States objected to the proposal to levy an additional cess on demerit goods.
Fourth Meeting, November 3-4, 2016, New Delhi
• GST Council agreed on a four-slab GST rates of 5, 12, 18 and 28 percent on goods. • The broad objective was to maintain equivalence to the existing tax burden on various goods.
Fifth Meeting, December 2-3, 2016, New Delhi
• Consensus could not be reached on the issue of sharing of administrative powers between the Centre and the States. • Certain headway was made on finalization of the draft legislations. • Due to the delay in building of consensus, GST implementation from April 1, 2016 became uncertain. • GST Council also deliberated on the impact of demonetisation on revenue.
Sixth Meeting, December 11-12, 2016, New Delhi
• This two-day meeting was convened to sort out the vexed issue of *cross empowerment*, or dual control of assessees. • The meeting was also expected to finalise three legislations—Central GST, Integrated GST and the Compensation Law—with the intent of placing these in Parliament during its ongoing Winter Session that ended on December 16, 2016. • However, the deadlock continued on the issue of dual control between the Centre and the States in the December 11 meeting. • December 12 meeting was cancelled.
Seventh Meeting, December 22-23, 2016, New Delhi
• It was decided to redraft the Compensation Bill to include *other receipts* apart from previously agreed cess on luxury and demerit goods as the source to fund compensation. • States voiced their concerns about a likely decline in their revenues following the scrapping of high-denomination currency notes. • Centre and the States failed to make a breakthrough over the vexed issue of division of control over tax assessees.
Eighth Meeting, January 3-4, 2017, New Delhi
• The issue of dual control remained unresolved. • Some States raised a new issue of split in tax rate in the ratio of 60:40 between States and the Centre instead of equally dividing GST between the Centre and the States. • Issues relating to administrative powers were left to be deliberated in the next meeting.
Ninth Meeting, January 16, 2017, New Delhi
• The possibility of implementing GST by the targeted deadline of April 1, 2017 receded with the Council failing to agree on the contentious issue of administrative control of GST. • The States wanted exclusive control on businesses with turnover below ₹ 1.5 crore (the existing threshold for central excise), including the service taxpayers. • Consensus was almost reached on the territorial control issue of levying GST on the high seas.

Tenth Meeting, February 18, 2017, Udaipur
• The Council managed to approve only one draft law pertaining to compensation to States, even as three crucial draft laws—Central GST (CGST), Integrated GST (IGST) and State GST (SGST)—got caught in a tussle between the States and the Centre. • There were clashes between the Centre and the States over the drafting of minutes of the previous GST Council meeting. • The dispute over the minutes related to the wordings over the division of new registrants, permission to States to tweak division of taxpayers and referral of disputes relating to imports and exports to the Centre.
Eleventh Meeting, March 4, 2017, New Delhi
• This meeting cleared the Central GST and Integrated GST Bills. • The State GST and the UT-GST Bills were under the review of the Law Commission and were postponed to be taken up in the next meeting of the Council. • Small restaurants and *dhabas* became eligible for composition scheme and they would pay GST of 5 percent, to be shared equally between the Central and the State Governments.
Twelfth Meeting, March 16, 2017, New Delhi
• The Council approved the Draft Bills for implementing GST in States and Union Territories (UTs). • The Council decided to levy cess on five categories of products (pan masala, chewing tobacco and cigarettes, luxury cars, aerated drinks and mineral water, coal and lignite) to create a fund with a corpus of around ₹ 50,000 crore for meeting potential compensation liability. • The Council, however, kept the option of adding more items to the list later. • It cleared a proposal to cap the cess on luxury cars and aerated drinks at 15 percent over the peak rate of 28 percent. • The Council also cleared a proposal for the nil rate to be applied for goods and services going to special economic zones (SEZs).
Thirteenth Meeting, March 31, 2017, New Delhi
• This meeting finalized five sets of rules relating to registration, refunds, returns, payment and invoice debit and credit. • It also gave its tentative nod to four more sets of rules dealing with composition scheme, valuation, input tax credit (ITC), and transitional provisions. • The Council was left with the vexatious and time-consuming work of fitting the various goods and services into the four tax slabs.
Fourteenth Meeting, May 18-19, 2017, Srinagar (J&K)
• The Council agreed on a four-tier tax structure for services, mirroring the GST rates on goods. • The fitment of rates of goods was discussed during the meeting and the Council approved the rate structure on majority of the goods and services. • The Council also approved seven sets of rules (out of nine), barring two sets of rules

(related to transitional provisions and returns) which were still to be vetted.
Fifteenth Meeting, June 3, 2017, New Delhi
• The main objective of this meeting was to decide tax rates on certain remaining items which included gold, textiles and footwear. • The Council decided to tax gold, gems, and jewellery at 3 percent. A nominal rate of 0.25 percent was decided on rough diamond. • The Council cleared all the pending rules related to transitional provisions and returns. • It decided to set up a committee to look into complaints regarding anti-profiteering clause. • All the States agreed to rollout GST from July 1, 2017.
Sixteenth Meeting, June 11, 2017, New Delhi
• The Council lowered tax rates on 66 goods and services which included packaged food, insulin, school bags and movie tickets. • The levy on job work for textiles, gems and jewellery, printing and leather was lowered from 18 percent to 5 percent. • The Council also widened the scope of a concessional tax payment scheme for small businesses and restaurants. It relaxed the turnover ceiling of ₹ 50 lakh to ₹ 75 lakh per annum for businesses to take part in the GST composition scheme. • Centre and all the States (except West Bengal) decided to rollout GST from July 1, 2017. • Tax rate for lottery, rules for electronic way (e-way), bills to replace the challans and anti-profiteering rules were left to be decided in the subsequent meetings of the Council.
Seventeenth Meeting, June 18, 2017, New Delhi
• Transport of goods by a vessel was made subject to GST rate of 5 percent with ITC in respect of input services and GST paid on ships, vessels including bulk carriers and tankers. • Accommodation in hotels, inns, guest houses, clubs, campsites or other commercial places meant for residential or lodging purposes where room tariff is ₹ 2,500 and above but less than ₹ 7,500 per room per day to attract GST rate of 18 percent with full ITC. • Accommodation in hotels including 5 star and above rated hotels, inns, guest houses, clubs, campsites or other commercial places meant for residential or lodging purposes, where room rent is ₹ 7,500 and above per day per room to attract GST rate of 28 percent with full ITC. • Supply of food/drinks in air-conditioned restaurant in 5-star or above rated hotels shall attract GST rate of 18 percent with full ITC. • It was decided that supply of lottery shall attract GST rates as under: (i) Lottery run by State Governments: 12 percent of face value of lottery ticket. (ii) Lottery authorized by State Governments: 28 percent of face value of lottery ticket.
Eighteenth Meeting, June 30, 2017, New Delhi
• This meeting of the Council was held hours before the final GST rollout on July 1, 2017. • The Council reduced the tax on fertilizers from 12 percent to 5 percent.

- Another decision, which also brought relief to farmers, was to reduce the tax rate on exclusive parts of tractors from 28 percent to 18 percent.
- While issues relating to farmers were discussed, the meeting was originally called just to thank the Council members for helping in the implementation of GST.

After the Introduction of GST on July 1, 2017

Nineteenth Meeting, July 17, 2017, Through Video Conferencing

- This was the first meeting of the Council since the launch of the GST on July 1, 2017.
- Unlike the earlier meetings, when the Centre and the States used to sit across the table and decide on a plethora of issues, this time the interaction was through video conferencing.
- Showing its ability to take quick decisions, the Council increased the fixed cess on cigarettes by 48 paise to 79 paise per stick (or ₹ 485 to ₹ 792 per thousand sticks).
- It is noteworthy that this fixed cess is over and above the GST rate of 28 percent plus 5 percent ad valorem cess on the commodity in question.

Twentieth Meeting, August 5, 2017, New Delhi

- The Council gave in-principle approval to the e-way bill rules, which envisaged a technology-driven tracking of movement of goods worth more than ₹ 50,000 and for sale beyond 10 kilometres distance.
- Approval was also given to constitution of Standing Committee and State-level Screening Committees as provided in the provisions relating to anti-profiteering.
- It was decided to cut the tax rate for job work throughout the textile chain and even for textile-related items (such as apparels, shawls, carpets) to 5 percent.
- The rate for certain tractor parts was reduced to 18 percent from 28 percent.
- Tax rate on agricultural services of post-harvest and storage nature was reduced to 12 percent from the earlier rate of 18 percent.
- The GST rate for government work contracts, for both Central and State Governments, was also cut to 12 percent with input tax credit from the earlier decided rate of 18 percent.

Twenty-first Meeting, September 9, 2017, Hyderabad

- A registered person (whether migrated or new registrant), who could not opt for composition scheme, was given the option to avail composition scheme till September 30, 2017 and such registered person was permitted to avail the benefit of composition scheme with effect from October 1, 2017.
- Previously, any person making inter-State taxable supplies was not eligible for threshold exemption of ₹ 20 lakh (₹ 10 lakh in special category states except J&K) and was liable for registration. It was decided to allow an exemption from registration to persons making inter-State taxable supplies of handicraft goods up to aggregate turnover of ₹ 20 lakh as long as the person has a permanent account number (PAN) and the goods move under the cover of an e-way bill, irrespective of the value of the consignment.
- Similarly, a job worker making inter-State taxable supply of job work service was not eligible for threshold exemption of ₹ 20 lakh (₹ 10 lakh in special category states except J&K) and was liable for registration. It was decided to exempt those job workers from obtaining registration who are making inter-State taxable supply of job

work service to a registered person as long as the goods move under the cover of an e-way bill, irrespective of the value of the consignment.

Twenty-second Meeting, October 6, 2017, New Delhi

- In this meeting, various decisions and changes pertaining to composition scheme, GST return filing, reverse charge mechanism were announced which significantly benefited the micro, small and medium enterprises (MSMEs).
- The composition scheme was made available to taxpayers having annual aggregate turnover of up to ₹ 1 crore as compared to the existing turnover of ₹ 75 lakh.
- This threshold of turnover for special category States, except Jammu and Kashmir (J&K) and Uttarakhand, was increased to ₹ 75 lakh from ₹ 50 lakh.
- The turnover threshold for J&K and Uttarakhand was decided to be ₹ 1 crore.
- It was also decided to constitute a Group of Ministers (GoM) to examine measures to make the composition scheme more attractive.
- Goods transport agencies (GTAs) were not willing to provide services to unregistered persons and were, in many cases, asking for GSTIN for transporting goods. In order to remove the hardship being faced by small unregistered businesses on this account, the services provided by a GTA to an unregistered person shall be exempted from GST.

Twenty-third Meeting, November 10, 2017, Guwahati (Assam)

- Decisions were taken relating to changes in GST rates, ITC eligibility criteria, and exemptions and clarifications on levy of GST on services.
- The Council decided to reduce tax rate on a wide range of mass use items from 28 percent to 18 percent. These items included, inter alia, chewing gums, detergents, chocolates, preparation for facial make-up, shaving and after-shave items, shampoo deodorants, washing powder, granite and marble.
- There was unanimity that in 28 percent category there should be only sin and demerit goods. Thus, the Council took a historic decision that in the 28 percent slab there will be only 50 items. Paints, cement, washing machines and air conditioners were retained in the 28 percent tax bracket.
- The rate of GST on job work services in relation to manufacture of those handicraft goods in respect of which the casual taxable person has been exempted from obtaining registration, was reduced to 5 percent with full ITC.
- GST on services by way of admission to *protected monuments* was exempted.

Twenty-fourth Meting, December 16, 2017, Through Video Conferencing

- The Council decided to make inter-State e-way bill compulsory from February 1, 2018. The system was to be ready by January 16, 2018. It was decided to introduce uniform system of e-way bill for inter-State as well as intra-State movement of goods across the country by June 1, 2018.
- Till such time as the nation-wide e-way bill was ready, the States were authorized to continue with their own separate e-way bill systems.

Twenty-fifth Meeting, January 18, 2018, New Delhi

- The Council declared yet another downward revision of GST rates on a number of goods and services. Specifically, the Council decided to reduce tax rate on 29 items and 53 categories of services with effect from January 25, 2018.

- GST rate on used (second-hand) medium and large cars and SUVs was reduced from 28 percent to 18 percent. The GST on used small cars and motor vehicles was reduced from 28 percent to 12 percent.
- GST on bio-diesel, drinking water packed in 20-litre bottles, drip irrigation system, mechanical sprayer, bio-pesticides, sugar boiled confectionery etc. was brought down from 18 percent to 12 percent.
- Tax on sales of liquefied petroleum gas (LPG) by private firms for domestic use and scientific equipment for satellite launch was reduced from 18 percent to 5 percent.
- Tax on diamonds and precious stones was reduced from 3 percent to 0.25 percent.
- A large number of essential services were exempted from GST tax entirely. These included services like education admission, the conduct of examinations, entrance fees for entrance examinations and transportation of students up to higher secondary schools.
- Decision on inclusion of real estate in GST was deferred.

Twenty-sixth Meeting, March 10, 2018, New Delhi

- Implement of inter-state e-way bill from April 1, 2018.
- Implement of intra-state e-way bill from April 15, 2018 in a phased manner by categorizing the states into 4 lots.
- Reverse charge mechanism (in case of supplies made by unregistered persons to registered persons) was delayed till July 1, 2018.
- Tax deduction at source (TDS) and tax collection at source (TCS) applicability was postponed until June 30, 2018.

Twenty-seventh Meeting, May 4, 2018, Through Video Conferencing

- The Council paved the way for single form GST return, based on the recommendations of the Group of Ministers (GoM) on IT simplification.
- GST return filing was made to happen only once every month compared to the three returns a month followed earlier.
- The Council gave green signal to making the GST Network a government entity as it was set to take over the 51 percent stake that was currently held by the private entities.

Twenty-eighth Meeting, July 21, 2018, New Delhi

- The Council recommended certain amendments to the CGST Act, 2017, IGST Act, 2017, UT-GST Act, 2017, and GST (Compensation to States) Act, 2017.
- GST rates were reduced on a variety of goods to provide relief to a cross-section of taxpayers.
- Threshold exemption limit for registration in the States of Assam, Arunachal Pradesh, Himachal Pradesh, Meghalaya, Sikkim and Uttarakhand was increased to ₹ 20 lakh from ₹ 10 lakh.
- Upper limit of turnover for opting for composition scheme was decided to be raised from ₹ 1 crore to ₹ 1.5 crore.
- Composition dealers were allowed to supply services (other than restaurant services),

for up to a value not exceeding 10 percent of turnover in the preceding financial year, or ₹ 5 lakh, whichever is higher. • Reverse charge mechanism (RCM) would remain suspended until September 2019. • The Council approved new return formats and associated changes in law. • The Council approved quarterly filing of return for the small taxpayers having turnover below ₹ 5 crore as an optional facility.
Twenty-ninth Meeting, August 4, 2018, New Delhi
• The Council decided to set up a sub-committee, headed by Minister of State for Finance, to look into various issues and concerns of micro, small and medium enterprises (MSMEs). • The Council also decided to experiment with a scheme to provide cash back for digital transactions.
Thirtieth Meeting, September 28, 2018, Through Video Conferencing
• The proposal of the State of Kerala for imposition of cess on SGST for rehabilitation and flood-affected works was discussed in this meeting of the Council. The Council decided to constitute a 7-member Group of Ministers (GoM) to examine the issue regarding modalities for revenue mobilization in case of natural calamities and disasters. The GoM was asked to submit its report by October 31, 2018.
Thirty-first Meeting, December 22, 2018, New Delhi
• 6 commodities were shifted from 28 percent to 18 percent rate category; 1 item from 28 percent to 5 percent; 3 items from 18 percent to 12 percent; 1 item from 18 percent to 5 percent; 3 items from 12 percent to 5 percent; 1 item from 12 percent to nil; and 2 items from 5 percent to nil rate category. • GST rate on cinema tickets above ₹ 100 was reduced from 28 percent to 18 percent and on cinema tickets up to ₹ 100 from 18 percent to 12 percent. • GST rate on third-party insurance premium of goods-carrying vehicles was reduced from 18 percent to 12 percent. • Exemption from GST on supply of gold by nominated agencies to exporters of article of gold Jewellery.
Thirty-second Meeting, January 10, 2019, New Delhi
• The Council decided to provide two threshold limits for supplier of goods for exemption from registration and payment of GST: ₹ 20 lakh and ₹ 40 lakh. • Threshold limits for service providers was kept unchanged, i.e. ₹ 20 lakh (₹ 10 lakh for Special Category States). • The limit of annual turnover in the preceding financial year for availing composition scheme for goods was increased from ₹ 1 crore to ₹ 1.5 crore. • Persons enrolled under the composition scheme were earlier required to file return every quarter. They were allowed to file one annual return, but making quarterly payment of taxes due. • Suppliers of services (or mixed suppliers) having an annual turnover in the preceding financial year up to ₹ 50 lakh were made eligible to enrol for the composition scheme.

• Kerala was allowed to levy cess on intra-State supply of goods and services at a rate not of not more than 1 percent for a period not exceeding 2 years.
Thirty-third Meeting, February 24, 2019, New Delhi
• GST rate for non-affordable housing was reduced from 12 percent to 5 percent without the benefit ITC. • GST rate for affordable housing was slashed from 8 percent to 1 percent without the benefit of input tax credit (ITC). Affordable housing was redefined under the GST law with a twin definition.
Thirty-fourth Meeting, March 19, 2019, via Video Conferencing
• Draft circulars/notifications on the rate cuts on housing announced in the Thirty-third Meeting were passed. • The Council approved the transition plan for the implementation of the new tax structure for housing units.
Thirty-fifth Meeting, June 21, 2019, New Delhi
• Tenure of NAA extended by 2 years to November 2021.
• Electronic invoicing (e-invoicing) for business-to business (B2B) transactions.
• Electronic ticketing (e-ticketing) for multiplexes.
• Aadhaar allowed as proof for obtaining registration under GST.

To sum up, GST Council is the linchpin of GST regime. So far, it has successfully resolved claims and counter claims of Central and State Governments. In the context of concurrent empowerment of the Centre and the States to levy and collect GST, GST Council is a unique institutional mechanism to ensure that decisions about the structure, design and operation of GST are taken jointly by the two layers of the government.

Endnotes

1. In the Constitution (One Hundred and Fifteenth Amendment) Bill, 2011, which lapsed with the dissolution of the 15th Lok Sabha, a Goods and Services Tax Dispute Settlement Authority was to be constituted. This body was judicial in nature and it was thought that its powers would override the supremacy of the Parliament and the State Legislatures. The Constitution (One Hundred and Twenty-second Amendment) Bill, 2014 departed from the lapsed GST Bill and proposed that the GST Council may decide about the modalities to resolve disputes arising out of its recommendation.
2. The gross annual turnover cut-off was increased to ₹ 75 lakh in the sixteenth meeting of the Council held on June 11, 2017 and further up to ₹ 1 crore in the twenty-second meeting of the council held on October 6, 2017.
3. It is noteworthy that presently funds are provided to cope with natural disasters under the National Disaster Relief Fund (NDRF).

9

Enactment of Central and State Legislations for Implementation of GST

Suitable legislations for the levy of GST drawing powers from the Constitution were needed to be passed by the Parliament and the State Legislatures. Unlike the constitutional amendment which required 2/3rd majority, the GST Bills needed to be passed by a simple majority. Obviously, the levy of the tax could commence only after the GST laws had been enacted by the Parliament and respective Legislatures.

Moreover, unlike the State VAT, the date of commencement of GST had to be synchronized across the Centre and the States. This was so because the IGST model could not have functioned unless the Centre and all the States participated in it simultaneously.

In short, both the Centre and States had to pass Central GST and State GST Bills respectively and rules had to be made under them.

9.1 Central Legislations

On March 20, 2017, the Union Cabinet approved the following 4 draft laws on GST which were needed to implement India's biggest tax reform:

1. Central Goods and Services Tax (CGST) Bill, 2017.
2. Integrated Goods and Services Tax (IGST) Bill, 2017.
3. Union Territory Goods and Services Tax (UT-GST), Bill, 2017.
4. Goods and Services Tax (Compensation to States), Bill, 2017.

All the 4 GST-related bills were taken up as money bills in the Parliament. Finance Minister Shri Arun Jaitley introduced the 4 GST-related Bills in the Lok Sabha on March 27, 2017 which were passed on March 29, 2017.

All the 4 GST-related Bills were passed by the Rajya Sabha on April 6, 2017. It is noteworthy that Rajya Sabha cannot reject a money bill as it only has powers to make recommendations on such legislation, which the Lok Sabha can choose to accept or reject.

All the 4 GST-related Bills passed by the Parliament received the assent of the President on April 12, 2017 and were notified on the same date.

It is noteworthy that the GST Council had already cleared all the 5 draft laws (the above 4 and the SGST law).

A brief explanation of the 4 GST-related enactments is as under:

9.1.1 Central Goods and Services Tax (CGST) Act, 2017: It makes provisions for the levy and collection of tax on intra-state supply of goods or services or both by the Central Government. It extends to the whole of India except the state of Jammu and

Kashmir. The CGST Act, 2017 is divided into 21 chapters which deal with matters connected with the levy, collection and administration of GST.

9.1.2 Integrated Goods and Services Tax (IGST) Act, 2017: It makes provisions for the levy and collection of tax on inter-state supply of goods or services or both by the Central Government. It extends to the whole of India except the state of Jammu and Kashmir.

9.1.3 Union Territory Goods and Services Tax (UT-GST), Act, 2017: It makes provisions for the levy and collection of tax on intra-UT supply of goods or services or both in the Union Territories without legislature. Thus, it extends to the Union territories of: (a) Andaman and Nicobar Islands, (b) Lakshadweep, (c) Dadra and Nagar Haveli, (d) Daman and Diu and (e) Chandigarh.

9.1.4 Goods and Services Tax (Compensation to States), Act, 2017: It provides for compensation to the states for loss of revenue arising on account of implementation of GST for first 5 years as per the provisions of Constitution (One Hundred and First Amendment) Act, 2016. It extends to the whole of India.

Compensation law provides for the levy of cess on top of the peak rate of approved tax on pan masala, tobacco, aerated waters, luxury cars and coal to create a fund for compensating states. Such cess has been capped at 135 percent in case of pan masala, ₹ 4,170 per thousand cigarette sticks or 290 percent on value (ad valorem), ₹ 400 per tonne on coal and 15 percent on aerated water and luxury cars. The compensation to states will be paid bi-monthly and the amount due would be calculated after considering a 14 percent growth rate in taxes over the base year of 2015-16.

9.2 State Legislations

Telangana was the first State to pass the SGST Act followed by Bihar, Rajasthan, Jharkhand, Chhattisgarh, Uttarakhand, Madhya Pradesh, Haryana, Gujarat, and Goa. Jammu and Kashmir (J&K) was the last to do so and that too post-GST implementation. More precisely, J&K passed the SGST Act on August 8, 2017 and the Central Government also subsequently extended the CGST Act to J&K.

Table 9.1 presents the enactment of SGST Acts by the States in chronological order.

On June 22, 2017, the first notification related to GST was issued. Since then a number of notifications under CGST Act have been issued from time-to-time notifying sections, rules, amendment to rules, rate revisions, waiver of penalty etc. Similarly, notifications have been issued, as and when required, under IGST Act, UT-GST Act and GST (Compensation to States) Act. Likewise, notifications have been issued by all the States under the respective SGST Acts. Apart from the notifications, circulars have also been issued by various GST authorities to facilitate the implementation of the tax and provide clarifications to assessees.

Although the dual GST model is being implemented through multiple statutes, the basic features of law—such as chargeability, definition of taxable event and taxable person, measure of levy including valuation provisions, basis of classification etc.—are uniform across these statutes as far as practicable.

Table 9.1: SGST Acts Enacted by the States in Chronological Order

S. No.	State	Date on which Act was Passed	S. No.	State	Date on which Act was Passed
1.	Telangana	April 9, 2017	17.	Maharashtra	May 22, 2017
2.	Bihar	April 24, 2017	18.	Tripura	May 24, 2017
3.	Rajasthan	April 26, 2017	19.	Sikkim	May 25, 2017
4.	Jharkhand	April 27, 2017	20.	Mizoram	May 26, 2017
5.	Chhattisgarh	April 28, 2017	21.	Nagaland	May 27, 2017
6.	Uttarakhand	May 2, 2017	22.	Himachal Pradesh	May 27, 2017
7.	Madhya Pradesh	May 3, 2017	23.	Delhi	May 31, 2017
8.	Haryana	May 4, 2017	24.	Manipur	June 5, 2017
9.	Gujarat	May 9, 2017	25.	Meghalaya	June 12, 2017
10.	Goa	May 9, 2017	26.	West Bengal*	June 15, 2017
11.	Odisha	May 11, 2017	27.	Karnataka	June 16, 2017
12.	Assam	May 11, 2017	28.	Punjab	June 19, 2017
13.	Arunachal Pradesh	May 12, 2017	29.	Tamil Nadu	June 19, 2017
14.	Uttar Pradesh	May 16, 2017	30.	Kerala*	June 21, 2017
15.	Andhra Pradesh	May 16, 2017	31.	Jammu & Kashmir	July 7, 2017
16.	Puducherry	May 17, 2017			

*Through ordinance route.

The laws, regulations and procedures for levy and collection of CGST, IGST, UT-GST and SGST have been harmonized to the extent possible. It is noteworthy that various laws related to GST depend on each other for meaning/definition of words and expressions used in relation to GST. Thus, section 20 of IGST Act, 2017 makes reference to 25 terms the meaning to which shall be the same as under CGST Act, 2017.

9.3 GST in Budget Speeches of the Finance Ministers

Hoping for the early implementation of the GST, Finance Minister Shri P. Chidambaram in his 2013-14 budget speech observed, "Hon'ble Members will recall that I had first mentioned the Goods and Services Tax (GST) in the Budget speech for 2007-08. At that time, it was thought that GST could be brought into effect from 1.4.2010. Alas, that was not to be, although all States swear by the benefit of GST.

However, my recent meetings with the Empowered Committee of State Finance Ministers has led me to believe that the State Governments—or, at least, the overwhelming majority—are agreed that there is need for a Constitutional amendment; there is need for State Governments and the Central Government to pass a GST law that will be drafted by the State Finance Ministers and the GST Council; and there is need for the Centre to compensate the States for loss due to the reduction in the CST rate.

I hope we can take this consensus forward in the next few months and bring to this House a draft Bill on the Constitutional amendment and a draft Bill on GST. Hope inspires courage. I propose to take the first decisive step by setting apart, in the Budget, a sum of ₹ 9,000 crore towards the first instalment of the balance of CST compensation. I appeal to the State Finance Ministers to realise the serious intent of the Government to introduce GST and come forward to work with the Government and bring about a transformational change in the tax structure of the country". [1]

In his budget speech to the Parliament on June 10, 2014, Finance Minister Shri Arun Jaitley made the following observations regarding GST, "The debate whether to introduce a Goods and Services Tax (GST) must now come to an end. We have discussed the issue for the past many years. Some States have been apprehensive about surrendering their taxation jurisdiction; others want to be adequately compensated.

I have discussed the matter with the States both individually and collectively. I do hope we are able to find a solution in the course of this year and approve the legislative scheme which enables the introduction of GST. This will streamline the tax administration, avoid harassment of the business and result in higher revenue collection both for the Centre and the States. I assure all States that government will be more than fair in dealing with them". [2]

In his budget speech to the Parliament on February 28, 2015, Finance Minister Shri Arun Jaitley observed on GST as follows, "We need to revive growth and investment to ensure that more jobs are created for our youth and benefits of development reach millions of our poor. We need an enabling tax policy for this.

I have already introduced the Bill to amend the Constitution of India for Goods and Services Tax (GST) in the last Session of this august House. GST is expected to play a transformative role in the way our economy functions. It will add buoyancy to our economy by developing a common Indian market and reducing the cascading effect on the cost of goods and services. We are moving in various fronts to implement GST from the next year". [3]

GST was finally implemented from July 1, 2017. GST has brought indirect system of India under one umbrella. In view of the roll out of GST, Finance Minister Shri Arun Jaitley in his budget speech to the Parliament on February 1, 2018 announced to change the name of Central Board of Excise and Customs (CBEC) to Central Board of Indirect Taxes and Customs (CBIC).

9.4 Chronology of Events that Led to the Introduction of GST

The long journey of GST commenced on February 28, 2005 when Union Finance Minister Shri P. Chidambaram proposed it in his 2005-06 budget speech to the Parliament. He again made a plea for GST in his Budget Speech to the Parliament for the year 2006-07.

Major milestones in the arduous journey of GST are presented in Table 9.2 in chronological order.

Table 9.2: Major Milestones in the Journey of GST

Month/date/year	Event
2003	Vijay Kelkar Task Force on Implementation of the Fiscal Responsibility and Budget Management Act, 2003 suggests a comprehensive Goods and Services Tax (GST) based on VAT principle.
February 28, 2005	Finance Minister Shri P. Chidambaran in his Budget Speech for the year 2005-06 states, as his medium to long-term goal, "...a goods and services tax, encompassing both the Centre and the States".
February 28, 2006	Finance Minister Shri P. Chidambaran in his Budget Speech for the year 2006-07 moots a proposal to introduce a National Level Goods and Services Tax (GST) by April 1, 2010. Since the proposal involved reform/restructuring of not only indirect taxes levied by the Centre but also the States, the responsibility of preparing a Design and Road Map for the implementation of GST is assigned to the Empowered Committee (EC) of State Finance Ministers. EC duly prepares a report on a Model and Road Map for GST.
May 10, 2007	EC sets up a Joint Working Group consisting of representatives of the EC and the Government of India for an in-depth study of the report prepared by it.
November 19, 2007	The Joint Working Group submits its report based on discussions and interactions with stakeholders.
November 28, 2007	EC discusses in detail the report of the Joint Working Group.
April 30, 2008	EC releases the final version of its views in the document titled, *A Model and Road Map for Goods and Services Tax in India.* The *model* detailed the operational issues which needed to be addressed, including the number of rates, exemptions and exclusions from GST, as well as the treatment of inter-state transactions. The *roadmap* outlined the legal and administrative steps which needed to be taken in order to comply with the April 1, 2010 deadline.
December 12, 2008	EC receives the comments of the Government of India on the above-mentioned document.
December 16, 2008	EC takes note of the comments of the Government of India and appoints a Committee to consider these comments in detail.
January 5-6, 2009	The Committee holds detailed deliberations and submits its recommendations to EC.
January 21, 2009	EC considers the recommendations of the Committee and accepts them in-principle. It forms a Working Group of concerned officials to submit their recommendations in detail on the structure of GST.

contd...

November 10, 2009	Based on the recommendations of the Working Group, EC releases the *First Discussion Paper on Goods and Services Tax in India.*
March 22, 2011	Constitution (One Hundred and Fifteenth Amendment) Bill, 2011 is introduced in the Parliament. The Bill lapses with the dissolution of the 15th Lok Sabha.
December 19, 2014	Constitution (One Hundred and Twenty-second Amendment) Bill, 2014 is introduced in the Lok Sabha.
May 6, 2015	The above Bill is passed by the Lok Sabha.
May 12, 2015	The Bill is referred to the Select Committee of Rajya Sabha.
July 22, 2015	Select Committee of Rajya Sabha submits its Report.
August 3, 2016	The Bill is passed by the Rajya Sabha with 9 amendments.
August 8, 2016	Lok Sabha passes the modified Bill approving all the 9 amendments by the Rajya Sabha.
September 8, 2016	After being approved by half of the States, President gives his assent to the Bill.
September 16, 2016	The Constitution (One Hundred and Twenty-second Amendment) Bill, 2014 is notified as the Constitution (One Hundred and First Amendment) Act, 2016.
March 20, 2017	Union Cabinet approves the 4 GST-related draft laws.
March 27, 2017	The 4 GST-related Bills are introduced in the Lok Sabha.
March 29, 2017	The 4 GST-related Bills are passed by the Lok Sabha.
April 6, 2017	The 4 GST-related Bills are passed by the Rajya Sabha.
July 1, 2017	GST is rolled out.

Endnotes

1. Government of India, Ministry of Finance, *Budget Speech of the Finance Minister, 2013-14.*
2. Government of India, Ministry of Finance, *Budget Speech of the Finance Minister, 2014-15.*
3. Government of India, Ministry of Finance, *Budget Speech of the Finance Minister, 2015-16,* para 96.

10

Current Constitutional Provisions Pertaining to Distribution of Taxation Powers between the Centre and the States

This chapter explains the constitutional provisions pertaining to taxation powers of different tiers of government in India. The Constitution makes elaborate, albeit complex, arrangements relating to the distribution, between the Union and the States, of taxes, the power of borrowing, and provision for grants-in-aid by the Union to the States. The underlying philosophy of these arrangements is to place at the disposal of the two tiers of government adequate financial resources to enable them to discharge their respective responsibilities under the Constitution.

10.1 Distribution of Taxation Powers

Article 265 of the Constitution specifically states that no taxes shall be levied or collected except by the authority of law.

Article 246 (read with Seventh Schedule of the Constitution) mentions the matters on which the Centre and the States can legislate. Thus, the Centre has exclusive powers to legislate in respect of matters contained in List I (Union List) of the Seventh Schedule. Entries 82 to 92C of this list refer to taxation powers of the Union Government (Table 10.1). Similarly, the States have exclusive powers to legislate in respect of matters contained in List II (State List) of the Seventh Schedule. Entries 45 to 63 of this list refer to taxation powers of the States (Table 10.2). Furthermore, the Centre and the States have concurrent powers to make laws on any matter contained in List III (Concurrent List) of the Seventh Schedule. However, this list does not contain any head of taxation.

The residual powers of taxation, as in general legislation, belong to the Union vide Article 248 read with Entry 97 of List I (Union List) in the Seventh Schedule. The Article reads, "(1) Subject to Article 246A, Parliament has exclusive power to make any law with respect to any matter not enumerated in the Concurrent List or State List.

(2) Such power shall include the power of making any law imposing a tax not mentioned in either of those Lists".

For example, gift tax was imposed by the Union Government in 1958 under these residual powers (gift tax was abolished in 1998). Similarly, prior to the Constitution (Eighty-eighth Amendment) Act, 2003, service tax was imposed under these residual powers.

As regards Union Territories, the Parliament has the power to impose any tax included in the State List.

A scrutiny of the taxation powers contained in List I Union List) and List II (State List) of the Seventh Schedule of the Constitution reveals that major and elastic sources of tax revenue belong to the Centre while relatively inelastic sources of revenue come under the purview of State Governments.

Table 10.1: Taxes within Union Jurisdiction as Enumerated in List I (Union List) in the Seventh Schedule (Read with Article 246) of the Constitution of India

Entry No. in List I	Description of the Tax/Duty	
	Before Constitution (One Hundred and First Amendment) Act, 2016	**After Constitution (One Hundred and First Amendment) Act, 2016**
82	Taxes on income other than agricultural income.	Same
83	Duties of customs including export duties.	Same
84	Duties of excise on tobacco and other goods manufactured or produced in India except: (a) alcoholic liquors for human consumption; (b) opium, Indian hemp and other narcotic drugs and narcotics, but including medicinal and toilet preparations containing alcohol or any substance, included in sub-paragraph (b) of this entry.	Duties of excise on the following goods manufactured or produced in India, namely: (a) petroleum crude; (b) high speed diesel; (c) motor spirit (commonly known as petrol); (d) natural gas; (e) aviation turbine fuel; and (f) tobacco and tobacco products.
85	Corporation tax.	Same
86	Taxes on the capital value of assets, exclusive of agricultural land, of individuals and companies, taxes on the capital of companies.	Same
87	Estate duty in respect of property other than agricultural land.	Same
88	Duties in respect of succession to property other than agricultural land.	Same
89	Terminal taxes on goods or passengers carried by railway, sea or air; taxes on railway fares and freights.	Same
90	Taxes other than stamp duties on transactions in stock exchanges and future markets.	Same
91[1]	Rates of stamp duty in respect of bills of exchange, cheques, promissory notes, bills of lading, letters of credit, policies of insurance, transfer of shares, debentures, proxies, and receipts.	Same
92	Taxes on the sale or purchase of newspapers and on advertisements published therein.	Omitted

contd...

92A[2]	Taxes on the sale or purchase of goods other than newspapers, where such sale or purchase takes place in the course of inter-State trade or commerce.	Same
92B[3]	Taxes on the consignment of goods (whether the consignment is to the person making it or to any other person), where such consignment takes place in the course of inter-State trade or commerce.	Same
92C[4]	Taxes on services.	Omitted
97[5]	Any other matter not enumerated in List II or List III including any tax not enumerated in either of these lists.	Same

1. To be read with Article 268.
2. Inserted by the Constitution (Sixth Amendment) Act, 1956; to be read with Article 269.
3. Inserted by the Constitution (Forty-sixth Amendment) Act, 1982; to be read with Article 269.
4. Inserted by the Constitution (Eighty-eighth Amendment) Act, 2003.
5. To be read with Article 248.

Source: Government of India, Ministry of Law and Justice, Legislative Department, *The Constitution of India* (as on July 31, 2018), Seventh Schedule, List I (Union List).

10.2 Special Provisions with Respect to Goods and Services Tax

Article 246A of the Constitution [1] makes special provision with respect to goods and services tax by the Centre and the States. It reads, "246A. (1) Notwithstanding anything contained in Articles 246 and 254, Parliament, and, subject to clause (2), the Legislature of every State, have power to make laws with respect to goods and services tax imposed by the Union or by such State. (2) Parliament has exclusive power to make laws with respect to goods and services tax where the supply of goods, or of services, or both takes place in the course of inter-State trade or commerce.

Explanation—The provisions of this article, shall, in respect of goods and services tax referred to in clause (5) of Article 279A, take effect from the date recommended by the Goods and Services Tax Council".

10.3 Restrictions on the Taxation Powers of the States

Constitution also imposes certain restrictions on the taxation powers of the States. Although a State legislature enjoys the power to levy Goods and Services Tax (GST) under Article 246A and any of the taxes mentioned in List II (State List) of the Seventh Schedule, in the case of certain taxes, this power is subject to restrictions imposed by substantive provisions of the Constitution. Some examples of these restrictions are as follows.

10.3.1 Restriction on States to Impose Tax on the Supply of Goods or Services or Both: Article 286 ensures that taxes imposed by the States do not interfere with imports and exports or inter-State trade and commerce which are matters of national importance. The Article reads as under:

Table 10.2: Taxes within State Jurisdiction as Enumerated in List II (State List) in the Seventh Schedule (Read with Article 246) of the Constitution of India

Entry No. in List II	Description of the Tax/Duty	
	Before Constitution (One Hundred and First Amendment) Act, 2016	**After Constitution (One Hundred and First Amendment) Act, 2016**
45	Land revenue, including the assessment and collection of revenue, the maintenance of land records, survey for revenue purposes and records of rights, and alienation of revenues.	Same
46	Taxes on agricultural income.	Same
47	Duties in respect of succession to agricultural land.	Same
48	Estate duty in respect of agricultural land.	Same
49	Taxes on lands and buildings.	Same
50	Taxes on mineral rights subject to any limitations imposed by Parliament by law relating to mineral development.	Same
51	Duties of excise on the following goods manufactured or produced in the State and countervailing duties at the same or lower rates on similar goods manufactured or produced elsewhere in India: (a) alcoholic liquors for human consumption; (b) opium, Indian hemp and other narcotic drugs and narcotics but not including medicinal and toilet preparations containing alcohol or any substance included in sub-paragraph (b) of this entry.	Same
52	Taxes on the entry of goods into a local area for consumption, use or sale therein.	Omitted
53	Taxes on the consumption or sale of electricity.	Same
54*	Taxes on the sale or purchase of goods other than newspapers, subject to the provisions of Entry 92A of List I.	Taxes on the sale of petroleum crude, high speed diesel, motor spirit (commonly known as petrol), natural gas, aviation turbine fuel and alcoholic liquor for human consumption, but not including sale in the course of inter-State trade or commerce or sale in the course of international trade or commerce of such goods.

contd...

55**	Taxes on advertisements other than advertisements published in the newspapers (and advertisements broadcast by radio or television).	Omitted
56	Taxes on goods and passengers carried by road or on inland waterways.	Same
57	Taxes on vehicles, whether mechanically propelled or not, suitable for use on roads, including tramcars subject to the provisions of Entry 35 of List III.	Same
58	Taxes on animals and boats.	Same
59	Tolls.	Same
60***	Taxes on professions, trades, callings and employment.	Same
61	Capitation taxes.	Same
62	Taxes on luxuries, including taxes on entertainment, amusements, betting and gambling.	Taxes on entertainments and amusements to the extent levied and collected by a panchayat or a municipality or a regional council or a district council.
63	Rates of stamp duty in respect of documents other than those specified in the provisions of List I with regard to rates of stamp duty.	Same

*Substituted by the Constitution (Sixth Amendment) Act, 1956: ** The words 'and advertisements broadcast by radio or television' inserted by the Constitution (Forty-second Amendment), Act, 1976: *** The scope of these taxes is spelt out in Article 276, clause (2) of which fixes the amount payable by a person on account of these taxes.

Source: Government of India, Ministry of Law and Justice, Legislative Department, *The Constitution of India* (as on July 31, 2018), Seventh Schedule, List II (State List).

"286. (1) No law of a State shall impose, or authorise the imposition of, a tax on the supply of goods or services or both, where such supply takes place: (a) outside the State; or (b) in the course of the import of the goods or services or both into, or export of the goods or services or both out of, the territory of India.

(2) Parliament may by law formulate principles for determining when a supply of goods or of services or both takes place in any of the ways mentioned in clause (1).

10.3.2 Exemption from State Taxes on Electricity Consumed by the Government of India (Article 287): The Article reads: "287. Save in so far as Parliament may by law otherwise provide, no law of a State shall impose, or authorise the imposition of, a tax on the consumption or sale of electricity (whether produced by a Government or other persons) which is:

(a) consumed by the Government of India, or sold to the Government of India for consumption by that Government; or (b) consumed in the construction, maintenance or operation of any railway by the Government of India or a railway company operating that railway, or sold to that Government or any such railway company for consumption in the construction, maintenance or operation of any railway, and any such law imposing, or authorising the imposition of, a tax on the sale of electricity shall secure that the price of electricity sold to the Government of India for consumption by that Government, or to any such railway company as aforesaid for consumption in the construction, maintenance or operation of any railway, shall be less by the amount of the tax than the price charged to other consumers of a substantial quantity of electricity".

10.3.3 Monetary Limit on Taxes on Professions etc.: A State legislature is empowered to levy a tax on professions, trade, calling or employment vide Entry 60 of List II. However, the total amount payable in respect of any one person to the State by way of such tax is not to exceed ₹ 2,500 per annum [Article 276(2)].

10.4 Exemption of Property of the Union from State Taxation

The property of the Centre is exempt from State taxation under Article 285(1) which reads as follows: "285. (1) The property of the Union shall, save in so far as Parliament may by law otherwise provide, be exempt from all taxes imposed by a State or by any authority within a State. (2) Nothing in clause (1) shall, until Parliament by law otherwise provides, prevent any authority within a State from levying any tax on any property of the Union to which such property was immediately before the commencement of this Constitution liable or treated as liable, so long as that tax continues to be levied in that State".

10.5 Exemption of Property and Income of a State from Union Taxation

Under Article 289 the property and incomes of the States are exempt from Union taxes, except that Parliament may by law provide for Central taxation of any trading activities of a State which are not incidental to the ordinary functions of Government. Article 289 reads as follows: "289. (1) The property and income of a State shall be exempt from Union taxation. (2) Nothing in clause (1) shall prevent the Union from imposing, or authorising the imposition of, any tax to such extent, if any, as Parliament may by law provide in respect of a trade or business of any kind carried on by, or on behalf of, the Government of a State, or any operations connected therewith, or any property used or occupied for the purposes of such trade or business, or any income accruing or arising in connection therewith. (3) Nothing in clause (2) shall apply to any trade or business, or to any class of trade or business, which Parliament may by law declare to be incidental to the ordinary functions of Government".

10.6 Sharing of Central Taxes

All the taxes and duties levied by the Union are not meant entirely for the purpose of the Union. In fact, revenues from certain taxes and duties leviable by the Union are totally assigned to States [2] or shared with them to supplement their revenues in accordance with their needs. It is a tribute to the foresight of the founding fathers that they realised that the sources of revenue allocated to the States may not prove sufficient in view of their growing welfare, maintenance, and developmental activities. Hence, specific provisions were made to set apart a portion of Central revenues for the benefit of States. These provisions indicate the flexibility of India's Constitution in terms of distribution of financial resources between different layers of the Government. They also make a distinction between the legislative power to *levy* a tax and the power to *appropriate* the proceeds of a tax so levied.

10.6.1 From Itemised Sharing to Global Sharing: Prior to the Constitution (Eightieth Amendment) Act, 2000, two main Central taxes were shared with the states, namely income tax (other than corporation tax) and the Union excise duties. The sharing of the income tax was mandatory under Article 270 while that of the Union excise duties was discretionary under Article 272. There were also two tax rental arrangements with the States, where the Union Government collected the tax on behalf of the States and then distributed the proceeds among the States on the basis of criteria recommended by the Finance Commission. These were: (i) additional duties of excise in lieu of sales tax on textiles, tobacco and sugar, and (ii) grant in lieu of tax on railway passenger fares.

The Constitution (Eightieth Amendment) Act, 2000, significantly changed the manner of distribution of Central tax collections between the Central and State Governments. It substituted a new Article for Article 270 and omitted the old Article 272. The new Article 270 provides for the sharing of the net proceeds of all Union taxes and duties with the States, subject to the provisions of Article 271 (explained below). In other words, all central taxes were brought into a shareable pool and it became mandatory to assign a share from each central tax to the States. Eleventh Finance Commission was the first to make recommendations in accordance with the new provisions of the Constitution.

It is noteworthy that only *net proceeds* are to be shared, and as such *cost of collection* has to be deducted to obtain the net proceeds as prescribed under Article 279. The proceeds are to be distributed among the States where the central taxes are *leviable* in *that year*.

Article 270 reads as follows: "270. (1) All taxes and duties referred to in the Union List, except the duties and taxes referred to in Articles 268, 269 and 269A, respectively, surcharge on taxes and duties referred to in Article 271 and any cess levied for specific purposes under any law made by Parliament shall be levied and collected by the Government of India and shall be distributed between the Union and the States in the manner provided in clause (2).

(1A) The tax collected by the Union under clause (1) of Article 246A shall also be distributed between the Union and the States in the manner provided in clause (2).

(1B) The tax levied and collected by the Union under clause (2) of Article 246A and Article 269A, which has been used for payment of the tax levied by the Union under clause (1) of Article 246A, and the amount apportioned to the Union under clause (1) of Article 269A, shall also be distributed between the Union and the States in the manner provided in clause (2).

(2) Such percentage, as may be prescribed, of the net proceeds of any such tax or duty in any financial year shall not form part of the Consolidated Fund of India, but shall be assigned to the States within which that tax or duty is leviable in that year, and shall

be distributed among those States in such manner and from such time as may be prescribed in the manner provided in clause (3).

(3) In this article, "prescribed" means—(i) until a Finance Commission has been constituted, prescribed by the President by order, and (ii) after a Finance Commission has been constituted, prescribed by the President by order after considering the recommendations of the Finance Commission".

The objective of the Constitution (Eightieth Amendment) Act, 2000 was to construct a pool of all central taxes for sharing so that a holistic view could be taken and both sides could share in the aggregate buoyancy of the central tax revenues.

10.7 Surcharges on Certain Duties and Taxes for the Purposes of the Union (Article 271)

The Article reads, "271. Notwithstanding anything in Articles 269 and 270, Parliament may at any time increase any of the duties or taxes referred to in those articles [except the goods and services tax under Article 246A [3] by a surcharge for purposes of the Union and the whole proceeds of any such surcharge shall form part of the Consolidated Fund of India".

10.8 Duties Levied by the Union but Collected and Appropriated by the States (Article 268)

These include such stamp duties as are mentioned in Entry 91 of List I (Union List) of the Seventh Schedule. The Article reads as follows: "268. (1) Such stamp duties as are mentioned in the Union List shall be levied by the Government of India but shall be collected: (a) in the case where such duties are leviable within any Union Territory by the Government of India, and (b) in other cases, by the States within which such duties are respectively leviable. (2) The proceeds in any financial year of any such duty leviable within any State shall not form part of the Consolidated Fund of India, but shall be assigned to that State".

Stamp duties are leviable on bills of exchange, cheques [4], promissory notes, bills of lading, letters of credit, policies of insurance, transfer of shares, debentures, proxies, and receipts. These documents are executed in the course of business and trade and they find place in the Union List to ensure uniformity of rates throughout the country for the smooth conduct of commercial and related transactions. Inter-State disparities in their rates and tax regulations can hinder, and even disrupt, the free flow of trade and commercial activities. The levy and collection of stamp duty is governed by the Indian Stamp Duty Act, 1899 which was last amended in 1976 when rates of stamp duty on certain instruments were revised. [5]

10.9 Taxes Levied and Collected by the Union but Assigned to the States (Article 269)

Article 269 reads as follows: "269. (1) Taxes on the sale or purchase of goods and taxes on the consignment of goods, except as provided in Article 269A, shall be levied and collected by the Government of India but shall be assigned and shall be deemed to have been assigned to the States on or after the 1st day of April, 1996 in the manner provided in clause (2).

Explanation—For the purposes of this clause: (a) the expression "taxes on the sale or purchase of goods" shall mean taxes on sale or purchase of goods other than newspapers, where such sale or purchase takes place in the course of inter-State trade or commerce and (b) the expression "taxes on the consignment of goods" shall mean taxes on the consignment of goods (whether the consignment is to the person making it or to any other person), where such consignment takes place in the course of inter-State trade or commerce.

(2) The net proceeds in any financial year of any such tax, except in so far as those proceeds represent proceeds attributable to Union territories, shall not form part of the Consolidated Fund of India, but shall be assigned to the States within which that tax is leviable in that year, and shall be distributed among those States in accordance with such principles of distribution as may be formulated by Parliament by law.

(3) Parliament may by law formulate principles for determining when a sale or purchase of, or consignment of, goods takes place in the course of inter-State trade or commerce".

The above two taxes correspond to Entries 92A and 92B in List I (Union List) of the Seventh Schedule. [6]

It is noteworthy that out of these two taxes only one was being levied till recently, viz. inter-State sales tax (Entry 92A). Central Sales Tax (CST) on inter-State sales was subsumed under GST.

10.9.1 Philosophy of Articles 268 and 269: Taxation arrangements under Articles 268 and 269 of the Constitution are of special importance. They place under the charge of the Union the taxes and duties which have inter-State character and require uniformity in rate structure for the smooth conduct of business and trade activities throughout the country. These two Articles mention taxes/duties which shall be levied by the Centre but assigned completely to the States within which they are leviable. [7]

10.10 Levy and Collection of Goods and Services Tax in the Course of Inter-State Trade or Commerce (Article 269A)

Inserted by Section 9 of the Constitution (One Hundred and First Amendment) Act, 2016 this new Article reads as follows: "269A. (1) Goods and services tax on supplies in the course of inter-State trade or commerce shall be levied and collected by the Government of India and such tax shall be apportioned between the Union and the States in the manner as may be provided by Parliament by law on the recommendations of the Goods and Services Tax Council.

Explanation—For the purposes of this clause, supply of goods, or of services, or both in the course of import into the territory of India shall be deemed to be supply of goods, or of services, or both in the course of inter-State trade or commerce.

(2) The amount apportioned to a State under clause (1) shall not form part of the Consolidated Fund of India.

(3) Where an amount collected as tax levied under clause (1) has been used for payment of the tax levied by a State under Article 246A, such amount shall not form part

of the Consolidated Fund of India.

(4) Where an amount collected as tax levied by a State under Article 246A has been used for payment of the tax levied under clause (1), such amount shall not form part of the Consolidated Fund of the State.

(5) Parliament may, by law, formulate the principles for determining the place of supply, and when a supply of goods, or of services, or both takes place in the course of inter-State trade or commerce".

10.11 Goods and Services Tax Council (GST Council) (Article 279A)

Section 12 of the Constitution (One Hundred and First Amendment) Act, 2016 inserted a new Article 279A in the Constitution to provide for the constitution of Goods and Services Tax Council (GST Council) to make recommendations to the Union and the States on various aspects of the Goods and Services Tax (GST). The new Article reads as follows: "279A. (1) The President shall, within sixty days from the date of commencement of the Constitution (One Hundred and First Amendment) Act, 2016, by order, constitute a Council to be called the Goods and Services Tax Council.

(2) The Goods and Services Tax Council shall consist of the following members, namely: (a) the Union Finance Minister...Chairperson; (b) the Union Minister of State in charge of Revenue or Finance...Member; (c) the Minister in charge of Finance or Taxation or any other Minister nominated by each State Government...Members.

(3) The Members of the Goods and Services Tax Council referred to in sub-clause (c) of clause (2) shall, as soon as may be, choose one amongst themselves to be the Vice-Chairperson of the Council for such period as they may decide.

(4) The Goods and Services Tax Council shall make recommendations to the Union and the States on: (a) the taxes, cesses and surcharges levied by the Union, the States and the local bodies which may be subsumed in the goods and services tax; (b) the goods and services that may be subjected to, or exempted from the goods and services tax; (c) model Goods and Services Tax Laws, principles of levy, apportionment of Goods and Services Tax levied on supplies in the course of inter-State trade or commerce under Article 269A and the principles that govern the place of supply; (d) the threshold limit of turnover below which goods and services may be exempted from goods and services tax; (e) the rates including floor rates with bands of goods and services tax; (f) any special rate or rates for a specified period, to raise additional resources during any natural calamity or disaster; (g) special provision with respect to the States of Arunachal Pradesh, Assam, Jammu and Kashmir, Manipur, Meghalaya, Mizoram, Nagaland, Sikkim, Tripura, Himachal Pradesh and Uttarakhand; and (h) any other matter relating to the goods and services tax, as the Council may decide.

(5) The Goods and Services Tax Council shall recommend the date on which the goods and services tax be levied on petroleum crude, high speed diesel, motor spirit (commonly known as petrol), natural gas and aviation turbine fuel.

(6) While discharging the functions conferred by this article, the Goods and Services Tax Council shall be guided by the need for a harmonised structure of goods and services

tax and for the development of a harmonised national market for goods and services.

(7) One-half of the total number of Members of the Goods and Services Tax Council shall constitute the quorum at its meetings.

(8) The Goods and Services Tax Council shall determine the procedure in the performance of its functions.

(9) Every decision of the Goods and Services Tax Council shall be taken at a meeting, by a majority of not less than three-fourths of the weighted votes of the members present and voting, in accordance with the following principles, namely: (a) the vote of the Central Government shall have a weightage of one-third of the total votes cast, and (b) the votes of all the State Governments taken together shall have a weightage of two-thirds of the total votes cast, in that meeting.

(10) No act or proceedings of the Goods and Services Tax Council shall be invalid merely by reason of: (a) any vacancy in, or any defect in, the constitution of the Council; or (b) any defect in the appointment of a person as a Member of the Council; or (c) any procedural irregularity of the Council not affecting the merits of the case.

(11) The Goods and Services Tax Council shall establish a mechanism to adjudicate any dispute: (a) between the Government of India and one or more States; or (b) between the Government of India and any State or States on one side and one or more other States on the other side; or (c) between two or more States, arising out of the recommendations of the Council or implementation thereof."

Section 15 of the Constitution (One Hundred and First Amendment) Act, 2016 also amended Article 368 of the Constitution which pertains to power of Parliament to amend the Constitution and procedure therefore. Thus, Article 279A (pertaining to GST Council) was included in the list of items amendments to which require ratification by the legislatures of not less than one-half of the States.

10.12 Taxes and Duties in List I (Union List) of the Seventh Schedule not being Levied at Present

These taxes/duties are discussed below individually along with the logic for retaining them with the Centre.

10.12.1 Entries 87 and 88: These two entries pertain to estate duty, and succession duty in respect of property other than agricultural land respectively. Since the incidence of both estate duty, and succession duty is on the same object, viz. property passing on the death of the owner to his successors, they are essentially similar in nature. However, while in the case of the estate duty, the value of the whole estate, even if situated in more than one State, is the base for taxation, the succession duty is relatable to the value of individual shares (i.e. parts of an estate) passing on to the successors.

The desirability of retaining both these duties with the Centre is self-evident. An individual may have properties located in more than one State and a total assessment of his estate can better be undertaken by the Union Government. Similarly, if succession duty is levied by the States, the persons inheriting properties in different States will have to deal with different tax rates and procedures. Moreover, if estate/succession duties are levied by the States, it may trigger unhealthy competition among the States, resulting into harassment of the assessees and hence litigation. On efficiency criterion (i.e. cost of collection) also it is desirable if these duties are levied and administered by the Union, thus avoiding duplication of tax administration. Moreover, the Union has better access to information and otherwise also it is in larger national interest to ensure uniformity with respect to these duties. It may be noted that estate duty was first imposed in India in 1953 when the Estate Duty Act of that year imposed a duty on the capital value of all property passing on the death of any person on or after October 15, 1953. It was abolished with effect from March 16, 1985.

10.12.2 Entry 89: It relates to terminal taxes on goods and passengers carried by railway, sea or air. However, under Entry 56 of List II, States are empowered to levy taxes on goods and passengers carried by road or on inland waterways. Thus, the taxation powers in regard to the services of the major means of transport rest with the Union.

In a developing and diversifying economy like India, the importance of transport sector is self-evident. The growth of this vital infrastructure enlarges the size of the market and determines, *inter alia*, the level of private enterprise. Lest the free flow of inter-State trade should be hampered by differential State levies, the taxation of transport services is, by and large, with the Union Government. The Fifth and the Eighth Finance Commissions examined the scope for levying these taxes but expressed themselves against their imposition on grounds of administrative difficulties and meagre revenue potential. It is noteworthy that there already exists a terminal tax on passengers carried by railway from or to certain places of pilgrimage or where fairs or exhibitions are held. The proceeds of the tax are credited to the Consolidated Fund of the concerned States. The tax is restrictive and limited in scope and not a general terminal tax on passengers carried by railways to all places.

Entry 89 also refers to taxes on railway fares and freights. The Eighth Finance Commission favoured levying tax on railway passenger fares but not until the present arrangement of giving grants in lieu of such a tax continues to exist.

10.12.3 Entry 90: It pertains to 'taxes other than stamp duties on transactions in stock exchanges and future markets'. Since stock exchanges and future markets [8] are at a formative stage and have an inter-State character therefore it is desirable to retain these taxes with the Union. The Eighth Finance Commission did not think it advisable to levy taxes on transactions in stock exchanges and future markets.

10.12.4 Entry 92: It refers to 'taxes on the sale or purchase of newspapers and on advertisements published therein'. This tax is retained with the Union to protect the freedom of the press, and avoid undue tax burden on newspaper industry, particularly the regional language newspapers. Since newspaper reading habit is not sufficiently developed and widespread in the country, it is not desirable to impose a tax on the sale or purchase of newspapers. Both the Fifth and the Eighth Finance Commissions did not recommend a tax on the sale or purchase of newspapers. However, both the Commissions opined that there was scope for tax on advertisements published in newspapers. The Eighth Commission cautioned that a tax on advertisement, if levied, should be borne by the advertisers themselves and not passed on to the newspapers and journals.

It is noteworthy that Entry 92 was omitted by Section 17 of the Constitution (One Hundred and First Amendment) Act, 2016.

10.13 Taxation Powers to Local Governments

The Constitution does not provide for any taxation powers to local governments. However, the implication of Article 276 is that the taxes on professions, trades, callings or employment are for the benefit of a State or of a municipality, district board, local board or any other local authority. The States on their own may assign any of the taxes in the State List to the local bodies. The taxes generally assigned to local governments are property taxes, and taxes on vehicles.

10.14 Powers of District Councils to Levy Taxes in Tribal Areas

Sixth Schedule of the Constitution [read with Articles 244(2) and 275(1)] pertains to provisions as to the administration of tribal areas in the States of Assam, Meghalaya, Tripura and Mizoram. Sub-paragraph (3) of paragraph 8 of the Sixth Schedule relates to powers of the District Council for an autonomous district to levy and collect all or any of the following taxes within such district: (a) taxes on professions, trades, callings and employments; (b) taxes on animals, vehicles and boats; (c) taxes on the entry of goods into a market for sale therein, and tolls on passengers and goods carried in ferries; (d) taxes for the maintenance of schools, dispensaries or roads; and (e) taxes on entertainment and amusements.

10.15 Freedom as to Payment of Taxes for Promotion of any Particular Religion

According to Article 27 of the Constitution of India, "No person shall be compelled to pay any taxes, the proceeds of which are specifically appropriated in payment of expenses for the promotion or maintenance of any particular religion or religious denomination".

10.16 Rationale for Constitutional Arrangements

The distribution of taxation powers between the Centre and the States is meant to minimise tax problems in a federal set up such as double taxation, tax rivalry among States, duplicate tax administration, and tax evasion. Constitutional division of taxation powers between the Union and the States in India rests on economic and administrative considerations. Taxes with an inter-State base, and those in the case of which uniformity in rates is desirable, are vested in the Central Government. Also, taxes which the taxpayer can evade by shifting his habitat, or where the place of residence is not a correct guide to the true incidence of the tax, belong to the Centre. Taxes which are location-specific and relate to subjects of local consumption are with the States.

Commenting upon the soundness of the constitutional arrangements regarding division of taxation powers, the Commission on Centre State Relations, 1988, observed, "A well balanced distribution of heads of taxation based on economic and administrative rationale between the Union and the States and adequate arrangements for sharing of resources is vital for the proper functioning of the two-tier polity. We are of the firm view that the basic scheme of the Constitution dividing the field of taxation between the Union and the States and incorporating adequate arrangements for sharing of resources between them, is sound and no major modifications in it are called for". [9]

Similarly, the Sixth Finance Commission made the following observations in this regard, "We must bear in mind that the country as a whole and every part thereof has gained significantly from the maintenance of a vast unified market within which there is free movement of goods and men. Having regard to the trends all over the world even for independent political entities to come together to forge closer economic links in the form of common markets and economic groupings, our best hopes of accelerated economic development lie in the further strengthening of our national market and in the promotion of fiscal arrangements that are most conducive to the effective functioning of this market. Given this basic fact, there can be no room for argument that the levy and administration of taxes with wide economic base such as income tax, corporation tax, Union excise duties and of course also import and export duties will have to remain with the Union Government. In fact the architects of our Constitution drew on the experience of some of the other federations in which the assignment of taxes with wide economic base to units had led to intractable problems of conflicting tax jurisdictions. They wisely averted the possibility of such conflicts by assigning such taxes right from the beginning to the Union Government. At the same time, the framers of our Constitution rightly allocated to the States' subjects such as agriculture, education, medical care, public health, irrigation and law and order that touch intimately the lives of the people. These can be efficiently administered in a vast country only by the State Governments which are closer to the people and are more keenly alive to their problems and needs. The heads of revenue and responsibilities were distributed on the basis of whether the Centre or the State was better equipped to deal with the particular head". [10]

10.17 Definitions

In relation to taxation, the Constitution provides the following definitions:

10.17.1 Goods: According to clause 12 of Article 366 of the Constitution, *goods* include all materials, commodities, and articles.

10.17.2 Goods and Services Tax: According to clause 12A [11] of Article 366 of the Constitution, *goods and services tax* means any tax on supply of goods, or services or both except taxes on the supply of the alcoholic liquor for human consumption.

10.17.3. Services: According to clause 26A [12] of Article 366 of the Constitution, *services* means anything other than goods.

10.17.4 State: According to clause 26B [13] of Article 366 of the Constitution, *State* with reference to Articles 246A, 268, 269, 269A and Article 279A includes a Union Territory with legislature.

10.18 Summary of Constitutional Provisions Pertaining to Taxes

Provisions regarding taxes in the Constitution of India are summarized in Table 10.3.

Table 10.3: Summary of Constitutional Provisions Pertaining to Taxes

Article	Brief Description
27	Freedom as to payment of taxes for promotion of any particular religion.
246 (read with Seventh Schedule of the Constitution)	Subject-matter (including taxes) of laws made by Parliament and by the Legislatures of States.
246A	Special provisions with respect to Goods and Services Tax (GST).
248 [read with Entry 97 of List I (Union List) of the Seventh Schedule]	Residuary powers of legislation, including taxes.
265	No tax shall be levied or collected except by authority of law.
268 [read with Entry 91 of List I (Union List) of the Seventh Schedule]	Duties levied by the Union but collected and appropriated by the States.
269 [read with Entries 92A and 92B of List I (Union List) of the Seventh Schedule]	Taxes levied and collected by the Union but assigned to the States.
269A	Levy and collection of Goods and Services Tax (GST) in the course of inter-State trade or commerce.
270	Taxes and duties levied and collected by the Union but distributed between the Union and the States.
271	Surcharges on certain duties and taxes for the purpose of the Union.
276(2)	Monetary limit on taxes on professions, trade, calling or employment.
279A	Goods and Services Tax Council (GST Council).
285(1)	Exemption of property of the Union from State taxation.
286	Restriction on States to impose tax on the supply of goods or services or both, where such supply takes place: (a) outside the State; or (b) in the course of the import of the goods or services or both into, or export of the goods or services or both out of, the territory of India.
287	Exemption from State taxes on electricity consumed by the Government of India.
289	Exemption of property and income of a State from Union taxation.
244(2) and 275(1) [read with sub-paragraph (3) of paragraph 8 of the Sixth Schedule]	Powers of District Councils to levy taxes in tribal areas.
366(12)	Definition of *goods.*
366(12A)	Definition of *goods and services tax.*
366(26A)	Definition of *services.*
366(26B)	Definition of *state* with reference to Articles 246A, 268, 269, 269A and 279A.

Endnotes

1. Article 246A was inserted in the Constitution by Section 2 of the Constitution (One Hundred First Amendment) Act, 2016.
2. See sections 10.8 and 10.9 of this chapter.
3. Inserted by Section 11 of Constitution (One Hundred and First Amendment) Act, 2016.
4. Stamp duty was payable on cheques prior to 1927 but was withdrawn in that year.
5. **Indian Stamp Act:** The Indian Stamp Act, 1899 is a fiscal statute laying down the law relating to tax levied in the form of stamps on instruments recording transactions and stamp duties on instruments specified in Entry 91 of List I (Union List) of the Seventh Schedule of the Constitution. Because of large scale changes in the usage of the instruments since the Indian Stamp Act, 1899 was introduced, a need to amend a good number of provisions of this Act is being felt for quite some time. Law Commission in its 67th report submitted in 1976 made extensive recommendations in this regard. Serious efforts are now being made to bring in large scale amendments in Indian Stamp Act, 1899 to bring this law in tune with the times. Stamp duties on instruments other than those mentioned in Entry 91 of List I above are levied by the States as per Entry 63 of List II (State List). Thus, stamp duty and registration fees are levied on the registration of property or other conveyances. Provisions other than those relating to rates of duty fall within the legislative power of both the Union and the States by virtue of Entry 44 of List III (Concurrent List) of the Seventh Schedule. Stamp duties on all the instruments are collected and kept by the concerned States.

   Till recently, the stamp duty rates were quite high in most states and the procedures for evaluating the conveyances were also complicated. In this context, the Tenth Five Year Plan (2002-07) remarked, "Stamp duty needs to be paid on all documents which are registered and the rate varies from state to state. With stamp duty rates of 13 percent in Delhi, 14.5 percent in Uttar Pradesh and 12.5 percent in Haryana, India has perhaps one of the highest levels of stamp duty. Some states even have double stamp incidence, first on land and then on its development. In contrast the maximum rate levied in most developed markets whether in Singapore or Europe is in the range of 1-2 percent. Even the National Housing and Habitat Policy, 1998, recommended a stamp duty rate of 2-3 percent. Most of the methods to avoid registration are basically to avoid payment of high stamp duty.

   Another fall out of high stamp duty rates is the understatement of the proceeds of a sale. This is also linked to payment of income tax and capital gains tax. When registration has not been effected, a transfer is not deemed to have taken place and hence capital gains tax can be totally avoided. Thus, the present provisions in various laws and their poor implementation have led to a situation where there is considerable financial loss to the exchequer on account of understatement of sale proceeds, non-registration and consequent non-payment of stamp duty and avoidance of capital gains tax" [Government of India, Planning Commission, *Tenth Five Year Plan* (2002-07), Volume II, pp. 833-834].

   Of late, states have undertaken reforms by reducing the duty rates and streamlining procedures for evaluation of property. After the reduction of rates, the general experience has been revenue-augmenting due to improved compliance of law.
6. Prior to the Eightieth Amendment of the Constitution, provisions of Article 269 were as follows.

   Taxes Levied and Collected by the Union but Assigned to the States (Article 269): These were: (a) duties in respect of succession to property other than agricultural land, (b) estate duty in respect of property other than agricultural land, (c) terminal taxes on goods or passengers carried by railway, sea or air, (d) taxes on railway fares and freights, (e) taxes other than stamp duties on transactions in stock exchanges and future markets, (f) taxes on the sale or purchase of newspapers and on advertisements published therein, (g) taxes on the sale or purchase of goods other than newspapers, where such sale or purchase takes place in the course of inter-State trade or commerce, and (h) taxes on the consignment of goods (whether the consignment is to the person making it or to any other person), where such consignment takes place in the course of inter-State trade or commerce. These taxes corresponded to Entries 87, 88, 89, 90, 92, 92A and 92B in the Union List.

7. **Assignment of Taxes:** Assignment of a tax means transfer of taxation power from a higher level to a lower level of government. Taxation power includes the following: the right to levy the tax, collect the tax, and appropriate the proceeds from the tax. Thus, there can be three interpretations of assignment of a tax. In the first case, the higher level government may levy and collect a tax but handover the entire proceeds to a lower level government. Taxes levied by the Government of India under Article 269 of the Constitution are a case in point. Secondly, the higher level government may levy a tax but allow the lower level government to collect it and retain fully the proceeds therefrom. Taxes levied by the Government of India under Article 268 of the Constitution fall under this category. Finally, the higher level government may transfer a tax to a lower level government lock, stock and barrel, a situation which defines assignment of a tax in its strictest sense.

   Assignment of taxes should not be unconditional. Along with the determination of tax domain for a state, the central government ought to prescribe conditions so that the underlying purpose of assignment is adequately served. Thus, it should be obligatory on the part of a state to levy the tax assigned to it. Not only this, the state should not have powers to alter the basic structure of the assigned tax. The state may enjoy flexibility in fixing the tax rates within a minimum and maximum range prescribed by the central government. Tax exemptions/concessions should be minimum because a state is not expected to serve national objectives through its tax policy. As at other levels, tax default through disputes should be discouraged by requiring full payments prior to disputing an assessment.

8. Future trading refers to contracts for sale and purchase of goods at a future date primarily with a view to avoid price fluctuations. Presently, future trading is allowed at specific centres in respect of four commodities, viz. jute products, paper, turmeric, and *gur*.
9. Government of India, *Report of the Commission on Centre State Relations* (Chairman: Justice R.S. Sarkaria) Part I, 1988, p. 271.
10. *Report of the Sixth Finance Commission*, 1973, p. 5.
11. Inserted by Section 14 of the Constitution (One Hundred First Amendment) Act, 2016.
12. Ibid.
13. Ibid.

Part III
Basics of GST

11

Meaning and Salient Features of GST

The basic objective of tax reform in any country should be to establish a tax system that is economically efficient, distributionally acceptable, and simple to administer.

GST is the most ambitious and remarkable indirect tax reform in India's post-Independence history. Its objective is to levy a single national uniform tax across India on all goods and services. GST has replaced a number of Central and State taxes, made India more of a national integrated market, and brought more producers into the tax net. By improving efficiency, it can add substantially to growth as well as government finances. Implementing a new tax, encompassing both goods and services, by the Centre and the States in a large and complex federal system, is perhaps unprecedented in modern global tax history.

After missing several deadlines and overcoming almost a decade of political differences—on how to replace a multi-layered set of Central and State taxes with a uniform nationwide tax—GST was finally introduced from July 1, 2017. GST subsumed a profusion of Central and State indirect taxes to create a single unified market. GST has make India a seamless national market, boosting trade and industry and hence growth rate.

11.1 What is GST?

GST was launched at the stroke of midnight hour of June 30-July 1, 2017 by Prime Minister Shri Narendra Modi, in the presence of President Shri Pranab Mukherjee from the Central Hall of Parliament.

It became applicable on whole of India with effect from July 1, 2017 (Jammu and Kashmir was covered from July 8, 2017).

GST is a multi-stage value added tax, with set-off provisions, levied on the supply of goods and services. Taxable event under GST is supply of goods or services or both.

GST is a tax on goods and services with comprehensive and continuous chain of set-off benefits up to the retailer level. It is essentially a tax only on value addition at each stage, and a supplier at each stage is permitted to set-off, through a tax credit mechanism, the GST paid on the purchase of goods and services. Ultimately, the burden of GST is borne by the end-user (i.e. final consumer) of the commodity/service. In short, GST is a single tax on the supply of goods and services, right from the manufacturer to the end-user. It aims, inter alia, to ensure all-India uniformity in the prices of goods and services.

According to clause 12A of Article 366 of the Constitution, *goods and services tax* means any tax on supply of goods, or services or both except taxes on the supply of the alcoholic liquor for human consumption. According to the same Article, *goods* includes all materials, commodities, and articles (clause 12), *services* means anything other than goods (clause 26A) and *State* with reference to Articles 246A, 268, 269, 269A and

Article 279A includes a Union Territory with legislature (clause 26B). [1]

The power to levy GST is derived from Article 246A of the Constitution which confers concurrent powers to both Parliament and State Legislatures to make laws with respect to GST. However, clause 2 of Article 246A read with Article 269A provides exclusive power to the Parliament to legislate with respect to inter-state trade or commerce. The taxable event under GST is the supply of goods and/or services. CGST and SGST are levied on intra-state supplies while IGST is levied on inter-state supplies.

The taxable event in GST is the *supply* of goods or services or both. Taxable event means the event which triggers tax liability under any tax law. The levy and collection of tax is based on the happening of the taxable event. Thus, earning of income is a taxable event under the Income Tax Act, 1961. During the pre-GST period, manufacturing of goods was a taxable event for the purpose of Central excise duty. Similarly, sale of goods was a taxable event for levying sales tax/VAT and Central sales tax.

GST belongs to the VAT family because tax is collected on the basis of value added. Unlike in the case of a pure commodity-based VAT system, GST includes services also. Hence, GST can be considered as an extended version of traditional VAT.

GST is generally paid to the Government by the supplier (i.e. the person who makes the supply) after collecting it from the recipient of supply. The supplier collects GST from the recipient as part of the consideration. However, in a few exceptional cases, the recipient is liable to pay GST to the Government on reverse charge basis.

The significance of GST can better be understood by comparing it with the pre-GST indirect tax structure of India.

11.2 Salient Features of GST

Salient features of this game-changing tax reform are explained below.

11.2.1 GST is Levied on Supply: Taxable event in law is the event the happening of which results in imposition of a tax. In other words, tax liability is activated when tax event takes place.

What is taxable event in GST? Taxable event in GST is the *supply* of goods or services or both. GST becomes applicable only if there is supply of goods/services. Therefore, the word *supply* holds the greatest significance in determining the taxability of various types of transactions. In fact, the concept of supply is the pivot around which GST revolves.

The concept of supply under GST includes all sorts of activities like manufacture, sale, barter, exchange, transfer etc. It also includes supplies made without consideration when such supplies are made in certain specified situations.

It is noteworthy that in the pre-GST system of indirect taxes, excise duties were imposed on manufacture/production of goods, sales tax (later VAT) on sale of goods and service tax on provision of services,

For details on the concept of supply, see chapter 13 of this book.

11.2.2 Applicability of GST: GST is leviable on the supply of all goods and services except in the following cases: [2]

1. **Goods outside the Purview of GST:** Alcohol for human consumption is a case in point.

2. **Goods within the Purview of GST but Currently Kept in Abeyance:** The following five petroleum products are part of the GST regime: (a) petroleum crude, (b) high speed diesel, (c) petrol, (d) natural gas and (e) aviation turbine fuel. However, the date on which GST would be levied on these petroleum products is yet to be decided by the GST Council, the constitutionally established joint forum of the Centre and the States.
3. **Goods and Services Exempted from GST:** Under GST law, Central and State Governments, on the recommendation of the GST Council, can exempt the supplies of desired goods and services from the levy of GST either generally or subject to conditions.
4. **Goods and Services Supplied by Businesses within Prescribed Threshold Limits of Aggregate Turnover:** Exemption from registration and payment of GST is allowed to small businesses the annual turnover of which is within prescribed limits. The limits of turnover are different for goods and services.
5. **Activities or Transactions which are Treated Neither as a Supply of Goods nor a Supply of Services:** Schedule III to the CGST Act, 2017 mentions certain activities or transactions which are treated neither as a supply of goods nor a supply of services. The list of such activities is popularly known as negative list though there is no such concept in GST.

11.2.3 Dual GST Model: GST is dual in nature, with the Centre and the States simultaneously levying it on a common base. GST levied by the Centre on intra-State supply of goods and services is called Central GST (CGST) and that levied by the States [including Union territories with legislature (Delhi and Puducherry)] is called State GST (SGST). The five Union territories without legislature—Andaman and Nicobar Islands, Lakshadweep, Dadra and Nagar Haveli, Daman and Diu, and Chandigarh— levy Union Territory GST (UT-GST). Area up to 12 nautical miles inside sea is part of State or Union Territory which is nearest.

CGST and SGST are levied simultaneously on every transaction of supply of goods and services. Further, both CGST and SGST are levied on the same price or value unlike the erstwhile State VAT which was levied on the value of the goods inclusive of Central Value Added Tax (CENVAT).

While the location of the supplier and the recipient within the country is immaterial for the purpose of CGST, SGST is chargeable only when the supplier and the recipient are both located within the same State.

This dual GST model is implemented through multiple statutes (one for CGST and one each SGST statute for every State). To the extent feasible, uniform procedures for collection of both CGST and SGST are prescribed in the respective legislations for CGST and SGST. The basic features of law such as chargeability, definition of taxable event and taxable person, measure of levy including valuation provisions, basis of classification etc. are uniform across these statutes as far as practicable.

CGST and SGST are paid electronically into the accounts of the Centre and the States separately.

The dual GST is in place in view of the federal structure in India. Prior to the enactment of the Constitution (One Hundred and First Amendment) Act, 2016 and the subsequent introduction of Goods and Services Tax (GST) from July 1, 2017, taxation powers between the Centre and the States were clearly demarcated in the constitution with no overlap between the respective domains. In other words, there were no concurrent powers of taxation (or joint occupancy of tax fields) by the two levels of government. The Centre had the powers to levy tax on the manufacture/production of goods while the States had the powers to levy tax on the sale of goods. In the case of inter-State sales, the Centre had the power to levy Central sales tax (CST), but the tax was collected and retained entirely by the originating States.

The enactment of the said Act, 2016 marked a clear departure from the initial scheme of distribution of tax powers between the Centre and the States envisaged in the constitution. Introduction of GST has concurrently empowered the Centre and the States to levy and collect it.

In order to address the issue of dual control over assessees and to ensure single interface, there is division of audit and assessment responsibilities between the Central and State Governments. Thus, all administrative control over 90 percent of taxpayers having turnover below ₹ 1.5 crore is vested with the State tax administration and the remaining 10 percent with the Centre. Assessees with a turnover above ₹ 1.5 crore are divided equally between the Centre and the States.

11.2.4 Integrated Goods and Services Tax (IGST): GST makes distinction between intra-state and inter-state supply of goods and services. Hence, IGST—as a part of GST regime—is levied on inter-State supply of goods and services. IGST also applies on imports.

IGST is a mechanism to monitor the inter-state supply of goods or services or both. It is levied by the Central Government on all inter-state transactions of taxable goods and services. It is levied and collected by the Centre so that the credit chain is not disrupted. IGST rate is broadly equal to CGST rate plus SGST rate. SGST component of IGST accrues to the consumer state. IGST maintains the integrity of input tax credit (ITC) chain in inter-state supplies.

For details, see section 12.4 of chapter 12 of this book.

11.2.5 Destination-based Consumption Tax: GST is a destination-based consumption tax as against the erstwhile origin-based sales tax (later VAT). This implies that all SGST collected ordinarily accrues to the State where the consumer of the goods/services sold resides. In other words, the tax accrues to the taxing authority which has jurisdiction over the place of consumption which is also termed as place of supply.

In the case of inter-State trade, the inter-State seller pays IGST on the supply of his goods/services to the Central Government. IGST rate is broadly equal to CGST rate plus SGST rate. SGST component of IGST accrues to the consumer state. If a computer is assembled in Bengaluru (Karnataka) but purchased eventually by a consumer in Chennai (Tamil Nadu), the SGST (or the SGST component of IGST) will accrue to Government of Tamil Nadu and not to Government of Karnataka.

For details, see section 6.6.1 of chapter 6 of this book.

11.2.6 Input Tax Credit (ITC): Seamless flow of input tax credit is a key feature of GST. In the pre-GST indirect tax system, the availability of ITC was limited in various respects. Thus, ITC of Central Sales Tax (CST), entry tax and luxury tax was not available. Similarly, ITC of Central excise duty and service tax was not admissible to dealers in goods. Under GST, ITC follows supply chain not only in intra-state but also in inter-state transactions. This has significantly reduced tax cascading.

For details, see chapter 14 of this book.

11.2.7 Rate Structure: The maximum tax burden under GST is 40 percent (20 percent CGST and 20 percent SGST). This is an enabling provision for financial emergencies. The actual rates in the four-slab structure are 5 percent, 12 percent, 18 percent and 28 percent. IGST, levied by the Centre, is CGST plus SGST on all inter-State transactions of taxable goods and services.

Many essential goods and services of mass consumption are either exempt from GST or bear nil rate of tax. For goods, examples include bread, fresh fruits and vegetables, fresh milk, curd, and hearing aids. For services, the two prominent examples are health and educational services.

Similarly, many essential goods and services are subject to 5 percent rate of tax which is affordable. Examples include sugar, tea, edible oils, and house-keeping services such as plumbing.

There are two standard rates of 12 percent and 18 percent.

About 40 items are subject to highest rate of 28 percent. These are mainly luxury and demerit goods like motor cars, air conditioners, *pan masala,* tobacco products and aerated waters.

A cess over the peak rate of 28 percent on certain specified luxury and *sin* goods like tobacco and tobacco products, pan masala, aerated waters, motor vehicles, is imposed to compensate States for any revenue loss on account of implementation of GST.

For details, see chapter 16 of this book.

11.2.8: Threshold Limits of Aggregate Turnover: Exemption from registration and payment of GST is allowed to small businesses the aggregate annual turnover of which is within prescribed limits. Threshold for exemption is built into GST to keep small businesses out of tax net.

For details, see chapter 35 of this book.

11.2.9 Composition Levy Scheme: The composition scheme is an important feature of GST to protect the interests of small traders and small-scale industries. A composition option (i.e. to pay tax at a flat rate without credits) is available to small manufacturers and traders whose annual aggregate turnover does not exceed ₹ 1.5 crore. Composition scheme allows small businesses to avail a hassle-free compliance regime. The objective of composition scheme is to bring simplicity and reduce compliance cost for the small taxpayers. It is noteworthy that these segments are large job creators and hence a priority area for the government.

For details, see chapter 36 of this book.

11.2.10 Reverse Charge Mechanism (RCM): Generally, the supplier of goods/services is liable to pay GST. However, in specified cases, the liability may be cast on the recipient under the reverse charge mechanism.

Reverse charge means the liability to pay tax is on the recipient of supply of goods/services instead of the supplier of such goods/services in respect of notified categories of supplies. Under reverse charge, the recipient of supplies becomes liable to pay the tax, i.e. the chargeability gets reversed.

In its Twenty-eighth Meeting held on July 21, 2018, the GST Council decided to apply GST on reverse charge basis on receipt of supplies from unregistered suppliers only on specified goods in case of certain notified classes of registered persons. RCM as such was suspended until September 2019.

For details, see section 22.4 of chapter 22 of this book.

11.2.11 Tax Deduction at Source (TDS): Tax deduction at source is a system of collecting tax from payments made. Intermediaries (or third parties) do the job on behalf of the government as regards assessment of the taxable base and the collection of tax thereon.

GST law provides for tax deduction at source (TDS) by specified categories of persons (called deductors) from the payment made to the suppliers of taxable goods/services (called deductees) at the prescribed rate.

Twenty-sixth Meeting of the GST Council held on March 10, 2018 decided to postpone the applicability of TDS until June 30, 2018. Provisions relating to TDS were again deferred for another 3 months till September-end, 2018.

Finally, the provisions for TDS were operationalized w.e.f. October 1, 2018.

For details, see section 22.2 of chapter 22 of this book.

11.2.12 Tax Collection at Source (TCS): There is obligation on electronic commerce operators to collect *tax at source* at the specified rates before making the payment to the supplier for proceeds of sale.

On September 13, 2018, Government notified the provision part of section 52 of the CGST Act, 2017 which had been kept in abeyance since the rollout of GST on July 1, 2017. As per the notification, TCS provisions under GST regime took effect from October 1, 2018. Rate of TCS for intra-state supplies is 1 percent of net taxable supplies (0.5 percent CGST plus 0.5 percent SGST). Rate of TCS for inter-state supplies (IGST) is 1 percent of net taxable supplies.

With the TCS provisions coming into force, tax authorities are empowered to monitor e-commerce transactions and ensure that suppliers selling their goods through e-commerce platforms do not get away with under-reporting their turnover. Hence, TCS is a tool to check tax evasion.

For details, see section 22.3 of chapter 22 of this book.

11.2.13 Exports and Imports: Under GST, exports are treated as *zero-rated supplies*. No tax is payable on exports of goods/services. However, input tax credit is available.

All exports (whether of goods or services) as well as supplies to SEZs have been categorized as zero-rated supplies in the IGST Act, 2017.

Zero-rated supply under Section 16 of the IGST Act, 2017 means any of the following supplies of goods or services or both, namely:

- Export of goods or services or both; or
- Supply of goods or services or both to a SEZ developer or a SEZ unit.

Import of goods is treated as inter-state supplies and hence subject to IGST in addition to the applicable customs duties. Import of services is treated as inter-state supplies and hence subject to IGST.

For details, see chapter 30 of this book.

11.2.14 E-way Bill: E-way bill is a bill for movement of goods which can be generated on the e-way bill portal. Transport of goods of more than ₹ 50,000 in value cannot be made by a registered person without an e-way bill.

Under GST, check-posts have been abolished across states. Rules and forms of e-way bill are uniform throughout the country. This has drastically reduced the time taken to transport goods and hence the transport cost.

E-way bill for inter-state transport became operational from April 1, 2018. The requirement of e-way bill for intra-state (within state) movement of goods started on April 15, 2018 in a phased manner by grouping states in four lots. Implementation of e-way bill system was completed by the all the states and UTs by June 16, 2018. This significant step has ensured smooth, swift and easy movement of goods throughout the country.

For details, see section 20.2 of chapter 20 of this book.

11.2.15 Registration: Registration is the most fundamental requirement in any tax system for identification of taxpayers to ensure tax compliance. Under GST, registration of any business entity implies obtaining a unique identification number from the concerned tax authority for the purpose of collecting tax on behalf of the government and to claim input tax credit for the taxes on its inward supplies.

Registration is required for each State separately where the taxable person has manufacturing or trading or service units. Single registration for each State is sufficient even if the taxpayer has multiple branches within that State. However, he can have more than one registration in one State if he has different *business verticals*. For each registration, a separate GST registration number (GSTIN) of 15 digits is allotted.

For details, see section 21.1 of chapter 21 of this book.

11.2.16 GST Council: GST Council is a joint forum of the Centre and the States created under Article 279A of the Constitution. The recommendations made by the Council act as benchmark or guidance to Union as well as State Governments.

The guiding principle of GST Council is to ensure harmonization on different aspects of GST between the Centre and the States as well as among States. It has been provided in Article 279A that the GST Council, in its discharge of various functions, shall be guided by the need for a harmonized structure of GST and for the development of a harmonized national market for goods and services.

For details, see chapter 8 of this book.

11.2.17 Goods and Services Tax Network (GSTN): GSTN is the information technology (IT) infrastructure of GST. In fact, it is GSTN the backbone of GST.

GSTN provides shared IT infrastructure and services to Central and State

Governments, tax payers and other stakeholders. GSTN is a special purpose vehicle (SPV) which aims to provide a standard and uniform interface to the taxpayers, and shared infrastructure and services to Central and State/UT Governments. It is the interface between the government and the taxpayers.

For details, see section 25.1 of chapter 25 of this book.

11.2.18 National Anti-profiteering Authority (NAA): GST law stipulates that any reduction in rate of tax on any supply of goods or services or the benefit of input tax credit should be passed on to the recipient by way of commensurate reduction in prices. NAA is the watchdog body constituted by the Central Government to examine whether such tax benefits availed by any registered person have actually resulted in a commensurate reduction in prices. NAA is the institutional mechanism under GST law to check unfair profit-making by the trading community.

The responsibility of NAA is to examine and check any profiteering activities and recommend punitive actions including cancellation of registration.

For details, see chapter 24 of this book.

To sum up, the introduction of GST is a very significant step in the field of indirect tax reforms in India. By amalgamating a large number of Central and State taxes into a single tax, it has mitigated cascading or double taxation in a major way and paved the way for a common national market. Introduction of GST has made Indian products competitive in the domestic and international markets. Moreover, GST, because of its transparent character, is easier to administer.

If the value added tax (VAT) was a major improvement over the pre-existing Central excise duty at the national level and the sales tax system at the State level, then GST is a further significant breakthrough towards a comprehensive indirect tax reform in the country.

It is noteworthy that GST is a tax on the supply of goods or services or both. It is irrelevant whether the supply is from the manufacturer to the wholesaler or from wholesaler to the retailer or from retailer to the consumer. Such distinctions were relevant in the pre-GST system when excise duties were imposed by the Central Government on the manufacture/production of goods and sales tax/VAT was imposed by State Governments on the sale of goods. Disputes, administrative wrangling and litigations were rampant regarding the jurisdiction, rate of tax/duty on various commodities, and exemptions and concessions.

Endnotes

1. Clauses 12A, 26A and 26B in Article 366 were inserted by Section 14 of the Constitution (One Hundred and First Amendment) Act, 2016.
2. For details, see chapter 15 of this book.

12

Components of GST

The introduction of GST on July 1, 2017 was a significant reform in the field of indirect taxes in India. Multiple taxes levied on goods and services by the Centre and the States were replaced by GST.

A dual GST model is in place in view of the federal structure of India. Centre and the States now simultaneously levy GST on every supply of goods or services or both which takes place within a State or Union Territory (i.e. intra-state trade). Hence, there are three components of GST so far as intra-state trade is concerned.

- Central Goods and Services Tax (CGST).
- State Goods and Services Tax (SGST).
- Union Territory Goods and Services Tax (UT-GST).

Another important component of GST is Integrated Goods and Service Tax (IGST) which is levied by the Centre on inter-state supply of goods or services or both. IGST rate is broadly equal to CGST rate plus SGST rate. SGST component of IGST accrues to the consumer state.

Similarly, a cess over the peak rate of 28 percent on certain specified goods is imposed to compensate States for any revenue loss on account of implementation of GST.

12.1 Central Goods and Services Tax (CGST)

GST levied by the Centre on intra-State supply of goods or services or both is called CGST. It is levied under Central Goods and Services Tax (CGST) Act, 2017 which makes provisions for the levy and collection of tax on intra-state supply of goods or services or both by the Central Government. The Act is divided into 21 chapters which deal with matters connected with the levy, collection and administration of GST.

As regards the levy and collection of the tax, Section 9 of the Act reads as follows:

"(1) Subject to the provisions of sub-section (2), there shall be levied a tax called the central goods and services tax on all intra-State supplies of goods or services or both, except on the supply of alcoholic liquor for human consumption, on the value determined under Section 15 [1] and at such rates, *not exceeding twenty per cent.*, as may be notified by the Government on the recommendations of the Council and collected in such manner as may be prescribed and shall be paid by the taxable person.

(2) The central tax on the supply of petroleum crude, high speed diesel, motor spirit (commonly known as petrol), natural gas and aviation turbine fuel shall be levied with effect from such date as may be notified by the Government on the recommendations of the Council.

(3) The Government may, on the recommendations of the Council, by notification, specify categories of supply of goods or services or both, the tax on which shall be paid

on reverse charge basis by the recipient of such goods or services or both and all the provisions of this Act shall apply to such recipient as if he is the person liable for paying the tax in relation to the supply of such goods or services or both.

(4) The central tax in respect of the supply of taxable goods or services or both by a supplier, who is not registered, to a registered person shall be paid by such person on reverse charge basis as the recipient and all the provisions of this Act shall apply to such recipient as if he is the person liable for paying the tax in relation to the supply of such goods or services or both.

(5) The Government may, on the recommendations of the Council, by notification, specify categories of services the tax on intra-State supplies of which shall be paid by the electronic commerce operator if such services are supplied through it, and all the provisions of this Act shall apply to such electronic commerce operator as if he is the supplier liable for paying the tax in relation to the supply of such services:

Provided that where an electronic commerce operator does not have a physical presence in the taxable territory, any person representing such electronic commerce operator for any purpose in the taxable territory shall be liable to pay tax:

Provided further that where an electronic commerce operator does not have a physical presence in the taxable territory and also he does not have a representative in the said territory, such electronic commerce operator shall appoint a person in the taxable territory for the purpose of paying tax and such person shall be liable to pay tax".

12.2 State Goods and Services Tax (SGST)

GST levied by the States on intra-state supply of goods or services or both under their respective SGST Acts is called SGST. Union territories with legislature (Delhi and Puducherry) are covered under the definition of *state*. However, Union territories without legislature are governed by Union Territory Goods and Services Tax (UT-GST), Act, 2017.

The Secretariat of the GST Council released the Model GST Law (MGL) in November 2016. The MGL provided a common draft of Central GST (CGST) Act and State GST (SGST) Act. MGL also included the draft of Integrated GST (IGST) Act as well as draft GST Valuation Rules.

Telangana was the first State to pass the SGST Act. Jammu and Kashmir was the last to do so and that too post-GST implementation. Dates of enactment of SGST Acts by different States, in chronological order, are given in Table 9.1 of chapter 9 of this book.

12.3 Union Territory Goods and Services Tax (UT-GST)

Union Territories without legislature are governed by a separate Act, namely the Union Territory Goods and Services Tax (UT-GST), Act, 2017 which makes provisions for the levy and collection of tax on intra-UT supply of goods or services or both in the Union Territories without legislature. Thus, it extends to the Union Territories of: (a) Andaman and Nicobar Islands, (b) Lakshadweep, (c) Dadra and Nagar Haveli, (d) Daman and Diu and (e) Chandigarh.

Why was there the need for a separate Act for UTs without legislature? It is notable that the Constitution (One Hundred and First Amendment) Act, 2016 inserted a new clause, viz. clause 26B in Article 366 of the Constitution. As per this clause, *State* with reference to Articles 246A, 268, 269, 269A and 279A includes a Union Territory with legislature. Delhi and Puducherry are Union Territories with legislature and hence covered under the definition of *State* for the purpose of GST.

Unlike States and Union Territories with legislature, Union Territories without legislature do not have their legislative assemblies. Hence, they do not have power to make Acts and Rules. As far as CGST is concerned, it applies to these territories also. However, a separate law, corresponding to SGST, was required for Union Territories without legislatures. Hence, the Central Government passed the Union Territory Goods and Services Tax (UT-GST), Act, 2017.

It is noteworthy in the above context that as per Article 246(4) of the Constitution, the Parliament has powers to make laws with respect to any matter for any part of the territory of India, which is not included in the State, including the matters enumerated in State List (List II) of the Seventh Schedule to the Constitution of India. Therefore, with the approval from the GST Council, the Central Government passed the UT-GST law in the Parliament.

Supply of goods/services within these Union Territories (for example supply by a trader from Chandigarh to another trader in Chandigarh) is subject to CGST plus UT-GST. For the purpose of GST, each of these territories is considered as a separate Union Territory. Thus, if a trader in Andaman and Nicobar Islands supplies goods to a trader in Lakshadweep, it will be treated as inter-state supply and hence subject to IGST.

12.4 Integrated Goods and Services Tax (IGST)

IGST is levied by the Centre on inter-state supply of goods or services or both.

12.4.1 Background: Before discussing the IGST model and its features, it is important to understand how inter-state trade or commerce was taxed in the pre-GST period. Inter-state trade or commerce was taxed under the Central Sales Tax (CST) Act, 1956, the authority for which was constitutionally derived from Article 269 of the Constitution. Further, as per Article 286 of the Constitution, no State could levy sales tax on any sales or purchase of goods that took place outside the State or in the course of the import of the goods into or export of the goods out of the territory of India. Only the Parliament could levy tax on such transactions. CST Act was enacted in 1956 to formulate principles for determining when a sale or purchase of goods takes place in the course of inter-state trade or commerce. The Act also provided for the levy and collection of taxes on sales of goods in the course of inter-state trade.

However, CST suffered from various shortcomings. CST was collected and retained by the origin state rather than the destination state. This was a travesty of the very philosophy of an indirect tax. Any indirect tax, by definition, is a consumption tax which should be borne by the consumer. Hence, the tax revenue must accrue to the destination state having jurisdiction over the consumer. Similarly, input tax credit of CST was not allowed to the buyers which resulted in tax cascading (tax-on-tax) in the supply chain. Moreover, various accounting forms were required to be filed under CST which added to the compliance costs of businesses. CST also hindered the free flow of trade across state borders.

12.4.2 What is IGST? IGST is a mechanism to monitor the inter-state supply of goods or services or both. It is levied by the Central Government on all inter-state transactions of taxable goods and services. IGST rate is broadly equal to CGST rate plus SGST rate. SGST component of IGST accrues to the consumer state. IGST maintains the integrity of input tax credit (ITC) chain in inter-state supplies.

GST makes distinction between intra-state and inter-state supply of goods and services. Hence, IGST—as a part of GST regime—is levied on inter-State supply (including stock transfers) of goods and services. It is levied and collected by the Centre so that the credit chain is not disrupted. IGST also applies on imports.

12.4.3 Constitutional and Legal Provisions: The Centre levies and collects IGST on all inter-State supplies of goods and services under Article 269A (1) of the Constitution. The said Article reads, "269A. (1) Goods and services tax on supplies in the course of inter-State trade or commerce shall be levied and collected by the Government of India and such tax shall be apportioned between the Union and the States in the manner as may be provided by Parliament by law on the recommendations of the Goods and Services Tax Council.

Explanation—For the purposes of this clause, supply of goods, or of services, or both in the course of import into the territory of India shall be deemed to be supply of goods, or of services, or both in the course of inter-State trade or commerce".

The relevant enactment for this purpose is the Integrated Goods and Services Tax (IGST) Act, 2017, chapter III of which (containing Sections 5 and 6 of the Act) makes provisions for the levy and collection of tax on inter-state supply of goods or services or both by the Central Government. The two sections read as follows:

"5. (1) Subject to the provisions of sub-section (2), there shall be levied a tax called the integrated goods and services tax on all inter-State supplies of goods or services or both, except on the supply of alcoholic liquor for human consumption, on the value determined under section 15 of the Central Goods and Services Tax Act and at such rates, *not exceeding forty percent*, as may be notified by the Government on the recommendations of the Council and collected in such manner as may be prescribed and shall be paid by the taxable person:

Provided that the integrated tax on goods imported into India shall be levied and collected in accordance with the provisions of section 3 of the Customs Tariff Act, 1975 on the value as determined under the said Act at the point when duties of customs are levied on the said goods under Section 12 of the Customs Act, 1962.

(2) The integrated tax on the supply of petroleum crude, high speed diesel, motor spirit (commonly known as petrol), natural gas and aviation turbine fuel shall be levied with effect from such date as may be notified by the Government on the recommendations of the Council.

(3) The Government may, on the recommendations of the Council, by notification, specify categories of supply of goods or services or both, the tax on which shall be paid on reverse charge basis by the recipient of such goods or services or both and all the

provisions of this Act shall apply to such recipient as if he is the person liable for paying the tax in relation to the supply of such goods or services or both.

(4) The integrated tax in respect of the supply of taxable goods or services or both by a supplier, who is not registered, to a registered person shall be paid by such person on reverse charge basis as the recipient and all the provisions of this Act shall apply to such recipient as if he is the person liable for paying the tax in relation to the supply of such goods or services or both.

(5) The Government may, on the recommendations of the Council, by notification, specify categories of services, the tax on inter-State supplies of which shall be paid by the electronic commerce operator if such services are supplied through it, and all the provisions of this Act shall apply to such electronic commerce operator as if he is the supplier liable for paying the tax in relation to the supply of such services.

Provided that where an electronic commerce operator does not have a physical presence in the taxable territory, any person representing such electronic commerce operator for any purpose in the taxable territory shall be liable to pay tax:

Provided further that where an electronic commerce operator does not have a physical presence in the taxable territory and also does not have a representative in the said territory, such electronic commerce operator shall appoint a person in the taxable territory for the purpose of paying tax and such person shall be liable to pay tax".

"6. (1) Where the Government is satisfied that it is necessary in the public interest so to do, it may, on the recommendations of the Council, by notification, exempt generally, either absolutely or subject to such conditions as may be specified therein, goods or services or both of any specified description from the whole or any part of the tax leviable thereon with effect from such date as may be specified in such notification.

(2) Where the Government is satisfied that it is necessary in the public interest so to do, it may, on the recommendations of the Council, by special order in each case, under circumstances of an exceptional nature to be stated in such order, exempt from payment of tax any goods or services or both on which tax is leviable.

(3) The Government may, if it considers necessary or expedient so to do for the purpose of clarifying the scope or applicability of any notification issued under sub-section (1) or order issued under sub-section (2), insert an Explanation in such notification or order, as the case may be, by notification at any time within one year of issue of the notification under sub-section (1) or order under sub-section (2), and every such Explanation shall have effect as if it had always been the part of the first such notification or order, as the case may be.

Explanation—For the purposes of this section, where an exemption in respect of any goods or services or both from the whole or part of the tax leviable thereon has been granted absolutely, the registered person supplying such goods or services or both shall not collect the tax, in excess of the effective rate, on such supply of goods or services or both".

12.4.4 Imports of Goods and Services: Import of goods and services are treated as inter-State supplies and are subject to IGST in addition to the applicable customs duties.

12.4.5 Non-vatable Additional Tax: For an initial period of 2 years—or as further extended on the recommendation of the GST Council—a non-vatable additional tax not exceeding 1 percent on inter-State supply of goods would be levied and collected by the Centre and assigned to the originating State.

12.4.6 Main Features of IGST: These are as follows:

1. IGST is charged on *movement of goods and services* from one state to another. For example, if goods are moved from Maharashtra to Karnataka, IGST will be levied on such goods. The revenue from IGST is shared between the Central Government and the importing state (Karnataka) as per the manner prescribed by the authorities.
2. IGST is designed to ensure seamless flow of input tax credit from one State to another. One State has to deal only with the Central Government to settle the tax amounts and not with every other state, thus making the process easier.
3. Any IGST input tax credit is first applied to set-off IGST (this will happen if there are two or more inter-State transactions of the same commodity), then CGST. The balance can be set-off against SGST.
4. IGST is broadly CGST plus SGST. The inter-State seller will pay IGST on value addition after adjusting available credit of IGST, CGST, and SGST on his purchases. The exporting State will transfer to the Centre the credit of SGST used in payment of IGST. The importing dealer will claim credit of IGST while discharging his output tax liability in his own State. The Centre will transfer to the importing State the credit of IGST used in payment of SGST. The relevant information is also submitted to the Central Agency which will act as a clearing house mechanism, verify the claims and inform the respective governments to transfer the funds.
5. Collections under the IGST are deposited into an IGST account administered by the Central Government and distributed between the Central Government and the consuming States on a mutually agreed formula epitomising the spirit of cooperative federalism.
6. IGST also applies to imports and exports of goods and services into/from India and any import/export of goods or services into/from Indian territory. In other words, imports and exports are deemed to be supply of goods and services as inter-state trade or commerce.
7. The amount of IGST not apportioned to the Centre or the States/UTs may, for the time being, on the recommendation of the GST Council, be apportioned at the rate of fifty percent to the Centre and fifty percent to the States/UTs, as the case may be, on ad hoc basis and this amount shall be adjusted against the amount finally apportioned.

12.4.7 Advantages of IGST Model: The major advantages of IGST model are as under:

1. Maintenance of uninterrupted input tax credit (ITC) chain on inter-State transactions.
2. No upfront payment of tax or substantial blockage of funds for the inter-State seller or buyer.
3. No refund claim in exporting State, as ITC is used up while paying the tax.
4. Self-monitoring mechanism.
5. Level of computerization is limited to inter-State dealers and Central and State Governments are able to computerize their processes expeditiously.

6. As all inter-State dealers are e-registered and correspondence with them is by email, the compliance level is substantially high.
7. IGST can take into account *business-to-business* as well as *business-to-consumer* transactions.
8. It facilitates the seamless flow of ITC across states as it is a destination-based tax, i.e., the IGST amount will be apportioned between the Centre and States although the power to levy and collect IGST lies with the Centre to ensure that a single coordinating agency administers it.

Thus, currently the following legislations are in force for the implementation of GST.

1. One CGST Act for CGST on intra-state supply of goods and/or services.
2. SGST Acts (1 each for 29 States and 1 each for 2 Union Territories with legislature, namely Delhi and Puducherry).
3. One UT-GST Act for the levy of GST in Union Territories without legislature.
4. One IGST Act for Central IGST on inter-sate supply of goods and/or services.

Chart 12.1 depicts the various components of GST.

Although the dual GST model is being implemented through multiple statutes, the basic features of law—such as chargeability, definition of taxable event and taxable person, measure of levy including valuation provisions, basis of classification etc.— are uniform across these statutes as far as practicable.

In the light of above discussion, following combinations of taxes are applicable for any transaction.

2. For supply of goods/services within a State (intra-State): CGST+SGST.
3. For supply of goods/services within Union Territories (intra-UT): CGST+UT-GST.
4. For supply of goods/services across States and/or Union Territories (inter-State/inter-UT): IGST.

Chart 12.1: Components of GST

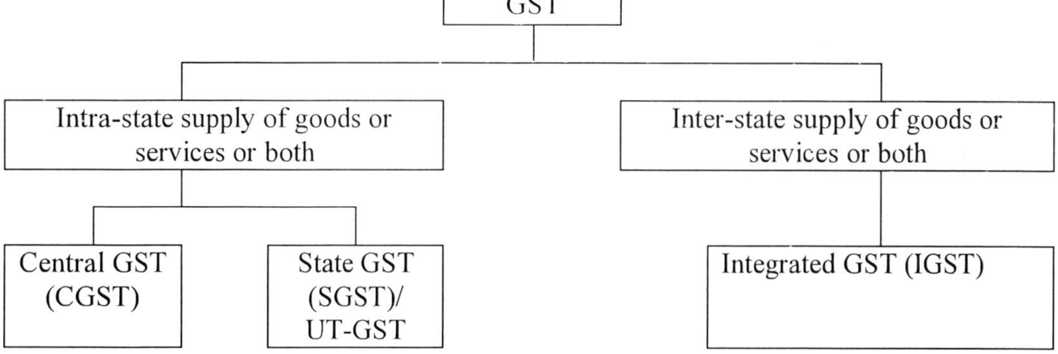

It is noteworthy that CGST, IGST and UT-GST laws are the exclusive domain of the Centre. Central Board of Indirect Taxes and Customs (CBIC)—formerly Central Board of Excise and Customs (CBEC)—is responsible for administration of the CGST, IGST and UT-GST laws. In addition, excise duty regime continues to be administered by the CBIC for levy and collection of Central excise duty on five specified petroleum products [2] as well as on tobacco products. [3] CBIC also continues to handle the work relating to levy and collection of customs duties.

SGST is administered by the respective State Governments through their commercial tax departments

12.5 Compensation Cess

It is a cess levied under section 8 of the Goods and Services Tax (Compensation to States) Act, 2017. It is applicable—in addition to the regular GST taxes (CGST + SGST/UT-GST on intra-state supplies and IGST on inter-state supplies—on the supply of certain notified goods/services. The following goods—which mostly belong to the luxury and demerit categories—have been notified for the purpose so far.

1. *Pan masala.*
2. Tobacco and tobacco products.
3. Coal.
4. Aerated waters.
5. Motor vehicles.

12.6 Rationale for Different Categories of GST

What is the logic for CGST, SGST, UT-GST and IGST? India is a federal polity where both the Centre and the States have been assigned the powers to levy and collect taxes. Both the levels of Government have distinct responsibilities to perform, as per the Constitution, for which they need to raise resources. Therefore, a dual GST is in keeping with the constitutional requirement of fiscal federalism. The Centre and States simultaneously levy GST.

In the pre-GST era, taxation powers between the Centre and the States were clearly demarcated in the constitution with no overlap between the respective domains. In other words, there were no concurrent powers of taxation (or joint occupancy of tax fields) by the two levels of government. Introduction of GST has concurrently empowered the Centre and the States to levy and collect it.

To sum up, GST is meant to evolve an efficient and harmonized consumption-based tax system in the country. GST is a consumption-based tax because the tax is received by the State in which the goods or services are consumed and not by the state in which such goods are manufactured. GST has replaced parallel systems of indirect taxation at the Central and State levels. The changeover to GST is a game-changing tax reform which will significantly contribute to the buoyancy of tax revenues, acceleration of growth, and generation of many positive externalities. Different components of GST are meant to ensure:

- One-country, one-tax and one-market.
- Adequate revenue for both the Centre and the States.

Endnotes

1. According to Section 15(1) of the Act, "The value of a supply of goods or services or both shall be the transaction value, which is the price actually paid or payable for the said supply of goods or services or both where the supplier and the recipient of the supply are not related and the price is the sole consideration for the supply".
2. Petroleum and petroleum products have been constitutionally included as *goods* under GST. However, it has also been provided that petroleum and petroleum products shall not be subject to the levy of GST till notified at a future date on the recommendation of the GST Council. The present taxes levied by the Centre and the States on petroleum and petroleum products—excise duty/CENVAT by the Centre and sales tax/VAT by the States—will continue to be levied in the interim period. The five petroleum products which have been kept in abeyance for the purpose of GST are the following: (a) petroleum crude, (b) motor spirit (petrol), (c) high speed diesel, (d) natural gas, and (e) aviation turbine fuel.
3. Tobacco and tobacco products would be subject to GST. In addition, the Centre would have the power to levy Central excise duty on these products.

13

Concept of Supply and Levy of GST

GST is levied on the supply of goods and services. The term *supply* is a legal term of broad sweep which covers under it various types of economic activities. In fact, the concept of supply is the pivot around which GST revolves. As against the erstwhile system of tax on manufacture of goods or on sale of goods or on provision of services, GST is applicable on supply of goods or services or both. The concept of supply under GST includes all sorts of activities like manufacture, sale, barter, exchange, transfer etc. It also includes supplies made without consideration when such supplies are made in certain specified situations.

According to clause 12 of Article 366 of the Constitution, *goods* include all materials, commodities, and articles. Similarly, as per clause 26A of Article 366 of the Constitution, *services* mean anything other than goods.

13.1 Supply is the Taxable Event in GST

In law, taxable event is the event the happening of which results in imposition of a tax. In other words, tax liability is activated when tax event takes place.

What is taxable event in GST? Taxable event under GST is the *supply* of goods or services or both. GST becomes applicable only if there is supply of goods/services. Therefore, the word *supply* holds the greatest significance in determining the taxability of various types of transactions.

GST is not applicable if the supplier is not in the business of supplying goods/services. A householder is not subject to GST if he sells his refrigerator because he is not in the business of selling refrigerators. Even if a person is engaged in the business of selling refrigerators, he may not attract GST if he is a non-taxable person. In other words, GST is applicable only when supply of goods/services is made by a taxable person. A taxable person means a person who is registered (or liable to be registered) under Sections 22 or 24 of the CGST Act. Every supplier whose aggregate turnover in a financial year exceeds a specified limit is required to get registered under GST in the State or Union Territory from where he supplies goods or services or both.

If a person—though not liable for registration—has taken voluntary registration, he will be considered a taxable person. Similarly, if a person—though liable for registration—has not taken registration, he will be considered a taxable person.

To attract GST, supply needs to be made by a taxable person. The recipient of supply may be a taxable person or non-taxable person. Also, supply by a non-taxable person to a taxable person may attract GST under reverse charge mechanism. [1]

13.2 Scope of Supply

In GST law, the definition of the word *supply* is inclusive which covers almost every transaction of goods and services unless specifically excluded. Section 7(1) of the CGST Act, 2017 defines the scope of the word *supply*. It states, "...supply includes: (a) all forms of supply of goods or services or both such as sale, transfer, barter, exchange, licence, rental, lease or disposal made or agreed to be made for a consideration by a person in the *course or furtherance of business*; [2] (b) import of services for a consideration whether or not in the course or furtherance of business; (c) the activities specified in Schedule I, made or agreed to be made without a consideration; and (d) the activities to be treated as supply of goods or supply of services as referred to in Schedule II".

According to Section 7(2), "(a) activities or transactions specified in Schedule III; or (b) such activities or transactions undertaken by the Central Government, a State Government or any local authority in which they are engaged as public authorities, as may be notified by the Government on the recommendations of the Council, shall be treated *neither as a supply of goods nor a supply of services*".

Thus, services by way of any activity in relation to a function entrusted to a *panchayat* under Article 243G of the Constitution have been notified neither as a supply of goods nor a supply of services.

Section 7(3) states, "...the Government may, on the recommendations of the Council, specify, by notification, the transactions that are to be treated as: (a) a supply of goods and not as a supply of services; or (b) a supply of services and not as a supply of goods.

As per Section 2(52) of CGST Act, 2017, "*goods* means every kind of movable property other than money and securities but includes actionable claim, growing crops, grass and things attached to or forming part of the land which are agreed to be severed before supply or under a contract of supply".

Similarly, according to Section 2(102) of the said Act, *services* means anything other than goods, money and securities but includes activities relating to the use of money or its conversion by cash or by any other mode, from one form, currency or denomination, to another form, currency or denomination for which a separate consideration is charged".

In view of the above definitions of *goods* and *services*, money and securities are the 2 common items which are neither goods nor services.

Generally, GST is applicable if supply of good/services is made for a consideration. [3] However, Schedule I in the above definition pertains to certain activities which, though made without consideration, are treated as supply under GST and hence chargeable to tax.

Schedule II to the CGST Act mentions activities which are to be treated as supply of goods or supply of services.

Schedule III to the CGST Act mentions activities or transactions which are treated neither as a supply of goods nor a supply of services. The list of such activities is popularly known as negative list though there is no such concept in GST.

Activities mentioned in Schedules I, II and III are given in Table 13.1.

Table 13.1: Activities Mentioned in Schedules I, II and III of the CGST Act, 2017

Schedule I: Activities which are to be treated as supply even if made without consideration: 1. Permanent transfer or disposal of business assets where input tax credit has been availed on such assets. 2. Supply of goods or services or both between related persons or between distinct persons as specified in Section 25, when made in the course or furtherance of business: Provided that gifts not exceeding fifty thousand rupees in value in a financial year by an employer to an employee shall not be treated as supply of goods or services or both. 3. Supply of goods—(a) by a principal to his agent where the agent undertakes to supply such goods on behalf of the principal; or (b) by an agent to his principal where the agent undertakes to receive such goods on behalf of the principal. 4. Import of services by a person from a related person or from any of his other establishments outside India, in the course or furtherance of business.
Schedule II: Activities or transactions which are to be treated as supply of goods or supply of services: 1. **Transfer:** (a) any transfer of the title in goods is a supply of goods; (b) any transfer of right in goods or of undivided share in goods without the transfer of title thereof, is a supply of services; (c) any transfer of title in goods under an agreement which stipulates that property in goods shall pass at a future date upon payment of full consideration as agreed, is a supply of goods. 2. **Land and Building:** (a) any lease, tenancy, easement, licence to occupy land is a supply of services; (b) any lease or letting out of the building including a commercial, industrial or residential complex for business or commerce, either wholly or partly, is a supply of services. 3. **Treatment or Process:** Any treatment or process which is applied to another person's goods is a supply of services. 4. **Transfer of Business Assets:** (a) where goods forming part of the assets of a business are transferred or disposed of by or under the directions of the person carrying on the business so as no longer to form part of those assets, whether or not for a consideration, such transfer or disposal is a supply of goods by the person; (b) where, by or under the direction of a person carrying on a business, goods held or used for the purposes of the business are put to any private use or are used, or made available to any person for use, for any purpose other than a purpose of the business, whether or not for a consideration, the usage or making available of such goods is a supply of services; (c) where any person ceases to be a taxable person, any goods forming part of the assets of any business carried on by him shall be deemed to be supplied by him in the course or furtherance of his business immediately before he ceases to be a taxable person, unless (i) the business is transferred as a going concern to another person; or (ii) the business is carried on by a personal representative who is deemed to be a taxable person. 5. **Supply of Services:** The following shall be treated as supply of services, namely: (a) renting of immovable property; (b) construction of a complex, building, civil structure or a part thereof, including a complex or building intended for sale to a buyer, wholly or partly, except where the entire consideration has been received after issuance of completion certificate, where required, by the competent authority or after its first occupation, whichever is earlier. 6. **Composite Supply:** The following composite supplies shall be treated as a supply of services, namely: (a) works contract as defined in clause (119) of Section 2; and (b) supply,

by way of or as part of any service or in any other manner whatsoever, of goods, being food or any other article for human consumption or any drink (other than alcoholic liquor for human consumption), where such supply or service is for cash, deferred payment or other valuable consideration.

7. **Supply of Goods:** The following shall be treated as supply of goods, namely: Supply of goods by any unincorporated association or body of persons to a member thereof for cash, deferred payment or other valuable consideration.

Schedule III: Activities or transactions which shall be treated neither as a supply of goods nor a supply of services:

1. Services by an employee to the employer in the course of or in relation to his employment.
2. Services by any court or tribunal established under any law for the time being in force.
3. (a) the functions performed by the Members of Parliament, Members of State Legislature, Members of *Panchayats*, Members of Municipalities and Members of other local authorities; (b) the duties performed by any person who holds any post in pursuance of the provisions of the Constitution in that capacity; or (c) the duties performed by any person as a Chairperson or a Member or a Director in a body established by the Central Government or a State Government or local authority and who is not deemed as an employee before the commencement of this clause.
4. Services of funeral, burial, crematorium or mortuary including transportation of the deceased.
5. Sale of land and, subject to clause (b) of paragraph 5 of Schedule II, sale of building.
6. Actionable claims, other than lottery, betting and gambling.
7. Supply of goods from a place in the non-taxable territory to another place in the non-taxable territory without such goods entering into India.
8. (a) Supply of warehoused goods to any person before clearance for home consumption. (b) Supply of goods by the consignee to any other person, by endorsement of documents of title to the goods, after the goods have been dispatched from the port of origin located outside India but before clearance for home consumption.

Note: Paragraphs 7 and 8 in Schedule III were inserted vide CGST (Amendment) Act, 2018. The new provisions became effective from February 1, 2019.

13.3 Different Kinds of Supply

First of all, it is very important to determine whether the supply is inter-state or intra-state. The kind of tax to be paid [IGST or (CGST + SGST)] depends on this distinction.

13.3.1 Inter-State Supply: Section 7 of IGST Act, 2017, comprehensively defines the term *inter-State supply.* It states, "(1)...supply of goods, where the location of the supplier and the place of supply are in: (a) two different States; (b) two different Union territories; or (c) a State and a Union territory, shall be treated as a supply of goods in the course of inter-State trade or commerce.

(2) Supply of goods imported into the territory of India, till they cross the customs frontiers of India, shall be treated to be a supply of goods in the course of inter-State trade or commerce.

(3)...supply of services, where the location of the supplier and the place of supply are in: (a) two different States; (b) two different Union territories; or (c) a State and a Union territory, shall be treated as a supply of services in the course of inter-State trade or commerce.

(4) Supply of services imported into the territory of India shall be treated to be a supply of services in the course of inter-State trade or commerce.

(5) Supply of goods or services or both: (a) when the supplier is located in India and the place of supply is outside India; (b) to or by a special economic zone developer or a special economic zone unit; or (c) in the taxable territory, not being an intra-State supply and not covered elsewhere in this section, shall be treated to be a supply of goods or services or both in the course of inter-State trade or commerce" (See Table 13.2).

The basis of charge in the case of inter-State supplies of goods/services is given by Section 5 of IGST Act, 2017. GST, in the case of inter-State supplies, is charged as IGST.

For details about IGST, see section 12.4 of chapter 12 of this book.

13.3.2 Intra-State Supply: It has been defined as any supply where the location of the supplier and the place of supply are in the same State or Union Territory

Section 8 of IGST Act, 2017, comprehensively defines the term *intra-State supply*. It states, "(1)...supply of goods where the location of the supplier and the place of supply of goods are in the same State or same Union territory shall be treated as intra-State supply: Provided that the following supply of goods shall not be treated as intra-State supply, namely: (i) supply of goods to or by a special economic zone developer or a special economic zone unit; (ii) goods imported into the territory of India till they cross the customs frontiers of India; or (iii) supplies made to a tourist.

(2)...supply of services where the location of the supplier and the place of supply of services are in the same State or same Union territory shall be treated as intra-State supply: Provided that the intra-State supply of services shall not include supply of services to or by a special economic zone developer or a special economic zone unit".

Intra-State supply of goods/services is chargeable simultaneously by the Centre and the States/UTs. The basis of charge is as under:

In the case of Central Government: Section 9 of CGST Act, 2017.

In the case of State Government: Section 9 of the SGST Act, 2017.

In the case of Union Territory: Section 7 of UT-GST Act, 2017.

It is noteworthy that to impose SGST on supply of goods/services within the State, each State has passed its own SGST Act which, for all practical purposes, is a copy of CGST Act, i.e. all provisions are identical. Thus, supply of a laptop by a trader in Kochi to a buyer in Kannur (both in Kerala) is taxable simultaneously under Section 9 of CGST Act, 2017 and Section 9 of Kerala GST Act, 2017. If GST rate is 18 percent, then 9 percent will be charged under CGST Act and 9 percent under Kerala GST Act.

There are 29 regular States in India. Out of 7 Union Territories, 2 (Delhi and Puducherry) have their own legislatures and they are considered as States for the purpose of GST. They have passed their own SGST Acts. Thus, there are 31 SGST Acts in all.

UT-GST Act has been passed for Union Territories which do not have legislature. Supply of goods/services within a Union Territory is taxable simultaneously under Section 9 of CGST Act and Section 7 of UT-GST Act. For the purpose of GST, each Union Territory is considered as a jurisdiction. Thus, if a trader of Chandigarh supplies goods to a trader of Lakshadweep, it will be treated as inter-State supply and hence subject to IGST.

Thus, whether the supply is inter-state or intra-state depends on the location of the supplier and the place of supply. Table 13.2 shows the difference between inter-state and intra-state supplies.

Table 13.2: Inter-state and Intra-state Supplies

Inter-state supply	Intra-state supply
Supply of goods from one state or union territory to another state or union territory.	Supply of goods within a state or union territory
Supply of services from one state or union territory to another state or union territory.	Supply of services within a state or union territory.
Import of goods and services.	
Export of goods and services.	
Supply of goods and services to/by SEZs	
Supplies to international tourists.	
Any other supply in the taxable territory which is not intra-state supply.	

13.3.3 Composite Supply: Charge of GST on the supply of individual goods/services is easy. Taxpayer has just to find out the applicable rate on a particular item. However, when two or more individual goods/services are supplied in conjunction with each other (called composite supply), it becomes difficult to find out the applicable GST rate. Composite supply is defined by Section 2(30) of the CGST Act, 2017. It is a supply comprising two or more supplies naturally bundled in ordinary course of business, one of which is principal supply. GST is chargeable on the entire consideration at the rate applicable on principal supply. A smart phone may be supplied for ₹ 40,000 along with a leather case, earphones and charger. In this case the principal supply is smart phone and hence the entire consideration of ₹ 40,000 will be subject to GST rate applicable on smart phone. Similarly, stay in a resort may be combined with such free services as body massage, steam bath, pedicure etc. Such services are ancillary to the principal service (lodging and boarding in the resort) and would be treated as services naturally bundled in the ordinary course of business.

13.3.4 Mixed Supply: Mixed supply is defined by Section 2(74) of the CGST Act, 2017. It comprises two or more supplies—not naturally bundled (and hence not composite supply)—for a single price. It will be treated as supply of that particular item in the mixed supply which attracts the highest GST rate. Consider the supply of a Diwali gift pack consisting of biscuits, chocolates, dry fruits and cans of aerated drinks. If the gift pack is supplied at a price of ₹ 1,200, then the entire consideration will be subject to GST rate of 28 percent (highest one) as applicable on aerated drinks.

Although the GST law provides definitions of composite supply and mixed supply yet no hard and fast rules can be laid down for the purpose. Rule of thumb has to be applied in different cases.

13.3.5 Continuous Supply: As per Section 2(32) of the CGST Act, 2017, "continuous supply of goods means a supply of goods which is provided, or agreed to be provided, continuously or on recurrent basis, under a contract, whether or not by means of a wire, cable, pipeline or other conduit, and for which the supplier invoices the recipient on a regular or periodic basis…".

According to Section 2(33), continuous supply of services means a supply of services which is provided continuously or on recurrent basis, under a contract. Such a contract is for a period exceeding 3 months with periodic payment obligations.

13.3.6 Taxable Supply: It means a supply of goods or services or both which is chargeable to GST [Section 2 (108) of the CGST Act]. Hence, non-taxable supply means a supply of goods or services or both which is not leviable to tax. Supply which is exempt under the law is not treated as taxable supply. However, exempt supply is included for the purpose of computation of aggregate turnover to determine threshold limit for small traders and composition scheme dealers.

13.3.7 Non-taxable Supply: According to Section 2(78) of CGST Act, 2017, *non-taxable supply* means a supply of goods or services or both which is not leviable to tax under CGST Act, 2017 or under IGST Act, 2017. Thus, supply of alcoholic liquor for human consumption is a non-taxable supply because it is excluded from the charging section (i.e. Section 9) of the CGST Act, 2017.

13.3.8 Exempt Supply: Section 2(47) of CGST Act, 2017 states, "*exempt supply* means supply of any goods or services or both which attracts nil rate of tax or which may be wholly exempt from tax under section 11, or under Section 6 of the Integrated Goods and Services Tax Act, and includes non-taxable supply".

Thus, exempt supply is a wider term and comprises the following three types of supply:

1. Supply which attracts nil rate of tax (0 percent tax) but does not form part of any exemption notification. Nil-rated supply has not been defined in the GST law.
2. Supply which may be wholly exempt from tax under Section 11 of CGST Act, 2017 or under Section 6 of IGST Act, 2017. Notifications for goods and services have been issued by using power given under Section 11. Thus, goods and services mentioned in these notifications are exempted goods/services as per definition of exempt supply. No tax is payable due to exemption notification.
3. Non-taxable supplies as defined by Section 2(78) of the CGST Act, 2017.

Tax need not be paid on these supplies. Although the three supplies are exempt from payment of tax yet they are differentiated due to following reasons:

- To meet reporting requirements of the tax authorities. There are separate columns for these supplies in GST return forms.
- The assessee is required to reverse input tax credit on inward supply which is used for exempt outward supply as per Rule 42 of the CGST Rules, 2017.
  See section 14.5 of chapter 14 of this book.
- The term *aggregate turnover* considers exempt supply for the purpose of calculating threshold limit for registration but does not consider non-GST supply (non-taxable supply).

No input tax credit can be claimed with respect to inputs and/or input services used for making exempt supplies.

See also section 15.4 of chapter 15 of this book.

13.3.9 Zero-rated Supply: In this regard, Section 16 of the IGST Act, 2017 makes the following provisions:

"(1) *zero rated supply* means any of the following supplies of goods or services or both, namely: (a) export of goods or services or both; or (b) supply of goods or services or both to a special economic zone developer or a special economic zone unit.

(2)...credit of input tax may be availed for making zero-rated supplies, notwithstanding that such supply may be an exempt supply.

(3) A registered person making zero rated supply shall be eligible to claim refund under either of the following options, namely: (a) he may supply goods or services or both under bond or Letter of Undertaking...without payment of integrated tax and claim refund of unutilised input tax credit; or (b) he may supply goods or services or both...on payment of integrated tax and claim refund of such tax paid on goods or services or both supplied".

In simple terms, zero-rated supply means any of the following supplies of goods/ services:

- Export of goods/services; or
- Supply of goods/services to a SEZ developer or a SEZ unit.

Input tax credit pertaining to such supplies is admissible even if such supplies are exempt supplies.

Taxes paid on zero-rated supplies are refunded.

See also section 30.1 of chapter 30 of this book.

Table 13.3 defines non-taxable supply, exempted supply, nil-rated supply and zero-rated supply with suitable examples.

Table 13.4 shows the difference between exempt supply and zero-rated supply.

13.3.10 Exempt Supply versus Zero-rated Supply: There is fundamental difference between the concepts of *exempt supply* and *zero-rated supply* in GST.

As per Section 2(47) of the CGST Act, 2017, a supply is said to be exempt when it attracts nil rate of tax or is specifically exempted by a notification or kept out of the purview of GST (non-taxable or non-GST supply).

Although the final product is exempt from tax yet the inputs which were used in the making of the product did suffer tax burden. If output is exempted and tax law does not allow input tax credit, as is the case for exempt supply, the entire supply chain cannot be considered free from taxation. The concept of zero rating is meant to rectify this anomaly.

Zero rating means the entire value chain of supply is exempt from tax. In other words, apart from the output being exempt from tax, the credit of taxes paid on inputs for making the output is also allowed.

Table 13.3: Meaning and Related Implications of Non-taxable Supply, Exempted Supply, Nil-rated Supply and Zero-rated Supply

Particulars	Exempt supply (Section 2(47) of the CGST Act, 2017			Zero-rated supply
	Non-taxable supply	Exempted supply	Nil-rated supply	
Meaning	Supply which is not leviable to tax under CGST Act or under IGST Act [section 2 (78) of CGST Act].	Supply which is wholly exempted from tax under section 11 of CGST Act or under section 6 of IGST Act. No tax is payable due to exemption notification.	Supply which attracts declared nil rate of tax (0 percent tax). Supply does not form part of any exemption notification.	Supply which is exported or sent to SEZ (section 16 of the IGST Act).
ITC availability	Not available	Not available	Not available	Available
GST applicability	Goods/services do not come under the purview of GST.	Goods and services come under the purview of GST.	Goods and services come under the purview of GST.	Goods and services come under the purview of GST.
Example	Supply of alcohol for human consumption.*	Bread, fresh fruits and vegetables, fresh milk, curd, inward supplies from unregistered dealers.	Salt, jaggery, contraceptives, sanitary napkins.	Export of sugar, handicrafts, gems and jewellery and other goods/services to various countries.

* States continue to levy duties of excise on alcoholic liquors for human consumption under Entry 51 of List II (State List) in the Seventh Schedule of the Constitution. If supply of alcohol is to be covered under GST, it will require amendment of the constitution.

Table 13.4: Difference between Exempt Supply and Zero-rated Supply

Exempt supply	Zero-rated supply
Exempt supply has the meaning assigned to it in Section 11 of the CGST Act, 2017 or Section 6 of the IGST Act, 2017.	*Zero-rated supply* has the meaning assigned to it in Section 16 of the IGST Act, 2017.
No tax on outward exempt supplies. Input supplies used for making exempt supplies are taxed.	No tax on outward supplies. Input supplies are also tax-free.
Input tax credit (ITC) is not available. ITC needs to be reversed, if taken.	Input tax credit (ITC) is available. ITC is available even if the supply is an exempt supply.
A person engaged exclusively in the business of supplying exempt supplies is not liable to registration under GST.	A person exclusively making zero-rated supplies may have to register to claim refunds of unutilized ITC or IGST paid.
A registered person supplying exempted good/services shall issue a bill of supply, instead of a tax invoice.	Normal tax invoice to be issued.

13.4 Location of Supplier and Place of Supply

Determination of the location of supplier, together with the place of supply of goods/services, is important to understand the nature of supply, i.e. whether the supply is intra-State or inter-State. CGST + SGST will be applicable if it is intra-State supply. In case of inter-State supply, the relevant form of GST will be IGST. Different combinations of location of supplier and place of supply are presented in Table 13.5.

Table 13.5: Different Combinations of Location of Supplier and Place of Supply

Location of supplier	Place of supply	Nature of supply	GST applicable
Kochi (Kerala)	Kannur (Kerala)	Intra-State	CGST + SGST
Kochi	Patna (Bihar)	Inter-State	IGST
Kochi	Lakshadweep (UT)	Inter-State	IGST
Lakshadweep	Lakshadweep	Intra-UT	CGST + UT-GST
Lakshadweep	Kochi	Inter-State	IGST
Lakshadweep	Chandigarh	Inter-UT	IGST
DTA in Kochi	SEZ in Kochi	Inter-State (export)	IGST
SEZ in Kochi	DTA in Kochi	Inter-State (import)	IGST

DTA = Domestic tariff area; SEZ = Special economic zone.

Note: Under GST, supplies made to and supplies made by SEZ units are treated as inter-State supplies and hence subject to IGST at the applicable rate. Supplies made to SEZ units from DTA units are considered as exports and as such are zero-rated. However, supplies made by SEZ units to DTA units are treated as imports and hence are subject to IGST. As per provisions of Section 2(19) of the IGST Act, 2017, SEZ has the same meaning as assigned to it in clause (za) of Section 2 of the Special Economic Zones (SEZ) Act, 2005. According to Section 2(i) of SEZ Act, 2005, DTA means "the whole of India but does not include the area of the special economic zones". For details on the applicability of IGST on exports and imports, see chapter 31 of this book.

Accurate determination of location of supplier and place of supply are important for businesses because wrong classification of supply (inter-State instead of intra-State or vice versa) can lead to hardships. Wrong taxes paid due to wrong classification necessitate claim of refund. Moreover, correct but delayed tax payment may invite interest payment for the delay.

13.4.1 Location of Supplier: In the case of goods, it is the geographical point (say premises of supplier) where the supplier is situated with goods, i.e. the place from where a supply is made. Thus, a place mentioned as the principal place of business in the GST registration certificate can be considered as location of the supplier.

Problems can arise when it comes to the location of the supplier of services. In fact, there are two concepts in this regard:

- Location of the supplier of services [Section 2(15) of IGST Act, 2017].
- Location of the recipient of services [Section 2(14) of IGST ACT, 2017].

A. Location of the Supplier of Services: The rules in this regard are as under:

Scenario	Location of supplier of services
Where a supply is made from a place of business for which the registration has been obtained.	Location of such place of business.
Where a supply is made from a place other than the place of business for which registration has been obtained (a fixed establishment elsewhere).	Location of such fixed establishment.
Where a supply is made from more than one establishment, whether the place of business or fixed establishment.	Location of the establishment most directly concerned with the provision of the supply.
In absence of such places.	Location of the usual place of residence of the supplier.

B. Location of the Recipient of Services: The rules in this regard are as under:

Scenario	Location of recipient of services
Where a supply is received at a place of business for which the registration has been obtained.	Location of such place of business.
Where a supply is received at a place other than the place of business for which registration has been obtained (a fixed establishment elsewhere).	Location of such fixed establishment.
Where a supply is received at more than one establishment, whether the place of business or fixed establishment.	Location of the establishment most directly concerned with the receipt of the supply.
In absence of such places.	Location of the usual place of residence of the recipient.

13.4.2 Place of Supply: One of the most important aspects of GST is determination of place of supply. Detailed provisions to determine the place of supply, separately for goods and services, are laid down in Sections 10 to 13 of the IGST Act, 2017.

GST is a destination-based (as against origin-based) tax, i.e. goods and services are taxed at the place where they are consumed. The State where they are consumed has the right to collect GST. So place of supply provisions determine the place, i.e. taxable jurisdiction where the tax should reach.

The place of supply determines whether a transaction is intra-state or inter-state. In other words, the place of supply of goods is required to determine whether a supply is subject to CGST plus SGST in a given State or else would attract IGST if it is an inter-state supply.

Provisions regarding place of supply are different in respect of goods and services.

A. Place of Supply of Goods: Provisions pertaining to place of supply of goods are different in respect of domestic supplies and cross-border supplies. Domestic supplies mean both the suppliers and recipients are in India. Domestic supplies are further categorized into intra-State (between two different States) and inter-State (Within the same State). Cross-border (international) supplies mean either the supplier or the recipient is outside India.

Sections 10 and 11 of the IGST Act, 2017 deal with the place of supply of goods.

(a) Section 10: Place of supply of goods other than supply of goods imported into, or exported from India.

(i) Place of Supply When there is Movement of Goods:

Scenario	**Place of supply**
Supply involves movement of goods, whether by the supplier or the recipient or by any other person	Location of the goods when the movement of goods terminates for delivery to the recipient.
Goods are delivered by the seller to a recipient on the direction of a third person	It is assumed that the third person has received the goods and the place of supply of such goods will be the principal place of business of the third person.

Case 1: Intra-State Sale: A in Kochi (Kerala) supplies smart phone to B in Kannur (Kerala). Since the supply takes place within the same State, CGST + SGST will be charged.

Case II: Inter-State Sale: A in Kochi (Kerala) supplies smart phone to B in Patna (Bihar). Since different States are involved, IGST will be charged.

Case III: Third Person Involvement: C in Chennai (Tamil Nadu) instructs A in Kochi (Kerala) to supply a smart phone to B (C's fiancée) in Patna (Bihar). It is deemed that C has received the goods. The place of supply is Chennai and IGST will be charged.

(ii) Place of Supply When There is no Movement of Goods:

Scenario	**Place of supply**
Supply involves no movement of goods, either by the supplier or the recipient.	Location of such goods at the time of the delivery to the recipient (at the time of transfer of ownership).
Goods are assembled or installed at the site.	Place of such installation or assembly.

(iii) Place of Supply When Goods are Taken On-board:

Scenario	**Place of supply**
Goods are supplied on-board a conveyance, including a vessel, an aircraft, a train or a motor vehicle.	Location at which such goods are taken on-board.

August Kranti Rajdhani Express departs from Delhi with supplies of evening snacks. Mr. A boards the train at Mathura (Uttar Pradesh) and orders snacks for himself and wife. Since the snacks were taken on board at Delhi, the place of supply is Delhi and hence CGST + SGST will be charged.

Note: Delhi is a Union Territory with legislature. Hence, it is SGST instead of UT-GST.

(iv) When Place of Supply of Goods Cannot be Determined: In such a case, the place of supply will be determined by rules framed by Parliament on the basis of the recommendations of GST Council.

(b) Section 11: Place of supply of goods imported into, or exported from India.

Scenario	**Place of supply**
Goods are imported into India	Location of the importer
Goods are exported from India	Location outside India (where goods are exported)

Business entity A imports smart phones from South Korea for its showroom registered in Chennai (Tamil Nadu). Place of supply is Chennai and IGST will be charged. Business entity B exports lady leather bags to USA. Place of supply is located outside India and GST is not chargeable.

In short, the place of supply of goods is the place where the goods are delivered, except in few cases. As goods are tangible, the determination of their place of supply, based on the consumption principle, is not difficult. Generally, the place of delivery of goods becomes the place of supply.

B. Place of Supply of Services: Sections 12 and 13 of the IGST Act, 2017 deal with the place of supply of services.

(a) Section 12: Place of supply of services where location of supplier and recipient is in India. The following rules are applicable except in certain specified cases:

Scenario	**Place of supply of services**
Supply made to a registered person	Location of recipient
Supply made to an unregistered person (Location of recipient available)	Location of recipient
Supply made to an unregistered person (Location of recipient not available)	Location of supplier

(b) Section 13: Place of supply of services where location of supplier or location of recipient is outside India. The following rules are applicable except in certain specified cases:

Scenario	**Place of supply of services**
Where the location of recipient of services is available	Location of recipient
Where the location of recipient of services is not available	Location of supplier

Services are essentially intangible in nature and as such cannot be viewed or touched by the consumers. Hence, it is not easy to determine the exact place where services are acquired, enjoyed and consumed.

The manner of delivery of service can be altered easily. For example, telecom service can change from post-paid to pre-paid. Similarly, billing address of provider/receiver of the service can change. Earlier the customers were required to go to the bank, but now they can avail banking services from anywhere. In other words, for supplying a service, a fixed location of service provider is not mandatory and even the service recipient may receive service while on the move. A couple of decades back no one could have thought of online booking of railway tickets, online shopping and mobile banking. Services are continuously evolving and would thus continue to pose newer challenges.

13.4.3 Supplies in Territorial Waters: According to Section 9 of the IGST Act, 2017, "...(a) where the location of the supplier is in the territorial waters, the location of such supplier; or (b) where the place of supply is in the territorial waters, the place of supply, shall be deemed to be in the coastal State or Union territory where the nearest point of the appropriate baseline is located". According to Section 25 of the CGST Act, 2017, every person who makes a supply from the territorial waters of India [4] shall obtain registration in the coastal State or Union territory where the nearest point of the appropriate baseline is located.

13.5 Point of Levy and Time of Supply

Point of levy means the point in time when goods are deemed to be supplied or services are deemed to be provided. Point of levy is significant to determine the rate of tax prevailing at that point. Point of levy (liability to pay GST) arises at the time of supply. There are separate provisions for time of supply for goods and time of supply for services.

13.5.1 Time of Supply for Goods: According to Section 12 of the CGST Act, 2017, the liability to pay tax on goods shall arise at the time of supply. The time of supply of goods shall be the earlier of the following dates:

- The date of issue of invoice by the supplier or the last date on which he is required...to issue the invoice with respect to the supply; or
- The date on which the supplier receives the payment with respect to the supply.

Thus, if the date of invoice is February 15, 2019 and the date of receipt of payment is March 19, 2019, then time of supply will be February 15, 2019.

13.5.2 Time of Supply of Services: According to Section 13 of the CGST Act, 2017 the liability to pay tax on services shall arise at the time of supply. The time of supply of services shall be the earliest of the following dates:

- The date of issue of invoice by the supplier; or
- The date of receipt of payment.

13.6 Value of Taxable Supply

The basis of charge of GST is given by Section 9 of the CGST Act, 2017. According to this section, GST shall be levied on the value of taxable supply of goods/services as determined by Section 15 of the same Act. Hence, Section 15 provides broad guidelines for determining value of taxable supply of goods/services which is normally the *transaction value*. In certain cases, transaction value is not considered for determination of tax liability. Thus, Rules 27 to 35 of the CGST Rules, 2017 prescribe specific mode of determination of taxable value of supply in different circumstances such as: (a) when consideration is not in money, (b) supply is between related persons and (c) supply is of second hand goods.

13.7 Stock Transfers

It is quite common for businesses having all-India presence to transfer stocks to their branches, depots, warehouses etc. to cater to timely delivery of orders from different geographical locations.

Under the GST regime, the taxable event is the supply of goods/services. As per paragraph 2 of Schedule I of the CGST Act, 2017, supply of goods or services or both between distinct persons is to be *treated as supply even if made without consideration.* Thus, if a person supplies goods or services from one of his establishments to another having different GSTIN, then it will be treated as supply even if made without consideration.

Since supply includes transfers to *distinct persons* therefore supply of goods/services between two distinct persons—having different GSTIN—in the course of business is subject to GST. Transfers are taxable as under:

13.7.1 Intra-State Stock Transfers: Intra-state self-supplies are not taxable. In other words, transfers from one branch to another branch in the same state do not attract GST and such transfer can be done with delivery challan. Transfers are taxable only when the entity has more than one registration in one state. These entities will be considered as *distinct persons*. Otherwise no GST will be levied on such transactions under section 9 of CGST Act, 2017.

13.7.2 Inter-State Stock Transfers: Inter-state self-supplies such as stock transfers, branch transfers or consignment sales are taxable under IGST even though such transactions may not involve payment of consideration. Transfers from branch in one state to branch in another state are taxable and invoice has to be raised for the same. In other words, transfers between two branches/units located in different states are always taxable and IGST is leviable in such type of transactions under Section 5 of the IGST Act, 2017. Thus, supply of goods/services by Punjab branch of business entity A to Haryana branch of A is subject to GST. However, input tax credit is available to Haryana branch.

Endnotes

1. Reverse charge means the liability to pay tax is on the recipient of supply of goods/services instead of the supplier of such goods /services in respect of notified categories of supply.
2. The term *business* has been defined in Section 2(17) of the CGST Act, 2017. It includes any trade, commerce, manufacture, profession, vocation etc., whether or not undertaken for a pecuniary benefit. Business also includes any activity or transaction incidental or ancillary to the said activities. In addition, any activity undertaken by the Central Government, a State Government or any local authority in which they are engaged as public authorities shall also be construed as business.
3. According to Section 2(31) of the CGST Act, 2017, consideration in relation to the supply of goods or services or both includes the following:

   "(a) any payment made or to be made, whether in money or otherwise, in respect of, in response to, or for the inducement of, the supply of goods or services or both, whether by the recipient or by any other person but shall not include any subsidy given by the Central Government or a State Government;

   (b) the monetary value of any act or forbearance, in respect of, in response to, or for the inducement of, the supply of goods or services or both, whether by the recipient or by any other person but shall not include any subsidy given by the Central Government or a State Government:

Provided that a deposit given in respect of the supply of goods or services or both shall not be considered as payment made for such supply unless the supplier applies such deposit as consideration for the said supply".

GST is applicable if goods/services are supplied for a *consideration*. Consideration may be in cash or in kind. If consideration is nil, GST is not applicable. However, activities given in Schedule I of the CGST Act, 2017 are subject to GST even if there is no consideration. Thus, supply of goods/services by a taxable person to a related person is subject to GST even if consideration is nil or even if supply is by way of gift. In other words, free gifts to a related person are subject to GST. It is noteworthy that employer and employee are treated as *related persons* for the purpose of GST. However, gifts up to ₹ 50,000 in a financial year to an employee are not subject to GST. Supply by way of gift between unrelated persons is not subject to GST. However, input tax credit claimed by the donor will have to be reversed.

4. See also endnote 1 of chapter 31 of this book.

14

Input Tax Credit (ITC)

One of the fundamental features of GST is the seamless flow of input tax credit across the supply chain and across the country. In the pre-GST indirect tax system, the availability of ITC was limited in various respects. Thus, ITC of Central Sales Tax (CST), entry tax and luxury tax was not available. Similarly, ITC of Central excise duty and service tax was not admissible to dealers in goods. [1]

Under GST, supplier of goods/services can take credit of input tax charged on any supply of goods/services to him which are used in the course of his business. ITC follows supply chain not only in intra-state but also in inter-state transactions. This has significantly reduced tax cascading (tax-on-tax).

Provisions regarding ITC are laid in Sections 16 to 21 of the CGST Act, 2017 and Rules 36 to 45 of the CGST Rules, 2017.

14.1 What is Input?

It means any goods other than capital goods used or intended to be used by a supplier in the course or furtherance of business [Section 2(59) of the CGST Act]. Apparently, it is a very broad-based definition and any goods used in the course or furtherance of business can be termed as inputs.

Input service means any service used or intended to be used by a supplier in the course or furtherance of business [Section 2(60) of the CGST Act]. Again, it is a very broad-based definition.

14.2 Input Tax

As per Section 2(62) of the CGST Act, 2017, *input tax*, in relation to a taxable person, means the Central tax, State tax, integrated tax or Union territory tax charged on any supply of goods and/or services to him…".

14.3 Input Tax Credit (ITC)

According to Section 2(63) of the CGST Act, 2017, *input tax credit* means the credit of input tax.

According to Section 16(1) of the CGST Act, 2017, "Every registered person shall, subject to such conditions and restrictions as may be prescribed and in the manner specified in section 49, be entitled to take credit of input tax charged on any supply of goods or services or both to him which are used or intended to be used in the course or furtherance of his business and the said amount shall be credited to the electronic credit ledger of such person".

In simple words, inputs mean goods and services which are used in the course of business. Input tax means CGST, SGST, UT-GST and IGST charged on supply of goods and services which are used in the course of business. Input tax credit means that a registered person under GST is entitled to take credit of input tax charged on supply of goods and services to him which are used in the course of his business and the said amount shall be credited to the electronic credit ledger of such person.

Suppose A is doing business and purchases goods/avails services for making further supplies in the course or furtherance of business. When such purchases are made by A from B (A's supplier), tax is charged and collected by B from A. If A can avail credit of the tax paid by him to B, it would be called input tax credit (ITC) for A. A can use this amount of credit for making payment of tax due from him on further supply made by him.

The illustration shown in Table 14.1 indicates, in terms of a hypothetical example, the working of input tax credit.

Table 14.1: Hypothetical Example of ITC Calculation

Stage of supply chain	Purchase value of inputs	Value addition	Value at which supply of goods and services made to next stage	Rate of GST (percent)	GST on output	Input tax credit	Net GST = GST on output – input tax credit
Manufacturer	100	30	130	10	13	10	13 - 10 = 3
Whole seller	130	20	150	10	15	13	15 - 13 = 2
Retailer	150	10	160	10	16	15	16 - 15 = 1

Source: The Empowered Committee of State Finance Ministers, *First Discussion Paper on Goods and Services Tax in India,* New Delhi, November 10, 2009, p. xxxix.

14.4 Eligibility and Conditions for Availing ITC

Section 16 of the CGST Act, 2017 deals with these matters which can be summarized as under:

1. ITC can be claimed by a person registered under GST. He has to fulfil all the conditions as prescribed in the law.
2. Registered person should be in possession of a tax invoice or debit note issued by a supplier registered under CGST Act, or such other tax paying documents as may be prescribed.
3. Registered person should have received the goods or services or both.
4. Where the goods against an invoice are received in lots or instalments, the registered person shall be entitled to take credit upon receipt of the last lot or instalment.
5. The tax charged in respect of such supply has been actually paid to the Government, either in cash or through utilisation of input tax credit admissible in respect of the said supply.
6. The registered person has furnished the return under Section 39.
7. Where a recipient fails to pay to the supplier of goods or services or both, the amount towards the value of supply along with tax payable thereon within a period of 180

days from the date of issue of invoice by the supplier, an amount equal to the input tax credit availed by the recipient shall be added to his output tax liability, along with interest thereon, in such manner as may be prescribed.

8. In case the tax on input is higher than the tax on output, the manufacturer is allowed to carry forward input tax or claim refund.
9. The time limit for claim of credit is 1 year from the date of the invoice. However, no credit pertaining to a financial year is allowed to be claimed post-filing of the return for September of the next financial year, or the filing of the annual return for the year to which the credit pertains, whichever is earlier.
10. Where the registered person has claimed depreciation on GST component of the cost of capital goods and plant and machinery under the provisions of the Income Tax Act, 1961, the input tax credit on the said GST component is not allowed.

It is also notable that ITC is available only when GST is leviable on outward supply of goods/services. In other words, if GST is not leviable on outward supply of goods/services, ITC is not available. However, there are certain output supplies which are zero-rated. In such cases, GST is not payable on outward supply, but ITC is still available. Zero-rated transactions are as under:

- Export of goods/services.
- Supply of goods/services to units in special economic zones (SEZs).

For details of zero-rated supplies, see section 13.3.9 of chapter 13 of this book.

14.5 Non-availability of ITC in Certain Cases

Input tax credit is available on almost all inward supply of goods/services used for making output taxable supply. However, a negative list of a few items is given by Section 17(5) of the CGST Act, 2017. In other words, the following input goods/services are not eligible for input tax credit.

1. Motor vehicles and other conveyances (with some exceptions).
2. Food and beverages, outdoor catering, beauty treatment, health services, cosmetic and plastic surgery (with some exceptions).
3. Membership of a club, health and fitness centre.
4. Rent-a-cab, life insurance and health insurance (with some exceptions).
5. Travel benefits extended to employees on vacation such as leave or home travel concession.
6. Works contract services when supplied for construction of an immovable property (other than plant and machinery (with some exceptions).
7. Goods/services received by a taxable person for construction of an immovable property (other than plant and machinery) on his own account including when such goods/services are used in the course or furtherance of business.
8. Goods/services on which tax has been paid by a person covered by composition scheme.
9. Goods/services received by a non-resident taxable person (except goods imported by him).

10. Goods/services used for personal consumption.
11. Goods lost, stolen, destroyed, written off or disposed of by way of gift or free samples.
12. Any tax paid in accordance with the provisions of Sections 74, 129 and 130 of the CGST Act, 2017. It means no input tax credit can be availed by a registered person in respect of any tax that has been paid in pursuance of any order where any demand has been confirmed on account of any fraud, wilful misstatement or suppression of facts.

14.6 Apportionment of ITC

According to Section 17(1) of the CGST Act, 2017, "where the goods or services or both are used by the registered person partly for the purpose of any business and partly for other purposes, the amount of credit shall be restricted to so much of the input tax as is attributable to the purposes of his business".

Similarly, as per Section 17(2) of the same Act, "Where the goods or services or both are used by the registered person partly for effecting taxable supplies (including zero-rated supplies)...and partly for effecting exempt supplies...the amount of credit shall be restricted to so much of the input tax as is attributable to the said taxable supplies (including zero-rated supplies)".

Apportionment of common credit is governed by Rule 42 of the CGST Rules, 2017.

Thus, in case of exempt supplies, amount of credit as attributable to exempt supplies shall be reversed. Credit attributable to exempt supplies is determined as follows.

Credit attributable to exempt supplies = (A/T) x C

Where:

A = Aggregate value of exempt supplies (all supplies other than taxable and zero-rated supplies).

T = Total turnover in the tax period.

C = Common credit (i.e. total input tax in a period minus tax attributable to non-business use of goods/services).

In short, the rules for claiming ITC are as under:

1. If the inputs are exempt from GST, the question of ITC does not arise.
2. If GST-paid inputs are used for effecting exempt supplies, ITC cannot be claimed. If ITC is allowed, it will be a case of negative taxation.
3. If GST-paid inputs are used for effecting zero-rated supplies (exports, supply to SEZs), ITC can be claimed. It is a case of negative taxation (hidden subsidy). The underlying objective of this facility is to encourage exports.
4. If GST-paid inputs are used for effecting taxable supplies, ITC is generally available.

14.7 Input Tax Credit for Capital Goods

ITC is available for capital goods under GST.

What are capital goods? Capital goods are assets such as buildings, machinery, equipment, vehicles and tools that an organization uses to produce goods or services.

Under GST law, capital goods are defined to mean goods, the value of which is capitalised in the books of account of the person claiming the input tax credit and which are used or intended to be used in the course or furtherance of business [Section 2(19) of the CGST Act, 2017].

There are special provisions in the GST law relating to calculation of ITC for capital goods, ITC availability and non-availability and calculation of reversal of ITC. Further there is special provision for capital goods which are used for both taxable as well as exempted supplies. In fact, GST paid on the purchase of a capital good can be claimed as credit in the same way as on inputs. In other words, ITC on capital goods can be availed in one go, i.e. 100 percent at the time of capitalization in book of account.

Rule 43 of the CGST Rules, 2017 describes the manner of determination of input tax credit in respect of capital goods and reversal thereof in certain cases. Main provisions of the said rule can be summarized as under.

1. When capital goods are used exclusively for business purpose, input tax credit is available under GST. To be eligible to claim input tax credit on capital goods, the transaction has to be reflected in the GST return filing.
2. Input tax credit on capital goods purchase is not available for capital goods used exclusively for effecting exempt supplies and for capital goods used exclusively for personal use.
3. In case a capital good is used for both business and personal use, then the input tax credit on the same has to be calculated as per the prescribed formula.
4. Where the registered person has claimed depreciation on the tax component of the cost of capital goods and plant and machinery under the provisions of the Income Tax Act, 1961, the input tax credit on the said tax component is not allowed.

14.7.1 Reversal of ITC: Following are the situations under which input tax credit availed on the capital goods needs to be reversed:

1. When taxpayers opts to pay tax under composition scheme.
2. When goods or services supplied by the taxpayer become exempted.
3. When there is supply of capital goods, on which input tax credit has been availed.
4. When the registration of registered tax payer has been cancelled, ITC involved in the remaining useful life of the asset in months will be computed on pro rata basis, taking the useful life of the asset as five years.

14.8 Input Service Distributor (ISD)

It means an office of the supplier of goods or services or both which receives tax invoices...towards the receipt of input services and issues a prescribed document for the purposes of distributing the credit of central tax, State tax, integrated tax or Union territory tax paid on the said services to a supplier of taxable goods or services or both having the same Permanent Account Number as that of the said office [Section 2(61) of the CGST Act].

Section 20 of the CGST Act describes the manner of distribution of credit by input service distributor. Similarly, Section 21 provides for the manner of recovery of credit distributed in excess by the input service distributor.

The concept of ISD under GST is a legacy carried over from the service tax regime of the Central Government of pre-GST era.

As is well-known, large-sized companies generally function by having a head office registered in one place along with one or multiple branches located in various other states. To maintain standardization, it is a common practice that the head office procures certain services which are utilized by all its branches, a typical example being advertising services. In such cases, it is logical that input tax credit available from common services is distributed to all the branches in a proportionate manner. This concept of distribution of common credit among various branches is known as *input service distribution* and the head office distributing such credit is known as *input service distributor* (ISD). There are certain rules to be followed in this regard. Some of these are as under:

1. ISD cannot distribute ITC relating to input goods and capital goods.
2. ITC of common input services can be distributed among those registered persons who have used these services in the course or for the furtherance of business.
3. ISD must issue an invoice. The invoice must indicate that it is issued for distribution purposes only.
4. ITC cannot be distributed relating to services where reverse charge mechanism is applicable.

Suppose company A is headquartered in Delhi and it is registered as input service distributor under the GST law. It has three branches located in Mumbai, Kolkata and Chennai. The Delhi office incurs advertisement expenses amounting to ₹ 1,20,000 to promote a new product. The input tax credit is distributable among all the three branches in the ratios of their respective turnovers to total turnover. Thus, the share of Mumbai branch can be calculated as follows:

$C_m = (T_m \div T) \times C$

Where:

C_m = credit to be allocated to Mumbai branch.

T_m = Turnover of the Mumbai branch.

T = Total turnover.

C = Total input tax credit.

Table 14.2 explains the distribution of ITC with a hypothetical numerical example.

Table 14.2: Hypothetical Numerical Example to Show the Distribution of Input Tax Credit among Recipients

Total turnover = ₹ 2,00,00,000; Total input tax credit = ₹ 1,20,000

Branch	Turnover	Share in input tax credit
Mumbai	₹ 80,00,000	(₹ 80,00,000 ÷ ₹ 2,00,00,000) x ₹ 1,20,000 = ₹ 48,000
Kolkata	₹ 70,00,000	(₹ 70,00,000 ÷ ₹ 2,00,00,000) x ₹ 1,20,000 = ₹ 42,000
Chennai	₹ 50,00,000	(₹ 50,00,000 ÷ ₹ 2,00,00,000) x ₹ 1,20,000 = ₹ 30,000

14.9 ITC in Case of Inverted Duty Structure (IDC)

As per Section 54(3) of the CGST Act, 2017, a registered person may claim a refund of unutilized input tax credit on account of inverted duty structure (rate of tax on inputs is greater than rate of tax on output) at the end of any tax period. In other words, IDC is a situation where the final output has lower levy than the input. For example, fabric makers face 5 percent levy but pay 15 percent on some of the yarn. Thus, input tax credit is allowed to fabric makers using raw material with higher GST rates.

A tax period is a period for which return is required to be furnished. Thus, a taxpayer can claim the refund of unutilized ITC on monthly basis. Such refund is not available in all cases. There are detailed rules in this regard.

14.10 ITC on Job Work

A principal manufacturer may send goods to a job worker for further processing. Job work means any treatment or process undertaken by a person on goods belonging to another registered person and the expression *job worker* shall be construed accordingly [Section 2(68) of the CGST Act, 2017].

Section 19 of the CGST Act, 2017 deals with ITC in respect of goods sent for job work. A principal manufacturer is allowed to take credit of tax paid on job work in both the cases, i.e. when goods are sent to job worker from principal's place of business or directly from the place of supply of the supplier of such goods.

However, to avail ITC the goods sent must be received back by the principal within 1 year (3 years in the case of capital goods).

14.11 ITC on Transfer of Business

Section 18 (3) of the CGST Act, 2017 pertains to cases when there is a change in the constitution of a registered person on account of sale, merger, demerger, amalgamation, lease or transfer of business with the provision of transfer of liabilities. In such a case, the registered person is allowed to transfer ITC which remains unutilized in his electronic credit ledger to such sold, merged, demerged, amalgamated, leased or transferred business.

14.12 Prescribed Order of Cross Utilization of ITC

There are well-defined rules in this regard.

Since CGST and SGST are two parallel taxes levied simultaneously on goods and services therefore the cross utilisation of CGST input tax credit for payment of SGST output tax liability and vice versa is not permitted. In other words, the two streams of ITC cannot be cross utilised, except in specified circumstances of inter-State supplies, for payment of IGST.

It is also noteworthy that there is no centralized registration under GST. Registration is required in all States/UTs from where one makes taxable supplies of goods/services. Each registration is treated as distinct person. Hence, ITC of one State cannot be used to set off output GST liability of another State.

The order of utilisation of the CGST credit is first towards CGST and then towards IGST. Similarly, SGST credit can be utilised first towards SGST liability and then towards IGST. Likewise, UT-GST credit can be utilized first towards UT-GST liability and then towards IGST. IGST credit can be utilized first towards IGST, then CGST, then SGST and the balance towards UT-GST liability. More specifically, ITC is permitted to be utilized in the following manner:

- ITC of CGST is allowed for payment of CGST and IGST in that order.
- ITC of SGST is allowed for payment of SGST and IGST in that order.
- ITC of UT-GST is allowed for payment of UT-GST and IGST in that order.
- ITC of IGST is allowed for payment of IGST, CGST, SGST and UT-GST in that order.
- ITC of GST compensation cess can be utilized only for payment of GST compensation cess.
- ITC of CGST cannot be used for payment of SGST/UT-GST and vice versa.

For further clarity, ITC utilization mechanism is shown in Table 14.3.

Table 14.3: ITC Utilization Mechanism

Tax on output	Availability of ITC (in descending order of priority)	ITC not available
CGST	CGST IGST	SGST, UT-GST and CC
SGST	SGST IGST	CGST, UT-GST and CC
UT-GST	UT-GST IGST	CGST, SGST and CC
IGST	IGST CGST SGST UT-GST	CC
CC	CC	CGST, SGST, UT-GST and IGST

CC = Compensation cess.

ITC is broad-based because it is available in respect of taxes paid on any supply of goods or services or both used or intended to be used in the course or furtherance of business. The law allows an assessee to carry forward his input tax credit and ensures that no ITC is lost while migrating to the new regime. There are detailed guidelines in this regard.

Accounts are settled periodically between the Centre and the State to ensure that the credit of SGST used for payment of IGST is transferred by the originating State to the Centre. Similarly, the IGST used for payment of SGST is transferred by Centre to the destination State.

Further, the SGST portion of IGST (IGST may contain CGST, SGST and Cess on luxury items) collected on B2C supplies is also transferred by the Centre to the destination State. The transfer of funds is carried out on the basis of information contained in the returns filed by the taxpayers.

In addition, the credits claimed need to be matched with the tax liability of the supplier, and in case of any discrepancies, the amount of excess credit claimed is added to the tax liability of the recipient.

Apart from the above, there are certain other provisions in the law pertaining to ITC. Thus, Section17 of the CGST Act, 2017 provides for the negative list with respect to the admissibility of ITC. Section 18 deals with availability of credit in special circumstances. Section 19 explains ITC in respect of inputs and capital goods sent for job work.

Providing ITC is a big administrative and technological work under the GST platform.

14.13 Invoice Matching for ITC

Every purchase invoice in GST regime must reconcile with sale invoice of the supplier on GST common portal for availing input tax credit.

For many businesses, GST has meant a complete overhaul of IT systems and major re-engineering work. Many small and medium businesses are now using technological tools for book-keeping and tax compliance purpose. It can be called the biggest change that businesses have witnessed in the post-Independence India. It also calls for patience and management reorientation from the business community for smooth transition.

The concept of invoice matching is possible only when both the buyer and the supplier are tightly integrated through an information system, which enables a seamless flow of information and fool-proof validations. Thus, it becomes critical for businesses to be highly compliant on a real-time basis and thus have a proper system in place to support it.

Invoice matching is a mechanism under which all the taxable supplies made under GST will be matched against all the taxable supplies received by the buyer.

Invoice matching is important because under GST input tax credit of purchase of goods and/or services is available only if the details of inward supply filed under GSTR-2 return of buyer match with the details of outward supplies filed in GSTR-1 of the supplier. This interlinking has been done by way of auto-population of data filed in GSTR-1 of supplier into GSTR-2 of the buyer.

Unless this matching reconciles the buyer will not be able to claim the input tax credit on purchases goods or services or both.

14.14 Hypothetical Numerical Examples to Explain the Working of CGST, SGST, IGST and ITC

Suppose a Mumbai-based businessman A is engaged in assembling computers. He purchases computer components (hard disk, mother board, monitor, key board, mouse etc.), assembles them and then supplies assembled computers to other parties. Let assembled computer (or simply computer) be called commodity X. The cost of components (inputs) per X is ₹ 10,000. To simplify the example, it is assumed that purchases of A are from a composition scheme dealer and hence A has no input tax credit (ITC) claim. [2]

14.14.1 Intra-state Single Transaction: A supplies X to B in Mumbai at a price of ₹ 20,000. Both the seller and the buyer are located in the same state (Maharashtra) and hence it is an intra-state transaction. GST is payable at the rate of 18 percent. In other words, CGST and SGST are separately and simultaneously payable at the rate of 9 percent, and hence form part of the invoice of A to B as under (all figures in ₹): [3]

Price of X	20,000
CGST @ 9 percent	1,800
SGST @ 9 percent	1,800
Total	23,600

A collects ₹ 1,800 as CGST and deposits it in the account of Central Government. Similarly, he collects ₹ 1,800 as SGST and deposits it in the account of Maharashtra Government. [4] Table 14.4 depicts the transaction.

Table 14.4: Intra-state Single Transaction of Commodity X

GST rate = 18 percent (CGST rate = 9 percent; SGST rate = 9 percent)

Sale	Nature of sale	Sale price (₹)	Amount (₹) received as GST by			
			Centre		Maharashtra	
1.	Intra-state (Maharashtra) sale of X from A to B	20,000	CGST	1,800	SGST	1,800

14.14.2 Intra-state Double Transaction: To continue the example given in Table 14.4 (A in Mumbai sells X to B in Mumbai for ₹ 20,000), now B sells X to C in Pune for ₹ 30,000. Again, being an intra-state transaction, CGST and SGST are payable and hence form part of the invoice of B to C as under (all figures in ₹):

Price of X	30,000
CGST @ 9 percent	2,700
SGST @ 9 percent	2,700
Total	35,400

B pays GST on his purchase of X. He charges GST on supply of X to C. Under GST law, B can take credit of the GST paid on X. In other words, the tax paid on purchase of X by B can be adjusted against the tax charged by B.

Thus, B collects ₹ 2,700 as CGST. After deducting CGST input tax credit of ₹ 1,800, he deposits ₹ 900 in the account of the Central Government. Similarly, he collects ₹ 2,700 as SGST. After deducting SGST input tax credit of ₹ 1,800, he deposits ₹ 900 in the account of Maharashtra Government. Table 14.5 depicts the transactions.

14.14.3 Inter-state Single Transaction: A in Mumbai (Maharashtra) sells X to B in Bengaluru (Karnataka) for ₹ 20,000. Being an inter-state transaction, IGST is payable at the rate of 18 percent and hence forms part of the invoice of A to B as under (all figures in ₹):

Price of X	20,000
IGST @ 18 percent	3,600
Total	23,600

Table 14.5: Intra-state Double Transactions of Commodity X

GST rate = 18 percent (CGST rate = 9 percent; SGST rate = 9 percent)
ITC = input tax credit

Sale	Nature of sale	Sale price (₹)	Amount (₹) received as GST by			
			Centre		Maharashtra	
1.	Intra-state (Maharashtra) sale of X from A to B	20,000	CGST	1,800	SGST	1,800
2	Intra-state (Maharashtra) sale of X from B to C	30,000	CGST (-) CGST ITC CGST (net)	2,700 1,800 900	SGST (-) SGST ITC SGST (net)	2,700 1,800 900
Total GST revenue				2,700		2,700

IGST so collected by A from B is deposited by the former in the account of the Central Government. The apportionment of the deposited amount between the Centre and the importing State (Karnataka in this case) is governed by Section 17 of the Integrated Goods and Services Tax Act, 2017 which reads as follows, "Out of the integrated tax paid to the Central Government…the amount of tax calculated at the rate equivalent to the central tax on similar intra-State supply shall be apportioned to the Central Government. The balance amount of integrated tax remaining in the integrated tax account in respect of the supply for which an apportionment to the Central Government has been done…shall be apportioned to the State where such supply takes place".

Broadly speaking, IGST (being the sum total of CGST and SGST) is apportioned between the Centre and the importing State in the ratio of 50:50. Table 14.6 depicts the transaction.

Table 14.6: Inter-state Single Transaction of Commodity X

IGST = 18 percent

Sale	Nature of sale	Sale price (₹)	Amount (₹) received as GST by					
			Centre		Maharashtra		Karnataka	
1.	Inter-state sale of X from A (Maharashtra) to B (Karnataka)	20,000	IGST	3,600	…	…		
Total GST revenue				3,600		…		
Adjustments of IGST between Centre and Karnataka								
			Transferred to Karnataka	1,800			Received from Centre	1,800
Final GST revenue				1,800				1,800

Just like exports from India are generally exempt from tax/duty, so also exports from one state to another are exempt from GST. Exporting state should be satisfied that goods produced by it are being consumed in other states. Enhanced production activities in the exporting state lead to more employment opportunities for its residents and profit earning by its entrepreneurs, apart from other benefits of higher production.

14.14.4 Inter-state Double Transaction: To continue the example given in Table 13.5 [A in Mumbai (Maharashtra) sells X to B in Bengaluru (Karnataka) for ₹ 20,000], now B in Bengaluru (Karnataka) sells X to C in Chennai (Tamil Nadu) for ₹ 30,000. Again, being an inter-state transaction, IGST is payable at the rate of 18 percent and hence forms part of the invoice of B to C as under (all figures in ₹):

Price of X	30,000
IGST @ 18 percent	5,400
Total	35,400

B collects ₹ 5,400 as IGST. After deducting IGST input tax credit of ₹ 3,600, he deposits ₹ 1,800 in the account of the Central Government. Table 14.7 depicts the transactions.

Table 14.7: Inter-state Double Transaction of Commodity X

IGST = 18 percent; ITC = input tax credit

Sale	Nature of sale	Sale price (₹)	Amount (₹) received as GST by					
			Centre		Maharashtra		Karnataka	
1.	Inter-state sale of X from A (Maharashtra) to B (Karnataka)	20,000	IGST	3,600	...	...		
2.	Inter-state sale of X from B (Karnataka) to C (Tamil Nadu)	30,000	IGST (-) IGST ITC IGST (net)	5,400 3,600 1,800				
Total GST revenue				5,400		...		
Adjustments of IGST between Centre and Karnataka								
			Transferred to Karnataka	2,700			Received from Centre	2,700
Final GST revenue				2,700				2,700

14.14.5 Intra-state and Inter-state Transactions:

A. Case I: A in Mumbai sells X to B in Mumbai for ₹ 20,000. Both the seller and the buyer are located in the same state (Maharashtra). Being an intra-state transaction, CGST and SGST are payable and hence form part of the invoice of A to B as under (all figures in ₹):

Price of X	20,000
CGST @ 9 percent	1,800
SGST @ 9 percent	1,800
Total	23,600

Now B sells the same X to C in Bengaluru (Karnataka) for ₹ 40,000. Being an inter-State transaction, IGST at the rate of 18 percent is payable and hence forms part of the invoice of B to C as under (all figures in ₹):

Price of X	40,000
IGST @ 18 percent	7,200
Total	47,200

IGST of ₹ 7,200 is collected by B from C. After deducting CGST input tax credit of ₹ 1,800 and SGST input tax credit of ₹ 1,800, B deposits IGST (net) of ₹ 3,600 into the account of Central Government.

Further, C sells the same X to D in Bengaluru (Karnataka) for ₹ 60,000. Being an intra-State transaction, it is subject to both CGST at the rate of 9 percent (₹ 5,400) and SGST at the rate of 9 percent (₹ 5,400). Invoice of C to D will be as under (all figures in ₹):

Price of X	60,000
CGST @ 9 percent	5,400
SGST @ 9 percent	5,400
Total	70,800

IGST input tax credit to the extent of ₹ 5,400 is set-off against the CGST of ₹ 5,400 by C and hence there is zero CGST (net) from C to Central Government. The remaining IGST input tax credit of ₹ 1,800 (₹ 7,200 - ₹ 5,400) is set-off against the SGST of ₹ 5,400 payable to Karnataka Government by C. Thus, C deposits ₹ 3,600 as SGST (net) into the account of Karnataka Government. [5]

The work of the taxpayers stops here.

(a) Adjustments of CGST, SGST and IGST among Centre, Maharashtra and Karnataka: As is known, GST is a consumption-based tax, i.e. the State where the goods are finally consumed will collect the tax. Thus, Maharashtra, where X was sold will not get any GST revenue. Central Government and Karnataka both, therefore, will get ₹ 5,400 each. Maharashtra (exporting state) will transfer to the Centre the credit of SGST of ₹ 1,800 used in payment of IGST. The Centre will transfer to Karnataka (importing state) ₹ 1,800 IGST credit used. Table 14.8 depicts the various transactions.

It is noteworthy that according to Table 14.7, the entire transfer received by the Centre from Maharashtra (₹ 1,800) is passed on to Karnataka.

B. Case II: We take another example to show that the transfer from Maharashtra to Centre is first used to compensate Karnataka for the IGST input tax credit deducted from SGST. The remaining amount is retained by the Centre. In other words, the transfer from Maharashtra to Centre is apportioned between Karnataka and the Centre.

A in Mumbai sells X to B in Mumbai for ₹ 15,000. Both the seller and the buyer are located in the same state (Maharashtra). Being an intra-state transaction, CGST and SGST are payable and hence form part of the invoice of A to B as under (all figures in ₹):

Price of X	15,000
CGST @ 9 percent	1,350
SGST @ 9 percent	1,350
Total	17,700

Table 14.8: Intra-state and Inter-state Transactions of Commodity X

GST rate = 18 percent (CGST rate = 9 percent and SGST rate = 9 percent)

IGST rate = 18 percent; ITC = Input tax credit

Sale	Nature of sale	Sale price (₹)	Amount (₹) received as GST by					
			Centre		Maharashtra		Karnataka	
1.	Intra-state (Maharashtra) sale of X from A to B	20,000	CGST	1,800	SGST	1,800	...	...
2.	Inter-state (Maharashtra and Karnataka) sale of X from B to C	40,000	IGST (-) CGST ITC (-) SGST ITC IGST (net)	7,200 1,800 1,800 3,600	...	...	...	...
3.	Intra-state (Karnataka) sale of X from C to D	60,000	CGST (-) IGST ITC* CGST (net)	5,400 5,400 0	...	...	SGST (-) IGST ITC (7,200 – 5,400) SGST (net)	5,400 1,800 3,600
Total GST revenue				5,400		1,800		3,600
Adjustments of CGST, SGST and IGST among Centre, Maharashtra and Karnataka								
			Received from Maharashtra (-) Transferred to Karnataka Net	1,800 1,800 0	Trans-ferred to Centre	1,800	Received from Centre	1,800
Final GST revenue				5,400		0		5,400

*Although IGST ITC is ₹ 7,200, CGST can set it off only to the extent of ₹ 5,400. The remaining IGST ITC of ₹ 1,800 will be set-off against SGST of Karnataka Government.

Now B sells the same X to C in Bengaluru (Karnataka) for ₹ 26,250. Being an inter-state transaction, IGST at the rate of 18 percent is payable and hence forms part of the invoice of B to C as under (all figures in ₹):

Price of X	26,250
IGST @ 18 percent	4,725
Total	30,975

IGST of ₹ 4,725 is collected by B from C. After deducting CGST input tax credit of ₹ 1,350 and SGST input tax credit of ₹ 1,350, B deposits IGST (net) of ₹ 2,025 into the account of Central Government.

Further, C sells the same X to D in Bengaluru (Karnataka) for ₹ 45,000. Being an intra-state transaction, CGST and SGST are payable and hence form part of the invoice of C to D as under (all figures in ₹):

Price of X	45,000
CGST @ 9 percent	4,050
SGST @ 9 percent	4,050
Total	53,100

IGST input tax credit to the extent of ₹ 4,050 is set-off against the CGST of ₹ 4,725 by C and hence there is zero CGST (net) from C to Central Government. The remaining

IGST input tax credit of ₹ 675 (₹ 4,725 - ₹ 4,050) is set-off against the SGST of ₹ 4,050 payable to Karnataka Government by C. Thus, C deposits ₹ 3,375 as SGST (net) into the account of Karnataka Government.

The work of the taxpayers stops here.

(a) Adjustments of CGST, SGST and IGST among Centre, Maharashtra and Karnataka: As is known, GST is a consumption-based tax, i.e. the State where the goods are finally consumed will collect the tax. Thus, Maharashtra, where X was sold will not get any GST revenue. Central Government and Karnataka both, therefore, will get ₹ 4,050 each instead of only ₹ 3,375 each. Maharashtra (exporting state) will transfer to the Centre the credit of SGST of ₹ 1,350 used in payment of IGST. The Centre will transfer to Karnataka (importing state) ₹ 675 IGST credit used. The remaining amount of ₹ 675 will be retained by the Centre.

Table 14.9 depicts the various transactions.

Table 14.9: Intra-state and Inter-state Transactions of Commodity X

GST rate = 18 percent (CGST rate = 9 percent and SGST rate = 9 percent)

IGST rate = 18 percent; ITC = input tax credit

Sale	Nature of sale	Sale price (₹)	Amount (₹) received as GST by					
			Centre		Maharashtra		Karnataka	
1.	Intra-state (Maharashtra) sale of X from A to B	15,000	CGST	1,350	SGST	1,350	...	...
2.	Inter-state (Maharashtra and Karnataka) sale of X from B to C	26,250	IGST (-) CGST ITC (-) SGST ITC IGST (net)	4,725 1,350 1,350 2,025	...	...	...	...
3.	Intra-state (Karnataka) sale of X from C to D	45,000	CGST (-) IGST ITC* CGST (net)	4,050 4,050 0	...	...	SGST (-) IGST ITC (4,725 - 4,050) SGST (net)	4,050 675 3,375
Total GST revenue				3,375		1,350		3,375
Adjustments of CGST, SGST and IGST among Centre, Maharashtra and Karnataka								
			Received from Maharashtra (-) Transferred to Karnataka Net	1,350 675 675	Trans-ferred to Centre	1,350	Received from Centre	675
Final GST revenue				4,050		0		4,050

*Although IGST ITC is ₹ 4,725, CGST can set it off only to the extent of ₹ 4,050. The remaining IGST ITC of ₹ 675 will be set off against SGST of Karnataka Government.

Although category of buyer is irrelevant from the viewpoint of supplier, it has implications for a better understanding of the working mechanism of GST. There can be at least four categories of buyers.

1. A buyer can be a householder who buys X for family entertainment (watching films

and playing video games). Since he buys computer for consumption purpose, the production-distribution process end with him, i.e. there are no further transactions.

2. The buyer can be a trader who offers his services in the distribution process. He buys X, pays GST, supplies X to another party at enhanced price and collects GST. He will deduct the GST paid on his inward supply from the GST collected on outward supply and deposit the remaining amount in the accounts of Central Government and the concerned state.
3. The buyer can be a shopping mall where X is used for issuing invoices and checking inventories etc. In this case, X is just one of the various inputs of the mall. Just like other inputs, GST paid on X will be adjusted against the GST collected.
4. The buyer can be an exporter. Exports are treated as inter-state supply and hence subject to IGST. Exports are also zero-rated supplies. Hence, the exporter can claim refund of IGST after verification of export obligation. Moreover, he is eligible for input tax credit on his purchases. Exports are zero-rated as a part of Government policy to promote exports. For details, see section 30.1 of chapter 30 of this book.

A distinction is made between B2B (business to business) and B2C (business to consumer) transactions because B2B transactions are *wash transactions* in the sense that ITC is availed by the registered person (recipient) and no real revenue accrues to the government. In the case of B2C transactions, revenue accrues to the government.

14.15 What is the Rationale for ITC?

The underlying philosophy of ITC is to avoid the double taxation of the same item in the production process. In the above example, hard disk is an item which is subject to GST (though, for simplicity, it was assumed to be an exempt item). In the production process it becomes part of the computer. Now if computer as such is subjected to GST, the hard disk will be taxed twice, first as an independent item and then as part of the computer. This is called tax-on-tax (or tax cascading) which must be avoided.

One can say that to avoid this kind of double taxation of the same item, inputs should be exempted from tax and only finished products should be taxed. This is not desirable because the tax system wants to distinguish between inputs used for business purpose and inputs used for consumption purpose. Hard disk purchased by a computer assembler is meant for further production of goods (computers). Contrarily, a hard disk purchased to replace a defective one in a computer being used for entertainment by a householder and his children is meant for consumption purpose. Similarly, tyres and tubes purchased by a motor car company are on a different footing than the same items purchased by a car owner—for the former the items are for production purpose while for the latter they are replacement items for consumption purpose. GST is a consumption-based tax. GST taxes consumption because consumption is a good indicator of the tax-paying capacity of a person along with income and wealth holding.

It is noteworthy that under GST there is a continuous chain of production and distribution. All entities under GST can pass on the tax burden except the end-user (i.e. the final consumer). The status of a manufacturer/trader differs from that of the consumer in the sense that the former can pass on the burden of tax to the latter, the latter cannot because the production-distribution process ends with him.

Those who can pass on the tax burden (called tax shifting) to succeeding entity suffer what the economists call *impact of the tax* (or initial tax burden). Those who cannot shift the tax burden (consumers) suffer *incidence of the tax*. Thus, the incidence of GST is on the consumer, i.e. consumer is the final bearer of GST burden. Or, to put it differently, kitchen of the householder is the final resting place of GST. This is a characteristic feature of an indirect tax.

Endnotes

1. For details, see section 5.3 of chapter 5 of this book.
2. A composition scheme dealer cannot collect any tax from his buyers. Hence, those who buy from a composition scheme dealer are not able to take credit of any input tax. For details of composition scheme, see chapter 36 of this book.
3. The four digit HSN code for computers is 8471. GST rate for computers is 18 percent. Computer monitors (not exceeding 32 inches) are also subject to 18 percent.
4. In fact, every registered person under GST has an electronic ledger. GST collected appears as tax liability and GST paid as tax credit. If GST collected is more than tax credit, the difference is deposited by the assessee.
5. This is in accordance with the prescribed order of cross utilization of ITC as explained in section 14.12 of this chapter.

15

Exclusions, Exemptions, Threshold Limits of Turnover, Negative List, and Composition Levy Scheme

Besides being the main source of revenue, both for the Central and State Governments, GST is an effective instrument to realise various socio-economic objectives of national policies. Exemptions/lenient tax treatment of essential goods and services of mass consumption serve the objective of tax equity. [1] Threshold limits benefit small traders. GST rates influence the relative prices of different goods and services and hence the allocation of resources among various sectors of the economy. Rate structure also determines the investment climate in the country and the aggregate demand and thus the scale of operations in the economy.

15.1 Scope of GST

GST is leviable on all goods and services except the following:

1. Goods outside the purview of GST (exclusions).
2. Goods within the purview of GST but currently kept in abeyance.
3. Goods and services exempted from GST.
4. Goods and services supplied by businesses within prescribed threshold limits of turnover.
5. Activities or transactions which are treated neither as a supply of goods nor a supply of services.

15.2 Goods outside the Purview of GST (Exclusions)

Alcohol for human consumption is outside the purview of GST. According to clause 12A of Article 366 of the Constitution, *goods and services tax* means any tax on supply of goods, or services or both except taxes on the supply of the alcoholic liquor for human consumption. Clause 12A was inserted by section 14 of the Constitution (One Hundred First Amendment) Act, 2016.

Hence, under GST law alcohol for human consumption is a *non-taxable supply*. According to Section 2(78) of the CGST Act, 2017, "*non-taxable supply* means a supply of goods or services or both which is not leviable to tax under this Act or under the Integrated Goods and Services Tax Act." Thus, supply of alcoholic liquor for human consumption is excluded from the charging section (i.e. Section 9) of the CGST Act, 2017.

In the case of alcohol for human consumption, States continue to levy the taxes presently being levied, i.e. State excise duty and sales tax/VAT. [2]

It is noteworthy that in the Constitution (One Hundred and Fifteenth Amendment) Bill, 2011, which lapsed with the dissolution of the 15th Lok Sabha on May 18, 2014, alcohol and five petroleum products—petroleum crude, high speed diesel, motor spirit (commonly known as petrol), natural gas and aviation turbine fuel)—were kept out of GST. This was done in view of the revenue importance of these items and the uncertainty which the States felt regarding the impact of the proposed GST on their tax revenue. However, in the Constitution (One Hundred and Twenty-second Amendment) Bill, 2014, only alcoholic liquor was kept outside GST. After passage of this Bill by both Houses of Parliament, ratification by State legislatures and receipt of assent by the President, it was notified as the Constitution (One Hundred and First Amendment) Act, 2016 with effect from September 16, 2016. It came into force from July 1, 2017.

See also sections 7.1 and 7.2 of chapter 7 of this book.

See also section 41.1 of chapter 41 of this book.

15.3 Goods within the Purview of GST but Currently Kept in Abeyance

As already noted above, in the Constitution (One Hundred and Fifteenth Amendment) Bill, 2011, which lapsed with the dissolution of the 15th Lok Sabha on May 18, 2014, alcohol and five petroleum products were kept out of GST. However, in the Constitution (One Hundred and Twenty-second Amendment) Bill, 2014—later notified as the Constitution (One Hundred and First Amendment) Act, 2016—only alcoholic liquor was kept outside GST.

Thus, by virtue of Article 279A(5) of the Constitution, the following five petroleum products are part of the GST regime: (a) petroleum crude, (b) high speed diesel, (c) motor spirit (commonly known as petrol), (d) natural gas and (e) aviation turbine fuel. However, the date on which GST would be levied on these petroleum products is yet to be decided by the Goods and Services Tax Council (GST Council), the constitutionally established joint forum of the Centre and the States.

Section 9(2) of the CGST Act, 2017 states, "The central tax on the supply of petroleum crude, high speed diesel, motor spirit (commonly known as petrol), natural gas and aviation turbine fuel shall be levied with effect from such date as may be notified by the Government on the recommendations of the Council".

Thus, the levy of GST on the five petroleum products continues to hang in balance till notified at a future date on the recommendations of the GST Council.

It is noteworthy that two other petroleum products (domestic LPG and PDS kerosene) are already subject to GST under 5 percent rate category.

In the absence of GST on the said five petroleum items, the Centre continues to levy excise duty on them. Likewise, the States are levying sales tax/VAT on them. While the rate of excise duty has uniform applicability throughout India, the rate of sales tax/VAT differs from state-to-state because each state has its own legislation for the purpose. This is the reason why prices of these five petroleum items (mainly petrol and diesel) vary in different states.

See also sections 7.1 and 7.2 of chapter 7 of this book.

See also section 41.2 of chapter 41 of this book.

15.4 Goods and Services Exempted from GST

Under GST law, Central and State Governments, on the recommendation of the GST Council, can exempt the supplies from the levy of GST either generally or subject to conditions. Hence, to understand the taxability of GST, it is important to know if an item is exempt or not under GST. It is noteworthy that most of the exempted goods and services are supplied by MSMEs.

For details, see chapter 34 of this book.

15.5 Goods and Services Supplied by Businesses within Prescribed Threshold Limits of Aggregate Turnover

Just like a basic exemption is allowed to individual taxpayers under the Income Tax Act, 1961, so also exemption from registration and payment of GST is allowed to small businesses the aggregate annual turnover of which is within prescribed limits. Threshold for exemption is built into GST to keep small businesses out of tax net.

For details, see chapter 35 of this book.

15.6 Activities or Transactions which Are Treated Neither as a Supply of Goods nor a Supply of Services

Schedule III to the CGST Act, 2017 mentions certain activities or transactions which are treated neither as a supply of goods nor a supply of services. The list of such activities is popularly known as negative list though there is no such concept in GST.

For details, see Table 13.1 of chapter 13 of this book.

15.7 Composition Levy Scheme

Composition scheme is an important feature of GST to protect the interests of small manufacturers, traders and service providers. A composition option (i.e. to pay tax at a flat rate without credits) is available to small taxpayers whose annual aggregate turnover does not exceed a specified limit. The objective of composition scheme is to bring simplicity and reduce compliance cost for small taxpayers. Composition scheme allows small businesses to avail a hassle-free compliance regime. It is noteworthy that these segments are large job creators and hence a priority area for the government.

For details, see chapter 36 of this book.

Endnotes

1. Tax equity refers to *fair* or *just* or *equitable* distribution of tax burden among taxpayers. Though fairness and justness in taxation are universally accepted, these terms are rarely defined rigorously and can be interpreted in various ways. Hence, there is no unanimity of opinion as to the type of tax system which results in the most equitable distribution of tax burden.

   Tax equity is the prime characteristic of a good tax system. It is the basic criterion for evaluating a tax system. This classical canon of taxation is based on the natural desire among people for justice.

   An inequitable tax system may hinder the establishment of a stable political, social, and economic order. The French and American Revolutions were partly the result of perceived inequity in the tax systems. In India, the duty on salt which hit the poor the most symbolised national protest against the British rulers during the freedom struggle. Tax equity ensures better tax compliance because unjust tax systems induce people to evade taxes. If properly defined and effectively implemented, an equitable tax system can prevent concentration of economic power in a few hands.

2. Under Entry 51 of List II (State List) in the Seventh Schedule of the Constitution, the States are empowered to levy, "duties of excise on: (a) alcoholic liquors for human consumption; (b) opium, Indian hemp and other narcotic drugs and narcotics; but not including medicinal and toilet preparations containing alcohol or any substance included in sub-paragraph (b) of this entry". The revenues accrue to the states in the form of licence duties from the vendors as well as the tax, which can be specific or ad valorem.

   Excise duties (on liquors and other narcotics) are an important source of States' own tax revenues. Some states have adopted the policy of prohibition (Gujarat and Bihar). However, it has resulted in export of the tax base to the neighbouring states.

   It is noteworthy that while in Western countries the main objective of duties on intoxicants is revenue collection, in India the overriding consideration in imposing these duties is to discourage consumption of intoxicants as a matter of public policy. Since demand for alcoholic beverages is generally price-inelastic, this tax provides a case for keeping high tax rates for controlling the level of consumption. In fact, high tax rates yield both high revenues and greater control on consumption.

16

Rate Structure of GST

Implementation of GST involved several issues which were debated in policy circles. Primary among them was the issue of the revenue neutral rate—the rate which would ensure that the migration to the proposed GST would not entail any revenue shortfall for the Centre and States from the current level. In order to achieve this goal, rates had to be appropriately set, exemplifying the true spirit of fiscal federalism, in which revenues are equitably shared by the Centre and States. To get the design of the GST right, it was necessary to aim at tax rates that would protect revenue, simplify administration, encourage compliance, avoid adding to inflationary pressures, and keep India in the range of countries with reasonable levels of indirect taxes.

16.1 Determination of the Revenue Neutral Rate (RNR)

The rationale for implementation of the GST was to reform the in-built inefficiencies in the prevalent tax structure. One of the most debated issues in GST implementation was the appropriate level of the *revenue neutral rate* (RNR). RNR refers to a single rate which preserves revenue at current level of taxation. Along with other factors such as administrative simplicity, inflation neutrality, compliance friendliness and lower tax burden for the public, RNR is an indicator of the success of the new tax system (GST in the present case). However, there is no clarity on whether a precise RNR exists. This is primarily due to growth uncertainties and its impact on different industries/sectors which impinges on tax revenue.

The Report of the Task Force on Goods and Services Tax, 2009 (Chairman: Arbind Modi), which was set up by the Thirteenth Finance Commission (XIII-FC), estimated RNR to be 11 percent exclusive of revenue gains from increased tax compliance and higher GDP. The report also recommended that formula-based devolution (based on recommendations of State Finance Commissions) of an amount equivalent to collection of State GST (SGST) at 2 percentage points should be made to the local bodies such as municipal corporations (as GST will lead to abolition of all entry and octroi taxes by state and other sub-national governments).

The Report on the Revenue Neutral Rate and Structure of Rates for the Goods and Services Tax (GST), 2015 (Chairman: Arvind Subramanian) cautioned that it was difficult to suggest one single number as the appropriate rate with any degree of confidence. Therefore, it recommended that the RNR be in a range of 15 to 15.5 percent, with a strong preference for the lower end of the range. It was argued that a higher rate in the initial stages of implementation may reduce tax compliance and increase dissatisfaction, besides being inflationary. Accordingly, a lower rate would be more prudent in terms of wider acceptability, ensuring better tax compliance.

A related issue was the revenue potential of the Centre and its capability to provide adequate compensation to the States. If revenues fell short and the fiscal position of both the Centre and States were affected, the Centre would find it difficult to compensate the States. Furthermore, multiple rates may be a problem as low rates on some goods have to be balanced through higher rates on other goods to ensure overall revenue neutrality. This would enhance the scope of tax evasion, besides posing administrative difficulties.

The debate on RNR highlighted a serious concern about the revenue mobilisation capacity of the proposed GST which had to yield more than the combined revenue of the existing Central excise and all the State level sales taxes/VATs. Any major shortfall would have caused a serious dent on the public finances of both the Centre and States. Therefore, the projected GST rate/rates had to be suitably calibrated.

16.2 GST Council Decisions on Rate Structure

The maximum tax burden under GST is 40 percent (20 percent CGST and 20 percent SGST). [1] This is an enabling provision for financial emergencies. IGST, levied by the Centre, is CGST plus SGST (i.e. 40 percent) on all inter-State transactions of taxable goods and services. [2]

CGST and SGST are levied at rates decided by the GST Council. These rates are later notified.

In this regard, the GST Council—in its Fourth Meeting held in New Delhi on November 3-4, 2016— settled for a 4-tier rate structure of 5, 12, 18 and 28 percent for goods which, it was thought, would not be inflationary and yet protect revenues of both Central and State Governments. It was broadly consistent with the RNR of 15-15.5 percent recommended by the Subramanian Committee. [3] It also indicated that there can be no single optimal rate for taxing commodities.

Similarly, at its Fourteenth Meeting held in Srinagar (J&K) on May 18-19, 2017, the Council agreed on a four-tier tax structure for services. The four slabs of 5, 12, 18 and 28 percent mirrored the GST rates on goods. In the same meeting it largely completed the exercise of fitment of various goods and services in different rate slabs. The fitment of goods and services in the various agreed slab rates was an important issue.

GST has been structured in a way that essential goods and services of mass consumption are either exempt from tax or placed in the lower tax brackets. Contrarily, luxury goods and services have been fitted in the higher tax brackets.

16.3 Rate Structure of GST on Goods

First of all there is a notified list of goods exempted from GST. The remaining goods have been organized rate-wise into 7 schedules as notified by the Central Board of Indirect Taxes and Customs (CBIC). These schedules are as under:

- Schedule I: List of goods at nil rate.
- Schedule II: List of goods at 0.25 percent rate.
- Schedule III: List of goods at 3 percent rate.
- Schedule IV: List of Goods at 5 percent rate.

- Schedule V: List of goods at 12 percent rate.
- Schedule VI: List of goods at 18 percent rate.
- Schedule VII: List of goods at 28 percent rate.

0.25 percent rate (for precious stones) and 3 percent rate (for gold and silver) are exceptions to *four-tax slabs-rule.*

Table 16.1 provides rate-wise illustrative lists of goods subject to GST.

Table 16.1: Rate-wise Illustrative Lists of Goods Subject to GST

GST rate (percent)	Illustrative list of goods
Exempted goods*	Bread • Fresh fruits and vegetables • Fresh milk and curd • Hearing aids.
Nil**	Salt • Jaggery • Contraceptives • Sanitary napkins • Bamboos • Music books.
0.25	Precious stones (other than diamonds).
3	Gold, silver and semi-precious stones.
5	Sugar • Tea • Roasted coffee beans • Edible oils • Skimmed milk powder • Milk food for babies • Packed food • Packed *paneer* • Newsprint • PDS kerosene • Domestic LPG • Building bricks • Renewable energy devices • Cotton and natural fibre • Apparel costing below ₹ 1,000 • Footwear costing below ₹ 1,000 • Cashew • *Agarbattis* • Insulin • Parts and accessories for the carriages for disabled persons • Coal (with compensation cess).
12	Mobiles • Medicines • Telephones • LED lights • Butter • *Ghee* •, Almonds • Sausages • Pickles • *Chutney* • *Morabba* • Toppings • Instant food mix • Packed coconut water • Umbrellas • Fertilizers • Exercise books • Cutlery.
18	Computers • Monitors and TVs of up to screen size of 32 inches • Digital cameras and video camera recorders •.Computer printers • Capital goods • Industrial intermediates • Hair oil • Soap • Toothpaste • Toilet and facial tissues • Iron and steel • Fountain pens • Man-made fibres • Footwear costing ₹ 1,000 and above • Insecticides • refractory bricks • Ball bearings • Plastic tarpaulin.
28	**Without Compensation Cess:** Cement • Air conditioners • Aircrafts for personal use • Dish washing machines.
	With Compensation Cess: *Pan masala*, tobacco and tobacco products, aerated waters and motor cars. For maximum permissible rate of compensation cess on these products, see Table 32.1 of chapter 32 of this book.

*Goods which are wholly exempt from tax under Section 11 of CGST Act or under Section 6 of IGST Act.

**Nil-rated goods are goods the declared rate of tax on which is 0 percent. Even 0 percent is a rate. Such goods do not form part of exemption notification. Goods taxable at nil rate (or 0 percent rate) must not be confused with zero-rated goods which have a different meaning in GST law. Zero rated goods are those on which no tax is payable but input tax credit pertaining to them is admissible. All exports (whether of goods or services) as well as supplies to SEZs have been categorized as zero-rated supplies in Section 16 of the IGST Act, 2017.

See also Table 13.3 of chapter 13 of this book.

Source: Government of India, Central Board of Indirect Taxes and Customs (CBIC) (website).

Analysis of rate structure of GST on goods reveals that many essential goods of mass consumption are exempt from GST, viz. bread, fresh fruits and vegetables, fresh milk, curd etc.

Similarly, many essential food items and mass consumption goods are subject to 5 percent rate of tax which is affordable. Examples include sugar, tea, edible oils, low cost apparel and footwear.

12 percent rate is applicable to mobiles, medicines, telephones, LED lights and semi-luxury goods like butter, *ghee* and almonds.

18 percent rate is leviable, among others, to most electronic items like computers, monitors, TVs, digital cameras, video camera recorders and computer printers.

The highest rate of 28 percent is applicable on luxury goods like air conditioners. Demerit and ultra-luxury goods like *pan masala,* tobacco and tobacco products, aerated waters and luxury motor cars are taxed at highest rate of 28 percent plus compensation cess. GST compensation cess is meant to compensate States for any revenue loss on account of implementation of GST. The cess has a sunset clause of 5 years.

There were about 229 items subject to 28 percent rate of tax when GST was rolled out on July 1, 2017. In due course of time, many items have been transferred to lower rate categories with the result that presently only about 31 items are subject to highest rate of 28 percent.

16.3.1 Classification of Goods: Harmonised System of Nomenclature (HSN) code is used for classifying goods under the GST regime. In order to apply a particular rate of tax, a taxable person is required to determine the classification of his supply as to whether it constitutes a supply of goods or services. Once the same is determined, it is also important to see whether it is composite supply or mixed supply. In the case of composite supply, he is required to determine the principal supply which decides the classification and applicable rate. Thus, classification in terms of HSN code is to be made by the assessee so as to arrive at the rate of tax which he is required to pay.

Under GST, the majority of dealers have to use two-, four-, or eight-digit HSN codes for their commodities, depending on their turnover the year prior.

1. Dealers with turnover of less than ₹ 1.5 crore are not required to mention HSN code in their invoices.
2. Dealers whose turnover is above ₹ 1.5 crore but below ₹ 5 crore are required to use two-digit HSN codes for their commodities.
3. Dealers with turnover exceeding ₹ 5 crore are required to use four-digit HSN codes for their commodities.
4. In the case of imports/exports, HSN codes of eight digits are compulsory, as GST has to be compatible with international standards and practices.

See also section 16.4.1 of this chapter for classification of services.

16.4 Rate Structure of GST on Services

First of all there is a notified list of services exempted from GST. The remaining services have been organized rate-wise into 5 lists as notified by the Central Board of Indirect Taxes and Customs (CBIC). These lists are as under:

- List of services at nil rate.
- List of services at 5 percent rate.
- List of services 12 percent rate.
- List of services at 18 percent rate.
- List of services at 28 percent rate.

Table 16.2 provides rate-wise illustrative lists of services subject to GST.

Table16.2: Rate Structure of GST on Services

GST rate (percent)	Illustrative list of services
Exempted services*	Healthcare services by a clinical establishment, an authorised medical practitioner or para-medics • Services provided by an educational institution to its students, faculty and staff • Services by government or a local authority. Services by the Reserve Bank of India • Services by a foreign diplomatic mission located in India • Services relating to cultivation of plants and rearing of all life forms of animals • Services provided by an arbitral tribunal • Services by way of admission to a museum, national park, wildlife sanctuary, tiger reserve or zoo • Services by way of training or coaching in recreational activities relating to arts or culture • Services by way of sponsorship of sporting events • Services provided by the Goods and Services Tax Network (GSTN) • Services by way of admission to *protected monuments*. Renting of hotels, inns, guest houses, clubs, campsites or other commercial places meant for residential or lodging purposes having room tariff below ₹ 1,000.
Nil**	Support services to agriculture, forestry, fishing, animal husbandry •Services by the Central Government, State Government, Union territory or local authority to governmental authority or government entity, by way of lease of land • Supply of land or undivided share of land by way of lease or sub-lease where such supply is a part of composite supply of construction of flats etc.
5	Transport of goods by rail • Transport of goods in a vessel • Renting of motorcab • Transport of passengers by air in economy class • Selling of space for advertisement in print media • Services by way of job work in relation to printing of newspapers • Leasing of aircrafts • Supply of tour operators' services• Stand-alone restaurants, irrespective of air-conditioned or otherwise • Food parcels (or takeaways) •. Restaurants in hotel premises having room tariff of less than ₹ 7,500 per unit per day.
12	Transport of passengers by air in other than economy class • Transport of goods in containers by rail by any person other than Indian Railways • Construction of a complex, building, civil structure or a part thereof, intended for sale to a buyer, wholly or partly • Renting of hotels, inns, guest houses, clubs, campsites or other commercial places meant for residential or lodging purposes having room tariff ₹ 1,000 and above but less than ₹ 2,500 per room per day • cinema tickets up to ₹ 100 • third-party insurance premium of goods-carrying vehicles.

contd...

18	Supply of food/drinks in restaurant having licence to serve liquor • Supply of food/drinks in outdoor catering • Services by way of admission or access to circus, Indian classical dance including folk dance, theatrical performance, drama • Composite supply of works contract • Restaurants in hotel premises having room tariff of ₹ 7,500 and above per unit per day (even for a single room) • Renting of hotels, inns, guest houses, clubs, campsites or other commercial places meant for residential or lodging purposes where room tariff of ₹ 2,500 and above but less than ₹ 7,500 per room per day • cinema tickets above ₹ 100.
28	Services by way of admission to entertainment events or access to amusement facilities • Services provided by a race club by way of totalisator or a licensed bookmaker in such club • Gambling • Accommodation in hotels including 5 star and above rated hotels, inns, guest houses, clubs, campsites or other commercial places meant for residential or lodging purposes, where room rent is ₹ 7,500 and above per night per room.***

*Services which are wholly exempt from tax under Section 11 of CGST Act or under Section 6 of IGST Act.
**Nil-rated services are services the declared rate of tax on which is 0 percent. Even 0 percent is a rate. Such services do not form part of exemption notification.
**Initially, GST was charged on the original published room rate, even when hotels offered rooms at a discount especially in off-season periods. As per the decision taken in the Twenty-eighth Meeting of the GST Council held on July 21, 2018, presently GST is levied only on the actual room rate, i.e. on invoice value, not on declared room tariff.
Source: Government of India, Central Board of Indirect Taxes and Customs (CBIC) (website).

Like goods, services can also be classified into two broad categories: essential services (e.g. health and education) and luxury services (e.g. entertainment and tourism). The rationale for exemption/lenient tax treatment of essential services is the same as for essential goods. Similarly, luxury services are taxed at a high rate like luxury goods.

The exempted services under GST are the same as the services exempted under the erstwhile service tax law. Services supplied by Goods and Services Tax Network (GSTN) are new addition to the list of exempted services under the abolished service tax law. It is noteworthy that health and educational services are exempt from GST.

5 percent rate is applicable on essential services like transport of goods by rail, transport of goods in a vessel, renting of motor cab, tour operators services, food parcels (or takeaways).

12 percent rate is applicable, among others, on cinema tickets up to ₹ 100 and third-party insurance premium of goods-carrying vehicles.

18 percent rate is applicable on cinema tickets above ₹ 100.

Highest rate of 28 percent is applicable on luxury services like services by way of admission to entertainment events or access to amusement facilities, services provided by a race club, gambling, accommodation in hotels including 5 star and above rated hotels where room rent is ₹ 7,500 and above per night per room.

16.4.1 Classification of Services: Similar to the international HSN Codes, India has adopted a Service Accounting Code (SAC) for all its services and which is a modified version of the United Nations Central Product Classification (UNCPC). GST has subsumed the erstwhile service tax which was levied by the Central Government at the national level. Since GST is a combination of both goods and services, an equable classification for services is also required.

HSN Code is an 8 digit number while SAC Code is a 6 digit number.

Using GST SAC code, the GST rates for services are fixed in five slabs, namely 0 percent, 5 percent, 12 percent, 18 percent and 28 percent.

If a service is not exempted from GST or if the GST rates are not provided, then the default GST rate of 18 percent is applicable for such services.

Services are classified as per the SAC. The SAC is strictly numeric having 6 digits. The first two digits (99) are the same for all services, the next two digits represent the major nature of service and the last two digits represent detailed nature of service.

SAC codes are used by the assessees and the tax administration as guiding tools for classification of services for the purpose of determining the rate of tax. Where a service is capable of differential treatment for any purpose based on its description, the most specific description is preferred over a more general description.

To understand this better, let us take an example of SAC code 9997 which pertains to *other services*. Breaking up this code reveals the nature of service or the classification of service as given in Table 16.3.

Table 16.3: Service Accounting Code (SAC) of Beauty and Physical Well-being Services

SAC code	Brief description of service
99	Common code.
9997	*Other services* (major nature of service).
99972	Beauty and physical well-being services.
999721	Hairdressing and barbers' services.
999722	Cosmetic treatment. This service code includes: • Face and beauty treatment. • Manicure and pedicure services. • Counselling services on beauty, face care and make-up.

See also section 16.3.1 of this chapter for classification of goods.

16.5 Downward Revision of Rates in the Twenty-third Meeting of the GST Council

At its Twenty-third Meeting held in Guwahati (Assam) on November 10, 2017, the GST Council took major decisions relating to GST rates, ITC eligibility criteria, and exemptions and clarifications on levy of GST on services.

The Council decided to reduce tax rate on a wide range of items of mass consumption from 28 percent to 18 percent. These items included, *inter alia*, furniture, mattresses, lamps and lighting fittings, ceramic tiles, musical instruments, detergents, chocolates, shaving and after-shave items, shampoo deodorants, washing powder, granite and marble. In fact, the Government was facing intense heat from opposition-ruled States over keeping mass-used goods in the 28 percent bracket which was meant for luxury and demerit goods. About 227 items were under 28 percent rate category. The Council pruned this list to 50. In other words, the Council cut rates on 177 goods.

There was unanimity that in 28 percent category there should be only luxury and demerit goods. Thus, the Council took a historic decision that in the 28 percent slab there would be only 50 items.

All stand-alone restaurants, irrespective of air-conditioned or otherwise, were made subject to 5 percent GST without ITC. Food parcels (or takeaways) would also attract 5 percent GST without ITC. Restaurants in hotel premises having room tariff of less than ₹ 7,500 per unit per day would attract GST of 5 percent without ITC. Restaurants in hotel premises having room tariff of ₹ 7,500 and above per unit per day (even for a single room) would attract GST of 18 percent with full ITC. Outdoor catering will continue to be at 18 percent with full ITC.

The rate of GST on job work services in relation to manufacture of those handicraft goods in respect of which the casual taxable person has been exempted from obtaining registration, was reduced to 5 percent with full ITC.

Services by way of admission to *protected monuments* were exempted from GST.

The above changes were made effective from November 15, 2017.

16.5.1 Rate Reduction on Goods:

From 28 Percent to 18 Percent:

1. Wires, cables, insulated conductors, electrical insulators, electrical plugs, switches, sockets, fuses, relays, electrical connectors.
2. Electrical boards, panels, consoles, cabinets etc. for electric control or distribution.
3. Particle/fibre boards and plywood. Articles of wood, wooden frame, paving block.
4. Furniture, mattress, bedding and similar furnishing.
5. Trunk, suitcase, vanity cases, brief cases, travelling bags and other hand bags, cases.
6. Detergents, washing and cleaning preparations.
7. Liquid or cream for washing the skin.
8. Shampoos; hair cream, hair dyes (natural, herbal or synthetic) and similar other goods; henna powder or paste, not mixed with any other ingredient.
9. Pre-shave, shaving or after-shave preparations, personal deodorants, bath preparations, perfumery, cosmetic or toilet preparations, room deodorisers.
10. Perfumes and toilet waters.
11. Beauty or make-up preparations.
12. Fans, pumps, compressors.
13. Lamp and light fitting.
14. Primary cell and primary batteries.
15. Sanitary ware and parts thereof of all kind.
16. Articles of plastic, floor covering, baths, shower, sinks, washbasins, seats, sanitary ware of plastic.

17. Slabs of marbles and granite.
18. Goods of marble and granite such as tiles.
19. Ceramic tiles of all kinds.
20. Miscellaneous articles such as vacuum flasks, lighters.
21. Wrist watches, clocks, watch movement, watch cases, straps, and parts.
22. Article of apparel and clothing accessories of leather, guts, furskin, artificial fur and other articles such as saddlery and harness for any animal.
23. Articles of cutlery, stoves, cookers and similar non-electric domestic appliances.
24. Razor and razor blades.
25. Multi-functional printers, cartridges.
26. Office or desk equipment.
27. Door, windows and frames of aluminium.
28. Articles of plaster such as board, sheet.
29. Articles of cement or concrete or stone and artificial stone.
30. Articles of asphalt or slate.
31. Articles of mica.
32. Ceramic flooring blocks, pipes, conduit, pipe fitting.
33. Wall paper and wall covering.
34. Glass of all kinds and articles thereof such as mirror, safety glass, sheets, glassware.
35. Electrical, electronic weighing machinery.
36. Fire extinguishers and fire extinguishing charge.
37. Fork lifts, lifting and handling equipment.
38. Bull dozers, excavators, loaders, road rollers.
39. Earth moving and levelling machinery.
40. Escalators.
41. Cooling towers, pressure vessels, reactors.
42. Crankshaft for sewing machine, tailor's dummies, bearing housings, gears and gearing; ball or roller screws; gaskets.
43. Electrical apparatus for radio and television broadcasting.
44. Sound recording or reproducing apparatus.
45. Signalling, safety or traffic control equipment for transports.
46. Physical exercise equipment, festival and carnival equipment, swings, shooting galleries, roundabouts, gymnastic and athletic equipment.
47. All musical instruments and their parts.
48. Artificial flowers, foliage and artificial fruits.
49. Explosive, anti-knocking preparation, fireworks.
50. Cocoa butter, fat, oil powder.
51. Extract, essence ad concentrates of coffee, miscellaneous food preparations.
52. Chocolates, chewing gum/bubble gum.
53. Malt extract and food preparations of flour, groats, meal, starch or malt extract.
54. Waffles and wafers coated with chocolate or containing chocolate.
55. Rubber tubes and miscellaneous articles of rubber.

56. Goggles, binoculars, telescope.
57. Cinematographic cameras and projectors, image projector.
58. Microscope, specified laboratory equipment, specified scientific equipment such as for meteorology, hydrology, oceanography, geology.
59. Solvent, thinners, hydraulic fluids, anti-freezing preparation.

From 28 Percent to 12 Percent:

1. Wet grinders consisting of stone as grinder.
2. Tanks and other armoured fighting vehicles.

From 18 Percent to 12 Percent:

1. Condensed milk.
2. Refined sugar and sugar cubes.
3. Pasta.
4. Curry paste, mayonnaise and salad dressings, mixed condiments and mixed seasoning.
5. Diabetic food.
6. Medicinal grade oxygen.
7. Printing ink.
8. Hand bags and shopping bags of jute and cotton.
9. Hats (knitted or crocheted).
10. Parts of specified agricultural, horticultural, forestry, harvesting or threshing machinery.
11. Specified parts of sewing machine.
12. Spectacles frames.
13. Furniture wholly made of bamboo or cane.

From 18 Percent to 5 Percent:

1. Puffed rice *chikki*, peanut *chikki*, sesame *chikki*, *revdi*, *tilrevdi*, *khaza*, *kazuali*, groundnut sweets *gatta*, *kuliya*.
2. Flour of potatoes put up in unit container bearing a brand name.
3. Chutney powder.
4. Fly ash.
5. Sulphur recovered in refining of crude.
6. Fly ash aggregate with 90 percent or more fly ash content.

From 12 Percent to 5 Percent:

1. Desiccated coconut.
2. Narrow woven fabric including cotton newar.
3. *Idli, dosa* batter.
4. Finished leather, chamois and composition leather.
5. Coir cordage and ropes, jute twine, coir products.
6. Fishing net and fishing hooks.
7. Worn clothing.
8. Fly ash bricks.

From 5 Percent to Nil: These were as under:

1. *Guar* meal.

2. Hop cone (other than grounded, powdered or in pellet form).
3. Certain dried vegetables such as sweet potatoes, maniac.
4. Unworked coconut shell.
5. Fish frozen or dried (not put up in unit container bearing a brand name).
6. *Khandsari* sugar.

16.6 Downward Revision of Rates in the Twenty-eighth Meeting of the GST Council

The Council in its Twenty-eighth Meeting held on July 21, 2018 reduced tax rates on a variety of goods to provide relief to a cross-section of taxpayers. The new rates became effective from July 27, 2018.

16.6.1 Rate Reduction on Goods:

From 28 percent to 18 percent:

1. Paints and varnishes (including enamels and lacquers).
2. Glaziers' putty, grafting putty, resin cements.
3. Refrigerators, freezers and other refrigerating or freezing equipment including water cooler, milk coolers, refrigerating equipment for leather industry, ice cream freezer etc.
4. Washing machines.
5. Lithium-ion batteries.
6. Vacuum cleaners.
7. Domestic electrical appliances such as food grinders and mixers and food or vegetable juice extractor, shaver, hair clippers etc.
8. Storage water heaters and immersion heaters, hair dryers, hand dryers, electric smoothing irons etc.
9. Televisions up to the size of 68 cm.
10. Special purpose motor vehicles, e.g. crane lorries, fire fighting vehicle, concrete mixer lorries, spraying lorries.
11. Works trucks of the type used in factories, warehouses, dock areas or airports for short transport of goods.
12. Trailers and semi-trailers.
13. Miscellaneous articles such as scent sprays and similar toilet sprays, powder-puffs and pads for the application of cosmetics or toilet preparations.

From 28 percent to 12 percent:

1. Fuel cell vehicles. Further, compensation cess shall also be exempted on fuel cell vehicles

From 18 percent, 12 percent and 5 percent to Nil:

1. Stone/marble/wood deities.
2. *Rakhi* (other than that of precious or semi-precious material of chapter 71).
3. Sanitary napkins.
4. Coir pith compost.
5. Sal leaves, siali leaves and their products and sabai rope.
6. *Phool Bhari Jhadoo* (raw material for *Jhadoo*).
7. *Khali dona.*

8. Circulation and commemorative coins sold by Security Printing and Minting Corporation of India Ltd. to Ministry of Finance.

From 12 percent to 5 percent:

1. Chenille fabrics and other fabrics under heading 5801.
2. Handloom dari.
3. Phosphoric acid (fertilizer grade only).
4. Knitted cap/topi having retail sale value not exceeding ₹ 1,000.

From 18 percent to 12 percent:

1. Bamboo flooring.
2. Brass kerosene pressure stove.
3. Hand operated rubber roller.
4. Zip and slide fasteners.

From 18 percent to 5 percent:

1. Ethanol for sale to oil marketing companies for blending with fuel.
2. Solid bio-fuel pellets.

16.6.2 Rate Change Made in Respect of Footwear: 5 percent GST was extended to footwear having a retail sale price up to ₹ 1,000 per pair. Footwear having a retail sale price exceeding ₹ 1,000 per pair would continue to attract 18 percent rate.

16.6.3 Reduction in Rates for Specified Handicraft Items:

From 18 percent to 12 percent:

1. Handbags including pouches, purses and jewellery box.
2. Wooden frames for painting, photographs, mirrors etc.
3. Artware of cork.
4. Stone artware and stone inlay work.
5. Ornamental framed mirrors.
6. Glass statues (other than those of crystal).
7. Glass artware including pots, jars, votive, cask, cake cover, tulip bottle, vase.
8. Artware of iron.
9. Artware of brass, copper/copper alloys, electro plated with nickel/silver.
10. Aluminium artware.
11. Handcrafted lamps (including panchloga lamp).
12. Worked vegetable or mineral carving, articles of wax etc.
13. *Ganjifa* card.

From 12 percent to 5 percent:

1. Handmade carpets and other handmade textile floor coverings.
2. Handmade lace.
3. Hand-woven tapestries.
4. Hand-made braids and ornamental trimming in the piece.
5. Toran.

16.6.4 GST on Services: As regards services, the Council took various decisions relating to exemptions, changes in GST rates, ITC eligibility criteria and rationalization of rates.

16.7 Downward Rate Revision by Thirty-first Meeting of the GST Council

GST Council in its Thirty-first meeting held in New Delhi on December 22, 2018 took the following decisions relating to changes in GST rates.

16.7.1 Rate Reduction on Goods:

From 28 percent to 18 percent:

1. Pulleys, transmission shafts and cranks, gear boxes etc.
2. Monitors and TVs of up to screen size of 32 inches.
3. Re-treaded or used pneumatic tyres of rubber.
4. Power banks of lithium ion batteries.
5. Digital cameras and video camera recorders.
6. Video game consoles and other games and sports requisites.

From 28 percent to 5 percent:

1. Parts and accessories for the carriages for disabled persons.

From 18 percent to 12 percent:

1. Cork roughly squared or debagged.
2. Articles of natural cork.
3. Agglomerated cork.

From 18 percent to 5 percent:

1. Marble rubble.

From 12 percent to 5 percent:

1. Natural cork.
2. Walking stick.
3. Fly ash blocks.

From 12 percent to Nil:

1. Music books.

From 5 percent Nil:

1. Vegetables, frozen, branded and put in a unit container.
2. Vegetable provisionally preserved but unsuitable in that state for immediate consumption.

It was clarified that rate of 5 percent/18 percent is to be applied based on transaction value of footwears.

16.7.2 Rate Reduction on Services:

1. GST rate on cinema tickets above ₹ 100 was reduced from 28 percent to 18 percent and on cinema tickets up to ₹ 100 from 18 percent to 12 percent.
2. GST rate on third-party insurance premium of goods-carrying vehicles was reduced from 18 percent to 12 percent.

In short, tax rates have been rationalized several times since GST was rolled out on July 1, 2017. At its Twenty-third Meeting held on November 10, 2017, the GST Council pruned the list of 227 items under 28 percent rate category to 50. In other words, the Council shifted 177 goods from 28 percent to 18 percent rate category. There was unanimity that 28 percent category should include only luxury and demerit goods.

In its Twenty-eighth Meeting held on July 21, 2018, GST Council reduced tax rates on a variety of goods to provide relief to a cross-section of taxpayers.

Again, in its Thirty-first Meeting held on December 22, 2018 various important decisions pertaining to reduction in GST rates were taken. Thus, 6 commodities were shifted from 28 percent to 18 percent rate category; 1 item from 28 percent to 5 percent; 3 items from 18 percent to 12 percent; 1 item from 18 percent to 5 percent; 3 items from 12 percent to 5 percent; 1 item from 12 percent to nil; and 2 items from 5 percent to nil rate category.

16.8 Dual Rate on Lotteries

Presently, private and state-run lotteries face differential rates. A state-organized lottery attracts 12 percent GST while a state-authorized lottery attracts 28 percent tax. An eight member group of state finance ministers could not reach a consensus on whether a uniform tax rate should be imposed on lotteries or the current differential tax rate system be continued.

In its Thirty-fifth Meeting held on June 21, 2019, the GST Council referred to the attorney general seeking his view on the issue, as there has been a Calcutta High Court judgement and there is a petition before the Supreme Court. The reference is limited to the point whether a product being one good can be taxed differently or not under the GST.

16.9 GST Rate on Electronic Vehicles (EVs)

In its Thirty-fifth Meeting held on June 21, 2019, the GST Council could not arrive at a decision on reducing GST on EVs. It, therefore, referred the proposal to cut GST rate on EVs from 12 percent to 5 percent and on electric chargers from 18 percent to 12 percent to the fitment committee. What the GST rate should be on leased EVs was also refereed to the committee.

To sum up, Government has followed the policy of *soft rates with better compliance.* This policy is continuing and more reductions in tax rates on goods and services are expected in the future.

It is notable that GST law stipulates that any reduction in rate of tax on any supply of goods or services or the benefit of input tax credit should be passed on to the recipient by way of commensurate reduction in prices. National Anti-profiteering Authority (NAA) is the watchdog body constituted by the Central Government to examine whether such tax benefits availed by any registered person have actually resulted in a commensurate reduction in prices. NAA is the institutional mechanism under GST law to check unfair profit-making by the trading community.

For details on anti-profiteering provisions of GST law, see chapter 24 of this book.

Endnotes

1. As per Section 9(1) of the CGST Act, 2017.
2. As per Section 5(1) of the IGST Act, 2017.
3. Earlier, the Centre had proposed a 4-slab structure of 6, 12, 16 and 26 percent.

Part IV
GST on Certain Special Entities/Sectors

17

GST on Casual and Non-resident Taxable Persons

17.1 GST on Casual Taxable Persons

Casual taxable person means a person who occasionally undertakes transactions involving supply of goods or services or both in the course or furtherance of business, whether as principal, agent or in any other capacity, in a State or a Union territory where he has no fixed place of business.

A casual taxable person making taxable supply in India has to compulsorily take registration. There is no threshold limit for registration. A casual taxable person cannot exercise the option to pay tax under composition levy. He has to apply for registration at least 5 days prior to commencing his business in India.

A casual taxable person has to make an advance deposit of tax in an amount equivalent to his estimated tax liability for the period for which the registration is sought.

17.1.1 Registration: There is no special form to register as a casual taxable person. The normal form GST REG-01 which is used by other taxable persons can be used for registration by casual taxable person. A casual taxable person, before applying for registration, will declare his permanent account number (PAN), mobile number, email address, State or Union territory in Part A of Form GST REG-01 on the common portal, either directly or through a facilitation centre notified by the Commissioner.

PAN shall be validated online by the common portal from the database maintained by the Central Board of Direct Taxes. The mobile number declared shall be verified through a one-time password sent to the said mobile number; and the email address shall be verified through a separate one-time password sent to the said email address. On successful verification of the PAN, mobile number and email address, a temporary reference number shall be generated and communicated to the applicant on the said mobile number and email address.

Using this reference number generated, the applicant shall electronically submit an application in Part B of Form GST REG-01, duly signed or verified through electronic verification code, along with the documents specified in the said Form at the common portal, either directly or through a Facilitation Centre notified by the Commissioner.

The applicant will be given a temporary reference number by the Common Portal for making the mandatory advance deposit of tax for an amount equivalent to the estimated tax liability of such person for the period for which the registration is sought. The registration certificate shall be issued electronically only after the said deposit appears in his electronic cash ledger. The amount deposited shall be credited to the electronic cash ledger of casual taxable person. On depositing the amount, an acknowledgement shall be issued electronically to the applicant in Form GST REG-02.

The casual taxable person can make taxable supplies only after the issuance of the certificate of registration. The certificate of registration shall be valid for the period specified in the application for registration or 90 days from the effective date of registration, whichever is earlier. In case the casual taxable person intends to extend the period of registration indicated in his application of registration, an application in Form GST REG-11 shall be submitted electronically through the Common Portal, either directly or through a Facilitation Centre notified by the Commissioner, before the end of the validity of registration granted to him. The validity period of 90 days can be extended by a further period not exceeding 90 days. The extension will be allowed only on payment of an additional amount of tax equivalent to the estimated tax liability for the period for which the extension is sought.

17.1.2 Returns: The casual taxable person is required to furnish the following returns electronically through the common portal, either directly or through a facilitation centre notified by the Commissioner:

- Form GSTR-1 giving the details of outward supplies of goods or services to be filed on or before the 10th day of the following month.
- Form GSTR-2, giving the details of inward supplies to be filed after 10th but before the 15th day of the following month.
- Form GSTR-3 to be filed after 15th day but before the 20th day of the following month.

However, a casual tax person shall not be required to file any annual return as required by a normal registered taxpayer.

17.1.3 Refund: The casual taxable person is eligible for the refund of any balance of the advance tax deposited by him after adjusting his tax liability. The balance advance tax deposit can be refunded only after all the returns have been furnished, in respect of the entire period for which the certificate of registration was granted to him had remained in force.

17.2 GST on Non-resident Taxable Person

17.2.1 Meaning of Non-resident Taxable Person: *Non-resident taxable person* means any person who occasionally undertakes transactions involving supply of goods or services or both, whether as principal or agent or in any other capacity, but who has no fixed place of business or residence in India. A non-resident taxable person making taxable supply in India has to compulsorily take registration. There is no threshold limit for registration. A non-resident taxable person cannot exercise the option to pay tax under composition levy. He has to apply for registration at least five days prior to commencing his business in India using a valid passport (and need not have a PAN number in India).

17.2.2 Registration Requirements: A business entity incorporated or established outside India, has to submit the application for registration along with its tax identification number or unique number on the basis of which the entity is identified by the Government of that country or its permanent account number, if available.

A non-resident taxable person has to make an advance deposit of tax in an amount equivalent to his estimated tax liability for the period for which the registration is sought.

A non-resident taxable person is not required to apply in normal application for registration being filed by other taxpayers. A simplified form GST REG-09 is required to be filled. A non-resident taxable person has to electronically submit an application, along with a self-attested copy of his valid passport, for registration, duly signed or verified through EVC, in Form GST REG-09, at least five days prior to the commencement of business at the Common Portal either directly or through a Facilitation Centre notified by the Commissioner.

The application for registration made by a non-resident taxable person has to be signed by his authorized signatory who shall be a person resident in India having a valid PAN. On successful verification of PAN, mobile number and e-mail address the person applying for registration as a non-resident taxable person will be given a temporary reference number by the Common Portal for making the mandatory advance deposit of tax for an amount equivalent to the estimated tax liability of such person for the period for which the registration is sought. The registration certificate shall be issued electronically only after the said deposit appears in his electronic cash ledger. The amount deposited shall be credited to the electronic cash ledger of the non-resident person.

The non-resident taxable person can make taxable supplies only after the issuance of the certificate of registration. The certificate of registration shall be valid for the period specified in the application for registration or ninety days from the effective date of registration, whichever is earlier.

17.2.3 Extension of Registration: In case the non-resident taxable person intends to extend the period of registration indicated in his application of registration, an application in Form GST REG-11shall be submitted electronically through the common portal, either directly or through a facilitation centre notified by the Commissioner, before the end of the validity of registration granted to him.

The validity period of ninety days can be extended by a further period not exceeding ninety days. The extension will be allowed only on payment of the amount of an additional amount of tax equivalent to the estimated tax liability for the period for which the extension is sought has to be deposited.

17.2.4 Input Tax Credit (ITC): ITC is not available in respect of goods or services or both received by a non-resident taxable person except on goods imported by him. The taxes paid by a non-resident taxable person shall be available as credit to the respective recipients.

17.2.5 Returns: The non-resident taxable person shall furnish a return in Form GSTR-5 electronically through the common portal, either directly or through a facilitation centre notified by the Commissioner, including therein the details of outward supplies and inward supplies and shall pay the tax, interest, penalty, fees or any other amount payable under the Act or these rules within twenty days after the end of a calendar month or within seven days after the last day of the validity period of registration, whichever is earlier.

17.2.6 Refund: The amount of advance tax deposited by a non-resident taxable person will be refunded only after the person has furnished all the returns required in respect of the entire period for which the certificate of registration granted to him had remained in force. Refund can be applied at serial no. 13 of the Form GSTR-5.

18

GST on Charitable and Religious Trusts

The provisions relating to taxation of activities of charitable institutions and religious trusts have been borrowed and carried over from the erstwhile service tax provisions. All services provided by such entities are not exempt. In fact, there are many services that are provided by such entities which would be within the ambit of GST.

18.1 Conditions for GST Exemption

Under GST, services by an entity registered under Section 12AA of Income Tax Act, 1961, by way of *charitable activities* are exempt from the whole of GST. However, exemption is given to the charitable trusts, only if the following conditions are satisfied.

1. Entities must be registered under Section 12AA of the Income Tax Act.
2. Such services or activities by the entity are by way of charitable activities.

Thus, it is essential that the activities must conform to the term *charitable activities* which means activities relating to:

1. Public health by way of:
- Care or counselling of: (a) terminally ill persons or persons with severe physical or mental disability; (b) persons afflicted with HIV or AIDS; and (c) persons addicted to a dependence-forming substance such as narcotics drugs or alcohol.
- Public awareness of preventive health, family planning or prevention of HIV infection.
2. Advancement of religion, spirituality or yoga.
3. Advancement of educational programmes or skill development relating to:
- Abandoned, orphaned or homeless children.
- Physically or mentally abused and traumatized persons.
- Prisoners.
- Persons over the age of 65 years residing in a rural area.
4. Preservation of environment including watershed, forests and wildlife.

GST law makes the exemption to charitable trusts available for charitable activities more specific. While the income from only those activities listed above is exempt from GST, income from the activities other than those mentioned above is taxable. Thus, there could be many services provided by charitable and religious trust which are not considered as charitable activities and hence, such services come under the GST net. The indicative list of such services could be renting of premises by such entities, grant of sponsorship and advertising rights during conduct of events/functions etc.

This is also borne out from the fact that in so far as renting out of religious precincts is concerned, there is a limited exemption available to such entities. Activities not covered by the specific exemption would be taxable.

18.2 Nature of Exemptions

GST law provides the following exemptions to entities registered under Section 12AA of the Income Tax Act, 1961:

1. Services by a person by way of conduct of any religious ceremony.
2. Renting of precincts of a religious place meant for general public, owned or managed by an entity registered as a charitable or religious trust under Section 12AA of the Income Tax Act, 1961 or a trust or an institution registered under sub-clause (v) of clause (23C) of Section 10 of the Income Tax Act or a body or an authority covered under clause (23BBA) of Section 10 of the said Income Tax Act:

Provided that this exemption shall not apply to: (a) renting of rooms where charges are ₹ 1,000 or more per day, (b) renting of premises, community halls, *kalian mandapam* or open area, and the like where charges are ₹ 10,000 or more per day, (c) renting of shops or other spaces for business or commerce where charges are ₹ 10,000 or more per month.

Thus, the law gives a limited exemption to renting of religious precincts or a religious place meant for general public by the entity registered under Section 12AA of the Income Tax Act.

This implies that if immovable properties owned by charitable trusts like marriage hall, convention hall, rest house for pilgrims, shops situated within the premises of a religious place are rented out, income from letting out of such property is wholly exempt from GST. But if such properties are not situated in the precincts of a religious place meaning thereby not within walls or boundary walls of the religious place, income from such letting out will lose this exemption and income from it will be liable to GST.

Income from a religious ceremony organised by a charitable trust is exempt. So the income from Navratri functions, other religious functions, and religious poojas conducted on special occasions like religious festivals by persons so authorised for this purpose by the charitable or religious trust are exempt from GST. But a careful perusal of this exemption shows that all income from such a religious ceremony is not exempt (services other than by way of conduct of religious ceremony are not exempt). Therefore, the nature of income is an essential factor for ascertaining whether it will be taxable or exempt. If income loses its religious nature, it is definitely chargeable to GST. For example, if with regard to Ganeshutsav or other religious functions, charitable trusts rent out their space to agencies for advertisement hoardings, income from such advertisement is chargeable to GST, as this will be considered as income from the advertisement services.

Further, if donation for religious ceremony is received with specific instructions to advertise the name of a donor, such donation income will be subject to GST. But if donation for religious ceremony is received without such instructions, it may not be subject to GST.

Similarly, following exemption is provided to an entity registered under Section 12AA of Income Tax Act, 1961.

Services by way of training or coaching in recreational activities relating to: (a) arts or culture, or (b) sports.

Thus, services provided by way of training or coaching in recreational activities relating to arts or culture or sports by a charitable entity are exempt from GST.

18.3 GST on Management of Educational Institutions by Charitable Trusts

If trusts are running schools, colleges or any other educational institutions specifically for abandoned, orphans, homeless children, physically or mentally abused persons, prisoners or persons over age of 65 years or above residing in a rural area, such activities will be considered as charitable activities and income from such supplies will be wholly exempt from GST.

18.4 GST on Hospital Managed by Charitable Trusts

GST law applicable to all persons including charitable trusts exempts healthcare services at clinical establishment, an authorised medical professional or paramedics. Healthcare services means any service by way of diagnosis or treatment or care for illness, injury, deformity, abnormality or pregnancy in any recognised system of medicines in India and includes services by way of transportation of the patient to and from a clinical establishment, but does not include hair transplant or cosmetic or plastic surgery, except when undertaken to restore or to reconstruct anatomy or functions of body affected due to congenital defects, developmental abnormalities, injury or trauma.

Therefore, all treatment or diagnosis or care for illness, injury, deformity, abnormality or pregnancy by a clinical establishment is covered. Such services provided by doctors and paramedics either provided as an employee (clinical establishment) or in their individual capacity is exempt. Transportation of patients to and from a clinical establishment is also exempt. The clinical establishment means a hospital, nursing home, clinic, sanatorium or any other institution by, whatever name called, that offers services or facilities requiring diagnosis or treatment or care for illness, injury, deformity, abnormality or pregnancy in any recognized system of medicines in India, or a place established as an independent entity or a part of an establishment to carry out diagnostic or investigative services of diseases.

So, if charitable trusts run a hospital and appoint specialist doctors, nurses and provide medical services to patients at a concessional rate, such services are not liable to GST. If hospitals hire visiting doctors/specialists and these deduct some money from consultation/visit fees payable to doctors and the agreement between hospital and consultant doctors is such that some money is charged for providing services to doctors, there may be GST on such amount deducted from fees paid to doctors.

18.5 Other Cases

18.5.1 Import of Services: If a charitable trust registered under Section 12AA of Income Tax Act, 1961, receives any services from provider of services located in non-taxable territory, for charitable purposes, such services received are not chargeable to

GST under the reverse charge mechanism.

18.5.2 Arranging Yoga and Meditation Camps: Charitable trusts organise yoga camps or other fitness camps and they generally are not free for participants, as trusts charge some amount from the participants in the name of accommodation or participation. If trusts are arranging residential or non-residential yoga camps by receiving donation or other charges from the participants, these will not be considered charitable activities (as it is different from advancement of religion, spirituality or yoga).

Since donation is received for participation, it will be considered commercial activity and it is covered under the GST. Similarly, if charitable trusts organise fitness camps in reiki, aerobics, etc., and receive donation from participants, such income will also be taxable.

18.5.3 Running of Public Libraries: No GST will be applicable if charitable trusts are running public libraries and lend books, other publications or knowledge-enhancing contents/material from their libraries.

18.5.4 Services Provided to Charitable Trusts: Services provided to charitable trusts are not out of ambit of GST. All services, other than those specifically exempted, provided to charitable trusts will be subject to GST.

18.5.5 Supply of Goods by Charitable Trusts: There is no exemption for supply of goods by charitable trusts. Thus, any goods supplied by such charitable trusts for consideration shall be liable to GST. For instance, sale of goods shall be chargeable to GST.

19

GST on Real Estate Sector

Real estate is an important sector of the Indian economy in terms of contribution to GDP and employment. In the pre-GST era, multiple taxes like service tax and VAT were applicable on this sector. Rates of VAT varied from state to state, causing considerable confusion among developers, builders and contractors. Now there is a single uniform tax, namely GST on this sector.

19.1 GST on Real Estate Transactions Prior to the Decisions of Thirty-third Meeting of the GST Council

Prior to the decisions of the GST Council taken in its Thirty-third Meeting held on February 24, 2019 in New Delhi, taxability of real estate transactions under GST was as shown in Table 19.1.

Table 19.1: GST on Real Estate Transactions Prior to the Decisions of Thirty-third Meeting of the GST Council

Particulars	GST applicability	Rate of GST
Ready-to-move-in properties for which completion certificates are issued	Not applicable because sale of building is treated as activity or transaction which is treated neither as a supply of good nor a supply of service as per Schedule III of CGST Act, 2017	–
Under construction properties [for homes purchased under credit-linked subsidy scheme (CLSS)]	Applicable as supply of services as per Schedule I of CGST Act, 2017	12 percent*
Under construction properties (other than above)	Applicable as supply of services as per Schedule I of CGST Act, 2017	12 percent
Resale of property is considered as ready-to-move-in property	Not applicable	–
Land purchase and sale	Not applicable. As per Schedule III, sale of land is neither supply of goods nor services.	–

*Homes purchased under CLSS attract 12 percent GST rate. The applicable rate is 8 percent after reducing the 1/3rd amount towards the cost of land. CLSS means purchase of property under Pradhan Mantri Awas Yojana (PMAY-Urban) and such other schemes.

In short, a single tax rate of 12 percent was applicable on properties under construction while GST was not applicable on completed or ready to sale properties.

19.2 Decisions Taken at the Thirty-third Meeting of GST Council

In its Thirty-third Meeting held on February 24, 2019, GST Council decided a rate cut for the under-construction properties covering the residential segment as follows:

1. GST rate for non-affordable housing was reduced from 12 percent to 5 percent without ITC.
2. GST rate for affordable housing was slashed from 8 percent to 1 percent without the benefit of input tax credit (ITC). Affordable housing was redefined under the GST law with a twin definition to it as follows:

- **In the Case of Metro Cities:** Flats with a value of up to ₹ 45 lakh with the carpet area of up to 60 square metres. Metro cities currently cover Bengaluru, Chennai, Hyderabad, Kolkata, Mumbai (the whole of MMR), and Delhi NCR (limited to Delhi, NOIDA, Greater NOIDA, Ghaziabad, Gurgaon, and Faridabad).
- **In the Case of Non-metro Cities:** Flats with a value up to ₹ 45 lakh with the carpet area of up to 90 square metres.

It was decided to draft all the changes by the law and fitment committee in a circular on or before March 10, 2019. These changes will be presented before the GST Council as recommendations. The notifications will be out soon after they are passed by the GST Council and will be made applicable from April 1, 2019.

The above concessions announced by the GST Council will boost the real estate selling henceforth and monitor one of the most unregulated sectors in India, by ensuring that the rate cut benefits are passed on to the neo and middle-class home buyers.

For the limited purpose of calculating the GST, stamp duty and registration charges are excluded. Stamp duty continues to be applicable on both completed properties and under-construction properties as was the case with pre-GST regime.

19.3 Decisions Taken at the Thirty-fourth Meeting of GST Council

Thirty-fourth Meeting of the GST Council, held on March 19, 2019, was convened to oversee and pass the circulars/notifications drafted by the rate fitment and legal committees on the rate cuts on housing announced in the Thirty-third Meeting held on February 24, 2019.

The meeting centred around the applicability of tax rates for under construction housing projects and the rules governing the transition from old rates to new rates for existing projects.

GST Council approved the transition plan for the implementation of the new tax structure for housing units in the following manner:

1. GST rates for new projects will be mandatory from April 1, 2019.
2. Builders of existing housing projects that are completing construction by March 31, 2019 can choose either of the two alternatives:

- Alternative 1: Choose the old rate of 12 percent (8 percent for affordable housing) and charge this GST rate in the invoices raised. Further, input tax credit (ITC) benefit is available and can be passed on to the buyer.

- Alternative 2: Choose to bear GST tax at the rate of 5 percent (1 percent for affordable housing as defined by GST law). The benefit of ITC is not available to the builder for procurements used in construction.

3. Those who choose the second alternative must reverse the accumulated ITC on their closing stock of under-construction properties in a proportion laid down in rules (to be notified) within 6 months.
4. New rate of 5 percent (1 percent for affordable housing) will apply to those residential properties whose construction is going on even after March 31, 2019 or any new projects launched after April 1, 2019. Here, the benefit of ITC on procurements will not be available to the builders.
5. 80 percent procurement of materials should be from the registered dealer.
6. Up to 15 percent of commercial space to be treated as residential property for GST purpose.

20

Services of Goods Transport Agencies (GTAs) and Electronic Way Bill (E-way Bill) System

---

20.1 Services of Goods Transport Agencies (GTAs)

20.1.1 Background: The levy of service tax on road transportation services has always been a contentious issue. The Finance Act, 1997 had levied service tax on goods transport operators w.e.f. November 16, 1997 which was subsequently withdrawn after nation-wide strike. Thereafter by the Finance Act, 2004 service tax was imposed on transport of goods by road services rendered by a goods transport agency with effect from September 10, 2004.

However, the levy was deferred until further notice again in view of transporters' strike. The Government thereafter constituted a Committee to deal with the issue and after taking into account the recommendations of the Committee, levied tax on transport of goods by road with effect from January 1, 2005. The legal position prevailing under service tax is being continued under the GST regime.

The services of transportation of goods by road (except services of GTAs) continue to be exempt even under the GST regime. In so far as the services of GTAs are concerned, if the services (of goods transportation) are provided (by the GTAs) to specified classes of persons, the tax liability falls on such recipients under the reverse charge mechanism. The following discussion will clarify the position.

20.1.2 Transportation of Goods: Presently, the following services are exempt from GST by way of transportation of goods.

1. By road except the services of:
- a goods transportation agency; or
- a courier agency.
2. By inland waterways.

Thus, transportation of goods by road, unless it is a service rendered by a GTA, is exempt from GST.

20.1.3 GTA Defined: As per Section 65B (26) of the Finance Act, 1994, "Goods Transport Agency means any person who provides service in relation to transport of goods by road and issues consignment note, by whatever name called". Therefore, in the service tax regime, issuance of consignment note (C/N) was integral and mandatory requirement before any road transporter could be brought within the ambit of GTA.

Under GST laws, the definition of GTA is provided in clause (ze) of notification no. 12/2017-Central Tax (Rate) dated 28.06.2017. Clause 'ze' reads, "goods transport agency means any person who provides service in relation to transport of goods by road and issues consignment note, by whatever name called".

Thus, it can be seen that issuance of a consignment note is *sine qua non* for a supplier of service to be considered as a GTA. If such a consignment note is not issued by the transporter, the service provider will not come within the ambit of goods transport agency. If a consignment note is issued, it indicates that the lien on the goods has been transferred (to the transporter) and the transporter becomes responsible for the goods till its safe delivery to the consignee. It is only the services of such GTA, who assumes agency functions, that is being brought into the GST net. Individual truck/tempo operators who do not issue any consignment note are not covered within the meaning of the term GTA. As a corollary, the services provided by such individual transporters who do not issue a consignment note [1] are exempt from GST.

20.1.4 Charge of GST on Services Provided by GTA: Services of GTA in relation to transportation of goods (including used household goods for personal use) attract 2.5 percent or 6 percent CGST. Identical rate would be applicable for SGST also, taking the effective rate to 5 percent or 12 percent. However, the rate of 5 percent is subject to the condition that credit of input tax charged on goods or services used in supplying the service has not been taken.

20.1.5 GTA Services Specifically Exempt: Following services provided by a GTA by way of transport in a goods carriage are exempt from payment of tax:

1. Agricultural produce.
2. Goods, where consideration charged for the transportation of goods on a consignment transported in a single carriage does not exceed one thousand five hundred rupees.
3. Goods, where consideration charged for transportation of all such goods for a single consignee does not exceed rupees seven hundred and fifty.
4. Milk, salt and foodgrains including flour, pulses and rice.
5. Organic manure.
6. Newspaper or magazines registered with the Registrar of Newspapers.
7. Relief materials meant for victims of natural or man-made disasters, calamities, accidents or mishap.
8. Defence or military equipments.

The above discussion shows that not all transport of goods by road is by GTAs. To qualify as services of GTA, the GTA should be necessarily issuing a consignment note. Only services provided by a GTA are taxable under GST. Services of transportation of goods by a person other than GTA are exempt. Moreover, in cases where the service of GTA is availed by the specified categories of persons in the taxable territory, the recipients who avail such services are the ones liable to pay GST and not the supplier of services unless the GTA opts for collecting and paying taxes @ 12 percent (6 percent CGST + 6 percent SGST). In all other cases where GTA service is availed by persons other than those specified, the GTA service supplier is the person liable to pay GST. The GTA service supplier is not entitled to take ITC on input services availed by him if tax is being charged @ 5 percent (2.5 percent CGST + 2.5 percent SGST).

In case the GTA service supplier hires any means of transport to provide his output service, no GST is payable on such inputs.

In a nutshell, the GST law continues the provisions prevailing under the service tax regime. The law recognizes that services of transportation of goods are mostly provided by persons in the unorganised sector and hence has specifically excluded such operators from the tax net. In respect of those who provide agency services in transport, the liability is cast on the recipients in most of the cases or unless option to pay under forward charge has been exercised by the GTA.

20.2 Electronic Way Bill [E-Way Bill (EWB)]

In the pre-GST era, different states had different requirements of documentation to allow goods pass through their check-posts. However, such check posts, by the very nature of their operations, generated enormous delays in road traffic. The arrangement also encouraged rent-seeking behaviour.

Introduction of e-way bill system is a fundamental shift from the earlier *departmental policing model* to *self-declaration model.* The new system envisages one EWB for movement of goods throughout the country, thereby ensuring a hassle-free movement for transporters throughout the country.

Under GST, check-posts have been abolished across states. Now EWB rules and forms are uniform throughout the country. This has drastically reduced the time taken to transport goods and hence the transport cost.

EWB rules were rolled out on a trial basis from January 16, 2018. EWB for inter-state transport was to be implemented from February 1, 2018. However, due to last minute glitches the decision was deferred. Finally, it became operational from April 1, 2018.

The requirement of EWB for intra-state (within state) movement of goods started on April 15, 2018 in a phased manner by grouping states in four lots. Implementation of EWB was completed by all the States and Union Territories by June 16, 2018. This significant step has ensured smooth, swift and easy movement of goods throughout the country.

20.2.1 What is EWB? EWB is a document required for movement of goods from one place to another. The movement may be either (a) from supplier to recipient and vice versa or (b) from manufacturer to job worker and vice versa or (c) between two premises of the same businessman or (d) for any other purpose.

20.2.2 When is EWB Required? EWB is required of every registered person causing movement of goods of consignment value (inclusive of GST) exceeding ₹ 50,000. For consignments even below ₹ 50,000, EWB is mandatory in case of inter-state movement of: (a) goods being sent for job work and (b) handicraft goods.

Any direct movement of goods between supplier and recipient warrants EWB, irrespective of distance. However, for intra-State movement of goods from supplier's premises to transporter and from transporter's premises to recipient, Part B is not mandatory, if the said distance is below 50 kilometres.

20.2.3 When is EWB not Required: It is not required when: (a) the mode of transport is non-motor vehicle, (b) goods transported from port, airport, air cargo complex or land customs station to inland container depot (ICD) or container freight station (CFS) for clearance by customs and (c) transport of specified goods is involved (e.g. sheep and goats).

Normally EWB is not required for exempted goods. In addition, there are few items [as detailed in Annexure to Rule 138(14) of the CGST Rules, 2017] for which EWB is not required.

20.2.4 Who is to Generate EWB? There can be following situations for movement of goods and hence generation of EWB:

1. **Registered Supplier to Registered Recipient:** EWB may be generated by either of them depending on terms of delivery, i.e. the person causing movement of goods is responsible for EWB generation.
2. **Registered Supplier to Unregistered Recipient:** EWB is to be generated mandatorily by the registered supplier.
3. **Unregistered Supplier to Registered Recipient:** In such supplies, the movement of goods is deemed to have been caused by registered recipient and hence he is required to generate EWB.
4. **Unregistered Supplier to Unregistered Recipient:** In such transaction, though EWB is not mandatory, it can be generated by either of them on voluntary basis.

Suppliers/recipients of goods can register themselves on the portal of EWB by using their GSTIN. EWB can be generated on the EWB portal and also through SMS. When an EWB is generated a unique EWB number (EBN) is allocated and becomes available to the supplier, recipient, and the transporter.

EWB can be cancelled by generator within 24 hours whereas it can be rejected by recipient within 72 hours or the time of delivery of the goods, whichever is earlier. If the recipient does not reject EWB within 72 hours, it would be deemed to have been accepted by him.

The main relevant form for EWB is GST EWB-01. Part A of this form asks for such information as GSTIN of supplier, place of dispatch, GSTIN of recipient, place of delivery, value of goods etc. Part B of the form requires information such as vehicle number, transport document number, temporary vehicle registration etc.

No changes can be made in Part A (i.e. consignment details) of EWB once generated. However, Part B (i.e. vehicle details) can be updated any number of times within the validity period. In case wrong details are fed, EWB can be cancelled by the generator within 24 hours provided it has not been verified in transit.

20.2.5 Validity Period of EWB: Validity is based on the distance travelled by the goods. For non-over dimensional cargo (ODC), the validity is 1 day for every 100 kilometres or part thereof. However, in the case of ODC cargo, 1 day is given for every 20 kilometres or part thereof. Validity starts from the time of Part B updation (i.e. vehicle number entry) and first day lasts till 12 midnight of next day.

20.2.6 Documents or Details Required to Generate E-way Bill: Following documents are required to generate an e-way bill.

1. Invoice/bill of supply/challan related to the consignment of goods.
2. Transport by road: Transporter's ID or vehicle number.

3. Transport by rail, air, or ship: Transporter's ID, transport document number, and date on the document.

20.2.7 Some Other Features of EWB System: These are as under:

- Supplier can authorize the transporter, courier agency or e-commerce operator to fill Part A of EWB on his behalf.
- Where the goods are transported by railways or by air or by vessel, EWB shall be generated by the registered supplier or registered recipient only and not by the transporter, and the same can be generated even after the commencement of the movement of the goods.
- Transporters of goods can register themselves on the portal of EWB by using their GSTIN.
- Railways have been exempted from generation and carrying of EWB. However, railways are required to carry invoice or delivery challan etc. But EWB has to be produced by the recipient before the delivery of goods by the railways.
- If the goods cannot be transported within the validity period of EWB, the supplier or transporter may extend the validity period in case of transhipment or in case of circumstances of exceptional nature.
- Where the goods are transferred from one conveyance to another, details of conveyance need to be updated by the transporter in Part B of Form GST EWB-01.
- The generation of EWB would be barred if a supplier or recipient does not file GST returns for 2 consecutive tax periods. This was made applicable from June 21, 2019.

20.2.8 Objectives of E-way Bill: These are as under:

1. To bring uniformity across the States for seamless inter-State movement of goods.
2. To ensure hassle-free movement of goods throughout the country.
3. To discontinue separate transit pass in each State for movement of goods.
4. To shift from departmental-policing model to self-declaration model for movement of goods.

20.2.9 Benefits of E-way Bill: These are as follows:

1. Taxpayers/transporters are not required to visit any tax officers/check posts for generation of e-way bill/movement of goods across States.
2. Unlike in the pre-GST period, there are no check posts under GST regime, resulting in saving of time. Saving of time and faster movement of goods ensure optimum utilization of vehicles and manpower.
3. E-way bill system is user-friendly. It can be generated easily and quickly.
4. It ensures checks and balances for smooth tax administration and process simplification.

In short, the introduction of EWB was a monumental shift from the earlier *departmental policing model* to a *self-declaration model*. It envisages one EWB for movement of goods throughout the country, thereby ensuring a hassle-free movement for transporters. New features in the EWB system have been introduced such as the auto calculation of distance based on PIN codes for the generation of EWB and blocking the generation of multiple EWBs against one invoice.

Endnote

1. Consignment note means a document, issued by a goods transport agency against the receipt of goods for the purpose of transport of goods by road in a goods carriage, which is serially numbered, and contains the name of the consignor and consignee, registration number of the goods carriage in which the goods are transported, details of the goods transported, details of the place of origin and destination, person liable for paying tax whether consignor, consignee or the goods transport agency.

Part V

Implementation, Administration and Technological Infrastructure of GST

21

Registration, Tax Invoice, Accounts and Records, and Returns

21.1 Registration for GST

Registration is the most fundamental requirement in any tax system for identification of taxpayers to ensure tax compliance. Under GST, registration of any business entity implies obtaining a unique identification number from the concerned tax authority for the purpose of collecting tax on behalf of the government and to claim input tax credit for the taxes paid on its inward supplies.

21.1.1 Persons Liable for Registration: Section 22 of the CGST Act, 2017 covers the persons liable for registration for the purpose of GST. Thus, every supplier is liable to be registered in the State or Union territory from where he makes a taxable supply of goods/services if his aggregate turnover in a financial year exceeds the prescribed limit. [1]

Threshold limit of aggregate turnover for exemption from registration and payment of GST for suppliers of goods is ₹ 40 lakh. It is ₹ 20 lakh in the case of Arunachal Pradesh, Manipur, Meghalaya, Mizoram, Nagaland, Puducherry, Sikkim, Telangana, Tripura and Uttrakhand. Both the limits are effective from April 1, 2019.

Threshold limit of aggregate turnover for exemption from registration and payment of GST for suppliers of services is ₹ 20 lakh. It is ₹ 10 lakh in the case of Manipur, Mizoram, Nagaland and Tripura.

In which state will a person be registered? A person liable to be registered has to apply for registration in each state from where he makes or intends to make outward supplies under GST. Within each state, generally only one registration is required to be obtained. However, taxpayers may opt for multiple registrations within a state/union territory in respect of multiple places of business located within the same state/union territory.

21.1.2 Persons not Liable for Registration: Section 23 of the CGST Act, 2017, mentions persons who are not liable for registration for the purpose of GST.

1. Any person who is engaged exclusively in the business of supplying goods/services that are not liable to GST or wholly exempt from GST [Section 23(1)(a)].
2. An agriculturist, to the extent of supply of produce out of cultivation of land.
3. Government may, on the recommendations of the GST Council, by notification, specify the category of persons who may be exempted from obtaining registration.

21.1.3 Compulsory Registration in Certain Cases: Under Section 24 of the CGST Act, 2017, registration is compulsory in the following cases even if aggregate turnover is less than the prescribed limit:

1. Persons making any inter-State taxable supply. However, suppliers of services, having turnover up to ₹ 20 lakh, making inter-state supplies are exempt from obtaining registration
2. Casual taxable persons making taxable supply.

3. Persons who are required to pay tax under reverse charge.
4. Electronic commerce operators as well as suppliers to electronic commerce operators. However, suppliers of services, having turnover up to ₹ 20 lakh, making supplies through e-commerce platforms are exempt from obtaining registration. Mandatory registration is required for only those e-commerce operators who are required to collect tax at source.
5. Non-resident taxable persons making taxable supply.
6. Persons who are required to deduct tax at source.
7. Persons who make taxable supply of goods or services or both on behalf of other taxable persons, whether as an agent or otherwise.
8. Input service distributor, whether or not separately registered under this Act.
9. Such other person or class of persons as may be notified by the Government on the recommendations of the GST Council.

21.1.4 Voluntary Registration: Businesses that have no requirement to register under GST can also choose to voluntarily register themselves under the new tax regime. Every provision under the tax that applies to registered entities shall be applicable to those who voluntarily get registered under GST. Voluntary registration under GST has several advantages such as more freedom in inter-state sales, passing on of input tax credit, good ratings, etc. However, it is important to also have the technology ready for online payments.

Initially, application for cancellation of registration by the concerned person who got registered voluntarily was only after 1 year from the date of registration. However, GST Council in its Twenty-fifth meeting held on January 18, 2018 allowed taxable persons who have obtained voluntary registration to apply for cancellation of registration even before the expiry of 1 year from the effective date of registration. Registration will remain temporarily suspended while cancellation of registration is under process, so that the taxpayer is relieved of continued compliance under the law.

21.1.5 Procedure for Registration: Section 25 of the CGST Act, 2017 explains the procedure for registration.

1. Every person who is liable to be registered under Section 22 or Section 24 shall apply for registration in every such State or Union territory in which he is so liable within thirty days from the date on which he becomes liable to registration.
2. A casual taxable person or a non-resident taxable person shall apply for registration at least five days prior to the commencement of business.
3. Every person who makes a supply from the territorial waters of India [2] shall obtain registration in the coastal State or Union territory where the nearest point of the appropriate baseline is located.
4. A person seeking registration shall be granted a single registration in a State or Union territory. Registration is required for each State separately where the taxable person has manufacturing or trading or service units. Single registration for each State is sufficient even if the taxpayer has multiple branches within that State.
5. A person having multiple business verticals in a State or Union territory may be

granted a separate registration for each business vertical. [3] For each registration, a separate GST registration number (GSTIN) of 15 digits is allotted.

6. A person, though not liable to be registered under Section 22 or Section 24, may get himself registered voluntarily.
7. A person who has obtained or is required to obtain more than one registration, whether in one State or Union territory or more than one State or Union territory shall, in respect of each such registration, be treated as distinct persons for the purposes of this Act.

There is no option for centralized registration under GST.

In its Twenty-fifth Meeting held on June 21, 2019, the GST Council allowed the use of Aadhaar as proof for obtaining registration under GST. The move was in line with the Government's policy to promote *ease of doing business*.

21.1.6 Goods and Services Taxpayer Identification Number (GSTIN): All the business entities registering under GST are provided a unique identification number known as GSTIN or GST Identification Number.

During pre-GST era, business entities were registered under various Central and State tax authorities. Under GST regime, different identification numbers have been replaced by a single registration number, i.e. GSTIN. This has ensured better administration by the authorities and greater tax compliance by taxpayers.

Every taxpayer is assigned a state-wise PAN-based GSTIN, which is 15 digits long as in the below hypothetical example.

27 ABCDEFGHIJ 2 Z 5

- The first two digits of GSTIN represent the state code according to Indian Census 2011. Each state has a unique two digit code like 27 for Maharashtra.
- The next ten digits of GSTIN are the PAN number of the taxpayer.
- The 13th digit indicates the number of registrations an entity has within a state for the same PAN. It is an alpha-numeric number (first 1-9 and then A-Z) and is assigned on the basis of number of registrations a legal entity (having the same PAN) has within one state. For example, if a legal entity has one registration only within a state then it will be assigned the number 1 as 13th digit of the GSTIN. If the same legal entity gets second registration for a second business vertical within the same state, then the 13th digit of GSTIN assigned to this entity will become 2 (as in the above hypothetical example). Similarly, if an entity has 10 registrations in the same state then it will be assigned letter A in the 13th place, B in case it has 11 registrations and so on up to Z. In this way, up to 35 (9 + 26) business verticals of any legal entity can be registered within a state using this system.
- The fourteenth digit currently has no use and therefore is Z by default.
- The last digit is a check code which is used for detection of errors.

Following are the two ways to get registered for GST after which GSTIN is provided.

1. GST online portal; or
2. GST Seva Kendras set up by Government of India.

It is mandatory to display the certificate of registration (Form GST REG-06) in a prominent location at the principal place of business and at every additional place(s) of business.

It is mandatory to display the GSTIN on the name board exhibited at the entry of the principal place of business and at every additional place(s) of business.

Persons registered under the Composition Scheme must mention the words "GST Composition Taxable Person" on every notice or signboard displayed at a prominent place at both the principal and the additional place(s) of business.

In its Twenty-eighth Meeting held on July 21, 2018, the GST Council took the following decisions as regards registration:

1. Taxpayers may opt for multiple registrations within a State/Union territory in respect of multiple places of business located within the same State/Union territory.
2. Mandatory registration is required for only those e-commerce operators who are required to collect tax at source.
3. Registration to remain temporarily suspended while cancellation of registration is under process, so that the taxpayer is relieved of continued compliance under the law.

21.1.7 Unique Identification Number (UIN) under GST: UIN is a special class of GST registration for foreign diplomatic missions and embassies which are not liable to taxes in the Indian territory. Any amount of tax (direct or indirect) collected from such bodies is refunded back to them.

The following organizations can apply for a UIN:

1. A specialized agency of the United Nations Organization.
2. A Multilateral Financial Institution and Organization notified under the United Nations (Privileges and Immunities) Act, 1947.
3. Consulate or Embassy of foreign countries.
4. Any other person or class of persons as notified by the Commissioner.

The organizations listed above are granted UIN. This allows the body to receive tax refund on inward supplies of goods and services (purchases).

GSTIN and UIN are two different types of identification numbers under GST.

Goods and Services Tax Identification Number (GSTIN) is allotted to regular taxpayers who are required to collect GST and file GST returns. UIN is allotted to only the above-mentioned organization.

The organization must apply for UIN using Form GST REG-13. If the proper officer is satisfied, he will assign a UIN and issue a certificate in Form GST REG-06 within 3 working days from the date of the submission of the application.

Every UIN holder must file GSTR-11 by 28th of next month in order to claim refund of the taxes paid on his inward supplies. GSTR-11 will contain details of such supplies of taxable goods and/or services.

GSTR-11 will contain details of such supplies of taxable goods and/or services.

A UIN holder is not allowed to add or modify any details in GSTR-11. The information is auto-populated information from seller's GSTR-1 (sales).

The taxable supplier (normal registered taxpayer under GST) while supplying to a UIN organization must:

1. Mention the UIN on the invoices.
2. Treat such sales as supplies to another registered person (B2B).
3. Invoices should be uploaded in the same manner as for normal B2B sales.

As mentioned before, refunds can be claimed only through GSTR-11. The return must be filed within 6 months from the last day of the quarter in which supply was received.

For example, consider a UIN holder that received purchases on October 10, 2018. The last day of the quarter of receiving the supplies is December 31, 2018. The deadline to claim the refund is 6 months from then, June 30, 2019. Beyond the 6 month deadline, the refund will lapse.

21.1.8 Advantages of Registration: Registration under GST regime confers the following advantages to the business:

1. Legally recognized as supplier of goods/services.
2. Legally authorized to collect tax from his purchasers.
3. Proper accounting of taxes paid on the inputs which can be utilized for payment of GST due on supply of goods/services by the business.

In short, without registration a person can neither collect GST from his customers nor claim any input tax credit.

21.2 Tax Invoice, Credit and Debit Notes

21.2.1 Tax Invoice: Invoicing forms a crucial function when it comes to the execution of a transaction. Invoice is the basic document for recording sale/purchase in books of account. In common parlance, invoice is a commercial instrument issued by a seller to a buyer. It: (a) identifies the seller and the buyer, (b) lists, describes and quantifies the items sold, (c) shows the date of transaction, (d) mentions the prices and discounts, if any and (e) records the terms of delivery and payment.

Under GST, tax invoice (or simply invoice) is an important document. It not only evidences the supply of goods or services, but is also an essential document for the purchaser to claim input tax credit. GST is chargeable at the time of supply. Invoice is an important indicator of the time of supply. [4]

A. Who is Liable to Issue a Tax Invoice? Every registered person (other than a composition scheme dealer or a person supplying exempted goods/services) supplying goods/services is required to issue tax invoice. Composition scheme dealer or a person supplying exempted goods/services shall issue a bill of supply instead of tax invoice.

Section 31 of the CGST Act, 2017 mandates the issuance of an invoice or a bill of supply for every supply of goods/services. [5]

A registered person may not issue tax invoice or bill of supply if the value of the goods/services supplied is less than ₹ 200, subject to the condition that the recipient is not a registered person and the recipient does not ask for such invoice. If the recipient asks for the invoice then the same must be issued, irrespective of the value. In such cases, the registered person shall issue a consolidated invoice at the end of the day in respect of all such supplies.

The law provides for issuance of tax invoice within prescribed period. Tax invoice for goods shall be issued on or before the time of removal/delivery of goods. In case of continuous supply of goods, it shall be issued on or before the time of issue of statement of accounts/receipt of payment. In the case of supply of services, it shall be issued within 30 days from the date of provision of service.

B. Contents of the Invoice: The law mentions the contents of the invoice issued by a supplier. The following items, among others, must be clearly mentioned on a tax invoice:

1. Supplier's GST identification number (GSTIN) and GSTIN of the recipient, if he/she is registered.
2. Taxable value, tax rate and tax amount payable.
3. Place of supply along with the name of the state, in case of inter-state supply.
4. Signature or digital signature of the supplier or his authorized representative.

Tax invoice should contain HSN code of goods/services. However, as a measure of relief for MSMEs, a taxpayer whose turnover in the preceding financial year did not exceed ₹ 1.5 crore is not required to mention HSN code in tax invoice. Similarly, a taxpayer whose turnover in the preceding year exceeded ₹ 1.5 crore but did not exceed ₹ 5 crore is required to mention only first two digits of HSN Code, i.e. chapter number. Furthermore, if such turnover exceeded ₹ 5 crore, the tax invoice should mention four digits of the Code.

Persons who are in the business of exports/imports are mandatorily required to follow eight digits HSN Code.

For the full list of items that must be included in a tax invoice, see Rule 46 of the CGST Rules, 2017.

In the case of supply of goods, tax invoice has to be prepared in triplicate. The original copy is meant for buyer, duplicate for transporter and triplicate for record of the seller. In the case of services, the invoice has to be prepared in duplicate, original for the buyer and duplicate for supplier.

21.2.2 Electronic Invoicing (E-invoicing): In its Thirty-fifth Meeting held on June 21, 2019, the GST Council decided to introduce e-invoicing in a phased manner for business-to business (B2B) transactions. Phase I is proposed to be voluntary and will be rolled out in January 2020. E-invoicing would help tax authorities in combating the menace of tax evasion.

21.2.3 Electronic Ticketing (E-ticketing) for Multiplexes: In its Thirty-fifth Meeting held on June 21, 2019, the GST Council made it mandatory for multiplexes to shift to an electronic ticketing system. Registered multiplexes shall be required to issue a tax invoice electronically. E-tickets issued by them shall be deemed to be tax invoices. This move was aimed at curbing possible tax evasion.

21.2.4 Credit and Debit Notes: Section 34 of the Act deals with credit and debit notes.

A registered supplier may issue to the recipient a credit note under the following circumstances:

1. Where a tax invoice has been issued for supply of any goods/services and the taxable

value or tax charged in that tax invoice is found to exceed the taxable value or tax payable in respect of such supply.

2. Where the goods supplied are returned by the recipient or where goods/services supplied are found to be deficient.

Barring the two cases mentioned above, credit note cannot be issued. A credit note should contain the details as prescribed by Rule 53 of the CGST Rules, 2017.

A registered supplier may issue to the recipient a debit note under the following circumstances:

1. Where a tax invoice has been issued for supply of any goods/services and the taxable value or tax charged in that invoice is found to be less than the taxable value or tax payable in respect of such supply.

A debit note should contain the details as prescribed by Rule 53 of CGST Rules, 2017.

21.3 Accounts and Records

21.3.1 Accounts and Other Records: In this connection, Section 35 of the CGST Act, 2017 reads as follows, "(1) Every registered person shall keep and maintain, at his principal place of business, as mentioned in the certificate of registration, a true and correct account of: (a) production or manufacture of goods; (b) inward and outward supply of goods or services or both; (c) stock of goods; (d) input tax credit availed; (e) output tax payable and paid; and (f) such other particulars as may be prescribed:

Provided that where more than one place of business is specified in the certificate of registration, the accounts relating to each place of business shall be kept at such places of business:

Provided further that the registered person may keep and maintain such accounts and other particulars in electronic form in such manner as may be prescribed".

Taxpayers having turnover exceeding the prescribed limit are also required to get their accounts audited by a chartered accountant or a cost accountant, and submit a copy of the audited annual accounts with the annual return. In addition, they would also be required to submit a reconciliation statement, reconciling the value of supplies declared in the return furnished for the year with the audited annual financial statement, and any other documents as may be prescribed.

21.3.2 Period of Retention of Records: Section 36 of the CGST Act, 2017, states, "Every registered person required to keep and maintain books of account or other records in accordance with the provisions of sub-section (1) of Section 35 shall retain them until the expiry of seventy-two months from the due date of furnishing of annual return for the year pertaining to such accounts and records".

21.4 Filing of Returns

Filing return under the GST regime is crucial as non-compliance or delay can result in penalties and adversely affect taxpayer's compliance rating and timely refunds. Sections 37 to 45 of the CGST Act, 2017 cover different types of GST returns.

21.4.1 General Guidelines: Under GST, a regular taxpayer needs to furnish monthly returns and one annual return. There are separate returns for a taxpayer registered under composition scheme, non-resident taxpayer, taxpayer registered as an input service distributor, a person liable to deduct or collect tax at source and a person granted unique identification number (UIN). It is noteworthy that a taxpayer is not required to file all types of returns. Actually, taxpayers are required to file returns depending on the activities they undertake.

Returns filed by taxpayers serve the following purposes:

1. Mode for transfer of information to tax administration.
2. Compliance verification programme of tax administration.
3. Finalization of the tax liabilities of the taxpayer within stipulated period of limitation; to declare tax liability for a given period.
4. Providing necessary inputs for taking policy decision.
5. Management of audit and anti-evasion programmes of tax administration.

Returns are self-assessed by the registered persons. A taxable person can take help of GST practitioner in filing returns etc. He can file return through GST Suvidha Providers (GSP). [6]

There is a provision for electronic filing of returns by different classes of persons at different cut-off dates. Returns, that allow the auto-population of data from the vendors and automated matching of invoices, are filed online by a normal/casual taxpayer in a sequential manner within different cut-off dates.

It may be noted that most of the returns are auto-generated by the GSTN system and the dealer is expected to validate the data and also fill in the missing data. The payment of tax due is a must for filing valid returns under the GST regime.

21.4.2 Simplification Measures: The return filing process, which faced severe criticism in the initial months of the roll out of GST, was subsequently revamped for simplification.

In its Twenty-seventh meeting held on May 4, 2018, the GST Council had approved the basic principles of GST return design and directed the law committee to finalize the return formats and changes in law. In its Twenty-eighth Meeting held on July 21, 2018, the GST Council approved the new return formats and associated changes in law to simplify the filing of returns. The formats and business processes approved in this meeting were in line with the basic principles approved in the Twenty-seventh meeting with one major change, i.e. the option of filing quarterly return with monthly payment of tax in a simplified return format by small taxpayers.

The layout of the three key forms SAHAJ, SUGAM and Normal (Monthly and Quarterly) were released on the GST portal. Also, the new Section 43A in the CGST (Amendment) Act laid a foundation for the new return filing system.

The new return filing system was introduced on a trial basis from April 1, 2019 and was scheduled to be introduced on mandatory basis from July 1, 2019. However, it was postponed to October 1, 2019.

21.4.3 New GST Return Filing System: On June 11, 2019, Government unveiled a transition plan for taxpayers under GST to switch to new and simpler return forms.

There are three main components to the new return: one main return (Form GST RET-1) and two annexures (Form GST ANX-1 and Form GST ANX-2).

From July 1, 2019, users would be able to upload invoices using the Form GST ANX-1 offline tool on trial basis for familiarisation. They would also be able to view and download, the inward supply of invoices using the Form GST ANX-2 offline tool under the trial programme.

For 3 months between July to September, 2019, the new return system (ANX-1 and ANX-2 only) would be available for trial for taxpayers to make themselves familiar with the new system. This trial would have no impact at the back end on the tax liability or input tax credit of the taxpayer. In this period, taxpayers shall continue to fulfil their compliances by filing Form GSTR-1 and Form GSTR-3B, i.e. taxpayers would continue to file their outward supply details in Form GSTR-1 on monthly or quarterly basis and return in Form GSTR-3B on monthly basis.

From October 1, 2019 onwards, Form GST ANX-1 shall be compulsory and Form GSTR-1 would be replaced by Form GST ANX-1.

Large taxpayers, with aggregate annual turnover over ₹ 5 crore in the previous financial year, would upload their monthly Form GST ANX-1 from October 1, 2019 onwards. However, small taxpayers, with turnover up to ₹ 5 crore, will need to file the first compulsory quarterly Form GST ANX-1 only in January, 2020 for the quarter October to December, 2019.

Form GST ANX-2 may be viewed simultaneously during this period but no action shall be allowed on such Form GST ANX-2.

For October and November, 2019, large taxpayers would continue to file Form GSTR-3B on monthly basis. They would file their first Form GST RET-01 for the month of December 2019 by 20th January 2020.

The small taxpayers would stop filing Form GSTR-3B and would start filing Form GST PMT-08 from October 2019 onwards. They would file their first Form GST-RET-01 for the quarter October 2019 to December 2019 from 20th January 2020. From January 2020 onwards, all taxpayers shall be filing Form GST RET-01 and Form GSTR-3B shall be completely phased out.

In its Twenty-fifth Meeting held on June 21, 2019, the GST Council decided that the new GST return filing system will be applicable fully from January 1, 2020.

21.4.4 Late Fee: Late fee forms an important component of the GST payment and is incurred by businesses in case of delay in submitting or filing GST returns. As per GST laws, late fee is an amount charged for delay in filing GST returns. It can be referred to as an overdue fine. When a GST registered business misses filing GST returns within the prescribed due dates, some amount of late fees is charged. The late fee is also applicable for the delay in filing NIL returns (i.e. no figures to declare for sales or purchases for the month). The amount of late fee depends upon the number of days of delay from the due date.

21.5 Compliance Controversy

Although much of the dust created by GST has settled down, still there are differences of opinion as regards the compliance burden of GST.

It may be recalled that in the pre-GST era, large businesses were required to file four returns dealing with Union excise duty, service tax, state VAT and Central sales tax (CST). Now, all these have been compressed into GST. The earlier process also involved filing of returns multiple times in a year and, in the case of VAT, returns had to be submitted in every state where goods were sold.

Post-GST, compliance burden, in general, has increased for service providers as compared to suppliers of goods. For example, a telecom company had to file two service tax returns annually in the pre-GST era. Post-GST, it is required to file one return every month in each state it operates in. Conversely, manufactures who had to file multiple returns under different tax laws are now required to file returns under a single GST law.

Frankly, business entities in India can broadly be classified into two groups: those which are doing business honestly and those which are following dubious methods like *Kuchha* bill or *purchi* system or some other hanky-panky mode for business transactions. The second category of business entities is finding it difficult to switch over to the new technology-based system. The old system was mainly manual and opaque while the new system is IT-based and hence transparent. Offline system has given way to online transactions. It would be better if *kuchha* bill practitioners adjust to the new system and get themselves registered under GST.

As regards honest business entities, again there are two categories: large business entities and small business entities. Large firms can hire the services of chartered accountants, software engineers, computer operators to meet the compliance requirements of GST regime. The real problem of compliance lies with small businesses who cannot afford the services of experts to comply with GST laws and procedures. However, there are provisions (threshold limit of turnover and composition scheme) to reduce compliance burden of small players, albeit such provisions need to be liberalized and strengthened.

To sum up, GST is a tax reform of revolutionary proportions. Some dislocations and disruptions are inevitable. It is unreasonable to expect a foolproof system from day one, much less in the case of a game-changing tax reform like GST. These transitory disruptions and dislocations suffered by individuals, families, firms and governments are the price a country pays to move forward with the comity of developed nations. Status quo is always comfortable. However, it is not a good option when the rest of the world is moving forward.

GST requires a very high level of compliance. The age of hand-written ledgers, account books, balance sheets and manual record-keeping is gone. Everything is now online—from tax payment to filing of returns and to claiming of refunds. Moreover, IT-based tax information has to be updated regularly.

Relevant authorities (GST Council and tax departments of Central and State Governments) are seized of the problems being faced by the GST assesses. Measures have been taken to solve problems, address concerns and redress grievances of assesses, particularly small businesses.

Endnotes

1. For the meaning of expression *aggregate turnover*, see section section 35.2 of chapter 35 of this book.
2. Every person who makes a supply from the territorial waters of India shall obtain registration in the coastal State or Union territory where the nearest point of the appropriate baseline is located (Section 25 of the CGST Act, 2017). States have the powers to levy tax on economic activity within territorial waters. Power to collect GST in territorial waters has been delegated by the Central Government to the States. Territorial waters of India extend to a distance of 12 nautical miles into sea from the nearest point of the appropriate baseline.
   With reference to supplies in territorial waters, Section 9 of the IGST Act, 2017 reads, "...(a) where the location of the supplier is in the territorial waters, the location of such supplier; or (b) where the place of supply is in the territorial waters, the place of supply, shall be deemed to be in the coastal State or Union territory where the nearest point of the appropriate baseline is located".
   See also endnote 1 of chapter 30 of this book.
3. **Business Vertical:** It means a distinguishable component of an enterprise that is engaged in the supply of individual goods or services or a group of related goods or services which is subject to risks and returns that are different from those of the other business verticals. Explanation—factors that should be considered in determining whether goods or services are related include: (a) the nature of the goods or services; (b) the nature of the production processes; (c) the type or class of customers for the goods or services; (d) the methods used to distribute the goods or supply of services; and (e) the nature of regulatory environment (wherever applicable), including banking, insurance, or public utilities [Section 2(18) of the CGST Act].
4. For details on time of supply, see section 13.5 of chapter 13 of this book.
5. For details on bill of supply, see endnote 4 of chapter 36 of this book.
6. GSPs are third-party service providers, having access to the GST system, who can help taxpayers for GST compliance. They have applications for return filing etc. for tax payers.

22

GST Payments, Tax Deduction at Source (TDS), Tax Collection at Source (TCS), Reverse Charge Mechanism (RCM) and Refunds

Every registered person is required to compute his tax liability on a monthly basis by setting off the input tax credit against the outward tax liability. If there is any balance tax liability, the same is required to be paid to the government.

22.1 GST Payments

Normally, GST is payable when supply is made or when payment is received, whichever is earlier.

GST payment is to be made by the taxable person at the time of supply of goods as explained in Section 12 of the CGST Act, 2017 and at the time of supply of services as explained in section 13 of the same Act. The time is generally the earliest of one of the three events, namely receiving payment, issuance of invoice or completion of supply. Different situations envisaged and different tax points have been explained in the aforesaid sections. Also, registered persons making supply of goods are required to make payment of tax at the time of the issuance of invoice and not at the time when advances are received.

GST of current month is payable by 20th of the following month. GST return filing requires that every month—once GSTR-1 is filed to report sales—one must file GSTR-3B to report the ITC and make necessary GST payment. Also, if a refund is to be claimed the same should be done by filing the relevant refund-related form.

Liability to pay tax arises when the taxable person crosses the threshold limits of turnover, except in certain specified cases where the taxable person is liable to pay GST even though he has not crossed the threshold limit. [1]

22.1.1 Categories of GST Payment: Tax to be paid under GST is mainly divided into 5 categories:

- **CGST:** This is paid into the account of the Central Government when supplies are made within a state/UT (intra-state supplies).
- **SGST:** This is paid into the account of the concerned State Government when supplies are made within that State (intra-state supplies).
- **UT-GST:** This is paid into the account of the concerned UT Administration when supplies are made within that UT (intra-UT supplies).
- **IGST:** This is paid into the account of the Central Government when inter-state supplies are made. IGST has components of both CGST and SGST.
- **Compensation Cess:** A cess on certain specified luxury and *sin* goods is imposed to compensate States for any revenue loss on account of implementation of GST. The revenue collected from compensation cess is credited to a non-lapsable fund known

as Goods and Services Tax Compensation Fund.

For details of various types of GST mentioned above, see chapter 12 of this book.

Apart from above payments, certain categories of registered persons are required to pay TDS and TCS into the government account.

22.1.2 Calculation of GST Payment: Ordinarily, ITC is reduced from outward tax liability to calculate the total GST payment to be made. TDS/TCS is reduced from the total GST to arrive at the net payable figure. Interest and late fees, if any, are added to arrive at the final amount. If GST is short paid, unpaid or paid late, interest at the rate of 18 percent is required to be paid by the dealer. Also, a penalty is to be paid which is higher of ₹ 10,000 or 10 percent of the tax short paid or unpaid. ITC cannot be claimed on interest and late fees. Both interest and late fees are required to be paid in cash.

In fact, the manner of calculation differs for different types of dealers.

A. Regular Dealers: A regular dealer is liable to pay GST on the outward supplies made and can also claim ITC on the purchases made by him. GST payable by a regular dealer is the difference between the outward tax liability and the ITC.

B. Composition Scheme Dealer: GST payment by a composition scheme dealer is relatively simpler. He has to pay a fixed percentage of GST on the total outward supplies made. GST is to be paid based on the type of business of a composition scheme dealer.

For details on composition scheme, see chapter 36 of this book.

22.1.3 Who Should Make the GST Payment? Following dealers are required to make GST payment.

1. A registered dealer if GST liability exists.
2. A registered dealer required to pay tax under reverse charge mechanism (RCM). This provision is not in force currently.
3. Agencies required to deduct tax at source (TDS).
4. E-commerce operators required to collect tax at source (TCS).

GST payment is to be made when GSTR-3 is filed, i.e. by 20th of the next month.

22.1.4 Methods of GST Payment: Payment of GST can be made electronically with a common *challan* (i.e. document for payment of taxes) for all the taxes.

GST payment can be made in 2 ways.

A. Payment through Credit Ledger: Taxpayers are allowed to take credit of taxes paid on inputs and utilize the same for payment of output tax. Payment can be made through debit of credit ledger of the taxpayer maintained on the common portal of GSTN. The credit can be taken only for payment of tax. Interest, penalty and late fees cannot be paid by utilizing ITC.

B. Payment through Cash Ledger: Payment can be made by debiting the cash ledger of the taxpayer maintained on the common portal of GSTN. Money can be deposited in the cash ledger by different modes, namely:

- E-payment (internet banking, credit card, debit card).
- Real time gross settlement (RTGS). [2]
- National electronic funds transfer (NEFT). [3]
- Over the counter payment in branches of banks authorized to accept deposit of GST.

GST payments can be made online or offline. The challan has to be generated on GST portal for both online and offline GST payments. Where tax liability is more than ₹ 10,000, it is mandatory to pay taxes online.

22.1.5 Electronic Ledgers: There are 3 ledgers prescribed by the government which are required to be maintained by every taxpayer. These ledgers are maintained electronically on the GST portal. [4]

A. Credit Ledger: It shows ITC as self-assessed in monthly returns. It records all the taxes paid on the inputs. The credit in this ledger can be used to make payment of *tax only* and no other amounts such as interest, penalty, fee etc.

B. Cash Ledger: It reflects all deposits made in cash, and TDS/TCS made on account of the taxpayer. This ledger can be used for making any payment on account of GST. It displays the total amount deposited by the taxpayer towards discharge of his tax liability.

C. Liability Register: It reflects the total tax liability of a taxpayer (after netting) for the particular month. This ledger is automatically displayed on the dashboard of a GST taxpayer.

22.1.6 GST Payment in Case of Job Work: Section 2(61) of the MGL provides that *job work* means undertaking any treatment or process by a person on goods belonging to another registered taxable person and the expression *job worker* shall be construed accordingly.

The principal has the option to send taxable goods without payment of GST to a job worker and bring it back, after processing, to any of his own place of business, for supplying such goods on payment of GST or export them. The principal also has the option to directly supply final products to end customers on payment of GST or export from the premises of job worker itself, subject to fulfilment of applicable conditions. GST credit is allowed in case of direct receipt of inputs or capital goods by the job worker, subject to receipt of goods back by the principal within specified period.

22.1.7 Features of GST Payment Process: The payment process under GST regime has the following features:

1. Electronically-generated *challan* from GSTN Common Portal in all modes of payment, i.e. use of manually prepared challan is not allowed.
2. Hassle free, anytime, anywhere mode of payment of tax.
3. Convenience of making payment online.
4. Logical tax collection data in electronic format.
5. Faster remittance of tax revenue to the government account.
6. Paperless transactions.
7. Speedy accounting and reporting.
8. Electronic reconciliation of all receipts.
9. Warehousing of digital challan.

22.2 Tax Deduction at Source (TDS)

22.2.1 What is TDS: Tax deduction at source (also called withholding tax) is a system of collecting tax from payments made. Intermediaries (or third parties) do the job on behalf of the government as regards assessment of the taxable base and the collection of tax thereon.

Generally, a fixed percentage is withheld from the payment made and the same is deposited in the government's account. At the time of filing the return, the taxpayer encloses withholding tax receipts, and in case of overpayment can claim refund of tax.

Tax deduction at source is beneficial for the government because it reduces the possibility of tax evasion, ensures prompt tax payment, and simplifies tax collection.

However, tax withholding involves additional paper work on the part of tax deductors. It also adds to the burden of taxpayers who have to obtain tax deduction certificates from deductors, fill additional tax forms, and wait for refunds.

There are provisions under various sections of the Income Tax Act, 1961 regarding TDS, e.g. deduction of tax from salaries (Section 192). Other incomes covered under the scheme of TDS include fees for professional/technical services, interest, dividends, rent from real estate, commission from insurance, sale of lottery tickets, winnings from lotteries, crossword puzzles and horse racing etc.

Persons responsible for making payments of such specified incomes are liable to deduct tax at source on such payments and deposit the same with the Government within the stipulated time.

22.2.2 TDS under GST Law: GST law provides for tax deduction at source (TDS) by specified categories of persons (called deductors) from the payment made to the suppliers of taxable goods/services (called deductees) at the prescribed rate.

In this connection, Section 51 of the CGST Act, 2017 reads as follows, "(1) Notwithstanding anything to the contrary contained in this Act, the Government may mandate: (a) a department or establishment of the Central Government or State Government; or (b) local authority; or (c) Governmental agencies; or (d) such persons or category of persons as may be notified by the Government on the recommendations of the Council, (hereafter in this section referred to as "the deductor"), to deduct tax at the rate of one percent from the payment made or credited to the supplier (hereafter in this section referred to as "the deductee") of taxable goods or services or both, where the total value of such supply, under a contract, exceeds two lakh and fifty thousand rupees:

Provided that no deduction shall be made if the location of the supplier and the place of supply is in a State or Union territory which is different from the State or as the case may be, Union territory of registration of the recipient".

Twenty-sixth Meeting of the GST Council held on March 10, 2018 decided to postpone the applicability of TDS until June 30, 2018. Provisions relating to TDS were again deferred for another 3 months till September-end, 2018.

Finally, the provisions for TDS were operationalized w.e.f. October 1, 2018.

22.2.3 Persons Liable to Deduct Tax: As per provisions of the GST law, the following persons are mandatorily required to deduct tax at source:

- A department or establishment of the Central Government or State Government; or
- Local authority; or
- Governmental agencies; or
- Such persons or category of persons as may be notified by the Government on the recommendations of the Council.

As per a notification dated September 15, 2017, the following class of persons are also required to deduct tax at source.

- An authority or a board or any other body: (i) set up by an Act of Parliament or a State Legislature; or (ii) established by any Government, with fifty-one percent or more participation by way of equity or control, to carry out any function.
- Society established by the Central/State Government or a Local Authority under the Societies Registration Act, 1860.
- Public sector undertakings.

Supply covers both goods and services by suppliers to the Government Departments and others as listed above. Some examples of supply of goods to such recipients include stationery items, furniture, air-conditioners, electrical goods, books and periodicals, and toiletry items. Examples of supply of services include procurement of security services, car rental services, maintenance services, rental of office machines etc. There can be supplies which are composite in nature as, for example, work contracts for roads, bridges, buildings, renovation and repairs.

22.2.4 When Tax Deduction is Required? Tax is required to be deducted from the payment made/credit to a supplier if the total *value of supply under a contract* in respect of supply of taxable goods or services or both exceeds ₹ 2,50,000. This value shall exclude taxes leviable under GST (CGST, SGST, UT-GST, IGST, compensation cess).

A. Conditions for and Rate of Deduction: TDS is required if the following conditions are satisfied:

1. Total value of taxable supply is greater than ₹ 2,50,000 under a single contract.
2. If the contract is made for both taxable supply and exempted supply, deduction will be made if the total value of taxable supply in the contract exceeds ₹ 2,50,000.
3. Where the location of the supplier and the place of supply are in the same state (Kerala), it is an intra-state supply and TDS @ 1 percent each for CGST and SGST is required (see row 2 of Table 22.1).
4. Where the location of the supplier is in State A (Delhi) and the place of supply is in State B (Kerala), it is an inter-state supply and TDS @ 2 percent for IGST is required if the deductor is registered in State B (Kerala) (see row 3 of Table 22.1).
5. Where the location of the supplier is in State A (Delhi) and the place of supply is in State B (Kerala), it is an inter-state supply and TDS @ 2 percent for IGST is required if the deductor is registered in State A (Delhi) (see row 4 of Table 22.1).
6. When advance is paid to a supplier for supply of taxable goods or services or both.

B. When Tax Deduction is not Required: TDS is not required in the following situations:

1. Total value of taxable supply is less than or equal to ₹ 2,50,000.
2. Contract value is greater than ₹ 2,50,000 for both taxable supply and exempted supply, but the value of taxable supply under the said contract is less than or equal to ₹ 2,50,000.
3. Receipt of goods which are exempt, e.g. hearing aids.
4. Receipt of services which are exempt, e.g. supply of labour for digging a pond for

the purpose of fisheries.

5. Goods on which GST is not leviable (alcohol for human consumption and five petroleum products, viz.: (a) petroleum crude, (b) high speed diesel, (c) motor spirit (commonly known as petrol), (d) natural gas and (e) aviation turbine fuel.
6. Where the location of the supplier is in State A (Delhi) and the place of supply is also in State A (Delhi), but the deductor is registered in State B (Kerala) (see row 5 of Table 22.1).
7. All activities or transactions specified in Schedule III of the CGST Act, 2017, irrespective of the value.
8. Where the tax is to be paid on reverse charge by the recipient, i.e. the deductee.
9. Where the payment is made to an unregistered supplier.
10. Where the payment relates to compensation cess component.

Table 22.1: Different TDS Scenarios Related to Location of Supplier, Place of Supply and State of Registration of Recipient

(Taxable contract value is greater than ₹ 2,50,000 in all cases)

Scenario	Location of supplier	Place of supply	State of registration of recipient	Type of supply	Tax applicable	TDS
Government of Kerala purchases taxable goods from a supplier in Kochi	Kochi	Kochi	Kerala	Intra-state	CGST + SGST	Yes
Government of Kerala purchases taxable goods from a supplier in Delhi	Delhi	Kerala	Kerala	Inter-state	IGST	Yes
Government of Delhi engages a contractor of Delhi for renovation of its guest house in Kerala.	Delhi	Kerala	Delhi	Inter-state	IGST	Yes
Government of Kerala engages a contractor of Delhi for renovation of Kerala House in Delhi	Delhi	Delhi	Kerala	Intra-state	CGST + SGST	No

C. Other TDS Requirements: These are as under:

1. Tax deductor is required to take registration and there is no threshold limit for this. Registration is to be done through common portal.
2. Payment of deducted tax is to be made within 10 days after the end of the month in which deduction was made. The payment is to be made to the appropriate government, i.e. Central Government in case of CGST and IGST and State Government in case of SGST.
3. Return in Form GSTR-7 is to be submitted within 10 days after the end of the month in which deduction was made. System generated TDS certificate in Form GSTR-7A

is to be furnished to the deductee within 5 days of crediting payment of TDS to the government, i.e. submitting Form GSTR-7 (Rule 66 of the CGST Rules, 2017).

4. There are provisions in the law for late fee, interest penalty etc.
5. There are provisions in the law for refund if excess amount is deducted.

With the deduction of tax and submission of return in Form GSTR-7, the amount deducted becomes available in Form GSTR-2A/4A of the registered deductee and the same is credited in his electronic cash ledger. The deductee can utilize this amount for discharging his tax liabilities.

22.3 Tax Collection at Source (TCS)

TCS means that any dealer selling through e-commerce will receive payment after deduction of tax at specified rate. Since TCS is mainly for e-commerce aggregators, it is necessary to understand what is e-commerce and who is an electronic commerce operator.

22.3.1 Electronic Commerce and Electronic Commerce Operator: Electronic commerce means the supply of goods or services or both, including digital products over digital or electronic network [Section 2(44) of the CGST Act, 2017]. Electronic commerce operator means any person who owns, operates or manages digital or electronic facility or platform for electronic commerce [Section 2(45) of the CGST Act, 2017].

As per Section 9(5) of the CGST Act, 2017, "The Government may, on the recommendations of the Council, by notification, specify categories of services the tax on intra-State supplies of which shall be paid by the electronic commerce operator if such services are supplied through it, and all the provisions of this Act shall apply to such electronic commerce operator as if he is the supplier liable for paying the tax in relation to the supply of such services:

Provided that where an electronic commerce operator does not have a physical presence in the taxable territory, any person representing such electronic commerce operator for any purpose in the taxable territory shall be liable to pay tax:

Provided further that where an electronic commerce operator does not have a physical presence in the taxable territory and also he does not have a representative in the said territory, such electronic commerce operator shall appoint a person in the taxable territory for the purpose of paying tax and such person shall be liable to pay tax".

It may be recalled that during pre-GST era supplying goods through e-commerce platform was not well-defined. E-commerce operators (like Amazon and Flipkart) were treated as facilitators by some states (like West Bengal and Kerala) and hence not required to register themselves for VAT. Contrarily, in some states (e.g. Uttar Pradesh) they were required to file a VAT declaration and other documents. Due to differential practices of states in this regard, there was lot of confusion and ambiguity. Under GST, there are clear-cut provisions applicable to e-commerce sector on all-India basis. There is no complication regarding inter-state movement of goods.

22.3.2 Legal Provisions for TCS: With regard to tax collection at source (TCS), sub-sections (1) and (3) of Section 52 of CGST Act, 2017 read as follows, " (1) Notwithstanding anything to the contrary contained in this Act, every electronic commerce operator (hereafter in this section referred to as the "operator"), not being an agent, shall collect an amount calculated at such rate not exceeding one percent, as may be notified by the Government on the recommendations of the Council, of the net value of taxable supplies made through it by other suppliers where the consideration with respect to such supplies is to be collected by the operator...(3) The amount collected under sub-section (1) shall be paid to the Government by the operator within ten days after the end of the month in which such collection is made, in such manner as may be prescribed".

Benefit of threshold exemption is not available to e-commerce operators and they are liable to be registered irrespective of the value of supply made by them.

Thus, Amazon is e-commerce operator because it is facilitating actual suppliers to supply goods through its platform.

If a person is supplying own products through his own hosting website then tax collection at source (TCS) will not take place because TCS is required when taxable supply is made through e-commerce operator by other supplier and consideration is collected by e-commerce operator. When someone is selling own product through own website there is no need for TCS. Here normal GST rate will be applicable.

If someone is purchasing goods from different vendors and selling such goods on his own website under his own billing, then TCS is not needed because supply is not made by other supplier.

Again, Amazon is e-commerce operator because it is facilitating suppliers to supply goods through its platform (popularly called market place model or fulfilment model). However, Amazon will not be treated as e-commerce operators in relation to those supplies which it makes on its own account (popularly called inventory model).

Twenty-sixth Meeting of the GST Council held on March 10, 2018 decided to postpone the applicability of TCS until June 30, 2018. Provisions relating to TCS were again deferred for another 3 months till September-end, 2018.

On September 13, 2018, Government notified the provision part of Section 52 of the CGST Act, 2017 which had been kept in abeyance since the rollout of GST on July 1, 2017. As per the notification, TCS provisions under GST regime took effect from October 1, 2018. Rate of TCS for intra-state supplies is 1 percent of net taxable supplies (0.5 percent CGST plus 0.5 percent SGST). Rate of TCS for inter-state supplies (IGST) is 1 percent of net taxable supplies.

Thus, e-commerce firms have to collect tax at the specified rate before making the payment to the supplier for proceeds of sale.

E-commerce operators had opposed TCS arguing that it would add to their compliance burden due to the cumbersome reporting provisions. E-commerce firms have to furnish a monthly statement and an annual statement containing details of the outward supplies. In addition, they have to deposit tax collected at source by 10th of the next month in which the tax was collected.

With the TCS provisions coming into force, tax authorities are empowered to monitor e-commerce transactions and ensure that suppliers selling their goods through e-commerce platforms do not get away with under-reporting their turnover.

TCS implementation as a tool to check tax evasion comes at a time when GST revenues are lagging behind budgeted targets and the tax authorities are struggling to stabilize revenues at higher level.

Government is hoping that TCS along with e-way bill implementation will prevent non-reporting and under-reporting of transactions thereby enlarging the taxpayer base.

22.3.3 No GST on Tax Collected at Source: Section 206C of the Income Tax Act, 1961 mandates a marginal tax to be collected at source on certain high-value transactions to ensure that those who make large purchases do not under-report their income. This tax is available as a credit at the time of making the income tax payment.

A circular issued in December 2018 had said that the value of the product on which GST is to be levied is inclusive of TCS. It led to confusion among traders as it amounted to a tax-on-tax.

In March 2019, the Finance Ministry provided relief to traders by withdrawing a rule that required them to charge GST on the compulsory income tax to be collected at source (TCS) from consumers who make high value purchases such as premium cars.

The Central Board of Indirect Taxes and Customs (CBIC) issued a circular in March 2019 clarifying that such income tax collected at source by dealers—over and above the value of the goods sold—and paid to the government on behalf of the consumer is not subject to GST.

CBIC said that the income tax department has clarified that the TCS was just an interim levy on the *possible income* of the buyer. There is a TCS of 1 percent on automobiles with an ex-showroom price of above ₹ 10 lakh.

For the purpose of determination of value of supply under GST, tax collected at source under the provisions of the Income Tax Act, 1961, would not be includible as it is an interim levy not having the character of tax.

The clarification came as a relief for businesses, especially in the automobile sector.,

22.4 Reverse Charge Mechanism (RCM)

Ordinarily, the supplier of goods/services is liable to pay GST. However, in specified cases like imports and other notified supplies, the liability may be cast on the recipient under the reverse charge mechanism.

22.4.1 What is Reverse Charge? As per Section 2(98) of the CGST Act, 2017, reverse charge means the liability to pay tax by the recipient of supply of goods or services or both instead of the supplier of such goods or services or both under sub-section (3) or sub-section (4) of Section 9 of the CGST Act, 2017, or under sub-section (3) or sub-section (4) of Section 5 of the IGST Act, 2017

Reverse charge means the liability to pay tax is on the recipient of supply of goods/services instead of the supplier of such goods/services in respect of notified categories of supply. Under reverse charge, the recipient of supplies becomes liable to pay the tax, i.e. the chargeability gets reversed. It is like a toll-free telephone number wherein the call is billed to the called party instead of the calling party.

22.4.2 Rationale for Reverse Charge: The rationale behind RCM is to enhance the tax base by covering unorganized sector. The best part about GST is its self-policing mechanism. Thus, a registered supplier shows the outward supplies in his return which, in turn, helps the recipient to be tracked, if he is a registered recipient. RCM comes in handy to track and check cases where supplier is unregistered and recipient is registered. Since registered taxpayers are required to pay GST on reverse charge basis when they purchase from an unregistered person, many registered businesses may stop transacting with micro and small businesses. Thus, RCM is a sort of indirect message to unregistered entities to fall in line by getting registered.

22.4.3 Two Kinds of Reverse Charge Scenario: There are two types of reverse charge scenarios provided in the GST law.

First is dependent on the nature of supply and/or nature of supplier. This scenario is covered by Section 9(3) of the CGST Act, 2017 and Section 5(3) of the IGST Act, 2017. As per these provisions, the Government may, on the recommendations of the GST Council, by notification, specify categories of supply of goods/services, the tax on which shall be paid on reverse charge basis by the recipient of such goods/services and all the provisions of these Acts shall apply to such recipient as if he is the person liable for paying the tax in relation to the supply of such goods/services.

Second scenario is covered by Section 9(4) of the CGST Act, 2017 and Section 5(4) of the IGST Act, 2017 where taxable supplies by any unregistered person to a registered person is covered. As per these provisions, the tax in respect of the supply of taxable goods or services or both by a supplier, who is not registered, to a registered person shall be paid by such person on reverse charge basis as the recipient and all the provisions of these Acts shall apply to such recipient as if he is the person liable for paying the tax in relation to the supply of such goods or services or both. Accordingly, wherever a registered person procures supplies from an unregistered supplier, he needs to pay GST on reverse charge basis. However, supplies, where the aggregate value of such supplies of goods/services received by a registered person from any or all the unregistered suppliers is less than ₹ 5,000 in a day, are exempted.

The provisions of Section 9(4) of the CGST Act, 2017 are not applicable to supplies made to a TDS deductor. Thus, Government entities which are TDS deductors under Section 51 of the CGST Act, 2017, need not pay GST under reverse charge in case of procurements from unregistered suppliers.

A person who is required to pay tax under reverse charge has to compulsorily register under GST and the threshold limit of turnover is not applicable to them.

A supplier cannot take ITC of GST paid on goods or services used to make supplies on which recipient is liable to pay tax.

22.4.4 Applicability of Reverse Charge: Reverse charge becomes applicable in following situations.

A. Supply from an Unregistered Person to a Registered Person: If a supplier, who is not registered under GST, supplies goods to a person who is registered, then reverse charge would apply. It means the tax will be paid by the recipient directly to the government, instead of the supplier. The registered dealer has to do self-invoicing [5] for the purchases made. For inter-state purchases, the buyer has to pay IGST, and for intra-state purchases he has to pay CGST and SGST.

B. Services through an E-commerce Operator: If an e-commerce operator supplies services, then reverse charge is applicable to him, i.e. he is liable to pay GST. If entity A provides services of beauticians and dieticians, then it is liable to collect GST from customers and pay it to the government, instead of the registered service providers.

C. Supply of Goods and Services Specified by Tax Authorities: Central Board of Indirect Taxes and Customs (CBIC) has issued a list of goods and services on which reverse charge is applicable.

GST paid under RCM would be available for input tax credit if goods/services purchased are used in the furtherance of business. If tax is payable under reverse charge, it has to be paid in cash through internet banking.

22.4.5 Time of Supply: The time of supply is the point when the supply is liable to GST. One of the factors relevant for determining time of supply is the person who is liable to pay tax. In reverse charge, recipient is liable to pay GST. Thus, time of supply for supplies under reverse charge is different from the supplies which are under forward charge.

In case of supply of goods, time of supply is earliest of the following:

1. Date of receipt of goods.
2. Date of payment as per books of account or date of debit in bank account, whichever is earlier.
3. Date immediately following thirty days from the date of issue of invoice or similar other document.

In case of supply of services, time of supply is earliest of the following:

1. Date of payment as per books of account or date of debit in bank account, whichever is earlier.
2. Date immediately following sixty days from the date of issue of invoice or similar other document.

Where it is not possible to determine time of supply using above methods, time of supply would be date of entry in the books of account of the recipient.

22.4.6 Compliances under RCM: In respect of supplies under RCM, following provisions of the law are noteworthy:

1. As per Section 31 of the CGST Act, 2017 read with Rule 46 of the CGST Rules, 2017, every tax invoice has to mention whether the tax in respect of supply in the invoice is payable on reverse charge. Similarly, this also needs to be mentioned in receipt voucher as well as refund voucher, if tax is payable on reverse charge.
2. Every registered person is required to keep and maintain records of all supplies attracting payment of tax on reverse charge.
3. Any amount payable under reverse charge shall be paid by debiting the electronic cash ledger. In other words, reverse charge liability cannot be discharged by using input tax credit. However, after discharging reverse charge liability, credit of the same can be taken by the recipient, if he is otherwise eligible.
4. Invoice level information in respect of all supplies attracting reverse charge, rate-

wise, are to be furnished separately in Table-4B of GSTR-1.

5. Advance paid for reverse charge supplies is also leviable to GST. The person making advance payment has to pay tax on reverse charge basis.

22.4.7 Supplies of Goods under RCM: These are listed in Table 22.2.

Table 22.2: Supplies of Goods under RCM

S. No.	Description of supply of goods	Supplier of goods	Recipient of goods
1.	Cashew nuts, not shelled or peeled	Agriculturist	Any registered person
2.	Bidi wrapper leaves (tendu)	Agriculturist	Any registered person
3.	Tobacco leaves	Agriculturist	Any registered person
4.	Silk yarn	Any person who manufactures silk yarn from raw silk or silk worm cocoons for supply of silk yarn	Any registered person
4A	Raw cotton	Agriculturist	Any registered person
5.	Supply of lottery	State Government, Union Territory or any local authority	Lottery distributor or selling agent
6.	Used vehicles, seized and confiscated goods, old and used goods, waste and scrap	Central Government, State Government, Union territory or a local authority	Any registered person
7.	Priority sector lending certificate	Any registered person	Any registered person

22.4.8 Supplies of Services under RCM: These are listed in Table 22.3.

Table 22.3 Supplies of Services under RCM

S. No.	Brief description of supply of services	Supplier of services	Recipient of services
1.	Goods transport agency (GTA) services	GTA which has not paid integrated tax at the rate of 12 percent.	Any factory, society, cooperative society etc. located in the taxable territory
2.	Legal services by advocate	An individual advocate including a senior advocate or firm of advocates	Any business entity located in the taxable territory
3.	Services supplied by an arbitral tribunal	An arbitral tribunal	Any business entity located in the taxable territory
4.	Services provided by way of sponsorship	Any person	Any body corporate or partnership firm

contd...

5.	Services supplied by the Central Government, State Government, Union territory or local authority (with some exceptions)	Central Government, State Government, Union territory or local authority	Any business entity located in the taxable territory
6.	Services supplied by a director of a company or a body corporate to the said company or the body corporate	A director of a company or a body corporate	The company or a body corporate located in the taxable territory
7.	Services supplied by an insurance agent to any person carrying on insurance business	An insurance agent	Any person carrying on insurance business, located in the taxable territory
8.	Services supplied by a recovery agent	A recovery agent	A banking company or a financial institution or a non-banking financial company, located in the taxable territory
9.	Services supplied by a person located in non-taxable territory by way of transportation of goods by a vessel from a place outside India up to the customs station of clearance in India	A person located in non-taxable territory	Importer located in the taxable territory
10.	Supply of services by an author, music composer, photographer, artist or the like	Author or music composer, photographer, artist, or the like	Publisher, music company, producer or the like, located in the taxable territory
11.	Supply of services by the members of Overseeing Committee to Reserve Bank of India	Members of Overseeing Committee constituted by the Reserve Bank of India	Reserve Bank of India

22.4.9: RCM in Abeyance: In its Twenty-second Meeting held on October 6, 2017, the GST Council suspended reverse charge mechanism till March 31, 2018 and called for the matter to be reviewed by a committee of experts.

In its Twenty-eighth Meeting held on July 21, 2018, the GST Council decided to apply GST on reverse charge basis on receipt of supplies from unregistered suppliers only on specified goods in case of certain notified classes of registered persons. RCM as such was suspended until September 2019.

It is all fine so long as registered taxpayers can purchase from unregistered persons without having to pay GST on reverse charge basis. Once the reverse charge provision comes into force, the situation may change to the disadvantage of small businesses.

22.5 Refunds

Ordinarily, when the tax paid is more than the liability, a situation of claiming refund arises. Section 54(1) of the CGST Act, 2017 states, "Any person claiming refund of any tax and interest, if any, paid on such tax or any other amount paid by him, may make an application before the expiry of two years from the relevant date in such form and manner as may be prescribed".

Under GST, the process of claiming a refund is standardized to avoid confusion. The process is online and time limits have also been set for the same.

22.5.1 Cases Where Refund Can be Claimed: These, *inter alia*, include as under:

1. ITC accumulation due to output being tax exempt or nil-rated.
2. Finalization of provisional assessment.
3. Refund of tax paid on purchases made by foreign embassies and UN bodies.
4. Export of goods/services.
5. Refund of tax for international tourists.

Suppose business entity A had GST liability of ₹ 1 lakh for the month of July. Owing to some mistake, it made a GST payment of ₹ 1.5 lakh. In other words, it made an excess GST payment of ₹ 50,000 which it can claim as refund. The time limit for claiming a refund is 2 years from the relevant date. The relevant date is different in different cases as shown in Table 22.4.

Table 22.4: Reasons and Relevant Dates for Claiming Refund

Reason for claiming refund	**Relevant date**
Excess payment of GST	Date of payment
Accumulated ITC because output is tax exempt or nil-rated.	Last date of financial year to which the credit belongs.
Finalization of provisional assessment	Date on which tax is adjusted.
Export of goods/services	Date of dispatch/loading/passing the frontier.

The refund application has to be made in Form RFD-01 within 2 years from the relevant date. The form should also be certified by a chartered accountant. If refund is paid with delay, an interest of 24 percent per annum is payable by the government.

Endnotes

1. For threshold limit of aggregate turnover for exemption from registration and payment of GST, see section 21.1.1 of chapter 21 of this book.
2. **National Electronic Funds Transfer (NEFT):** NEFT is an electronic message-based payment system which was introduced by the Reserve Bank of India (RBI) in November 2005. NEFT is a nation-wide payments system facilitating one-to-one fund transfer up to ₹ 2 lakh, usually on the same day.
3. **Real Time Gross Settlement (RTGS) System:** RTGS system was operationalised in March 2004. The system started operations with four banks and settled only inter-bank transactions.

Subsequently, the system was opened for settlement of customer transactions. RTGS is meant for large-value instantaneous fund transfers. The minimum amount to be remitted through RTGS is ₹ 2 lakh with no upper or maximum ceiling.

On June 6, 2019, RBI announced waiving off charges on NEFT and RTGS. The waiver became effective July 1, 2019.

4. The official GST portal www.gst.gov.in is a one-stop solution website for all information, filing, queries and other technicalities related to the new GST regime. The portal also has all the GST-related laws and downloadable files which a taxpayer requires under GST.
5. Self-invoicing is to be done when a registered person purchases goods/services from an unregistered supplier *and* such purchases fall under reverse charge. This is so because the supplier cannot issue a GST-compliant invoice to the buyer who becomes liable to pay tax on his behalf. Hence, self-invoicing becomes necessary.

23

Assessment, Scrutiny, Audit, Advance Ruling, Appeals, and Offences and Penalties

In order to address the issue of dual control over assessees and to ensure single interface, there is division of audit and assessment responsibilities between the Central and State Governments. Thus, all administrative control over 90 percent of taxpayers having turnover below ₹ 1.5 crore is vested with the State tax administration and the remaining 10 percent with the Centre. Assessees with a turnover above ₹ 1.5 crore are divided equally between the Centre and the States. Powers under the IGST Act are also cross-empowered on the same basis as under CGST and SGST Acts with few exceptions.

23.1 Assessment of Tax Payable

Assessment means determination of tax liability under GST law.

23.1.1 Self-assessment: Section 59 of the CGST Act, 2017 states, "Every registered person shall self-assess the taxes payable under this Act and furnish a return for each tax period as specified under Section 39".

23.1.2 Provisional Assessment: Proper officer can be requested for provisional assessment (with reasons) in the following two cases:

1. When a taxable person is unable to determine the value of goods/services.
2. When a taxable person is unable to determine applicable rate of GST.

Final assessment can be made within 6 months from the date of communication of the order of provision assessment. Taxable person shall be liable to pay interest as well if tax liability as per the final assessment is higher than in provisional assessment

23.2 Scrutiny of Returns

Section 61 of the CGST Act, 2017 deals with the scrutiny of returns. The provisions in this regard are as under:

1. If the return furnished by the registered person is selected for scrutiny, the proper officer may scrutinize the same and related particulars furnished by the registered person to verify the correctness of the return.
2. In case any discrepancy is found, the proper officer shall inform him, through notice, of the same and seek his explanation thereto.
3. The registered person is required to submit his explanation within a period of thirty days from the date of service of the notice.
4. In case the explanation is found acceptable, the registered person shall be informed accordingly and no further action shall be taken in this regard.
5. The registered person may accept the discrepancy mentioned in the notice and pay

the tax and any other amounts arising from such discrepancy.

6. In case no satisfactory explanation is furnished within a period of thirty days of being informed by the proper officer or where the registered person, after accepting the discrepancies, fails to take the corrective measure, the proper officer may initiate appropriate action including those under Section 65 or Section 66 or Section 67, or proceed to determine the tax and other dues under Section 73 or Section 74.

23.3 Audit of Registered Persons

GST is a trust-based tax regime under which the assessee is required to self-assess his returns and determine tax liability. A tax regime which relies on self-assessment has to put in place a robust audit mechanism to ensure compliance with the provisions of the law by the taxable person. Thus, audit of registered persons is conducted to verify compliance with the provisions of the law.

As per Section 2(13) of the CGST Act, 2017, "*audit* means the examination of records, returns and other documents maintained or furnished by the registered person under this Act...to verify the correctness of turnover declared, taxes paid, refund claimed and input tax credit availed, and to assess his compliance with the provisions of this Act or the rules made thereunder."

Section 65 of the CGST Act, 2017 states, "(1) The Commissioner or any officer authorised by him, by way of a general or a specific order, may undertake audit of any registered person for such period, at such frequency and in such manner as may be prescribed".

Section 66 of the CGST Act, 2017 makes provision for special audit. During the scrutiny, inquiry or investigation of a registered person, the proper officer may be of the opinion that the value has not been correctly declared or the credit availed is not within the normal limits. In special audit, the registered person can be directed to get his records (including books of account) examined and audited by a chartered accountant/cost accountant during any stage of scrutiny, inquiry or investigation, depending on the complexity of the case.

In short, every registered person whose turnover during a financial year exceeds the prescribed limit is required to get his accounts audited by a chartered accountant or a cost accountant. However, as a trade facilitation measure for MSMEs, registered persons having annual turnover up to ₹ 2 crore are exempted from getting their accounts audited by a chartered accountant or a cost accountant.

23.4 Inspection, Search, Seizure and Arrest

23.4.1 Power of Inspection, [1] **Search** [2] **and Seizure** [3]**:** Section 67 of the CGST Act, 2017 states, "(1) Where the proper officer, not below the rank of Joint Commissioner, has reasons to believe that: (a) a taxable person has suppressed any transaction relating to supply of goods or services or both or the stock of goods in hand, or has claimed input tax credit in excess of his entitlement under this Act or has indulged in contravention of any of the provisions of this Act or the rules made thereunder to evade tax under this Act; or (b) any person engaged in the business of transporting goods or an owner or operator of a warehouse or a godown or any other place is keeping goods which have escaped payment of tax or has kept his accounts or goods in such a manner as is likely to cause evasion of tax payable under this Act, he may authorise in writing any other officer of central tax to inspect any places of business of the taxable person or the persons engaged in the business of transporting goods or the owner or the operator of warehouse or godown or any other place.

(2) Where the proper officer, not below the rank of Joint Commissioner, either pursuant to an inspection carried out under sub-section (1) or otherwise, has reasons to believe that any goods liable to confiscation or any documents or books or things, which in his opinion shall be useful for or relevant to any proceedings under this Act, are secreted in any place, he may authorise in writing any other officer of central tax to search and seize or may himself search and seize such goods, documents or books or things".

23.4.2 Power to Arrest [4]**:** Under Section 69 of the CGST Act, 2017 where the Commissioner has reasons to believe that a person has committed any offence specified in various provisions of the Act, he may, by order, authorize any officer of central tax to arrest such person.

23.5 Demands and Recovery (and Limitation Period)

GST is payable on a self-assessment basis. If the assessee pays the tax correctly, then there is no problem. However, if there is any short payment or wrong utilization of ITC, the tax authorities will initiate demand and recovery proceedings against the assessee.

A valid demand by the tax department can only be raised and enforced if the same is within the period of limitation as prescribed under law. Thus, GST law also prescribes period of limitation for recovery of tax not paid or short paid or erroneously refunded, or where input tax credit has been wrongly availed or utilized. The provisions in this regard are as under:

1. *For any reason, other than the reason of fraud or any wilful mis-statement or suppression of facts to evade tax:* Within three years from the due date or the actual date, whichever is earlier, for filing of annual return for the year for which demand is proposed to be raised (Section 73 of the CGST Act, 2017).
2. *On account of reason of fraud or any wilful mis-statement or suppression of facts to evade tax:* Within a period of five years from the due date or the actual date, whichever is earlier, for filing of annual return for the year to which the demand relates (Section 74 of the CGST Act, 2017).

23.5.1 Tax Collected but not Paid to the Government: Section 76 of the CGST Act, 2017 has provisions related to the recovery of the amount collected by a person as tax from another person but not deposited with the Government.

The law says that it is mandatory to pay the amount of tax collected from another person to the government regardless of whether the supplies in respect of which such amount collected is taxable or not.

For any such unpaid tax, the proper officer may issue show cause notice for its recovery and charge penalty equivalent to such amount.

23.6 Advance Ruling

Advance ruling is issued by the tax administration of a country regarding the manner in which a particular future activity/transaction would be treated for tax purposes. Entrepreneurs planning certain business initiatives may approach tax authorities to find out tax implications of their intended activity. A request for advance ruling is generally in the form of an application containing all relevant facts and surrounding circumstances. A modest fee may also be charged for the purpose. By binding the tax administration, an advance ruling creates certainty in the mind of the entrepreneur about the tax consequences of his activity.

Section 97 of the CGST Act states, "(1) An applicant desirous of obtaining an advance ruling under this Chapter may make an application in such form and manner and accompanied by such fee as may be prescribed, stating the question on which the advance ruling is sought.

(2) The question on which the advance ruling is sought under this Act, shall be in respect of: (a) classification of any goods or services or both; (b) applicability of a notification issued under the provisions of this Act; (c) determination of time and value of supply of goods or services or both; (d) admissibility of input tax credit of tax paid or deemed to have been paid; (e) determination of the liability to pay tax on any goods or services or both; (f) whether applicant is required to be registered; and (g) whether any particular thing done by the applicant with respect to any goods or services or both amounts to or results in a supply of goods or services or both, within the meaning of that term".

Advance ruling can be obtained easily as one Advance Ruling Authority has been constituted for all the States. GST laws provide for the facility of appeal against the advance ruling.

The objectives of having a mechanism of advance ruling are the following:

1. To provide certainty in tax liability in advance in relation to an activity proposed to be undertaken by the applicant.
2. To attract foreign direct investment (FDI).
3. To reduce litigation.
4. To pronounce ruling expeditiously in transparent and inexpensive manner.

23.7 Appeals and Revisions (Dispute Resolution Mechanism)

Tax laws, like other laws, impose obligations which are broadly of two kinds: (a) tax-related and (b) procedure-related. A taxpayer's compliance with these obligations is verified by the tax authorities through various means such as scrutiny and audit. Sometimes, there are situations of actual or perceived non-compliance. If the difference in views persists, it results into a dispute which is then required to be resolved.

It is for this reason that the laws provide for appeal. An appeal under any law is an application to a higher court for a reversal of the decision of a lower court. Appeals arise when there are any legal disputes.

Since the right to appeal is a legal right, the law also places certain fetters on the exercise of that right. The time limits prescribed by the statute for filing of appeals, and the requirement of a pre-deposit of a certain sum before the appeal can be heard by the competent authority are examples of such fetters on the statutory right.

An elaborate adjudication and appellate procedure is prescribed under the GST law. There is a separate appellate tribunal called the Goods and Services Tax Appellate Tribunal (GST Appellate Tribunal) to deal with disputes. The Tribunal hears appeals against the orders passed by the Appellate Authority or the Revisional Authority. States would adopt the provisions relating to Tribunal in respective SGST Act.

23.7.1 Appeal to Appellate Authority: Section 107 of CGST Act states, "(1) Any person aggrieved by any decision or order passed under this Act or the State Goods and Services Tax Act or the Union Territory Goods and Services Tax Act by an adjudicating authority may appeal to such Appellate Authority as may be prescribed within three months from the date on which the said decision or order is communicated to such person.

(2) The Commissioner may, on his own motion, or upon request from the Commissioner of State tax or the Commissioner of Union territory tax, call for and examine the record of any proceedings in which an adjudicating authority has passed any decision or order under this Act or the State Goods and Services Tax Act or the Union Territory Goods and Services Tax Act, for the purpose of satisfying himself as to the legality or propriety of the said decision or order and may, by order, direct any officer subordinate to him to apply to the Appellate Authority within six months from the date of communication of the said decision or order for the determination of such points arising out of the said decision or order as may be specified by the Commissioner in his order".

In its Twenty-eighth Meeting held on July 21, 2018, the GST Council capped the amount of pre-deposit payable for filing of appeal before the Appellate Authority at ₹ 25 crore.

23.7.2 Constitution of Appellate Tribunal: Section 109 of the CGST Act states, "(1) The Government shall, on the recommendations of the Council, by notification, constitute with effect from such date as may be specified therein, an Appellate Tribunal known as the Goods and Services Tax Appellate Tribunal (GSTAT) for hearing appeals against the orders passed by the Appellate Authority or the Revisional Authority".

In its Twenty-eighth Meeting held on July 21, 2018, the GST Council capped the amount of pre-deposit payable for filing of appeal before the Appellate Tribunal at ₹ 50 crore.

In its Twenty-fifth Meeting held on June 21, 2019, the GST Council decided on the location of state and area benches for GSTAT for various states and Union Territories with legislature. It was decided to have a common state bench for Sikkim, Nagaland, Manipur and Arunachal Pradesh.

23.7.3 Appeal to High Court: Section 117 of the CGST Act states, "(1) Any person aggrieved by any order passed by the State Bench or Area Benches of the Appellate Tribunal may file an appeal to the High Court and the High Court may admit such appeal, if it is satisfied that the case involves a substantial question of law".

23.7.4 Appeal to the Supreme Court: Section 118 of the CGST Act states, "(1) An appeal shall lie to the Supreme Court: (a) from any order passed by the National Bench or Regional Benches of the Appellate Tribunal; or (b) from any judgment or order passed by the High Court in an appeal made under Section 117 in any case which, on its own motion or on an application made by or on behalf of the party aggrieved, immediately after passing of the judgment or order, the High Court certifies to be a fit one for appeal to the Supreme Court".

23.8 Offences and Penalties

Being a destination-based and transaction-wise tax, GST has strict compliance procedures for all the taxpayers. Since every transaction is recorded and tracked between the source and destination, it is obligatory for the taxpayers to maintain and declare information with utmost accuracy.

To ensure an honest movement of goods, intra-state and inter-state, and to reduce corruption, GST defines strict guidelines pertaining to offences and penalties.

Section 122(1) of the CGST Act, 2017 mentions the following 21 offences [5] for which penalty [6] is leviable.

Thus, where a taxable person who:

1. Supplies any goods/services without any invoice or issues a false invoice.
2. Issues any invoice or bill without supply of goods/services in violation of the provisions of GST.
3. Collects any amount as tax but fails to pay the same to the Government beyond a period of 3 months.
4. Collects any tax in contravention of the provisions of law but fails to pay the same to the Government beyond a period of 3 months.
5. Fails to deduct the tax in accordance with the provisions of law or deducts an amount which is less than the amount required to be deducted.
6. Fails to collect tax in accordance with the provisions of law or collects an amount which is less than the amount required to be collected.
7. Takes or utilises input tax credit without actual receipt of goods/services.
8. Fraudulently obtains refund of tax.
9. Takes or distributes input tax credit in contravention of law.
10. Falsifies or substitutes financial records or produces fake accounts or documents or furnishes any false information or return with an intention to evade payment of tax due under the law.
11. Is liable to be registered but fails to obtain registration.
12. Furnishes any false information with regard to registration particulars.
13. Obstructs or prevents any officer in discharge of his duties under the law.
14. Transports any taxable goods without the cover of documents as may be specified in this behalf.
15. Suppresses his turnover leading to evasion of tax.
16. Fails to keep, maintain or retain books of account and other documents in accordance with the provisions of the law.
17. Fails to furnish information or documents called for by an officer in accordance with

the provisions of the law.

18. Supplies, transports or stores any goods which he has reasons to believe are liable to confiscation under the law.
19. Issues any invoice or document by using the registration number of another registered person.
20. Tampers with, or destroys any material evidence or document.
21. Disposes off or tampers with any goods that have been detained, seized, or attached under the law.

Shall be liable to pay a penalty of ₹ 10,000 or an amount equivalent to the tax evaded or the tax not deducted or short deducted or deducted but not paid to the Government or tax not collected or short collected or collected but not paid to the Government or input tax credit availed of or passed on or distributed irregularly, or the refund claimed fraudulently, whichever is higher.

For any offence committed by a company, both the officer-in-charge (such as director, manager, secretary) as well as the company will be held liable for such an offence.

Endnotes

1. *Inspection* is a softer provision than search to enable officers to access any place of business of a taxable person and also any place of business of a person engaged in transporting goods or who is an owner or an operator of a warehouse or godown.
2. As per law dictionary and as noted in different judicial pronouncements, the term *search*, in simple language, denotes an action of a government machinery to go, look through or examine carefully a place, area, person, object etc. in order to find something concealed or for the purpose of discovering evidence of a crime. The search of a person or vehicle or premises etc. can only be done under proper and valid authority of law.
3. The term *seizure* has not been specifically defined in the MGL. In Law Lexicon Dictionary, *seizure* is defined as the act of taking possession of property by an officer under legal process. It generally implies taking possession forcibly contrary to the wishes of the owner of the property or who has the possession and who was unwilling to part with the possession.
4. The term *arrest* has not been defined in the MGL. However, as per judicial pronouncements, it denotes 'the taking into custody of a person under some lawful command or authority'. In other words, a person is said to be arrested when he is taken and restrained of his liberty by power or colour of lawful warrant.
5. An offence is a breach of a law or rule, i.e. an illegal act. Likewise, an offence under GST is a breach of the provisions of GST Acts and Rules.
6. The word *penalty* has not been defined in the GST law but judicial pronouncements and principles of jurisprudence have laid down the nature of a penalty as: (a) a temporary punishment or a sum of money imposed by statute, to be paid as punishment for the commission of a certain offence and (b) a punishment imposed by law or contract for doing or failing to do something that was the duty of a party to do.

   A penalty can be both corporal (jail) or pecuniary (monetary), civil or criminal. Both corporal and pecuniary penalties are applicable under GST.

24

Anti-profiteering Provisions

Introduction of GST is generally believed to have inflationary tendency, i.e. increase in prices across the board. This happens in spite of the availability of input tax credit at every stage of value addition in the production process which should actually reduce the final prices. Prices increase because suppliers do not pass on the benefits of tax concessions to the consumers and thereby indulge in illegal profiteering. India followed examples of Malaysia and Australia which had to put in place mechanisms to prevent unethical profiteering.

Therefore, India's GST law requires that any reduction in rate of tax on any supply of goods or services or the benefit of input tax credit should be passed on to the recipient by way of commensurate reduction in prices.

24.1 Consumer Protection in India

At the root of consumer protection is the recognition of an unequal relationship between consumers and producers. Protection of consumers is accomplished by setting minimum quality specifications and safety standards for both goods and services and establishing mechanisms to redress their grievances.

The consumer movement in India is as old as trade and commerce. In Kautilya's Arthashastra, there are references to the concept of consumer protection against exploitation by the trade and retailer with respect to quality, short weight, measurement and adulteration of goods.

Yet until the late 1970s, there was no systematic movement in the country for safeguarding the interest of consumers. However, now it is widely acknowledged that the level of consumer awareness and protection is a true indicator of development of the country and progressiveness of civil society.

The main reason for this is the rapidly increasing variety of goods and services which modern technology has made available. In addition, the growing size and complexity of production and distribution systems, the high level of sophistication in marketing and selling practices and in advertising and other forms of promotion, mass marketing methods and consumers' increased mobility resulting in reduction of personal interaction between buyers and sellers, have contributed to the increased need for consumer protection.

24.1.1 Consumer Protection Act, 1986: This Act was enacted with the objective to provide better protection of the interests of the consumers. The Act provides for effective safeguards to consumers against various types of exploitations and unfair dealings, relying on mainly compensatory rather than punitive or preventive approach. The Act applies to all goods and services unless specifically exempted and covers private, public and co-operative sectors and provides for speedy and inexpensive adjudication. The consumer rights under the Act are the following:

1. Right to be protected against marketing of goods and services, which are hazardous to life and property.
2. Right to be informed about quality, quantity, potency, purity, standard and price of goods and services, as the case may be, to protect consumer against unfair trade practices.
3. Right to be assured of access to a variety of goods and services at competitive prices.
4. Right to be heard and assured that consumer interest will receive due consideration at appropriate fora.
5. Right to seek redressal against unfair trade practices or restrictive trade practices or unscrupulous exploitation of consumers.
6. Right to consumer education.

24.1.2 Central Consumer Protection Council (CCPC): The objective of CCPC, established under the Consumer Protection Act, 1986, is to promote and protect consumer rights that include the right to be informed and the right to consumer education.

24.2 CGST Act, 2017 on Anti-profiteering

Chapter XXI of the CGST Act, 2017, deals with miscellaneous provisions. Anti-profiteering provision is an important item under these miscellaneous provisions.

As per Section 171 of the Act, any reduction in rate of tax on any supply of goods or services or the benefit of input tax credit shall be passed on to the recipient by way of *commensurate* reduction in prices.

Section 171 of the Act reads as follows, "(1) Any reduction in rate of tax on any supply of goods or services or the benefit of input tax credit shall be passed on to the recipient by way of commensurate reduction in prices.

(2) The Central Government may, on recommendations of the Council, by notification, constitute an Authority, or empower an existing Authority constituted under any law for the time being in force, to examine whether input tax credits availed by any registered person or the reduction in the tax rate have actually resulted in a commensurate reduction in the price of the goods or services or both supplied by him.

(3) The Authority referred to in sub-section (2) shall exercise such powers and discharge such functions as may be prescribed".

24.3 Institutional Mechanism for Anti-profiteering

24.3.1 State Screening Committee: All applications (after confirming prima facie evidence of profiteering) from interested parties on issues of profiteering of local nature are first examined by the State-level Screening Committee constituted in each State by the State Governments consisting of an officer of the State Government, to be nominated by the Commissioner, and an officer of the Central Government, to be nominated by the Chief Commissioner.

The Screening Committee on being satisfied that the supplier has not passed on the reduction in rate of tax on any supply of goods or services or the benefit of input tax credit on to the recipient by way of commensurate reduction in prices, will forward the application with its recommendations to the Standing Committee on Anti-profiteering, which consists of such officers of the State Government and Central Government as may be nominated by the GST council, for further action.

24.3.2 Standing Committee: If the Standing Committee is satisfied that there is a prima facie evidence to show that the supplier has not passed on the benefit of reduction in the rate of tax on the supply of goods or services or the benefit of input tax credit to the recipient by way of commensurate reduction in prices, it shall refer the matter to the Director General of Safeguards, Central Board of Indirect Taxes and Customs (CBIC) for a detailed investigation.

It is noteworthy that if the profiteering has all-India character, the affected consumers may file an application in the prescribed format directly before the Standing Committee on Anti-profiteering, after confirming prima facie evidence of profiteering,

24.3.3 Director General of Anti-profiteering: The Director General of Anti-profiteering (formerly Director General of Safeguards) shall conduct investigation and collect evidence necessary to determine undue profiteering and before initiation of the investigation, issue a notice to the interested parties (and to such other persons as deemed fit for a fair enquiry into the matter) containing, *inter alia*, information on the following:

1. Description of the goods or services in respect of which the proceedings have been initiated.
2. Summary of the statement of facts on which the allegations are based.
3. Time limit allowed to the interested parties and other persons who may have information related to the proceedings for furnishing their reply.

The evidence or information presented to the Director General of Safeguards by one interested party can be made available to the other interested parties, participating in the proceedings. The evidence provided will be kept confidential and the provisions of Section 11 of the Right to Information Act, 2005 shall apply mutatis mutandis to the disclosure of any information which is provided on a confidential basis.

The Director General of Safeguards can seek opinion of any other agency or statutory authorities in the discharge of his duties. He, or an officer authorised by him, will have the power to summon any person necessary either to give evidence or to produce a document or any other thing. He will also have same powers as that of a civil court and every such inquiry will be deemed to be a judicial proceeding.

The Director General of Safeguards will complete the investigation within a period of 3 months or within such extended period not exceeding a further period of 3 months for reasons to be recorded in writing, as allowed by the Standing Committee and, upon completion of the investigation, furnish to the National Anti-profiteering Authority, a report of its findings along with the relevant records.

24.3.4 National Anti-profiteering Authority (NAA): Any reduction in rate of tax on any supply of goods or services or the benefit of input tax credit should be passed on to the recipient by way of commensurate reduction in prices. However, it has been the experience of many countries that when GST was introduced there was a marked increase in the prices of the commodities (inflation). This happened in spite of the availability of the tax credit right from the production stage to the final consumption stage which should have actually reduced the final prices. This was obviously happening because the suppliers were not passing on the benefit to the consumers and thereby indulging in illegal profiteering. NAA was, therefore, constituted by the Central Government to examine whether input tax credits availed by any registered person or the reduction in the tax rate have actually resulted in a commensurate reduction in prices.

NAA is the institutional mechanism under GST law to check the unfair profit-making activities by the trading community.

The responsibility of NAA is to examine and check such profiteering activities and recommend punitive actions including cancellation of Registration. The chairman, NAA along with 4 Technical members and with the help of the Standing Committee, Screening Committee in every state and the Directorate General of Anti-profiteering in the Central Board of Indirect Taxes and Customs (CBIC), will work together on the anti-profiteering front.

NAA shall (after granting an opportunity of hearing to the interested parties if so requested) within a period of 3 months from the date of the receipt of the report from the Director General of Anti-profiteering determine whether a registered person has passed on the benefit of the reduction in the rate of tax on the supply of goods or services or the benefit of input tax credit to the recipient by way of commensurate reduction in prices.

NAA follows a simple test to judge if benefit of tax cuts has been passed on to the consumers or not—comparing the prices of individual items immediately before the tax cut and the price at which the item is sold after the tax revision.

Where the NAA determines that a registered person has not passed on the benefit of the reduction in the rate of tax on the supply of goods or services or the benefit of input tax credit to the recipient by way of commensurate reduction in prices, it may order: (a) reduction in prices, (b) return to the recipient, an amount equivalent to the amount not passed on by way of commensurate reduction in prices along with interest, (c) imposition of penalty as specified under the Act and (d) cancellation of registration under the Act.

Any order passed by NAA shall be immediately complied with by the registered person failing which action shall be initiated to recover the amount in accordance with the provisions of the IGST Act, 2017 or the CGST Act, 2017 or the UT-GST Act, 2017 or the SGST Act, 2017 of the respective States, as the case may be. NAA can direct any authority of Central tax, State tax or Union territory tax to monitor the implementation of the order passed by it.

NAA is a mechanism devised to ensure that prices remain under check and to ensure that businesses do not pocket all the gains from GST because profit is fine, but undue profiteering at the expense of the common man is not.

A. Composition of NAA: NAA was constituted by the Central Government to examine whether input tax credits availed by any registered person or the reduction in the tax rate have actually resulted in a commensurate reduction in the price of the goods or services or both supplied by him? This is to ensure that the consumer is protected from arbitrary price increase in the name of GST.

NAA shall be a five member committee consisting of a Chairman who holds or has held a post equivalent in rank to a Secretary to the Government of India; and four Technical Members who are or have been Commissioners of State tax or Central tax or have held an equivalent post under existing laws. The Additional Director General of Safeguards under the CBEC shall be the Secretary to NAA. NAA shall cease to exist after the expiry of two years from the date on which the Chairman enters upon his office unless the GST Council recommends otherwise.

If the Members of NAA differ in opinion on any point, the point shall be decided according to the opinion of the majority.

B. Powers to Determine Methodology and Procedures: NAA can determine the methodology and procedure for determination as to whether the reduction in the rate of tax on the supply of goods or services or the benefit of input tax credit has been passed on by the registered person to the recipient by way of commensurate reduction in prices.

C. Duties of NAA: NAA would have the following duties:

1. To determine whether any reduction in the rate of tax on any supply of goods or services or the benefit of input tax credit has been passed on to the recipient by way of commensurate reduction in prices.
2. To identify the registered person who has not passed on the benefit of reduction in the rate of tax on supply of goods or services or the benefit of input tax credit to the recipient by way of commensurate reduction in prices.
3. To order:

- Reduction in prices.
- Return to the recipient, an amount equivalent to the amount not passed on by way of commensurate reduction in prices along with interest at the rate of 18 percent from the date of collection of the higher amount till the date of the return of such amount or recovery of the amount not returned, as the case may be, in case the eligible person does not claim return of the amount or is not identifiable, and depositing the same in the Consumer Welfare Fund. [1]
- Imposition of penalty. [2]
- Cancellation of registration.

Director General of Anti-profiteering of CBIC has been mandated to conduct detailed enquiries on anti-profiteering cases and give his recommendations for consideration by NAA.

D. NAA in Action: On September 18, 2018, NAA passed an order asking the Gurugram-based (Haryana) real estate firm Pyramid Infratech to refund over ₹ 8.22 crore to 2,476 flat owners within 3 months with 18 percent interest. The firm had failed to pass on the GST reduction benefit to the homebuyers. Tax commissioner of Haryana was ordered to monitor the compliance and submit a report within 4 months.

Homebuyers had filed a complaint of profiteering against the builder in two affordable housing projects in Gurugram. They had alleged that the builder had not passed on the benefit of lower tax arising out of availing of input tax credit (ITC) post roll out of GST and hence had indulged in profiteering.

After investigation by the Director General of Anti-profiteering (DGAP), NAA maintained that excess ITC was available to the firm and it was required to be passed on to the buyers.

E. Tenure of NAA: According to Rule 137 under Chapter XV of the Central Goods and Services Tax (CGST) Rules, 2017, "Tenure of Authority: The Authority shall cease to exist after the expiry of two years from the date on which the Chairman enters upon his office unless the Council recommends otherwise".

Government may extend the term of NAA beyond its original 2-years transition period mandate. The 2-years term has been specified only in the Rules rather than in the CGST Act, 2017. Therefore, it would be easier to extend the term of NAA.

The Union Cabinet approved the constitution of NAA on November 16, 2017.

The GST Council in its Thirty-fifth Meeting held on June 21, 2019 extended the tenure of NAA by another 2 years to November 2021 in order to protect consumers' interests.

NAA needs to function for a longer period in the light of frequent rate changes in GST. Moreover, GST on five petroleum products is still to be levied. As and when this happens, services of NAA would be needed to ensure passing on of benefits, if any.

To sum up, Government is committed to ensure all consumers enjoy the benefits of lower prices of goods and services under GST. Under GST, suppliers of goods and services must pass on any reduction in the rate of tax or the benefit of input tax credit to consumers by way of commensurate reduction in prices. If this is not done, the consumer's interest is protected by NAA. Government has warned the industry time and again that it should pass on the benefit of lower taxes to consumers or face anti-profiteering action provided under the GST law.

Although the law and the institutional set-up are in place, public awareness about these arrangements is equally important. For this purpose, the Central Board of Indirect Taxes and Customs (CBIC) has been educating the people about their rights through advertisements in the print and electronic media.

NAA should make efforts to ensure that businesses make suitable price revisions and pass on tax cut benefits to buyers at the beginning of the supply chain itself, rather than wait for the end-user (i.e. consumer) to file complaint.

The problem of *unjust profiteering* is akin to the problem of *unjust enrichment* under the erstwhile excise duty system. [3]

However, industry circles maintain that rules in this regard are vaguely worded, which makes them prone to misuse. In a complex production system where a variety of inputs go into manufacturing of a product, reaching a definitive conclusion on *commensurate* is difficult. The best way to check profiteering, and hence protect consumer welfare, is to ensure competition.

Endnotes

1. Section 57 of the CGST Act, 2017, refers to the constitution of Consumer Welfare Fund.

2. The GST Council in its Thirty-fifth Meeting held on June 21, 2019 approved the imposition of an additional penalty of up to 10 percent of the profiteered amount if the money is not deposited within 30 days of the order being issued. Currently, the penalty is capped at ₹ 25,000.
3. The term *unjust enrichment* was used to describe a situation when a person undeservedly got enriched. In the context of refund of Union excise duty, the principle of unjust enrichment was the first and foremost principle which was kept in mind by the sanctioning authorities. If the manufacturer had charged excise duty to his buyer, it was clear that he had passed on the burden to the buyer and had already recovered duty from his customer. In such cases, refund of excess duty paid to the manufacturer would amount to excess and undeserved profit to him. It would not be equitable to refund the duty to him as he would get double benefit—first from the customer and again from the Excise Department. This is called unjust enrichment. Refund of duty should, ideally, be paid to the customer who had borne the burden of duty. Since it is practically not feasible to identify such customers on individual basis, the amount of refund was credited to Consumer Welfare Fund in accordance with section 12C of the Central Excise Act, 1944. The principle of unjust enrichment was held valid and constitutional by the Supreme Court in the famous case of Mafatlal Industries Ltd. (1997).

25

Technological Infrastructure and Institutional Set-up for GST

An important objective of tax reform is simplification of tax administration and compliance, which is dependent on three factors. The first determining factor for simplicity is the tax design itself. Generally, the more rational and neutral the tax design, the simpler it would be to administer and encourage compliance. If the tax is levied on a broad base at a single rate, there would be few classification disputes and the tax-specific record keeping requirements for vendors would be minimal. It would simplify enforcement, and encourage voluntary compliance.

The second factor is the infrastructure for tax administration, including the design of tax forms, data requirements, system of tax rulings and interpretations, and the procedures for registration, filing and processing of tax returns, tax payments and refunds, audits, and appeals. A modern tax administration focuses on providing services to taxpayers to facilitate compliance. It harnesses information technology to enhance the quality of services, and to ensure greater transparency in administration and enforcement.

The third factor in a federation (such as India) is the degree of harmonization among the taxes levied by the Centre and the States. Thus, under the dual GST—consisting of a Centre GST and a State GST—harmonization of the Centre and State GSTs would be critical to keep the overall compliance burden low. Equally important is harmonization of GSTs across the states.

25.1 Goods and Services Tax Network (GSTN)

Among the various steps that had been taken for the introduction of GST was the establishment of a strong information technology (IT) infrastructure. For this purpose the Government had set up an Empowered Group (Chairman: Nandan Nilekani). Significant efforts were made for the conceptualization and design of the GSTN—a common portal for the Centre and States that would enable electronic processing of the key business processes of registration, returns, and payments.

The structure of GSTN was approved by the Empowered Committee (EC). National Securities Depository Limited (NSDL) was the technology partner for incubating GSTN. In this regard, NSDL set up a pilot project in collaboration with 11 States prior to GST roll out across the country. Three Joint Working Groups of officials were also constituted comprising officials from the Central Government, State Governments, and the Empowered Committee (EC) of State Finance Ministers to work on legislation, business procedures and IT infrastructure respectively.

GSTN was incorporated as a private limited company on March 28, 2013. It is a section

8 company under the Companies Act, 2013 and hence is a not-for-profit entity.

GSTN provides shared IT infrastructure and services to Central and State Governments, tax payers and other stakeholders. GSTN is a special purpose vehicle (SPV) which aims to provide a standard and uniform interface to the taxpayers, and shared infrastructure and services to Central and State/UT Governments. It is the interface between the government and the taxpayers.

GSTN is a state-of-the-art comprehensive IT infrastructure including the common GST portal which provides front-end services of registration, payments and returns to taxpayers. It also assists some States with back-end IT modules that include processing of returns, registrations, audits, assessments, appeals etc. All States, accounting authorities, Reserve Bank of India (RBI) and banks are also preparing their IT infrastructure for the administration of GST. There is no manual filing of returns. All taxes can also be paid online. All mis-matched returns are auto-generated, and there is no need for manual interventions. Most returns are self-assessed.

The functions of the GSTN, *inter alia*, include the following:

1. Facilitating registration.
2. Forwarding the returns to Central and State authorities.
3. Computation and settlement of IGST.
4. Matching of tax payment details with banking network.
5. Providing various MIS reports to the Central and the State Governments based on the tax payer return information.
6. Providing analysis of tax payers' profile.
7. Running the matching engine for matching, reversal and reclaim of input tax credit.

GSTN is a unique and complex IT initiative. It is unique as it seeks, for the first time, to establish a uniform interface for the taxpayer and a common and shared IT infrastructure between the Centre and States.

GSTN renders the following services through the common GST Portal:

1. Registration (including existing taxpayer master migration and issue of PAN-based registration number).
2. Payment management including payment gateways and integration with banking systems.
3. Return filing and processing.
4. Taxpayer management, including account management, notifications, information, and status tracking.
5. Tax authority account and ledger management.
6. Computation of settlement (including IGST settlement) between the Centre and States; clearing house for IGST.
7. Processing and reconciliation of GST on imports and integration with EDI systems of customs.
8. MIS including need-based information and business intelligence.
9. Maintenance of interfaces between the Common GST Portal and tax administration systems.

10. Providing training to stakeholders.
11. Providing analytics and business intelligence to tax authorities.
12. Carrying out research, study best practices and provide training to stakeholders.

GSTN is a National Information Utility. GSTN implements common PAN-based registration, returns filing and payments processing for all States on a shared platform. The use of PAN as a common identifier in both direct and indirect taxes, has enhanced transparency and checked tax evasion.

GSTN has appointed Infosys Ltd. as managed service provider for a period of 5 years.

In September 2017, a Group of Ministers (GoM) was set up to look into the technical issues faced by GSTN.

On September 26, 2018, the Union Cabinet cleared a proposal to convert GSTN into a government-owned company. 50 percent stake will be owned by the Centre and the remaining by the states on pro-rata basis in the new structure.

Earlier, the GST Council had approved the proposal to convert GSTN into 100 percent government-owned company.

Currently, the Centre and the States together hold 49 percent stake in GSTN, the company which provides IT backbone to the GST regime. The remaining 51 percent is held by 5 private financial institutions, viz. HDFC Limited, HDFC Bank Limited, ICICI Bank Limited, NSE Strategic Investment Company and LIC Housing Finance Limited.

In short, GSTN is the backbone of GST. It is important in the following ways:

1. GSTN provides shared IT infrastructure and services to the tax authorities, taxpayers and other stakeholders.
2. It provides online services of registration, return filing, processing and payment management.
3. It provides offline tools for ease of filing various returns.
4. GSTN has a highly competent multi-layered security system to prevent cyber attacks on critical tax payer's data.

25.2 Ministry of Finance

25.2.1 Department of Revenue: It exercises control in respect of matters relating to all the Direct and Indirect Union Taxes through two statutory Boards namely, the Central Board of Direct Taxes (CBDT) and the Central Board of Indirect Taxes and Customs (CBIC) [formerly Central Board of Excise and Customs (CBEC)]. Each Board is headed by a Chairman who is also ex-officio Special Secretary to the Government of India. Matters relating to the levy and collection of all Direct taxes are looked after by the CBDT whereas those relating to levy and collection of indirect taxes and customs fall within the purview of the CBIC. The two Boards were constituted under the Central Board of Revenue Act, 1963.

25.2.2 Central Economic Intelligence Bureau (CEIB): CEIB was setup in the year 1985. Functioning under the Ministry of Finance, it is responsible for co-ordination, intelligence sharing, and investigations at national as well as regional levels amongst various law enforcement agencies.

It is the nodal agency for economic intelligence mandated to ensure effective interaction and co-ordination among all the concerned agencies in the area of economic offences. It also functions as the clearing house of all economic intelligence and provides a platform for such exchange between various agencies within the Department of Revenue and other intelligence and enforcement agencies including Intelligence Bureau (IB), Research and Analysis Wing (RAW), Central Bureau of Investigation (CBI) and other such agencies.

In terms of organizational structure, CEIB has three wings:

A. Administration and Co-ordination Wing (AC): This wing acts as the Secretariat to the Economic Intelligence Council (EIC) chaired by the Finance Minister. It looks after the work relating to the EIC and Working Group and also monitors the working of the 21 Regional Economic Intelligence Councils (REICs) all over the country. In addition to this, the wing is also responsible for general administration of CEIB.

B. Economic Intelligence Wing (ECOINT): This wing co-ordinates at the central level the exchange of information and intelligence relating to economic offences including drug trafficking, smuggling, foreign exchange violations, supply of counterfeit currency, hawala transactions, financial frauds in stock markets, money laundering, tax evasion etc.

C. COFEPOSA Wing: This wing deals with work relating to the COFEPOSA Act. Smugglers and foreign exchange racketeers can be detained for a period of 1 year under COFEPOSA Act, 1974, with a view to prevent them from indulging in prejudicial activities in future.

25.2.3 Economic Intelligence Council (EIC): It came into existence in 2003 and is chaired by the Finance Minister and comprises senior functionaries of various ministries and intelligence agencies, including the Governor of RBI and the Chairman of the Securities and Exchange Board of India (SEBI). The EIC meets at least once a year to discuss and take decisions regarding trends in economic offences and strategies on intelligence sharing, coordination etc. Implementation of decisions taken by the EIC is monitored by the Working Group on Intelligence Apparatus, set up for this purpose within the EIC.

25.2.4 Financial Intelligence Unit (FIU): The FIU-IND was established by the Government of India on November 18, 2004 for coordinating and strengthening efforts for national and international intelligence by investigation and enforcement agencies in combating money laundering and terrorist financing. FIU-IND is the national agency responsible for receiving, processing, analysing, and disseminating information relating to suspect financial transactions. It is an independent body reporting to the Economic Intelligence Council headed by the Finance Minister. For administrative purposes, the FIU-IND is under the control of the Department of Revenue, Ministry of Finance.

25.2.5 Central Board of Indirect Taxes and Customs (CBIC): CBIC is a part of the Department of Revenue under the Ministry of Finance, Government of India. It deals with the tasks of formulation of policy concerning levy and collection of indirect taxes and customs, prevention of smuggling, and administration of matters relating to indirect taxes and customs to the extent under the CBIC's purview.

After Independence in 1947, a need was felt to have a centralized agency in India to deal with cases of violations of Central excise and customs laws, having ramifications beyond the geographical jurisdiction of localized field formations and for collection, co-ordination and correlation of intelligence with respect to violation of these laws and also to furnish specialized know-how.

In 1953, Government of India established a new Government agency which was focused to do preventive services. The agency was named as Central Revenue Intelligence Bureau (CRIB), and charged with the responsibility of dealing with all matters connected with anti-smuggling and anti-corruption in the Customs and Central Excise Organizations all over India. Later on the CRJB was split in two parts: Directorate of Revenue Intelligence (DRI) and Directorate General of Central Excise Intelligence (DGCEI). The responsibility of dealing with all matters connected with anti-smuggling and customs laws was given to DRI and the responsibility of dealing with all matters connected with Central excise offences was given to DGCEI which was renamed as Directorate General of GST Intelligence (DGGSTI) after the implementation of GST in 2017.

A. Directorate General of Central Excise Intelligence (DGCEI): DGCEI was the apex intelligence organization functioning under CBIC. It was entrusted with the responsibility of detecting evasion of Central excise duties and service tax. It developed intelligence, especially in new areas of tax evasion through its intelligence network across the country and disseminated information in this respect by issuing modus operandi circulars and alert circulars to apprise field formations of the latest trends in tax evasion. Wherever found necessary, DGCEI on its own, or in co-ordination with field formations, organised operations to unearth evasion of indirect taxes.

B. Directorate General of GST Intelligence (DGGSTI): Rapid liberalization of Indian economy and its gradual integration with the world economy has resulted in rapid growth in services as well as manufacturing sectors. The said growth has necessitated closer monitoring of new nerve centres of economy. Need for closer monitoring of these booming sectors of economy has cast upon DGGSTI an onerous responsibility of checking and preventing misuse of the liberalized economic environment by unscrupulous and manipulative elements in the trade and industry.

DGGSTI works under CBIC and is headquartered in New Delhi.

DGGSTI has 25 zones across India to check GST evasion. It is part of National Intelligence Grid (NATGRID) which means it enjoys the following prime powers given by Government of India:

1. Sharing and exchanging sensitive information with other intelligence and security agencies like RAW, IB, CBI, DRI, Enforcement Directorate and Narcotics Control Bureau.
2. DGGSTI is protected by RTI Laws.
3. It is also protected by several structural and procedural safeguards and oversight mechanisms including that of external audits and technology safeguards.
4. It enjoys power of phone tapping and tracking.

25.3 National Academy of Customs, Excise and Narcotics (NACEN)

One of the biggest challenges is to train the indirect tax officials of both the Central and State Governments about the concepts, processes and procedures of GST. NACEN—the apex training institution for capacity building in indirect taxation under the Central Board of Indirect Taxes and Customs—has been mandated to impart training on GST to Central and State Government officers. NACEN is conducting a mammoth capacity building exercise to train about 60,000 indirect tax officers of the Centre and the States so that officers are well-equipped to implement GST. NACEN has already created a team of almost 2,000 trainers across the country to train the field officers. Apart from classroom training, NACEN is also planning to use advanced information technology tools such as virtual classrooms and e-learning modules, to ensure larger coverage.

As part of this capacity building exercise, the NACEN has prepared a compilation of frequently asked questions (FAQs)—based on inputs gathered while conducting training and interactive sessions—as a training tool for helping the officers as well as public, to get acquainted with the Model GST Law and its nuances.

25.4 Serious Frauds Investigation Office (SFIO)

It functions under the Ministry of Corporate Affairs and takes up for investigation complex cases having inter-departmental and multidisciplinary ramifications and substantial involvement of public interest, either in terms of monetary misappropriation or in terms of persons affected. It also takes up cases where investigation has the potential of contributing towards a clear improvement in systems, laws, or procedures.

Part VI
Impact of GST on the Indian Economy

26

GST: An All-India Unified, Uniform and Harmonized Indirect Tax System

The pre-GST system of indirect taxes was marked by multiplicity of taxes and rates at the Central and State levels. This resulted in a complex tax structure which was ridden with hidden costs for trade and industry. There was no uniformity of tax rates and collection procedures across States.

In sharp contrast to the earlier system, GST has ensured uniform exemption list, uniform rates and uniform collection procedures throughout the country. It has paved the way for a common national market. The country has moved from an inefficient and fragmented indirect tax system to an efficient and unified tax regime in the form of GST. The old system was mainly manual and opaque while the new system is technology-based and hence transparent.

26.1 From Fragmented to Unified Indirect Tax System

Prior to the introduction of GST, the indirect tax system of India was fragmented and complicated.

The Central Government imposed excise duty on the manufacture/production of commodities. These duties were imposed on almost all industrial products at varying rates. Apart from the basic excise duty, there were additional excise duties, surcharges and cesses. Exemptions and concessions were an integral part of the excise system. Excise preferences and reliefs were given to promote a wide spectrum of socio-economic objectives.

Excise taxation in India was an interesting example of multitude of rates which were subject to frequent revisions. Numerous considerations contributed to the complexity of excise rates. The labyrinthine intricacies of the tariff often led to confusion and litigation amongst the taxpayers and revenue authorities.

Moreover, there were different procedures to assess and collect excise duties, viz. physical control system, self-removal procedure (SRP) and compounded levy scheme.

All Union duties of excise were abolished—except those on petroleum products and tobacco—to pave way for the introduction of GST.

During the pre-GST system, States were precluded from taxing services. Centre had the exclusive authority to tax services.

In all, 8 Central taxes, including the above-mentioned, were abolished to pave way for the roll out of GST from July 1, 2017. [1]

States Governments, on their part, imposed sales tax (later VAT) on almost the same commodities as were subject to excise duties. All the States had their own Sales Tax

Acts. Lists of exemptions, rates of taxation, compounding schemes and rules and regulations varied across States. It was a nightmare for a business entity doing business in more than one State.

Differential rates of sales tax on the same set of commodities in different States often led to uneconomic diversion of trade as well as production centres. It was not uncommon for people of one State making purchases in other States to avoid or reduce sales tax liability.

Apart from sales tax, states also imposed various types of cesses and taxes of local nature like entry tax, octroi, terminal tax etc.

Then there was the Central Sales Tax (CST). When goods were sold within the State, sales tax was levied, collected and appropriated by the concerned state. In case goods were sold in the course of inter-State trade, then CST was levied by the Centre but collected and appropriated by the exporting state.

In all, 9 state taxes/duties were abolished, including the above-mentioned, to prepare ground for the introduction of GST. [2]

In sum, GST subsumed under it 17 taxes/duties (8 Central and 9 State). GST is a single tax on the supply of goods or services or both, right from the manufacturer to the consumer. Credits of input taxes paid at each stage are available in the subsequent stage of value addition, which makes GST essentially a tax only on value addition at each stage. This exercise at consolidation and unification of taxation of goods and services was historic and unprecedented.

26.2 From Differing to Uniform Tax Practices

In the pre-GST era, multiple taxes were imposed at different levels of the government. Businesses had to keep multiple-record-keeping for a variety of taxes. In the case of sales tax, every State had its own rate structure, exemption list and collection procedures. Many of the administrative processes were manual, not benefiting from the efficiencies of automation. All this not only increased the costs of compliance, but also undermined revenue collection.

In fact, there was no national policy as regards the burden of taxes on different goods. The scenario has changed with the introduction of GST. Instead of multiple taxes at different levels of the government, there is one tax with common base, exemption list, rate structure and administrative procedures. This has reduced investment of resources and manpower in maintaining records. GST has improved the ease-of-doing-business and transportation of goods across the country.

Apart from reducing compliance costs, common tax rates and procedures across the country have made business tax neutral, irrespective of the choice of place of doing business.

26.3 From Tax Rivalry to Tax Harmony

26.3.1 Centre-state Tax Rivalries: In the pre-GST system of indirect taxes, the Centre had a commanding position over the States in the sense that the former had the first right to levy tax (excise duties) on a wide range of industrial products. State levied sales tax (later VAT) on almost the same set of commodities, but with whatever little scope left after the imposition of excise duties. In other words, States played second fiddle to the Centre in terms of revenue from commodity taxation. Since the Centre and States acted independently without co-ordination among themselves, there was hardly any possibility to harmonize commodity tax system successfully. Similarly, as excise duty and sales tax were levied by different layers of Government, it became difficult to determine judiciously the impact of these levies on production, investment, and the consumers.

Another point of rivalry was the taxation of services. In the pre-GST regime, services per se remained outside the scope of state taxation powers. In other words, Centre had the exclusive power to tax services. Exclusion of services from the state taxation powers had negative impact on the buoyancy of State tax revenues. With the growth in per capita incomes, services were accounting for a growing fraction of the total consumer basket, which the states could not tax. With no powers to levy tax on fastest growing components of consumer expenditures, the States had to rely almost exclusively on compliance improvements or rate increases for any buoyancy in their *own-source revenues*.

Centre-State revenue antagonism has subsided with the imposition of GST on goods and services. Article 246A of the Constitution confers concurrent powers to both Parliament and State Legislatures to make laws with respect to GST. The dual GST imposes tax on the same taxable event—supply of goods and services—simultaneously by both the Centre and the States. Both the Centre and the States are empowered to levy GST across the value chain from the stage of manufacture to consumption.

The assignment of concurrent jurisdiction to the Centre and the States for the levy of GST requires a unique institutional mechanism that would ensure that decisions about the structure, design and operation of GST are taken jointly by the two. GST Council is the institutional mechanism for this purpose with constitutional force.

GST has charted out a new course for co-operative federalism in India, focusing on mutual understanding and accommodation between the Centre and States as regards the structure of taxation of goods and services. It is pertinent to note that in all the 35 meetings of the GST Council held so far, all decisions have been taken unanimous or through consensus. In other words, no occasion has arisen so far that required voting to decide any matter.

26.3.2 Inter-state Tax Rivalry: In the pre-GST era, State Governments levied sales tax/VAT on a wide range of commodities at different rates with diverse procedures and rules for its collection. The rate structure of sales tax/VAT was further complicated in view of different lists of exemptions/concessions in each of the States. In order to attract trade and industry to their respective areas, some States indulged in a kind of *rate war* (competitive reductions in sales tax/VAT rates). It is true that some States lacked infrastructural facilities and to compensate for that sales tax concessions came handy to attract industries, but this shortcut eroded the resource-base of the States, so vital for the development of infrastructure which alone could guarantee their speedy development on permanent footing.

GST has ensured uniform exemption list, uniform rates and uniform collection procedures throughout the country. GST represents fiscal integration of the country on the same pattern as political integration of India after attaining Independence in 1947.

Table 26.1 provides a comparison, in summarized form, of pre-GST and post-GST systems of taxation of goods and services in India.

Table 26.1: Pre-GST and Post-GST Systems of Taxation of Goods and Services in India: A Comparison

Pre-GST system	Post-GST system
Centre and the States enjoyed mutually exclusive powers of taxation. No concurrent powers of taxation and hence no joint occupancy of tax fields.	Centre and the States are concurrently empowered to levy GST on goods and services (i.e. common tax fields).
Centre levied excise duty on the *manufacture* of goods while States levied sales tax/VAT on the *sale* of goods.	GST is levied on the *supply* of goods or services or both.
Centre had the exclusive power to tax services.	Centre and the States both tax goods and services under GST.
Origin-based taxation.	GST is destination-based consumption tax.
Structure of VAT in different states differed due to different exemption lists, different VAT rates and different collection procedures.	Uniform exemption list, uniform rates and uniform collection procedures throughout the country under GST.
Limited use of IT under VAT.	GST is completely IT-based.

Endnotes

1. For a list of these 8 taxes/duties, see section 7.4.1 of chapter 7 of this book.
2. For a list of these 9 taxes/duties, see section 7.4.2 of chapter 7 of this book.

27

GST, Gross Domestic Product (GDP), Employment Generation and Formalization of the Economy

As the world economy slows, and increasing financial volatility and turbulence become the *newest normal*, only a few economies have the resilience to be a refuge of stability and the potential to be an outpost of opportunity. India is one of those few. Macroeconomic stability seems reasonably assured for India. This bedrock of stability coupled with reforms can propel the economy to a high growth trajectory. Key amongst these reforms is the national level GST.

GST is an initiative that has commanded broad consensus across the political spectrum. It has also been a model of co-operative federalism in practice with the Centre and States coming together as partners in embracing growth and employment-enhancing reforms. It was a long-awaited reform and its implementation has validated expectations of important government actions and effective political will to modernize the economy.

Many benefits of GST are claimed for the Indian economy.

27.1 GST and GDP Growth

India is recording highest GDP growth rate among all the major economies of the world. According to *World Economy Outlook* (January 2019 update) of IMF, India would remain the fastest growing economy among the major economies of the world. India is projected to grow at 7.5 percent in 2019-20 and 7.7 percent in 2020-21.

Similarly, World Bank's Report titled *Global Economic Prospects*, released in January 2019 has kept India's growth projections unchanged at 7.3 percent for 2018-19 and 7.5 percent in 2019-20.

On January 7, 2019, Central Statistics Office (CSO) released the first advance estimates of GDP growth for the year 2018-19. It projected an overall economic growth of 7.2 percent for the year 2018-19.

India's growth performance needs to be seen in the context of the slowing down of the world economy. Global growth is expected to slow to 2.9 percent in 2019-20. International trade and investment are moderating, trade tensions remain elevated, and financing conditions are tightening. Amid recent episodes of financial stress, growth in emerging market and developing economies has lost momentum. Financial market pressures and trade tensions can escalate, denting global activity.

Amidst this gloomy landscape, India stands out as a haven of stability and an outpost of opportunity. These achievements are creditable because they have been accomplished in the face of global headwinds.

IMF has praised India for implementing important reforms including the introduction of GST, inflation targeting and Insolvency and Bankruptcy Code. It has observed that "sleeping Indian elephant has started running". Once the elephant starts running, it is very difficult to stop it.

High GDP growth rate clearly indicates that several structural reforms have started paying rich dividends. The economy is back on the rails after short-term dislocations and disruptions caused by demonetization of high currency notes on November 8, 2016 and the implementation of the GST from July 1, 2017. Now the time has come to reap the benefits of GST.

The contribution of GST to enhanced growth rate of India's GDP cannot be ignored. GST has moved the country from Inspector Raj to Technology Raj. Everything is now online—from tax payment to filing of returns and to claiming of refunds.

Business has become attractive. There are more entrepreneurs and start-ups in the country. India was placed at 77th position in World Bank's *Doing Business Report 2019*, making it the highest-ranked South Asian country. India was ranked at 142 in 2015, 130 in 2017 and 100 in 2018. Thus, the country has performed remarkably well by jumping 65 places since 2015.

The positive contribution of GST to GDP is not unexpected. Pre-GST studies by reputed research organizations had estimated that introduction of GST would lead to 2 to 3 percent increase in GDP. A study by the National Council of Applied Economic Research (NCAER) had suggested that growth would increase by 0.9-1.7 percent of GDP, purely based on the elimination of the cascading of taxes on exports. [1]

27.2 GST and Employment Generation

GST has contributed, though indirectly, to employment generation in many ways.

27.2.1 Concessions and Reliefs for Small Businesses: In view of the role of micro, small and medium enterprises (MSMEs) in employment creation and development of the economy, lenient tax treatment of this sector in GST laws has been a priority area for the tax authorities. MSMEs are the pampered child of GST. Small-scale traders, manufacturers and service providers have been given special consideration under the GST regime.

For a detailed discussion on this topic, see Part VII of this book.

27.2.2 Higher Investment: Under the pre-GST system, Union excise duties/CENVAT and States' sales tax/VAT applied to all capital goods, but the input tax credits were generally limited to manufacturing plant and equipment. For example, no input tax credits were allowed for the Union excise duties on capital equipment acquired for use in transportation, infrastructure, distribution, or construction sectors because these sectors were all outside the scope of excise duties which were applicable to manufacturing only. Similarly, no credit was allowed for the State VAT on capital goods acquired by the service sector (e.g. telecommunications, transportation, finance, insurance, and IT services).

GST provides a seamless and efficient crediting of taxes paid on capital goods. Prices of capital goods can be expected to come down, thereby increasing their demand, boosting investment and hence growth.

In fact, investment was discouraged under the earlier system through the application of excise duties and VAT to capital goods, for which no set-off or input tax credit was provided. This increased the cost of capital goods and reduced investment which, in turn, led to lower employment and output.

27.3 GST and Formalization of the Economy

Unorganized (or informal) sector of the Indian economy is very large. Many small traders, manufacturers and service providers do business through cash transactions which are not properly recorded and hence lack transparency. The availability of input tax credit (ITC) under GST has forced lakhs of small business entities to come under the umbrella of GST. This has led to enhanced formalization of the economy. [2]

27.4 GST and Black Money

The Government of Prime Minister Shri Narendra Modi has placed a great deal of emphasis on controlling black money. This has been reflected in a series of measures taken recently. [3] These measures can be significantly complemented by GST which is a self-policing system, and hence more effective way of reducing corruption and rent-seeking. The complementary role of GST in curbing black money has, at least, two aspects.

The first relates to the self-policing incentive inherent in GST. To claim input tax credit, each dealer has an incentive to request documentation from the dealer behind him in the value-added/tax chain. Provided the chain is not broken through wide ranging exemptions, especially on intermediate goods, this self-policing feature of GST can work very powerfully.

According to Pomeranz, "Value added tax (VAT) is a stark example of a tax believed to facilitate enforcement through a built-in incentive structure that generates a third party reported paper trail on transactions between firms, which makes it harder to hide the transaction from the government". [4]

Second, GST has a dual monitoring structure—one by the States and one by the Centre. Hence, there is greater probability that evasion will be detected. Even if one tax authority overlooks and/or fails to detect evasion, there is the possibility that the other overseeing authority will catch the culprits.

Endnotes

1. National Council for Applied Economic Research, "Moving to Goods and Services Tax in India: Impact on India's Growth and International Trade", 2009.
2. There are many different definitions of formality/informality. The most common ones are: (a) whether a worker has a formal contract; (b) whether a worker is a regular/salaried worker (as opposed to self-employed or casual); (c) whether a firm is registered with any branch of the government; (d) whether the firm pays taxes; and (e) whether a worker receives social security.
3. In recent years, the issue of corruption and black money has come to the forefront after a series of financial scandals. Generation of black money—and its stashing abroad in tax havens and offshore financial centres—has dominated discussions and debates in public fora during the recent past. Members of the Parliament, the Supreme Court of India and the public at large have

unequivocally expressed concern on the issue, particularly after some reports suggested enormous estimates of such unaccounted wealth being held abroad.

After uproar in the Parliament, the Government of India came out with a *White Paper* on Black Money in May 2012. The *White Paper* presented the different facets of black money and its complex relationship with policy and administrative regime in the country. It also reflected upon the policy options and strategies that the Government had been pursuing to address the issue of black money and corruption in public life.

4. Pomeranz, Dina, "No Taxation without Information: Deterrence and Self-Enforcement in the Value Added Tax," Harvard University and NBER, 2013.

28

GST, Industry and Trade

The benefits of GST for industry and trade can be listed as under.

28.1 Unified, Uniform and Harmonized Indirect Tax System

Prior to the introduction of GST from July 1, 2017, the indirect tax system of India was marked by multiplicity of taxes and rates at the Central and State levels. This resulted in a complex tax structure which was ridden with hidden costs for trade and industry. There was no uniformity of tax rates and collection procedures across States.

GST has ensured uniform exemption list, uniform rates and uniform collection procedures throughout the country. It has paved the way for a common national market. The country has moved from an inefficient and fragmented indirect tax system to an efficient and unified tax regime in the form of GST. The old system was mainly manual and opaque while the new system is technology-based and hence transparent.

For details, see chapter 26 of this book.

28.2 One-country, One-tax, and One-market

Pre-GST tax structure unmade India by fragmenting markets along state lines. This had the collateral consequence of favouring imports and disfavouring domestic production. These distortions were caused mainly by the following three features of the then existing tax system:

1. Central sales tax (CST) on inter-state sales of goods.
2. Other numerous inter-state taxes like entry tax.
3. Extensive nature of exemptions from additional duties of customs [commonly known as countervailing duty (CVD)] [1] and special additional duty of customs (SAD). [2]

28.2.1 Abolition of Central Sales Tax (CST): CST on inter-state sales of goods led to inefficiencies in the supply chain of goods. Goods produced locally within the jurisdiction of consumption attracted lower tax than those produced outside. This tax encouraged geographic fragmentation of production. The tax could be avoided partially through branch/stock transfers by manufacturers. However, the tax savings from branch transfers got substantially offset by the incremental costs of logistics and warehousing of goods in multiple locations.

28.2.2 Elimination of other Inter-state Taxes: Prior to the introduction of GST, there were inter-state taxes that were levied by the States in addition to the CST. These included entry tax not in lieu of octroi and entry tax in lieu of octroi. These taxes caused horrible difficulties for transporters. Highlighting the problems of transporters, *Economic Survey, 2016-17* remarked, "Images of queues of trucks in India, idling at state borders with their drivers haggling for official clearances or being subject to extortion are legion. The consequent damages to trade and economic activity too have been extensively catalogued". [3] All these taxes have now been folded into the GST with enormous benefits.

There is ample evidence to suggest that logistical costs within India are high. One study suggests that in one day, trucks in India drive 280 kilometres while the figure for US is 800 kilometres. This raises direct costs (wages to drivers, passed on to firms), indirect costs (firms keeping larger inventory), and location choices (locating closer to suppliers/customers instead of lowest-cost location in terms of wages, rent etc.). Further, only about 40 percent of the total travel time is spent driving, check points and other official stoppages take up almost one-quarter of total travel time. Eliminating check point delays could keep trucks moving almost 6 hours more per day, equivalent to additional 164 kilometres per day, thus, pulling India above global average and to the level of Brazil. [4]

All of these barriers to inter-state trade become even more important in India because the share of roads in freight traffic is high (about 72 percent). The implication is that it is especially important for India to reduce costs to inter-state trade because of the excessive reliance on roads for movement of goods.

28.2.3 CVD and SAD Exemptions: It is a well-accepted proposition in tax theory that achieving neutrality of incentives between domestic production and imports requires that all domestic indirect taxes should also be levied on imports. So, if a country levies excise duty/sales tax/GST on domestic production/sales, it should also levy them on imports. In India, this was achieved through CVD and SAD which were levied on imports to offset the impact of the excise duty and sales tax/VAT levied on domestically manufactured goods.

However, in some cases there were CVD and SAD exemptions which acted perversely to favour foreign production over domestically produced goods, i.e. they provided negative protection for Indian manufacturing. Moreover, CVD and SAD were not applied on the whole range of imports.

Two arguments in favour of CVD and SAD exemptions were typically given. First, that CVD and SAD exemptions on inputs helped manufacturers by reducing their input costs. The second rationale advanced for exempting many imported goods from CVD and SAD was that there was no competing domestic production. This argument was faulty because the absence of competing domestic production was by itself the result of not having the neutrality of incentives that the CVD created. In other words, domestic producers might have chosen not to enter because the playing field was not level.

Now if an exemptions-free GST is levied on imports, as seems to be the case, it would ensure neutrality of incentives. In effect, India would be promoting domestic manufacturing without becoming protectionist and without violating any of its international trade obligations under the World Trade Organization (WTO) or under India's free trade agreements (FTAs).

28.3 Absence of Tax Cascading

By amalgamating a large number of Central and State taxes into a single tax and allowing set-off of prior-stage taxes, GST has mitigated the ill effects of cascading and pave the way for a common national market. A system of seamless tax credits throughout the value-chain, and across boundaries of States, has ensured that there is minimal cascading of taxes. This would reduce hidden costs of doing business.

See also section 5.3 of chapter 5 of this book.

28.4 Hassles-free Movement of Goods

In the pre-GST era, most States had put in place a system of check posts on their border roads. There were many reasons for putting such physical barriers to trade. These included the following:

1. Enforcement of state excise, market cess, forest and vehicle fitness regulations.
2. Applicability of lower taxes on inter-state trade than on intra-state trade.
3. There being no tax on stock transfers.
4. Levy of entry tax on specified goods.
5. Levy of octroi by some municipalities.
6. Internal security.

However, such check posts, by the very nature of their operations, generated enormous delays in road traffic. The arrangement also encouraged rent-seeking behaviour. The same vehicle had to pass through two check posts—the exporting State's check post and the importing State's check post—while crossing one border. Both these check posts were often located within a couple of kilometres of each other and a transport vehicle had to spend considerable time at both. Truck drivers often had to queue up for hours to pay octroi/entry tax and get their consignments and papers checked, causing delays and adding to costs.

Soon after the introduction of GST from July 1, 2017, most of the States dismantled border check posts for commercial taxes. Many State Governments, through advisories to their field staff, are ensuring that truckers are not harassed. This has significantly reduced travel time, minimized delays and reduced transaction costs.

28.5 Easy Compliance

In the pre-GST system, there were multiple compliances required for taxes such as Central excise, service tax, state level sales tax/VAT, entry tax etc.

GST has ensured single and uniform compliance for indirect taxes across the country. GST has been designed to have minimal human interface. It is being implemented through a strong IT platform by GSTN. Practically every activity is done online.

A robust and comprehensive IT system is the foundation of GST regime in India. Therefore, all taxpayer services such as registrations, returns, payments, refunds etc. would be available to the taxpayers online, which would make compliance easy and transparent. Electronic matching of input tax credits across India will make the process more transparent and accountable. Improved environment of compliance would encourage more paper trail of transactions. [5]

28.6 Reduced Interface between Taxpayer and Tax Collector

All interactions under GST are through the common GSTN portal and hence there will be less public interface between the taxpayer and the tax administration. Timelines have been provided for important activities like obtaining registration, refunds etc.

In short, GST is a comprehensive indirect tax levy on manufacture, sale and consumption of goods as well as services at the national level. GST is an indirect tax for the whole of India to make it one unified common market. GST is designed to give India a world class tax system and improve tax collections. It would end the long-standing distortions of differential treatment of manufacturing sector and services sector. GST will facilitate seamless credit across the entire supply chain and across all States under a common tax base.

See also Part VII of this book for interface between GST and micro, small and medium enterprises (MSMEs).

Endnotes

1. Under Section 3(1) of the Customs Tariff Act, 1975, an additional duty on goods imported into the country was leviable. The rate of this duty was equal to the excise duty on like articles if produced or manufactured in India. The underlying philosophy of this countervailing duty was to ensure that the protection provided by the import duty to domestic industry was not reduced.
2. This duty was also known as special CVD and was levied under Section 3(5) of the Customs Tariff Act, 1975. This duty was in addition to basic customs duty and CVD levied under Sections 3(1) and 3(3) respectively of the said Act. It was equal to sales tax/VAT, local tax or any other charge on a like article on its sale, purchase or transportation in India.
3. Government of India, *Economic Survey, 2016-17*, p. 233.
4. JPS Associates (2011), "Economic Cost of Inter-State Barriers in Goods Traffic".
5. For various types of compliance costs, see section 1.6.2 of chapter 1 of this book.

29

GST and Prices

Price rise, general or commodity-specific, can be due to many reasons. Tax is just one component of the price of a commodity or service. If price of petrol increases, it can be due to costlier crude oil imports and/or enhanced Central excise duty/State VAT.

Cross-country experience shows that introduction of GST has inflationary tendency. This happens in spite of the availability of input tax credit at every stage of value addition in the production process which should actually reduce the final prices. Prices increase because suppliers do not pass on the benefits of tax concessions to the consumers and thereby indulge in illegal profiteering. India followed examples of Malaysia and Australia which had to put in place mechanisms to prevent unethical profiteering. Therefore, India's GST law requires that any reduction in rate of tax on any supply of goods or services or the benefit of input tax credit should be passed on to the recipient by way of commensurate reduction in prices.

Luckily, price situation in India has remained comfortable after the implementation of GST from July 1, 2017. Rate of inflation has been hovering around 3 to 4 percent which is within tolerable limits. Following reasons can be identified for this price stability.

29.1 Why Prices Have Not Increased Post-GST?

First, many essential goods and services of mass consumption are either exempt from GST or bear nil rate of tax. For goods, examples include bread, fresh fruits and vegetables, fresh milk, curd, and hearing aids. For services, the two prominent examples are health and educational services.

Second, many essential goods and services are subject to 5 percent rate of tax which is affordable. Examples include sugar, tea, edible oils, and house-keeping services such as plumbing.

Third, there were about 227 items subject to 28 percent rate of tax when GST was rolled out. In due course of time, many items have been transferred to lower rate categories with the result that presently only about 40 items are subject to highest rate of 28 percent. These are mainly luxury and demerit goods like motor cars, air conditioners, *pan masala,* tobacco products and aerated waters.

Fourth, GST law stipulates that any reduction in rate of tax on any supply of goods or services or the benefit of input tax credit should be passed on to the recipient by way of commensurate reduction in prices. National Anti-profiteering Authority (NAA) is the watchdog body constituted by the Central Government to examine whether such tax benefits availed by any registered person have actually resulted in a commensurate reduction in prices. NAA is the institutional mechanism under GST law to check unfair profit-making by the trading community.

For details on anti-profiteering provisions under GST law, see chapter 24 of this book.

In short, prices have not increased post-GST because Government has followed a policy of soft rates with improved compliance.

29.2 Pre- and Post-GST Indirect Tax Burden

In the pre-GST system, goods were subject to Central excise duties, State level VAT, entry tax and various kinds of cesses. The rate of VAT differed from state-to-state. It was difficult to estimate the total burden of taxes/duties on different goods. GST has ensured uniform tax rates on different goods and services throughout the country. Therefore, comparison of pre-GST tax burden on a commodity with post-GST burden is a ticklish exercise. Nevertheless, calculations show that GST burden on many goods is less than pre-GST tax burden. For example, detergents are subject to 18 percent rate under GST while it was much higher earlier (12 percent excise duty + 13 percent VAT).

In the case of services, there was a uniform service tax rate of 15 percent imposed by the Central Government. Pre- and post-GST comparison of tax burden on different services is relatively easier. Thus, erstwhile service tax of 15 percent was leviable on insurance services, banking services, telecommunication services, and services of beauty parlours. These services are subject to 18 percent rate of GST. Apparently, these services have become a bit costlier due to GST. Conversely, eating out in a restaurant attracted 15 percent service tax but under GST it is 5 percent. Thus, eating out has become cheaper in the post-GST period.

29.2.1 Single and Transparent Tax Proportionate to the Value of Goods and Services: In the pre-GST regime, cost of most goods and services in the country was laden with a host of hidden taxes due to multiple indirect taxes being levied by the Centre and the States, with incomplete or no input tax credits available at progressive stages of value addition. Under GST, there is only one tax from the manufacturer to the consumer, leading to transparency of taxes paid by the final consumer.

29.3 Relief in Overall Tax Burden

For the consumers, the biggest gain is in terms of a reduction in the overall tax burden on goods. Due to efficiency gains and prevention of leakages, GST is claimed to have reduced overall tax burden on most commodities, benefiting the consumers. As already noted, many essential items of mass consumption are either exempt from GST or bear 5 percent rate of tax.

Government has generally followed the policy of *soft rates with improved compliance.* This policy is continuing and more reductions in tax rates on goods and services are expected in the future.

The evolving GST design is aimed at tax rates that would protect revenue, simplify administration, encourage compliance, avoid adding to inflationary pressures, and keep India in the range of countries with reasonable levels of indirect taxes.

Table 29.1 lists the items on which tax incidence under GST is lower than pre-GST incidence of indirect taxes.

Table 29.1: Items on which Tax Incidence under GST is Lower than Pre-GST Incidence of Indirect Taxes

(percent)

S. No.	Description of item	Pre-GST incidence*	GST rate
1.	Wheat	2.5	0
2.	Rice	2.75	0
3.	Unbranded flour	3.5	0
4.	Curd, *lassi*, butter milk	4	0
5.	Unbranded natural honey	6	0
6.	Ultra high temperature (UHT) milk	6	5
7.	Tea	6	5
8.	Milk powder	6	5
9.	Sugar	6	5
10.	Sweatmeats	7	5
11.	Vegetable edible oils	6	5
12.	Spices	6	5
13.	Ketchup and sauces	12	12
14.	Mustard sauce	12	12
15.	Toppings, spreads and sauces	12	12
16.	Mineral water	27	18
17.	Sugar confectionery	21	18
18.	Children's drawing/colouring books etc.	7	0
19.	Footwear up to ₹ 500 per pair	10	5
20.	Kerosene pressure lanterns	8	5
21.	Coal	9	5
22.	Toothpowder	17	12
23.	LED	15	12
24.	X-ray films for medical use	23	12
25.	Diagnostic kits and reagents	16	12
26.	Fixed speed diesel engines	16	12
27.	Fly ash bricks and fly ash blocks	16	12
28.	Sewing machines	16	12
29.	Hair oil	27	18
30.	Toothpaste	27	18
31.	Soap	27	18
32.	Other footwear	21	18
33.	LGP stove	21	18
34.	Aluminium foils	19	18
35.	School bags	22	18
36.	Printers	19	18

contd...

37.	Staplers	27	18
38.	Tractor rear tyres and tubes	20	18
39.	Helmets	20	18
40.	CCTV	19	18
41.	Baby carriages	27	18
42.	Plastic tarpaulin	19	18
43.	Bamboo furniture	23	18
44.	Headgears and parts thereof	27	18
45.	Cement	29	28

*Pre-GST tax incidence would be higher if the tax incidence on account of Central sales tax (CST), octroi, entry tax etc. (which was more than 2 percent) is also included.

Source: Government of India, Central Board of Indirect Taxes and Customs (CBIC), [formerly, Central Board of Excise and Customs (CBEC)] (website).

30

GST, Exports and Imports

30.1 GST and Exports

30.1.1 Significance of Exports: Export promotion is a key objective of economic policy in India. Exports help to improve the country's economic growth, employment and balance of payments. Exports have acquired added significance in the wake of liberalisation wave sweeping across the world. The trend towards market economy in almost all the countries of the world has increased the role of exports in developmental efforts. Exports have become an important indicator of a country's economic performance.

Department of Commerce, Ministry of Commerce and Industry, Government of India is the nodal agency for the regulation, development and promotion of India's international trade and commerce. Goals are realized through the formulation of appropriate international trade and commercial policy and its effective implementation. The long-term vision is to make India a major player in world trade by 2020, and assume a role of leadership in international trade organizations commensurate with India's growing importance.

Foreign Trade Policy (FTP) for the period 2015-20 announced by the Government on April 1, 2015 visualises increase in India's exports of merchandise and services from US$ 465.9 billion in 2013-14 to approximately US$ 900 billion by 2019-20 and to raise India's share in world exports from 2 percent to 3.5 percent.

Against this backdrop, the greatest challenge facing the Indian economy is to enhance its productivity and competitiveness so as to achieve a sustained growth in exports of goods and services. Growth prospects can be enhanced considerably by tapping the opportunities offered by the international economy in terms of markets, investment and technologies along with improvement in efficiency and absorbing excess capacity available in the economy.

In short, export promotion is a key objective of the economic policy of the Government of India. The rationale for the same is to maintain the balance of payments, create job opportunities and boost economic growth. To boost exports, government provides certain reliefs and benefits to business houses. One such relief provided under GST regime is the provision of zero-rated supplies. Taxes that go into production of goods that are exported are refunded to keep competitiveness of India's exports in world markets.

30.1.2 Meaning of Export of Goods and Services: According to Section 2(5) of the IGST Act, 2017, "export of goods means taking goods out of India to a place outside India". [1]

As per Section 2(6) of the same Act, "export of services means the supply of any service when:

1. the supplier of service is located in India;
2. the recipient of service is located outside India;
3. the place of supply of service is outside India;

4. the payment for such service has been received by the supplier of service in convertible foreign exchange; and
5. the supplier of service and the recipient of service are not merely establishments of a distinct person in accordance with Explanation 1 in Section 8.

30.1.3 Exports are Inter-state Supplies: Section 7 of the IGST Act, 2017, comprehensively defines the term *inter-State supply.* [2] As part of the comprehensive definition of inter-state supply, Section 7(5) of the Act treats the supply of goods/services as inter-state supply: (a) when the supplier is located in India and the place of supply is outside India and (b) when supply is made to or by a special economic zone (SEZ) developer or a SEZ unit. [3]

30.1.4 Exports are Zero-rated Supplies: What is zero-rated Supply? Zero rated supply is a supply of goods/services on which no tax is payable but input tax credit pertaining to that supply is admissible.

All exports (whether of goods or services) as well as supplies to SEZs have been categorized as zero-rated supplies in the IGST Act. [4]

Zero-rated supply under Section 16(1) of the IGST Act, 2017 means any of the following supplies of goods/services namely:

1. Export of goods or services or both; or
2. Supply of goods or services or both to a SEZ developer or a SEZ unit.

For a comparison between *exempt supply* and *zero-rated supply*, see Tables 13.3 and 13.4 of chapter 13 of this book.

The concept of zero rating of supplies requires the supplies as well as the inputs used in supplying the supplies to be GST-free. This is ensured by employing the following means:

1. Taxes paid on the supplies which are zero-rated are refunded.
2. Credit of input taxes is allowed.
3. Wherever the supplies are exempted, or the supplies are made without payment of tax, the tax paid on inputs (i.e. unutilized input tax credit) is refunded.

As per Section 16(2) of the IGST Act, 2017 credit of input tax may be availed for making zero-rated supplies, notwithstanding that such supply may be an exempt supply.

Thus, even if a supply is exempted (e.g. sanitary napkins), the credit of input tax may be availed for making zero-rated supplies.

Explanation to Section 54 of the CGST Act, 2017 defines refund as under:

"*refund* includes refund of tax paid on zero-rated supplies of goods or services or both or on inputs or input services used in making such zero-rated supplies, or refund of tax on the supply of goods regarded as deemed exports [5], or refund of unutilised input tax credit as provided under sub-section (3)". [6]

30.1.5 Options for the Exporters: According to Section 16(3) of the IGST Act, 2017, "A registered person making zero rated supply shall be eligible to claim refund under either of the following options, namely: (a) he may supply goods or services or both under bond or Letter of Undertaking…without payment of integrated tax and claim refund of unutilised input tax credit; or (b) he may supply goods or services or both…on payment of integrated tax and claim refund of such tax paid on goods or services or both supplied, in accordance with the provisions of section 54 of the Central Goods and Services Tax Act or the rules made thereunder".

A registered person making zero-rated supply can claim refund under either of the following options.

1. Export under bond [7] or letter of undertaking (LUT) [8] without payment of tax.
2. Export along with tax payment and claim refund later.

Any registered taxpayer exporting goods can make use of LUT. However, any person who has been prosecuted for tax evasion for an amount of ₹ 2.5 crore or more under the GST laws is not eligible to furnish LUT. The validity of such LUT is for a period of 1 year (till the end of financial year). An exporter furnishing LUT is required to furnish fresh LUT for each financial year. If the conditions mentioned in LUT are not satisfied within the time-limit, the privileges are revoked and the exporter will have to furnish bond.

For all the other assesses (including the ones who have been prosecuted for tax evasion of ₹ 2.5 crore or more under the GST laws), bond is to be furnished if the export is being made without payment of IGST.

30.1.6 Grant of Provisional Refund in Case of Zero-rated Supplies: Section 54(6) of the CGST Act, 2017 provides for grant of provisional refund of 90 percent of the total amount of refund claimed, on account of zero-rated supply of goods/services by a registered person. The remaining 10 percent can be refunded later after due verification of documents furnished by the applicant.

Provisional refund would be paid within 7 days after giving the acknowledgement. The acknowledgement of refund application is normally issued within a period of 14 days but in case of refund of integrated tax paid on zero-rated supplies, the acknowledgement would be issued within a period of 3 days.

The amount of provisional refund is credited directly to the claimant's bank account.

There is a condition attached to provisional refunds. The provisional refund is not granted if the applicant has been prosecuted for any offence under the GST law or earlier law within past 5 years. The amount of tax evaded in such prosecution shall be more than ₹ 2.5 crore.

30.1.7 Non-applicability of Principle of Unjust Enrichment: As per Section 54(8) of the CGST Act, 2017, the principle of unjust enrichment shall not be applicable in case of refund of taxes paid wherever such refund is on account of zero-rated supplies. [9]

30.1.8 Refund Problems: Refund is the main problem of exporters. Twenty-second meeting of the GST Council held on October 6, 2017, provided a comprehensive relief package for exporters. [10]

Government has organized special refund drives for exporters from time-to-time. Dedicated refund cells and help desks have been established in each commissionerate to help exporters to get their refund claims processed.

However, there are procedural problems and delays in getting refunds because export documents are to be verified and refund claims passed. Because of this delay, the working capital of the exporters gets blocked which adversely affects their capacity to export.

30.1.9 Failure to Export Goods and Services: What happens if goods and services are not exported? The provisions laid in Rule 96A of the CGST Rules, 2017 in this regard are as under:

(1) Any registered person availing the option to supply goods or services for export without payment of IGST shall furnish, prior to export, a bond or a letter of undertaking binding himself to pay the tax due along with interest:

(a) if goods are not exported outside India within 3 months of issuing the export invoice. The tax shall be paid within 15 days from the end of such three months period or

(b) if the payment for goods is not received in convertible foreign exchange within one year. The tax shall be paid within 15 days from the expiry of such one year.

(2) The details of the export invoices furnished on the common portal shall be electronically transmitted to the system designated by Customs and a confirmation that the goods covered by the said invoices have been exported out of India shall be electronically transmitted to the common portal from the said system.

(3) Where the goods are not exported within the time specified in sub-rule (1) and the registered person fails to pay the amount mentioned in the said sub-rule, the export as allowed under bond or letter of undertaking shall be withdrawn forthwith and the said amount shall be recovered from the registered person in accordance with the provisions of Section 79 of the CGST Act, 2017.

(4) The export as allowed under bond or letter of undertaking withdrawn in terms of sub-rule (3) shall be restored immediately when the registered person pays the amount due.

(5) Authorities, by way of notification, may specify the conditions and safeguards under which a letter of undertaking may be furnished in place of a bond.

(6) The provisions of sub rule (1) shall apply, mutatis mutandis, in respect of zero-rated supply of goods or services or both to a SEZ developer or a SEZ unit without payment of integrated tax.

30.1.10 Export of Goods and Services to Nepal and Bhutan: In GST law, export of goods and export of services are treated differently. As already noted, definition of *export of goods* under Section 2(5) of the IGST Act, 2017 attaches no condition other than 'taking goods out of India to a place outside India'. However in case of export of services, Section 2(6) of the same Act mandates, *inter alia*, the receipt of payment in *convertible foreign exchange*.

In case export proceeds from Nepal and Bhutan are received in Indian rupees, they will qualify as export in terms of goods but not in terms of services. If the payment is not received in freely convertible currency, then such services will not be treated as exports and in such situations the service provider has to discharge the tax liability.

Consequent upon the recommendations made by the GST Council in its Twenty-third meeting held in Guwahati on November 10, 2017, services to Nepal and Bhutan are treated as export of services irrespective of realization of payment in Indian Rupee. Such services are exempt from payment GST and allowed ITC.

In short, goods and services exported to Nepal and Bhutan are exports, irrespective of realization of payment in India rupee.

30.1.11 Refund of IGST Paid on Supply of Goods to Tourist Leaving India: According to Section 15, "The integrated tax paid by tourist leaving India on any supply of goods taken out of India by him shall be refunded in such manner and subject to such conditions and safeguards as may be prescribed.

Explanation—For the purposes of this section, the term "tourist" means a person not normally resident in India, who enters India for a stay of not more than six months for legitimate non-immigrant purposes".

30.2 GST and Imports

30.2.1 Meaning of Imports of Goods and Services: Import of goods means bringing goods into India from a place outside India. Import of services means the supply of any service where

- the supplier of service is located outside India;
- the recipient of service is located in India; and
- the place of supply of service is in India.

30.2.2 Imports are Inter-state Supplies: As per explanation to clause (1) of Article 269A of the Constitution, IGST (CGST plus SGST) will be levied on all imports into the territory of India. Thus, import of goods is treated as inter-state supplies and hence subject to IGST in addition to the applicable customs duties. Import of services is treated as inter-state supplies and hence subject to IGST.

30.2.3 Rationale for IGST on Imports: Under Section 12 of the Customs Act, 1962 (the main enactment), duty of customs is levied, at such rates as may be specified under Customs Tariff Act, 1975, on goods imported into, or exported from India. This is known as basic customs duty (BCD).

As per Section 2 of the Customs Tariff Act, 1975, the rates at which duties of customs shall be levied are indicated in the First Schedule and the Second Schedule of this Act. First Schedule deals with import tariff and Second Schedule with export tariff.

BCD on imports indicates the *level of protection* which the Government wants to provide to domestic industries, subject to WTO rules, regulations and norms.

The duty may be a percentage of the value of the goods or at a specific rate. The Central Government has the power to reduce or exempt any goods from these duties.

IGST on imports ensures *level playing field* between imported goods and domestically produced goods.

In the pre-GST era, *level playing field* was ensured through Additional Duty of Customs [commonly known as Countervailing Duty (CVD)] under Section 3(1) of the Customs Tariff Act, 1975, on goods imported into the country. The rate of this duty was equal to the excise duty on like articles if produced or manufactured in India. [11] Similarly, Special Additional Duty of Customs (SAD), also known as Special CVD, was levied under Section 3(5) of the Customs Tariff Act, 1975. This duty was equal to sales tax/VAT, local taxes or any other charge on a like article on its sale, purchase or transportation in India. Again, the purpose of SAD was to counter balance various state level taxes and provide *level playing field* to indigenous goods which had to bear these taxes/charges.

With effect from July 1, 2017, these duties (CVD and Special CVD) were replaced by IGST. As already stated, the underlying philosophy of IGST is to endure *level playing field* between imported goods and domestically produced goods. In other words, IGST ensures that that the *level of protection* provided by the basic import duty (under Section 2 of the Customs Tariff Act, 1975) to domestic industry is not reduced.

30.2.4 Applicability and Calculation of IGST: IGST is applicable by virtue of section 3 (7) of the Customs Tariff Act, 1975. This section was amended with effect from July 1, 2017. The amended version provides that any article which is imported into India shall be liable to IGST at such rate which is leviable under Section 5 of the IGST Act, 2017 on a like article on its supply in India.

Section 3(7) of the Customs Tariff Act, 1975 reads as follows, "any article which is imported into India shall, in addition, be liable to integrated tax at such rate, not exceeding forty percent, as is leviable under section 5 of the Integrated Goods and Services Tax Act, 2017 on a like article on its supply in India, on the value of the imported article...".

While the full set-off is available of the IGST paid on import of goods and services, BCD paid on import is not eligible for set-off.

The incidence of tax follows the destination principle and the tax revenue in case of SGST accrues to the State where the imported goods and services are consumed. Unlike in the past, the States where imported goods are consumed now gain their share from the IGST paid on imported goods.

IGST is calculated on the aggregate of the following:

- Assessable value.
- Basic customs duty.
- Social welfare surcharge (10 percent of basic customs duty).

GST compensation cess over the peak rate of 28 percent of IGST on certain specified items, mainly luxury and *sin* goods (pan masala, tobacco and tobacco products, coal, aerated waters, motor vehicles), is imposed to compensate States for any revenue loss on account of implementation of GST.

Other notable points are as under:

1. IGST is applicable in case of import of goods/services.
2. IGST is not applicable on baggage.
3. Input tax credit pertaining to IGST paid is available.
4. If an exemption is given on inter-State supply under the IGST Act, 2017, it is taken into consideration while calculating IGST for the purpose of import.

30.2.5 Exemptions from IGST on Imports: At its Twenty-third Meeting held in Guwahati (Assam) on November 10, 2017, the GST Council took major decisions relating to GST rates, ITC eligibility criteria, and exemptions and clarifications on levy of GST on services. In the context of imports it approved the following exemptions:

1. Exemption from IGST on imports of lifesaving medicine supplied free of cost by overseas supplier for patients, subject to certification by DGHS of Centre or State

and certain other conditions.

2. Exemption from IGST on imports of goods (other than motor vehicles) under a lease agreement if IGST is paid on the lease amount.
3. Exemption from IGST on imports of specified goods by a sports person of outstanding eminence, subject to specified conditions.
4. Exemption from GST on specified goods, such as scientific or technical instruments, software, and prototype supplied to public funded research institution or a university or IISc, or IITs or NIT.
5. Coverage of more items, such as temporary import of professional equipment by accredited press persons visiting India to cover certain events, broadcasting equipments, sports items, testing equipment, under ATA carnet system. These goods are to be re-exported after the specified use is over.

Endnotes

1. Section 2(56) of the CGST Act, 2017 defines *India* to means the territory of India as referred to in Article 1 of the Constitution, its territorial waters, seabed and sub-soil underlying such waters, continental shelf, exclusive economic zone or any other maritime zone as referred to in the Territorial Waters, Continental Shelf, Exclusive Economic Zone and other Maritime Zones Act, 1976, and the air space above its territory and territorial waters.

   While territorial waters extends to a distance of 12 nautical miles into sea from the nearest point of the appropriate baseline, the Continental Shelf extends beyond the limit of the territorial waters to the outer edge of the continental margin or to a distance of 200 nautical miles from the baseline. Similarly, Exclusive Economic Zone is an area beyond and adjacent to the territorial waters, and the limit of such zone is 200 nautical miles from the baseline. Accordingly, it may be inferred that the jurisdiction of GST law would extend to 200 nautical miles into sea.
2. See section 13.3.1 of chapter 13 of this book.
3. **Special Economic Zones (SEZs):** India was one of the first in Asia to recognize the effectiveness of the export processing zone (EPZ) model in promoting exports, with Asia's first EPZ set up in Kandla (Gujarat) in 1965. However, the EPZs were not able to emerge as effective instruments for export promotion on account of multiplicity of controls and clearances, absence of world-class infrastructure and an unstable fiscal regime.

   Considering the need to enhance foreign investment and promote exports from the country and realising the need that level playing field must be made available to the domestic enterprises and manufacturers to be competitive globally, the Special Economic Zones (SEZs) Policy was announced in April 2000. This policy intended to make SEZs an engine for economic growth supported by quality infrastructure complemented by an attractive fiscal package, both at the Centre and the State level, with the minimum possible regulations. SEZs in India functioned from November 1, 2000 to February 9, 2006 under the provisions of the Foreign Trade Policy and fiscal incentives were made effective through the provisions of relevant statutes.

   To instil confidence in investors and signal the Government's commitment to a stable SEZ policy regime and with a view to impart stability to the SEZ regime thereby generating greater economic activity and employment through the establishment of SEZs, a comprehensive draft SEZ Bill was prepared after extensive discussions with the stakeholders. The Special Economic Zones Act, 2005, was passed by Parliament in May 2005 which received Presidential assent on June 23, 2005. After extensive consultations, the SEZ Act, 2005, supported by SEZ Rules, came into effect on February 10, 2006, providing for drastic simplification of procedures and for single window clearance on matters relating to Central as well as State Governments. The main objectives of the SEZ Act are the following:

- Generation of additional economic activity.
- Promotion of exports of goods and services.
- Promotion of investment from domestic and foreign sources.
- Creation of employment opportunities.
- Development of infrastructure facilities.

4. In its Twelfth Meeting held on March 16, 2017, the GST Council cleared a proposal for the zero rate to be applied for goods and services going to special economic zones (SEZs). In other words, supplies made to SEZs are zero-rated and considered as physical exports. In the earlier decision—in case of procurement of supplies by SEZs—tax was to be paid and then refund claimed of such tax paid but as per the discussion in the said meeting the same supplies were accepted as zero-rated.
5. As per Section 2(39) of the CGST Act, 2017, "*deemed exports* means such supplies of goods as may be notified under Section 147". According to section 147 of the same Act, "The Government may, on the recommendations of the Council, notify certain supplies of goods as deemed exports, where goods supplied do not leave India, and payment for such supplies is received either in Indian rupees or in convertible foreign exchange, if such goods are manufactured in India".
6. Sub-section (3) of Section 54 of the CGST Act, 2017 states, "...a registered person may claim refund of any unutilised input tax credit at the end of any tax period: Provided that no refund of unutilised input tax credit shall be allowed in cases other than: (i) zero-rated supplies made without payment of tax; (ii) where the credit has accumulated on account of rate of tax on inputs being higher than the rate of tax on output supplies (other than nil rated or fully exempt supplies), except supplies of goods or services or both as may be notified by the Government on the recommendations of the Council: Provided further that no refund of unutilised input tax credit shall be allowed in cases where the goods exported out of India are subjected to export duty: Provided also that no refund of input tax credit shall be allowed, if the supplier of goods or services or both avails of drawback in respect of central tax or claims refund of the integrated tax paid on such supplies".
7. **Bond:** It has a surety (another person) who guarantees the performance on the part of the obligor (person furnishing the bond).
8. **Letter of Undertaking (LUT):** It is a type of bank guarantee, under which a bank allows its customer to raise money from another Indian bank's foreign branch as a short-term credit.
9. For meaning of the term *unjust enrichment*, see endnote 3 of chapter 24 of this book.
10. See section 8.5.4 (I) of chapter 8 of this book.
11. Till the early 1960s, countervailing duty was levied on a select basis on products which were considered to erode the margin of protection to the domestic industry on account of the excise duty. In course of time when the number of excisable goods increased, the selective use of countervailing duty was found to be inadequate and complicated. Therefore, the Indian Tariff Act, 1934, was amended in 1963 to insert a new Section 2A to provide for the levy of countervailing duty in all cases where excise duty was leviable on a similar indigenous commodity.

31

GST and Government Revenues

GST is a non-intrusive electronic tax system under which the scope for black transaction is minimal. Moreover, it is a self-regulating system. These are positive features of GST in terms of government revenues.

Prior to the introduction of GST, it was made clear by the Central Government and the GST Council that the new nationwide tax would be revenue neutral. In other words, the revenue from GST would be almost the same as from taxes/duties proposed to be subsumed under GST. The natural growth in tax revenue, as a result of expanding economy, both at the level of Central and State Governments would be taken into account.

Central and State Governments stand to gain from GST in the following manner:

31.1 Reduction in Operating Costs

Since major Central and State indirect taxes have got subsumed under GST, the multiplicity of taxes has been substantially reduced which, in turn, would decrease the operating costs of the country's tax system. [1] The uniformity in tax rates and procedures across the country will go a long way in reducing compliance costs.

Backed by a robust end-to-end IT system, GST is simpler and easier to administer than all the erstwhile indirect taxes of the Centre and the States. GST, with common bases and common rates (across goods and services and across States and between the Centre and States) has facilitated administration and improved compliance while also rendering manageable the collection of taxes on inter-State supplies.

31.2 Controls on Leakages and Revenue Efficiency

Due to the seamless transfer of input tax credit from one stage to another in the chain of value additions, there is an in-built mechanism in the design of GST that incentivizes tax compliance by assessees. Uniform GST rates have reduced the incentive for evasion by eliminating rate arbitrage between neighbouring States and that between intra- and inter-State sales. [2]

GST is expected to decrease the cost of collecting taxes and will, therefore, lead to higher revenue efficiency. [3] There may also be revenue gain for the Centre and the States due to widening of the tax base, increase in trade volumes and improved tax compliance. Also, because of its transparent character, GST would be easier to administer.

31.3 Abolition of Central Cesses

26 Central cesses have been subsumed under GST. Apparently, it has increased the size of the divisible pool of resources to the advantage of the States.

For the list of Central cesses abolished, see Table 7.2 in chapter 7 of this book.

31.4 Inclusion of Services in the Tax Base

Prior to the introduction of GST, services were taxed by the Central Government under Entry 97 of List I (Union List) in the Seventh Schedule of the Constitution. Apart from the Centre, the States also had powers to tax certain services specified in clause (29A) of Article 366 of the Constitution. This sort of division of taxing powers created a grey zone which led to confusion and legal disputes. This problem was solved with the implementation of GST.

In fact, tax base of State Governments has significantly increased with the inclusion of the tax on services as well as the tax on manufactures. The tax base of the Centre, on the other hand, has increased only to the extent of tax on sales.

For details, see chapter 3 of this book.

31.5 States' Share in IGST on Imports

Additional duty of customs [commonly known as countervailing duty (CVD)] and special additional duty of customs (SAD) levied on imports have been replaced by IGST with the implementation of GST from July, 1, 2017. As per explanation to clause (1) of Article 269A of the Constitution, IGST is levied on all imports into the territory of India. Unlike during the pre-GST period, States—where imported goods are consumed—now gain their share from IGST paid on imported goods.

31.6 Compensation Provisions

Due to a shift from origin-based to destination-based indirect tax structure, some States may face drop in revenue in the initial years. To help the States during this transitional phase, the Centre has committed to compensate loss of revenue to any State for a period of 5 years. Section 18 of Constitution (One Hundred First Amendment) Act, 2016 provides for compensation to States by law, on the recommendation of the GST Council, for loss of revenue arising on account of implementation of GST for a period of 5 years. Thus, it is a Constitutional obligation on the part of the Centre to compensate a State if it suffers loss of revenue on account of switch over to GST.

For details, see chapter 32 of this book.

GST revenue figures made available by the Ministry of Finance from time-to-time show that revenue from GST is on expected lines, in fact slightly on the higher side. It can be concluded that the burden of indirect taxation, by and large, has remained the same. If GST revenue is extraordinarily high, then government should provide relief to taxpayers, in one form or the other.

Central Budget (Final) for the year 2019-20 presented to the Parliament on July 5, 2019 estimated GST revenue at ₹ 6,63,343 crore with the following break-up: CGST ₹ 5,26,000 crore; IGST ₹ 28,000 crore; GST compensation cess ₹ 1,09,343 crore.

Endnotes

1. **Operating Costs of a Tax:** These are made up of administrative costs plus compliance costs of a tax. See section 1.6 of chapter 1 of this book.

2. During the pre-GST period, differential rates of sales tax on the same set of commodities in different States often led to uneconomic diversion of trade as well as production centres. It was not uncommon for people of one State making purchases in other States to avoid or reduce sales tax liability.
3. Every tax involves some revenue yield and a corresponding cost of collection. The main items comprising the latter are wages of the officials and costs of materials. Cost of collection when expressed as a proportion of tax revenue is called cost-yield ratio. It is indicative of the overall efficiency of tax administration. Thus, the lower the cost of collection, the more productive is the tax and vice versa. Unusually high cost-yield ratios prove drag on public exchequer. Cost-yield ratios may be used to evaluate administration of competing taxes. Administrative costs are generally high in developing economies which are in the process of evolving tax system and tax administration. Widespread illiteracy and lack of accounting practices make assessment procedures extremely difficult in these countries.

32

GST and the Changed Landscape of Fiscal Federalism in India

Enactment of the Constitution (One Hundred and First Amendment) Act, 2016 and the subsequent introduction of Goods and Services Tax (GST) from July 1, 2017 marked a clear departure from the initial scheme of distribution of taxation powers between the Centre and the States envisaged in the Constitution. [1]

32.1 From Mutually Exclusive to Concurrent Powers of Taxation

Prior to the said Act, 2016 taxation powers between the Centre and the States were clearly demarcated in the constitution with no overlap between the respective domains. In other words, there were no concurrent powers of taxation (or joint occupancy of tax fields) by the two levels of government. The Centre had the powers to levy tax on the manufacture of goods (except alcoholic liquor for human consumption, opium, narcotics etc.) while the States had the powers to levy tax on the sale of goods. In the case of inter-State sales, the Centre had the power to levy Central sales tax (CST), but the tax was collected and retained entirely by the originating States.

Taxes with inter-state base and those in the case of which all-India uniformity in rates was desirable, to facilitate industry and trade, were vested in the Central Government. Taxes which were location-specific and related to subjects of local consumption were with the States. As for services, it was the Centre alone that was empowered to levy service tax. Broadly speaking, taxes on production and services were levied by the Centre and taxes on sale and purchase by the State Governments. The absence of joint occupancy of tax fields had successfully minimised double taxation, tax rivalry between the Centre and the States, and duplicate tax administration.

The above-mentioned Act, 2016 inserted Article 246A in the constitution which now confers concurrent powers to both Parliament and State Legislatures to make laws with respect to Goods and Services Tax (GST). The dual GST imposes tax on the same taxable event—supply of goods and services—simultaneously by both the Centre and the States. Both the Centre and the States are empowered to levy GST across the value chain from the stage of manufacture to consumption. The credit of GST paid on inputs at every stage of value addition is available for the discharge of GST liability on the output, thereby ensuring GST is charged only on the component of value addition at each stage. This has ensured that there is no *tax-on-tax*.

As already stated, introduction of GST has concurrently empowered the Centre and the States to levy and collect it. The assignment of concurrent jurisdiction to the Centre and the States for the levy of GST requires a unique institutional mechanism that would ensure that decisions about the structure, design and operation of GST are taken jointly by the two levels of government. Goods and Services Tax Council (GST Council) is the institutional mechanism for this purpose with constitutional force.

32.2 Compensation to States for the Loss of Revenue Due to GST Implementation

In the pre-GST era, when goods were sold within the State, then sales tax (later VAT) was levied, collected and appropriated by the concerned state. In case goods were sold in the course of inter-State trade, then Central Sales Tax (CST) was levied by the Central Government but the revenue was collected and appropriated by the exporting State (State of origin) where production or sale took place rather than the State where consumption happened (importing State).

Switchover from origin-based sales tax/VAT to destination-based GST was a thorny issue in the designing of the new tax. Many manufacturing States expressed concerns over the loss of revenue on account of such a shift. To allay their fears, it was decided to compensate states which may suffer revenue loss consequent upon the introduction of GST.

For details on this issue, see section 6.6.1 of chapter 6 of this book.

32.3 Constitutional Provisions and the Law for Compensation to States

Despite the sincere attempts made by the Empowered Committee (EC) of State Finance Ministers on the determination of revenue neutral GST rates, it was difficult to estimate accurately as to how much the States would gain from service taxes and how much they would lose on account of removal of cascading effect, payment of input tax credit and phasing out of CST. In view of this, it was essential to provide adequately for compensation for loss that might emerge during the process of implementation of GST. The payment of this compensation was ensured in terms of special grants to be released to the States on the basis of neutrally-monitored mechanism. Section 18 of the Constitutional (One Hundred First Amendment) Act, 2016—reproduced below—incorporated provisions for such compensation.

"Compensation to States for Loss of Revenue on Account of Introduction of Goods and Services Tax: 18. Parliament shall, by law, on the recommendation of the Goods and Services Tax Council, provide for compensation to the States for loss of revenue arising on account of implementation of the goods and services tax for a period of five years".

Goods and Services Tax (Compensation to States) Act, 2017 was enacted to levy compensation cess for providing compensation to the States for the loss of revenue arising on account of implementation of the goods and services tax with effect from July 1, 2017, for a period of 5 years or for such period as may be prescribed on the recommendations of the GST Council.

Compensation to the affected states is provided through GST compensation cess.

In the very First Meeting of GST Council held on September 22-23, 2016, it was decided, *inter alia*, that Financial year 2015-16 would be the base year for compensating the States in case of any revenue loss to States following the implementation of GST.

Growth rate of revenue for a state during the 5 year period is assumed to be 14 percent.

The base year tax revenue consists of revenue from: (a) state VAT, (b) Central sales tax, (c) entry tax, octroi, local body tax, (d) taxes on luxuries and (e) taxes on advertisements etc. In other words, revenue from all taxes of a state—subsumed under GST—in 2015-16 is the base year revenue. However, any revenue among these taxes related to supply of alcohol for human consumption, and five specified petroleum products, is not accounted as part of the base year revenue.

32.4 GST Compensation Cess

It is a cess levied under Section 8 of the Goods and Services Tax (Compensation to States) Act, 2017. It is applicable—in addition to the regular GST taxes (CGST + SGST/UT-GST on intra-state supplies and IGST on inter-state supplies—on the supply of certain notified goods/services. The following goods—which mostly belong to the luxury and demerit categories—have been notified for the purpose so far.

1. *Pan masala.*
2. Tobacco and tobacco products.
3. Coal.
4. Aerated waters.
5. Motor vehicles.

32.4.1 Purpose of Compensation Cess: GST cess is levied to compensate states which may suffer any loss of revenue due to the implementation of GST from July 1, 2017. The revenue collected from compensation cess is credited to a non-lapsable fund known as Goods and Services Tax Compensation Fund. The Fund is used for compensating tax revenue loss to states on account of GST implementation.

The Act specifies that compensation payable to states has to be released at the end of every two months. The cess will be levied for a period of 5 years (transition period) from the date of implementation of GST.

32.4.2 Collection and Calculation of Cess: All taxable persons supplying the notified goods, except taxpayers registered under composition scheme, are liable to collect and remit the cess to the Government. The cess is calculated on the basis of the taxable value of the supply and as per the rate schedule for compensation cess. It is levied in addition to the regular GST taxes, i.e. CGST + SGST/UT-GST in the case of intra-state supplies and IGST in the case of inter-state supplies.

A. On Exports: Compensation cess is not charged on goods exported by an exporter under bond and the exporter is eligible for refund of input tax credit of cess relating to goods exported. In case goods are exported on the payment of cess, the exporter is eligible for refund of cess paid on goods exported by him, along with refund of input tax credit of cess relating to goods exported.

B. On Imports: In case compensation cess is applicable on goods imported into India, then it is levied and collected in accordance with the provisions of Section 3 of the Customs Tariff Act, 1975, at the point when duties of customs are levied on the said goods under section 12 of the Customs Act, 1962, on a value determined under the Customs Tariff Act, 1975.

The cess is levied and collected along with customs duty and IGST.

Table 32.1 presents maximum permissible rate of GST compensation cess on notified goods.

Table 32.1: Maximum Permissible Rate of GST Compensation Cess

S. No.	Description of supply of goods or services	Maximum rate of GST compensation cess
1.	Pan Masala	One hundred and thirty-five percent. Ad valorem
2.	Tobacco and manufactured tobacco substitutes, including tobacco products	Four thousand one hundred and seventy rupees per thousand sticks or two hundred and ninety percent ad valorem or a combination thereof, but not exceeding four thousand one hundred and seventy rupees per thousand sticks plus two hundred and ninety percent ad valorem
3.*	Coal, briquettes, ovoids and similar solid fuels manufactured from coal, lignite, whether or not agglomerated, excluding jet, peat (including peat litter), whether or not agglomerated.	Four hundred rupees per tonne
4.	Aerated waters	Fifteen percent ad valorem
4A.**	Motor vehicles for the transport of not more than thirteen persons, including the driver	Twenty-five percent ad valorem
5.	Motor cars and other motor vehicles principally designed for the transport of persons (other than motor vehicles for the transport of ten or more persons, including the driver), including station wagons and racing cars	Twenty-five percent ad valorem*
6.	Any other supplies	Fifteen percent ad valorem

*Compensation cess on coal is the new *avtaar* of clean energy cess which was levied under Central excise law but with a difference. Clean energy cess was levied only on raw coal, lignite and peat raised and dispatched from a coal mine. GST compensation cess is levied at every point of sale of coal.
**Inserted by Section 2 of Goods and Services Tax (Compensation to States) Amendment Act, 2017.
Source: Government of India, Ministry of Finance, Department of Revenue, Central Board of Indirect Taxes and Customs (CBIC) (website).

32.4.3 Input Tax Credit (ITC): ITC can be availed on compensation cess paid on inward supplies of the notified goods. However, the credit of the cess paid can be utilized only towards payment of cess liability.

32.4.4 Laws and Rules Applicable: The provisions of the CGST Act, 2017 and the rules made thereunder—including those relating to assessment, input tax credit, appeals, offences and penalties—apply in relation to the levy and collection of the cess on the intra-state supply of goods and services. Similarly, in the case of inter-state supplies the provisions of the IGST Act, 2017 and the rules made thereunder shall apply.

32.5 GST and Co-operative Federalism

Tax revenue is generally the main source of financing public expenditure at different levels of the government. In most democratic countries, taxation powers of central, state and local governments are mentioned in the constitution itself. Taxation powers of the government at different levels may be mutually exclusive or overlapping. The joint occupancy of tax fields often causes friction not only between the federal and provincial governments but also among the provinces themselves. This conflict concerns the manner in which the tax capacity of a particular tax base is shared between the two levels, i.e. how the tax room is apportioned.

In this connection, it is pertinent to note the relevance of co-operative federalism. To quote, "The essence of a co-operative federalism is that the Centre and the State Governments should be guided by the broader national concerns of using the available resources for the benefit of the people. Co-operative federalism encourages the Government at different levels to take advantage of a large national market, diverse and rich natural resources and the potential of human capabilities in all parts of the country and from all sections of the society for building a prosperous nation. Co-operative federalism makes it possible to raise all the available resources by the Government at different levels in a co-ordinated way and channel them for use for the common good of the people. This requires a harmonious relationship and co-operative spirit between the Centre and the States and among the States themselves. While a healthy competition among the States for evolving efficient and socially desirable policies and programmes is welcome, any competition which nullifies each other's advantages in development and erodes the resource base of the States should be avoided. Co-operative federalism is intended to ensure a minimum bundle of basic services and a nationally acceptable level of living for all the people of the country". [2]

GST has charted out a new course for co-operative federalism in India, focusing on mutual understanding and accommodation between the Centre and States as regards the structure of taxation of goods and services. It is pertinent to note that in all the 35 meetings of the GST Council held so far, all decisions have been taken unanimous or through consensus. In other words, no occasion has arisen so far that required voting to decide any matter. It may be recalled that economic reforms initiated in 1991 did not seek to consult the states. In contrast, every state was taken on board at every stage of the implementation of GST.

Highlighting the significance of GST Council, *Economic Survey, 2017-18* observed, "India has created one of the most effective institutional mechanisms for cooperative federalism, the GST Council. At a time when international events have been marked by a retreat into economic nativism and the attendant seizing of control, Indian states and the centre have offered up a refreshing counter-narrative, voluntarily choosing to relinquish and then pool sovereignty for a larger collective cause.

Co-operative federalism is of course not a substitute for states' own efforts at furthering economic and social development. But it is a critical complement, needed to tackle a wide array of difficult structural reforms that involve the states. For example, the "co-operative federalism technology" of the GST Council could be used to create a common agricultural market, integrate fragmented and inefficient electricity markets, solve interstate water disputes, implement direct benefit transfers (DBT), make access to social benefits portable across states, and combat air pollution". [3]

32.6 Enhanced Need for Co-operative Federalism in the 21st Century

India is making strides in the global sphere and this momentum cannot be maintained and carried forward without shared partnership of the State Governments in the development process. Hence, whenever development programmes are touched by international agreements, the well-conceived demands of states should be met in order to promote truly co-operative, co-ordinative and multi-dimensional centre-state relations.

Environmental challenges of global nature like climate change do not recognise state frontiers. Pollution and conservation issues reflect the uncomfortable tension between decision-making process of the governments at the centre-state-local levels. Disaster management transcends inter-state boundaries too.

Terrorism, militancy, organised crimes, rehabilitation of internally displaced persons, all require that the country as a whole comes together and the institutional bodies under State Governments help the Centre by collectively making available the necessary information and resources.

Globalisation has reinforced the need for concurrence between the geographical, climatic, environmental and technological diversities so that they may link with global processes. The experiences felt at the global level are also being felt at the local level.

Regrettably, sporadic voices of autonomy and separatism have vitiated the political and social fabric of the federal structure. Some ill-informed political leaders view all problems from a narrow parochial outlook. This not only weakens the nation but also makes the land fertile for the growth of terrorism and insurgency.

It has been argued that GST has led to loss of fiscal autonomy for states as it has curbed their ability to levy new taxes, change the existing tax rates or give exemptions to any class of goods or services. However, this criticism is outweighed when seen in the light of benefits of GST. GST has provided an all-India unified, uniform and harmonized indirect tax system to the country. It has ensured uniform exemption lists, uniform tax rates and uniform collection procedures throughout the country. It has paved the way for a common national market. The country has moved from an inefficient and fragmented indirect tax system to an efficient and unified tax regime in the form of GST. The old system was mainly manual and opaque while the new system is technology-based and hence transparent.

GST has successfully ensured tax harmony (instead of tax rivalry) not only between the Centre and the States but also among the States themselves.

Both the Centre and the States must attend to the task of preserving India's unity through constructive co-operative federalism which requires a great deal of commitment.

See also section 40.6 of chapter 40 of this book.

To sum up, post-GST, taxation powers of the Centre and the States overlap and the two tiers of the government will have to agree on GST rates, exemption lists, compliance procedures and other matters related to the smooth functioning of the new tax. The implementation of GST is the single most important tax reform undertaken since Independence in 1947 with far reaching fiscal consequences for the federal polity of India.

Endnotes

1. For enactment of the Constitution (One Hundred and First Amendment) Act, 2016 and its main provisions, see chapter 7 of this book.
2. Government of India, Planning Commission, *Ninth Five Year Plan* (1997-2002), Volume I, p. 241.
3. Government of India, *Economic Survey, 2017-18*, Volume I, p. 3.

Part VII
GST-MSMEs Interface

33

Why Are MSMEs Important in the Indian Economy?

MSMEs sector has emerged as a highly vibrant and dynamic sector of the Indian economy over the years. It contributes significantly in the economic and social development of the country by fostering entrepreneurship and generating largest employment opportunities, at comparatively lower capital cost than large industries, next only to the agricultural sector. MSMEs are complementary to large industries as ancillary units and this sector contributes significantly in the inclusive industrial development of the country. The MSMEs are widening their domain across sectors of the economy, producing diverse range of products and services to meet demands of domestic as well as global markets. MSMEs also help in industrialization of rural and backward areas, thereby reducing regional imbalances, and assuring more equitable distribution of national income and wealth.

In view of the crucial role of MSMEs in employment generation and development of the economy, it is imperative for the Government to make it easier for this sector to do business and comply with rules and regulations in force. In recognition of the same, relief to this sector in GST laws has been a priority area for the tax authorities. In fact, MSMEs sector is the pampered child of GST. Small manufacturers, traders and service providers have been given special consideration under the GST regime.

33.1 Estimated Number of MSMEs

As per the National Sample Survey (NSS) 73rd round, conducted by National Sample Survey Office, Ministry of Statistics and Programme Implementation during the period 2015-16, there were 633.88 lakh unincorporated non-agriculture MSMEs in the country engaged in different economic activities (196.64 lakh in manufacturing, 230.35 lakh in trade and 206.84 lakh in other services (Table 33.1).

Table 33.1: Estimated Number of MSMEs: Activity-wise

(in lakh)

Activity	Rural	Urban	Total	Percent share
Manufacturing	114.14	82.50	196.65	31
Trade	108.71	121.64	230.35	36
Other services	102.00	104.85	206.85	33
All	324.85	309.00	633.85	100

Source: Government of India, Ministry of Micro, Small and Medium Enterprises, *Annual Report, 2017-18*, Table 2.2, p. 24.

33.2 Share of MSMEs in Gross Domestic Product (GDP)

Recent trends in the contribution of MSMEs to GDP are shown in Table 33.2.

Table 33.2: Contribution of MSMEs to GDP at Current Prices

(₹ crore)

Year	Total GDP	Percent share of MSMEs in GDP
2011-12	87,36,329	29.57
2012-13	99,44,013	29.94
2013-14	1,12,33,522	29.76
2014-15	1,24,45,128	29.39
2015-16	1,36,82,035	28.77

Source: Government of India, Ministry of Micro, Small and Medium Enterprises, *Annual Report, 2017-18*, Table 2.1, p. 22.

33.3 Estimated Employment in MSMEs

As per the National Sample Survey (NSS) 73rd round conducted during the period 2015-16, MSMEs sector has been creating 11.10 crore jobs (360.41 lakh in manufacturing, 387.18 lakh in trade and 362.82 lakh in other services in the rural and the urban areas across the country (Table 33.3).

Table 33.3: Estimated Employment in MSMEs Sector: Activity-wise

(in lakh)

Activity	Rural	Urban	Total	Percent share
Manufacturing	186.56	173.86	360.41	32
Trade	160.64	226.54	387.18	35
Other services	150.53	211.69	362.22	33
All	497.73	612.09	1,109.81	100

Source: Government of India, Ministry of Micro, Small and Medium Enterprises, *Annual Report, 2017-18*, Table 2.8, p. 28.

33.4 Social Face of MSMEs

Being the largest source of employment after agriculture, MSMEs sector in India enables lakhs of men, women and children living in urban slums, upcoming towns, remote villages and isolated hamlets to use indigenous knowledge, cultural wisdom, and entrepreneurial skills for the sustenance of their lives and livelihoods. Apart from contributing to national income, MSMEs are instruments of inclusive growth, touching the lives of the most vulnerable, the most marginalized, viz. women, Muslims, scheduled castes (SCs) and scheduled tribes (STs). For many families, it is the only source of livelihood. For others, it supplements family income. Thus, instead of taking a welfare approach, this sector seeks to empower people to break the cycle of poverty and deprivation. It focuses on people's skills and agency.

Different segments of the MSMEs sector are dominated by different social groups. Women are mostly found in the unregistered sector—food processing enterprises, manufacturing enterprises and weaving—and often work part-time in family enterprises. Women and small children roll *bidis*, make *agarbattis*, do *zari* and sequin work for meagre wages. Muslims in large number are found in the unorganised weaving sector and in powerlooms. STs produce handcrafted articles and are involved in sericulture. In the North-East of India, most women engage in weaving.

33.5 Advantages of MSMEs

MSMEs have been recognised as engines of economic growth worldwide. In India, MSMEs manufacture products ranging from handloom sarees, carpets, soaps, pickles, *papads* to machine parts for large industries. Not only do MSMEs generate the highest employment per capita investment, they also go a long way in checking rural urban migration by providing villagers and people living in isolated areas with a sustainable source of employment. Among the MSMEs in India, the dispersed food products sector generates maximum employment. MSMEs often act as ancillary industries for the large scale industries providing them with raw materials, vital components and backward linkages.

Ever since the announcement of the Industrial Policy Resolution of 1948, small-scale industries have occupied a prominent place in the overall strategy of industrial development in India. Successive Five Year Plans allocated increasing resources for the development of small industries. In view of the abundance of labour, scarcity of capital, and rural nature of the economy, the preference for small industries is natural. The main arguments in favour of small industries are the following.

33.5.1 High Employment Potential: As development in a country takes place, the share of agriculture in providing employment and in GDP decreases. Small-scale industries provide maximum employment next only to the agricultural sector. Small industries are generally labour-intensive and therefore promise wider employment possibilities for the ever increasing population of India. They are also suitable as a supplementary source of employment for the Indian farmers who remain out of work during lean period of agricultural season. Small industries offer promising opportunities to educated unemployed in the urban areas to become self-employed gainfully.

The dispersed, unorganized and often household-based micro and small enterprises are capital-saving, labour-intensive and environment-friendly. In India, they are the largest source of employment after agriculture and are found in both rural as well as urban areas.

In view of the decline in agriculture's contribution to GDP and the near constant proportion of workers dependent on it, there is need for rapid generation of off-farm employment. There is need for diversification within agriculture (to sericulture, horticulture, pisciculture) to expand the scope for off-farm rural livelihoods. The real potential for employment generation however rests with the MSE sector which comprises weavers, artisans, and people engaged in food processing, hawkers, vendors, carpenters.

33.5.2 Widely Dispersed Entrepreneurial Base: On the eve of Independence in 1947, industries in India were located at certain selected places and were managed by a few communities like Parsis, Marwaris, and Chettiars. The Directive Principles of Indian

Constitution prohibit the concentration of economic power in few hands. Small industries ensure widest possible participation by different regions and different classes in the industrial growth of the country. These industries can be set up easily in any part of the country with modest skills and resources.

33.5.3 Relatively Low Capital Investment: As is well-known, India is a capital scarce country. One chief criticism of the pattern of industrial development has been the undue emphasis on capital-intensive large-scale industries. It is probably due to this wrong policy that the industrial sector has not been able to generate sufficient employment for the massive work force. Small industries require low capital investment and that too in indigenously produced machines, tools, and implements.

MSMEs are often driven by individual creativity. A major strength of the sector is its potential for greater innovation both in terms of products and processes. An inherent strength of the sector is that these enterprises can be set up with very small amounts of investments and have the locational flexibility to be located anywhere in the country. They are amenable to ancilliarisation and thus have natural linkages with large enterprises.

33.5.4 Regional Balanced Development: Balanced development of all the regions of the country has been an accepted objective of national economic policy. Many districts of the country, particularly in tribal and hilly areas have remained industrially undeveloped/underdeveloped as compared to certain other regions of the country. It may not be feasible to set up modern large-scale industries in backward areas. Therefore, these areas can be developed through a network of cottage and small industries.

33.5.5 Export Potential: MSMEs dominate in exports of sports goods, readymade garments, woollen garments and knitwear, plastic products, processed food and leather products. It is interesting to note that handicrafts have emerged as a leading revenue-earning item in India's exports. There is tremendous potential to expand the quantum of exports by small enterprises which produce handcrafted and hence eco-friendly items. Further, while small firms are unable to take advantage of economies of scale, they are ideal for meeting small orders from bulk exporters of ready-made garments, home furnishings etc.

33.6 Nature of MSMEs

MSMEs sector in India is highly heterogeneous in terms of the size of the enterprises, variety of products and services produced the levels of technology employed. These could be broadly grouped into the following three categories, based on the different sets of constraints faced and requirements of policy interventions.

33.6.1 High Growth Enterprises: These include MSMEs in sectors like textiles and garments, leather and leather products, auto components, drugs and pharmaceuticals, food processing, information technology (IT) hardware and electronics, paper, chemicals and petrochemicals, telecom equipment etc. Such enterprises not only have high potential for growth but could also contribute significantly in enhancing India's exports. One of the major constraints in growth of such enterprises is access to equity capital. Presently, there is almost negligible flow of equity capital into this sector despite the fact that overall such capital inflow has witnessed significant increase in the recent years.

There is, therefore, a need to promote inflow of equity capital into this sector by providing suitable incentives to MSME-focused angel/venture capital funds as well as by setting up of SME Exchanges/platforms.

Technology is another aspect that is critical for the growth of MSMEs. Given their scale of operations, it is not only difficult for them to invest in research and development activities but even to acquire modern and latest technologies available in the market due to high costs. The Government has launched the National Manufacturing Competitiveness Programme with the objective of enhancing the competitiveness of MSMEs. The programme includes several new and innovative schemes (viz. lean manufacturing, design clinics, quality management standards, quality technology tools, and incubators) for assisting the MSMEs in adoption of best international practices to enhance their competitiveness. Simultaneously, there is a need to make massive efforts for dissemination of information on the latest/modern technologies among the MSMEs and supporting them for undertaking technology upgradation, acquisition, adaptation and innovation. In addition, the Government also needs to encourage R&D in the engineering/technical institutions through suitable tax incentives and setting up of business incubators.

33.6.2 Enterprises Operating under Sub-contracting: Promotion of sub-contracting has been one of the important ingredients of the policy envisaged for the development of MSMEs in the country. Several measures have been taken by the Government towards this endeavour such as ancilliarisation, vendor development programmes, and buyer-seller meets. This has resulted in a significant number of micro and small enterprises operating under some system of sub-contracting with large enterprises. Such arrangements have not only helped in providing marketing linkages but have also resulted in technological linkages through provision of product specification and design. However, in view of the dependent relationship of such enterprises with the large enterprise, they also face several problems. Some of the major problems include the following:

1. Delays in payments.
2. In case of rejection, the small firms end up with practically no option but to dispose off their products.
3. Linkages such as financial and supply of raw material are seldom provided by the buyer enterprises.
4. Buyer enterprises are not bothered to ensure that such enterprises operate with minimum working conditions or comply with various regulations related to their working.

In the present globalised regime, there is an increasing pressure on industries to reduce costs to withstand the domestic as well as international competition. Sub-contracting offers significant scope for cost reduction and may lead to higher incidence of sub-contracting among micro and small enterprises. It is, therefore, important to address the constraints faced by the enterprises operating under such arrangements. While the Micro, Small and Medium Enterprises Development Act, 2006 provides for more rigorous provisions to counter the problems of delayed payments to the MSEs, the sense of insecurity of contract prevents them from taking legal action for recovery of dues. The MSE facilitation councils constituted in the States have to become more active to help MSEs in quick resolution of disputes relating to delayed payments. Further, the MSMEs need to be supported through appropriate programmes/schemes with focus on skill development and technology upgradation for improving the quality of their products so that rate of rejection is minimized. Also, there is a need to provide enabling legal environment—by suitably amending the labour and urban zoning laws—that is conducive to setting up of new enterprises as well as functioning of existing enterprises.

33.6.3 Unorganised Sector Enterprises: No discussion on MSMEs can be complete without a full treatment of the unorganized sector in which enterprises are typically established through own funds or funds obtained through non-institutional sources. They lack managerial bandwidth, do not have established channels for marketing and are cantered around a single traditional technology.

According to the final report of the National Commission for Enterprises in the Unorganised Sector (NCEUS) [Chairman: Arjun Sengupta] released in April 2009, workers in the unorganized (or informal) sector constitute more than 93 percent of the total workforce of India. Unorganized sector workers are those who do not have any job security, income security or social security and are therefore extremely vulnerable to exogenous shocks. The Commission defined an unorganized enterprise as enterprise employing less than 10 workers. It estimated such enterprises at 58 million with total employment of 104 million persons.

33.7 GST and the Ministry of MSMEs

Following the rollout of GST on July 1, 2017, the Ministry of MSMEs took the following steps involving all the stakeholders:

All field organisations under the Ministry of MSMEs—namely Office of Development Commissioner (Micro, Small and Medium Enterprises), Khadi and Village Industries Commission (KVIC), National Small Industries Corporation (NSIC), Coir Board, National Institute for Micro, Small and Medium Enterprises (Ni-MSME), Mahatma Gandhi Institute for Rural Industrialization (MGIRI)—opened GST Cells in their respective offices to provide requisite support to MSMEs with respect to GST issues. More than 20,000 persons were trained in the various nuances of GST through workshops by Ministry of MSMEs and all its field organizations.

A special issue of *Laghu Udyog Samachar* was brought out fully dedicated to GST related issues. A GST-specific window was opened within the Internet Grievance Redressal System (IGMS) of the Ministry of MSMEs. Ministry set up a 24x7 helpline in NSIC to attend to queries. On July 13, 2017, the Ministry conducted a wider consultation workshop with all associations in which sector experts pertaining to MSMEs of the GST Council made presentations and clarified the queries and concerns related to GST.

To sum up, while MSMEs sector continues to script an exciting success story in India, there are inherent weaknesses and systemic failures which require bold policy initiatives and massive resource allocation. The sector is a blend of tradition and modern with an alarming level of informal sector enterprises at the bottom. The process of liberalization and global market integration has opened up wide opportunities for the sector, as also new challenges. Transparent and efficient policy-regulatory framework is the need of the hour. Government and other stakeholders should make concerted efforts to adopt bold strategies, best practices and progressive policies to unleash the potential of MSMEs.

34

Goods and Services Exempted from GST

Under GST law, Central and State Governments, on the recommendation of the GST Council, can exempt the supplies from the levy of GST either generally or subject to conditions. Hence, to understand the taxability of GST, it is important to know if an item is exempt or not under GST. It is noteworthy that most of the exempted goods and services are supplied by MSMEs.

34.1 Constitutional and Legal Provisions

Article 279A (4) of the Constitution reads, "The Goods and Services Tax Council shall make recommendations to the Union and the States on: (a) the taxes, cesses and surcharges levied by the Union, the States and the local bodies which may be subsumed in the goods and services tax; (b) the goods and services that may be subjected to, or exempted from the goods and services tax".

The power to grant exemption is given by Section 11 of the CGST Act, 2017 (or Section 6 of IGST Act, 2017). Section 11 reads, "(1) Where the Government is satisfied that it is necessary in the public interest so to do, it may, on the recommendations of the Council, *by notification*, exempt generally, either absolutely or subject to such conditions as may be specified therein, goods or services or both of any specified description from the whole or any part of the tax leviable thereon with effect from such date as may be specified in such notification.

(2) Where the Government is satisfied that it is necessary in the public interest so to do, it may, on the recommendations of the Council, *by special order* in each case, under circumstances of an exceptional nature to be stated in such order, exempt from payment of tax any goods or services or both on which tax is leviable".

In simple terms, following are the features of grant of exemptions under GST law:

1. Exemption should be in public interest.
2. It must be recommended by the GST Council
3. Generally, it is by way of issue of notification. [1]
4. Under exceptional circumstances, exemption may be granted by way of special order (not notification).
5. Exemption may be absolute or conditional.
6. Exemption may be grant from whole of tax leviable or part of tax leviable.

Provisions of Sections 11(1) and 11(2) of the CGST Act, 2017 are shown in Table 34.1.

Furthermore, Section 2(47) of the CGST Act, 2017 states, "*exempt supply* means supply of any goods or services or both which attracts nil rate of tax or which may be wholly exempt from tax under section 11, or under section 6 of the Integrated Goods and Services Tax Act, and includes non-taxable supply".

For details on exempt supply, see section 13.3.8 of chapter 13 of this book.

Table 34.1: Provisions of Sections 11(1) and 11(2) of the CGST Act, 2017

Taxable goods/services of any specified description	
Government is satisfied that it is necessary to do so in public interest	
Section 11(1)	**Section 11(2)**
Exempt generally	Exempt
Absolutely or subject to conditions	Under circumstances of an exceptional nature
Whole of tax leviable or part of tax leviable	Whole of tax leviable
By notification	By special order in each case

34.2 Classification of Exemptions

This can be as follows:

1. **Supply-specific Exemptions:** Certain supplies due to their nature and type are exempt from GST. All supplies that are notified become eligible for exemption, irrespective of who the supplier is, e.g. services by way of sponsorship of sport events and services by way of public conveniences.
2. **Supplier-specific Exemptions:** Exemption to the person making supplies, i.e. to the supplier, regardless of the nature of outward supply as, for example, services by Securities and Exchange Board of India (SEBI) and Reserve Bank of India (RBI).

34.3 Kinds of Exemptions

Exemptions can be of the following types:

34.3.1 Absolute Exemptions: These exemptions are given without any condition as, for example, transmission or distribution of electricity by an electricity transmission or distribution utility.

34.3.2 Conditional Exemptions: These exemptions are given subject to certain conditions as, for example, services by a hotel, guest house etc. for residential or lodging purposes, having declared tariff of a unit of accommodation of less than ₹ 1,000 per day.

34.3.3 Partial Exemptions: These are another type of exemptions subject to conditions. For example, intra-state supplies of goods and/or services from an unregistered person by a registered person are exempt from payment of GST under RCM (reverse charge mechanism) provided the aggregate value of all such supplies received by the registered person from all or any of the suppliers does not exceed ₹ 5,000 in a day.

Exempted goods are within the purview of GST but their supply does not attract any GST rate. There is a list of exempted goods which is harmonized for the Centre and the States as well as across States as far as possible.

Some of the exempted goods under GST law include bread, fresh fruits and vegetables, fresh milk, curd, and hearing aids. Similarly, exempted services include, *inter alia*, electricity [2], services provided by an educational institution to its students, faculty and staff, and healthcare services by a clinical establishment, an authorised medical practitioner or paramedics.

It is noteworthy that notification for exemption issued under Section 11(1) or 11(2) of the CGST Act, 2017 is deemed to be issued under the UT-GST Act, 2017 and the SGST Acts of respective States.

Exemption under the CGST Act, 2017 has no auto-application under the IGST ACT, 2017. Similarly, exemption under the IGST Act, 2017 has no auto-application under the CGST Act, 2017. In other words, GST exemption allowed in the case of inter-state transactions is not the same as GST exemption available in case of intra-state transactions and vice versa.

Choices which the GST Council makes regarding exemptions are critical. The more the exemptions, the higher will be the average GST rate.

Endnotes

1. The following two important notifications issued for exemption from payment of GST are noteworthy.

- Notification number 02/2017 dated June 28, 2017 which exempted supplies of around 149 items of goods in terms of section 11 (1) of the CGST Act, 2017. Salt, fresh fruits, plastic bangles were some of the items included in the list. The notification has been amended from time to time.
- Notification number 12/2017 dated June 28, 2017 which exempted supply of specified services under the CGST Act, 2017. The exempted services were almost the same as provided under the erstwhile service tax law. The notification has been amended from time to time.

2. Under Entry 53 of List II (State List) in the Seventh Schedule of the Constitution, the electricity duty is charged to consumers along with the electricity consumption rates. The rates are meant for the providers of electricity (electricity boards) while the electricity duty is meant for the state treasury.

35

Goods and Services Supplied by Businesses within Prescribed Threshold Limits of Aggregate Turnover

Just like a basic exemption is allowed to individual taxpayers under the Income Tax Act, 1961, so also exemption from registration and payment of GST is allowed to small businesses the aggregate annual turnover of which is within prescribed limits.

35.1 Purpose of Threshold Limit of Aggregate Turnover:

Threshold for exemption is built into a tax regime to keep small businesses out of tax net. This has following advantages:

1. Administrative cost of dealing with small businesses is relatively high.
2. Compliance costs and efforts are saved for small businesses.
3. Small businesses get relative advantage over large enterprises on account of lower or nil tax incidence.

Prior to the introduction of GST from July 1, 2017, thresholds prescribed in different VAT Acts of States varied from State-to-State.

35.2 Methodology to Compute Aggregate Turnover

In the context of GST, the methodology to compute *aggregate turnover* is given in Section 2(6) of the CGST Act, 2017 which states, "*aggregate turnover* means the aggregate value of all taxable supplies (excluding the value of inward supplies on which tax is payable by a person on reverse charge basis), exempt supplies, exports of goods or services or both and inter-State supplies of persons having the same Permanent Account Number, to be computed on all India basis but excludes Central tax, State tax, Union territory tax, integrated tax and cess".

Accordingly, aggregate turnover means the aggregate value of the following:

- All taxable supplies (excluding the value of inward supplies on which tax is payable by a person on reverse charge basis).
- Exempt supplies.
- Exports of goods/services.
- Inter-State supplies of persons having the same PAN, to be computed on all India basis.

However, aggregate turnover does not include the amount of GST (i.e. CGST, SGST/UT-GST, IGST and compensation cess).

35.3 Provisions Prior to April 1, 2019

Acknowledging the desirability of a uniform threshold across States, GST Council, in its First Meeting held on September 22-23, 2016 decided that businesses with an annual turnover of less than ₹ 20 lakh would be exempted from GST. Also, the threshold was decided to be ₹ 10 lakh in the case of special category States, which have been given a carve-out in the Constitution (One Hundred and First Amendment) Act, 2016 that paved the way for the introduction of GST. Thus, under Article 279A (4)(g) of the Constitution, GST Council can make recommendations to the Union and the States on special provision with respect to the 11 States of Arunachal Pradesh, Assam, Jammu and Kashmir, Manipur, Meghalaya, Mizoram, Nagaland, Sikkim, Tripura, Himachal Pradesh and Uttarakhand.

Due to smaller businesses, the threshold is lower in Special Category States. It is noteworthy that a lower threshold had prevailed in these States during the VAT regime.

In its Twenty-eighth Meeting held on July 21, 2018, the GST Council increased the threshold limit for registration in the six States of Assam, Arunachal Pradesh, Himachal Pradesh, Meghalaya, Sikkim, and Uttrakhand from ₹ 10 lakh to ₹ 20 lakh. In other words, only five States (Manipur, Mizoram, Nagaland, Tripura and Jammu and Kashmir) were left with threshold limit of ₹ 10 lakh.

Threshold limit of turnover was drastically recast in the Thirty-second Meeting of the GST Council held on January 10, 2019 in New Delhi. In the case of suppliers of goods, the Council decided to provide two threshold limits for exemption from registration and payment of GST: ₹ 20 lakh and ₹ 40 lakh. Depending on their revenue consideration, States were given the option to decide about one of the limits. It is noteworthy that the limits are not applicable for businesses selling goods inter-state.

As regards service providers, they were required to register for GST once they crossed a turnover of ₹ 20 lakh (₹ 10 lakh for Special Category States).

35.4 Provisions Effective April 1, 2019

Threshold limit of aggregate turnover for exemption from registration and payment of GST for the suppliers of goods is ₹ 40 lakh. It is ₹ 20 lakh in the case of Arunachal Pradesh, Manipur, Meghalaya, Mizoram, Nagaland, Puducherry, Sikkim, Telengana, Tripura and Uttrakhand.

The benefit of threshold exemption, however, is not available in the case of inter-state supplies of goods.

Threshold limit of aggregate turnover for exemption from registration and payment of GST for the suppliers of services is ₹ 20 lakh. It is ₹ 10 lakh in the case of Manipur, Mizoram, Nagaland, and Tripura.

35.5 To Be or Not to Be

An exempt business is outside the GST system. If its purchases are subject to GST, it will have to pay tax on them but it cannot recover the tax paid. Many small entrepreneurs feel that they can bypass GST if their turnover is less than the prescribed limit. However, this exemption has its own flip side. If a business is not under GST, the businesses it supplies to cannot get the benefit of input tax credit. They may eventually switch to vendors who are registered under GST and can issue invoices which include GST.

It is not necessarily an advantage to be exempt rather than standard-rated. A trader selling almost entirely to the general public will usually gain by being exempt, but he may find exemption a disadvantage if he is selling to registered traders in competition with registered traders. His potential customers in that case will prefer to buy from registered traders because then they can offset input tax against their output tax, which they cannot do if they purchase from an unregistered dealer.

Thus, even if a business is small with a turnover of less than the prescribed limit, it may be desirable for it, particularly a manufacturer supplying components to a large firm, to get itself registered under GST. The threshold limit scheme is optional. A business unit may be eligible for threshold exemption but it may still want to be part of the GST chain.

If a business obtains voluntary registration despite the turnover being below the prescribed limit, it would be treated as a normal taxable person. Every provision under the tax that applies to registered entities shall be applicable to it. Voluntary registration under GST has several advantages such as more freedom in inter-state sales, passing on of input tax credit etc. However, it is important to also have the technology ready for online payments.

Thus, to opt or not for GST registration depends upon the nature of business, judgement and business circumstances of an individual.

36

Composition Levy Scheme for MSMEs

Composition levy scheme (or simply composition scheme) is an important feature of GST for the benefit of MSMEs.

36.1 What is Composition Scheme under GST?

Composition scheme is an important feature of GST to protect the interests of small manufacturers, traders and service providers. A composition option (i.e. to pay tax at a flat rate without credits) is available to small taxpayers whose annual aggregate turnover does not exceed a specified limit. It is a kind of presumptive tax. [1] The objective of composition scheme is to bring simplicity and reduce compliance cost for small taxpayers. Composition scheme allows small businesses to avail a hassle-free compliance regime. It is noteworthy that these segments are large job creators and hence a priority area for the government.

In fact, composition scheme acknowledges the importance of MSMEs by granting lenient tax rates and compliance procedures.

Section 10 of the CGST Act, 2017, deals with the composition scheme.

36.2 Who Can Opt for Composition Scheme?

As per provisions effective April 1, 2019, small businessmen—being suppliers of goods and suppliers of restaurant services—with annual aggregate turnover up to ₹ 1.5 crore are eligible for the scheme. [2] In the case of Arunachal Pradesh, Manipur, Meghalaya, Mizoram, Nagaland, Sikkim, Tripura, and Uttarakhand, the eligibility limit is ₹ 75 lakh.

Aggregate turnover of the taxpayer in the immediately preceding financial year is considered. The methodology to compute *aggregate turnover* in the context of GST is given in Section 2(6) of the CGST Act, 2017. [3]

Rates of tax on turnover applicable for different categories of composition scheme dealers are given in Table 36.1.

Table 36.1: Rates of Tax on Turnover Applicable for Composition Scheme Dealers

S. No.	Category of registered person	Rate of tax
1.	Manufacturers and traders (goods)	1 percent (0.5 percent CGST plus 0.5 percent SGST) of the turnover
2.	Restaurants (not serving alcohol)	5 percent (2.5 percent CGST plus 2.5 percent SGST) of the turnover

Earlier, composition scheme dealers were required to file return every quarter. Effective April 1, 2019, they are allowed to file one annual return but making quarterly payment of taxes due. Composition scheme dealers are allowed to pay self-assessed tax on a quarterly basis till 18th of the month succeeding such quarter and furnish a return till April 30 for the previous financial year.

Composition scheme is not available to inter-state suppliers and specified category of manufacturers.

GST Council in its Thirty-second Meeting held on January 10, 2019 extended the composition scheme to service providers. Thus, effective April 1, 2019, suppliers of services (or mixed suppliers) having an annual turnover in the preceding financial year up to ₹ 50 lakh are eligible to enrol for the composition scheme.

Such service providers would have to pay GST at the rate of 6 percent (3 percent CGST + 3 percent SGST) of turnover. They are liable to file one annual return with quarterly payment of taxes (along with a simple declaration).

36.3 Persons Not Eligible for Composition Scheme

Following persons are not allowed to opt for the composition scheme.

1. Suppliers whose aggregate turnover in the preceding financial year crossed ₹ 1.5 crore (₹ 75 lakh in the case of Arunachal Pradesh, Manipur, Meghalaya, Mizoram, Nagaland, Sikkim, Tripura, and Uttarakhand.
2. A casual taxable person or a non-resident taxable person.
3. Suppliers making any supply of goods through an electronic commerce operator who is required to collect tax at source.
4. A manufacture of following goods: (a) ice cream and other edible ice, whether or not containing cocoa, (b) pan masala and (c) tobacco and manufactured tobacco substitutes.
5. Persons supplying goods which are not taxable under GST law.
6. Supplier who has purchased any goods or services from unregistered supplier unless he has paid GST on such goods or services on reverse charge basis.
7. Persons making any inter-State outward supplies of goods.

In short, composition scheme is not available to inter-state suppliers and specified category of manufacturers.

Taxable person who was not eligible for the composition scheme would be liable to pay tax, interest and in addition he shall also be liable to a penalty equivalent to the amount of tax payable.

36.4 Conditions for Availing Composition Scheme

1. A person under composition scheme cannot issue tax invoice. This is so because he is not allowed to charge GST from his customers. Hence, he has to issue a bill of supply. [4]
2. Such a person will have to pay tax on his total turnover out of his pocket as per the rates prescribed.

3. Input tax credit is not available to composition dealers. Similarly, input tax credit is not available to the person who gets supply of goods/services from a dealer under composition scheme.
4. A dealer under composition scheme cannot make any inter-state supply of goods.
5. He has to mention the words *Composition Taxable Person* on every notice or signboard displayed prominently at his place of business.
6. He has to mention the words *Composition Taxable Person* on every bill of supply issued by him.
7. Compulsory withdrawal from composition scheme is required if a person crosses the turnover of ₹ 1.5 crore/₹ 75 lakh. The option to pay tax under composition scheme shall lapse from the day on which his aggregate turnover during the financial year exceeds the prescribed limits. Once he crosses the limit, he shall file an intimation for withdrawal from the scheme in Form GST CMP-04 within 7 days of the occurrence of such event. He shall also furnish a statement in Form GST ITC-01 containing details of the stock of inputs and capital goods as per the rules in this regard. This would help him join the input tax credit chain and avail credit of tax that he has paid on his inputs/goods lying in stock on the day he crosses over.

36.5 How to Opt for Composition Scheme?

Composition scheme is optional. Intimation that the option has been availed should be made electronically in Form GST CMP-01. A person who has already obtained registration and opts for payment under composition scheme subsequently needs to give intimation electronically in Form GST CMP-02. This can be done online by logging into the GST portal. [5] This intimation should be given at the beginning of every financial year.

If a person has registration in multiple States, he cannot opt for payment of tax under composition scheme only in one State. In other words, the option to pay tax under composition scheme has to be exercised for all States. An intimation that composition scheme has been availed in one state shall be deemed to be an intimation in respect of all other places of business registered on the same PAN in other states.

36.5.1 Validity of Composition Levy: The option exercised by a registered person to pay tax under composition scheme shall remain valid so long as he satisfies all the conditions specified in the law. The option is not required to be renewed.

36.6 How to Withdraw from Composition Scheme?

A registered person who intends to withdraw from the composition scheme can file a duly signed or verified application in Form GST CMP-04. In case he wants to claim input tax credit on the stock of inputs and inputs contained in semi-finished or finished goods held in stock by him on the date of withdrawal, he is required to furnish a statement in Form GST ITC-01 containing the details of such stock within a period of 30 days of withdrawal.

Any intimation or application for withdrawal in respect of any place of business in any state or union territory, shall be deemed to be an intimation for withdrawal in respect of all other places of business registered on the same PAN.

36.7 Tax Payment under Composition Scheme

A registered person under composition scheme has no input tax credit. He would make all his tax payments by debit in the cash ledger maintained at the common portal. He can deposit cash at any time in the electronic cash ledger at his convenience. The payment in cash ledger can be made through all modes available like e-payment through net-banking, credit card/debit card, over the counter of banks, RTGS or NEFT.

36.8 Returns, Accounts and Records under Composition Scheme

A person opting to pay tax under composition scheme is required to furnish electronically, in Form GSTR-4, a quarterly return of turnover in the State or Union Territory, inward supplies of goods/services, tax payable and tax paid with in 18 days after the end of such quarter.

Rules on accounts and records provide details of the accounts to be maintained. They are maintained as per normal course of business by any small manufacturer. The details to be maintained in accounts consist of bills of supply, credit notes, debit notes, receipt vouchers, payment vouchers etc. The requirement to maintain detailed accounts of stocks in respect of goods received and supplied, work in progress, goods lost and destroyed does not apply to a manufacturer under composition scheme. A person under composition scheme need not maintain account of input tax, input tax credit claimed etc. because he is neither allowed to avail input tax credit nor can he issue an invoice showing tax so that the buyer may avail input tax credit.

A registered person under composition scheme need not specify HSN code of the products in the bill of supply.

36.9 Advantages and Disadvantages of Composition Scheme

36.9.1 Advantages: These are as under:

1. Rate structure under composition scheme is less burdensome than the regular GST rates.
2. A registered person has to pay GST on monthly basis on or before 20th of the succeeding month. A composition scheme dealer pays GST on a quarterly basis on or before the 18th day of the month after the end of the quarter.
3. Dealers under composition scheme are allowed to switch over to normal scheme during the year if they intend to do so.
4. Composition scheme is optional.
5. A dealer registered under composition scheme is not required to maintain detailed records. In other words, compliance burden—in terms of returns, maintenance of records, issuance of invoices etc.— is less for a composition dealer.

36.9.2 Disadvantages: Though the composition scheme requires lesser GST compliance, it has several drawbacks, particularly for the manufacturers.

1. A dealer under composition scheme cannot make any inter-state outward supply of goods. Hence, limited territory of business.
2. A person paying tax under composition scheme cannot make exports or supply goods to SEZ units because such supplies are treated as inter-State supplies. Similarly, he cannot be involved in imports.
3. A taxable person opting to pay tax under composition scheme is out of the credit chain. He cannot take input tax credit on the supplies received.
4. A composition scheme dealer cannot issue a tax invoice to his buyer. Instead, he issues a bill of supply. He cannot collect any tax on the supplies made by him on his bill of supply and is required to show only the price charged for the supply. Consequently, a registered person buying goods from a composition scheme dealer cannot take input tax credit.
5. If a composition scheme dealer purchases from a registered dealer, the former cannot avail credit of tax paid on his inputs.
6. Option availed by a registered person lapses with effect from the day on which his aggregate turnover during a financial year exceeds the limit specified under the scheme.
7. Composition scheme dealer is not eligible to supply goods through an e-commerce portal.
8. A person under composition scheme cannot do job work for other entities. Job work is a supply of service and hence not eligible for composition scheme. A person who wishes to carry out job work for others is not eligible for composition scheme.

Taking into account the advantages and disadvantages of the composition scheme mentioned above and his business circumstances, a person can decide whether to opt or not for the composition scheme.

Table 36.2 presents a comparison between regular dealer and a composition scheme dealer in terms of GST requirements.

Table 36.2: Regular versus Composition Scheme Dealer

Particulars	Regular dealer	Composition scheme dealer
Registration	• Threshold limit for the suppliers of goods: ₹ 40 lakh (₹ 20 lakh in the case of Arunachal Pradesh, Manipur, Meghalaya, Mizoram, Nagaland, Puducherry, Sikkim, Telengana, Tripura and Uttrakhand) • Threshold limit for the suppliers of services: ₹ 20 lakh (₹ 10 lakh in the case of Manipur, Mizoram, Nagaland, and Tripura)	• Threshold limit for suppliers of goods and suppliers of restaurant services: ₹ 1.5 crore (₹ 75 lakh for Arunachal Pradesh, Manipur, Meghalaya, Mizoram, Nagaland, Sikkim, Tripura, and Uttarakhand) • Threshold limit for suppliers of services (or mixed suppliers): ₹ 50 lakh

contd...

Particulars	Regular dealer	Composition scheme dealer
Territory of business	Intra-state as well as inter-state	Only intra-state
Input tax credit	Generally available	Not available
Business through e-commerce	Allowed	Not allowed
GST collection from buyer	Allowed	Not allowed
Tax invoice	Allowed	Not allowed; bill of supply instead
GST returns	Monthly	Quarterly
Switchover from regular to composition or vice versa	Relatively high compliance procedure	Compulsory registration under regular provisions once threshold is crossed

Endnotes

1. Presumptive tax relates to the use of appropriate indicators of income, wealth, sales etc. instead of the actual records of these tax bases. The chief advantage of presumptive taxation is its simplicity, both for the tax collectors and the taxpayers. It is, therefore, cost-effective for the administration. The simplicity attribute may also encourage tax compliance. Presumptive taxation particularly suits the developing countries with a large unorganised business sector consisting of small retail establishments, and self-employed professionals. It is easy to administer this tax which can become an effective source of revenue.
2. Initially, the turnover ceiling was ₹ 50 lakh which was increased to ₹ 75 lakh by the GST Council in its Sixteenth Meeting held on June 11, 2017. The limit for availing composition scheme was further relaxed to ₹ 1 crore in the Twenty-second Meeting of the GST Council held on October 6, 2017. In its Twenty-eighth Meeting held on July 21, 2018, the GST Council recommended this limit to be raised to ₹ 1.5 crore, requiring amendment in Section 10 of the CGST Act, 2017. The required amendment was passed by the Lok Sabha on August 9, 2018. The amendment was notified w.e.f. February 1, 2019. The enhanced eligibility limit became effective from April 1, 2019.
3. For the meaning of aggregate turnover, see section 35.2 of chapter 35 of this book.
4. **What is a Bill of Supply?** A business registered under GST issues a tax invoice to the buyer. Such an invoice mentions the GST rate charged on the goods and services sold. However, some businesses even though registered under GST cannot charge any tax on the invoice issued by them. Such dealers have to issue a bill of supply. A bill of supply is issued when GST is not applicable on a transaction or when GST is not to be recovered from the customer.

   How a tax invoice is different from a bill of supply? The difference lies both in name and details contained. While most of the details to be provided in a bill of supply are similar to a tax invoice, the former does not contain the rate of tax and the amount of tax charged as the same cannot be collected.

   Who Should Issue Bill of Supply? The following registrants should issue bill of supply:

   Composition Dealer: A taxpayer whose turnover is less than ₹ 1.5 crore can opt for composition scheme. A dealer opting for composition scheme has to deposit tax on their receipts themselves, they are not allowed to collect any tax from their buyers. The GST has to be paid out of pocket by the composition dealer. They cannot charge GST in the invoice.

   Thus a composition dealer has to raise a bill of supply instead of a tax invoice.

The composition dealer has to mention the words 'composition taxable person not eligible to collect taxes on supplies' on the bill of supply.

Exporters: An exporter is also not required to charge GST on his invoice. This is so because export supplies are zero-rated. Hence, a taxpayer exporting goods can issue a bill of supply in place of a tax invoice.

The dealer has to mention the following in his bill of supply:

Supply meant for export on payment of IGST; or

Supply meant for export under bond or letter of undertaking without payment of IGST.

Exempted Goods Supplier: When a registered dealer supplies exempt goods or services, he is required to issue bill of supply.

Contents of Bill of Supply: The GST law has specified certain particulars that should be present in a bill of supply. These are as under:

- Name, address, and GSTIN of the supplier.
- Bill of supply number.
- Date of issue.
- If the recipient is registered then the name, address, and GSTIN of the recipient.
- Description of goods/services.
- Value of the goods/services.
- HSN Code of goods or Accounting Code for services. The number of digits that are required to be mentioned based on turnover is as given in table below.

Turnover	**Number of HSN digits**
If turnover is less than ₹ 1.5 crore	HSN code is not required
If turnover is between ₹ 1.5 and 5 crore	2-digit HSN code
If turnover is above ₹ 5 crore	4-digit HSN code

- Signature or digital signature of the supplier.

5. The official GST portal-www.gst.gov.in is a one-stop solution website for all information, filing, queries and other technicalities related to the new GST regime. The portal also has all the GST-related laws and downloadable files which a taxpayer requires under GST.

37

Soft Tax Rate Policy for MSMEs

GST Council has taken measures in its various meetings for the benefit of MSMEs. Resultantly, goods predominantly manufactured and/or used in the unorganized MSMEs sector are either exempt or bear low rate of GST. Rate on jute and coir goods (like hand bags, ropes etc.), which are produced mainly in the cottage sector, has been reduced from 12 percent to 5 percent. Similarly, rate on fishing hooks, largely used by the fishermen, and the industry being labour-intensive, has been reduced from 12 percent to 5 percent. Electrical switches and wires, pipelines, plastic products etc. are largely produced by MSMEs and tax rate on these has been brought down from 28 percent to 18 percent.

37.1 Soft Tax Rate Policy in Relation to Goods

Following the recommendations of GST Council in its various meetings, GST rates on goods produced mainly in the MSMEs sector have been reduced from time-to-time. Table 37.1 depicts these rate reductions.

Table 37.1: Reduction of GST Rates on Goods Produced Mainly in the MSMEs Sector

Description of the item	**GST rate (percent)**	
	From	**To**
Twenty-first Meeting, September 9, 2017, Hyderabad		
• Rubber bands.	28	12
• Idols of wood and stone including marble and metals (other than those made of precious metals).	28	12
• Idols made of clay.	28	Nil
• Textile caps.	18	12
• Cotton quilts.	18	5 and 12*
• Rough industrial diamonds including unsorted diamonds.	3	0.25
Twenty-second Meeting, October 6, 2017, New Delhi		
• *Khakra.*	12	5
Twenty-third Meeting, November 10, 2017, Guwahati (Assam)		
• Wet grinder consisting of a stone as a grinder.	28	12
• Refined sugar and sugar cubes, pasta and curry paste.	18	12
• Puffed rice *chikki*, peanut *chikki*, sesame *chikki, gajak*.	18	5
• Finished leather.	12	5
• *Idli, dosa.*	12	5

contd...

• Fly ash bricks.	12	5
• Bangles of lac/shellac.	3	Nil
Twenty-fifth Meeting, January 18, 2018, New Delhi		
• Bamboo wood.	18	12
• Boiled sugar confectionary.	18	12
• Tamarind kernel powder.	18	5
• *Mehendi* paste in cones.	18	5
• Articles of straw, basketware and wickerwork.	12	5
Twenty-eighth Meeting, July 21, 2018, New Delhi		
• *Rakhi*, sanitary napkins, coir pith compost, sal leaves.	18, 12, 5	Nil
• Handloom dari, knitted caps.	12	5
• Bamboo flooring, brass kerosene pressure stove, zips and slide fasteners.	18	12
• Solid biofuel pellets.	18	5

*5 percent on those not exceeding ₹ 1,000 per piece and 12 percent on those exceeding ₹ 1,000 per piece.

37.2 Soft Tax Rate Policy in Relation to Services

Following the recommendations of GST Council in its various meetings, GST rates on services provided/received mainly by MSMEs sector have been reduced as under.

1. Two major services—in which large number of MSMEs are engaged, namely healthcare services provided by clinical establishments and educational services provided by educational institutions—are exempt from GST.
2. GST rate on most of the job work services, particularly in textile, leather, food processing, printing, jewellery and diamonds, handicrafts, has been reduced from 28 percent to 5 percent.
3. GST rate on government contracts for construction of roads, bridges, canals has been reduced from 18 percent to 12 percent.
4. Effective GST rate on construction of houses for poor under Pradhan Mantri Awas Yojana (PMAY) has been reduced from 12 percent to 5 percent.
5. GST rate on services provided by restaurants has been reduced from 18 percent to 5 percent (except restaurants in hotels having tariff of ₹ 7,500 per unit per day or more).
6. Hotel accommodation having tariff of less than ₹ 1,000 per day has been exempted and those having tariff up to ₹ 2,500 per day attract reduced rate of 12 percent. Both these types of accommodation are mainly provided by hotels in MSMEs sector.
7. Services of goods transport agencies (GTAs), which are mainly in the MSMEs sector, have been kept under reverse charge mechanism (RCM), thereby shifting the compliance burden on recipient of services. GTAs have also been given option to pay GST at 12 percent with full input tax credit (ITC) under forward charge.
8. Services supplied by an insurance agent, recovery agent or individual direct selling agents have been kept under RCM, thereby shifting the compliance burden on the recipient of services.

38

Simplified Compliance Procedures for MSMEs

It is understandable that the cost of compliance in terms of statutory laws is proportionately much higher for MSMEs as compared to large companies. Hence some relaxation benefits are necessary in order to help them cope with sudden increase or change in compliance challenges.

Large companies can hire the services of chartered accountants, software engineers, and computer operators to meet the compliance requirements of GST regime. The real problem of compliance lies with small businesses who cannot afford the services of experts to comply with GST laws and procedures.

38.1 Simplified Return Filing

Filing return under the GST regime is crucial as non-compliance or delay can result in penalties and adversely affect taxpayer's compliance rating and timely refunds.

Returns are self-assessed by the registered persons. A taxable person can take help of GST practitioner in filing returns etc. He can file return through GST Suvidha Providers (GSP). GSPs are third-party service providers, having access to the GST system, who can help taxpayers for GST compliance.

There is a provision for electronic filing of returns by different classes of persons at different cut-off dates. Returns, that allow the auto-population of data from the vendors and automated matching of invoices, are filed online by a normal/casual taxpayer in a sequential manner within different cut-off dates.

It may be noted that most of the returns are auto-generated by the GSTN system and the dealer is expected to validate the data and also fill in the missing data. The payment of tax due is a must for filing valid returns under the GST regime.

The return filing process, which faced severe criticism in the initial months of the roll out of GST, has been revamped for simplification. In its Twenty-eighth Meeting held on July 21, 2018, the GST Council approved the new return formats and associated changes in law to simplify the filing of returns.

On June 11, 2019, Government unveiled a transition plan for taxpayers under GST to switch to new and simpler return forms.

For details, see section 21.4 of chapter 21 of this book.

38.2 GST on Advances Received

Earlier, whenever a taxable person received advance, an *advance receipt voucher* was issued and the GST on the advance received was remitted to the Government. In case supply was later not provided and refund of advance was provided to the customer, then the supplier had to claim refund.

The requirement to pay GST on advances received was proving to be burdensome for small dealers and manufacturers. In order to mitigate their inconvenience on this account, the Twenty-second Meeting of the GST Council held on October 6, 2017 decided that taxpayers having annual aggregate turnover up to ₹ 1.5 crore shall not be required to pay GST at the time of receipt of advances on account of supply of goods. The GST on such supplies shall be payable only when the supply of goods is made.

38.3 Other Trade-friendly Measures for MSMEs

GST Council in its various meetings has been recommending trade-friendly measures for the benefit of MSMEs. Some of these measures are as under:

- Small retailers doing a large number of small transactions for up to a value of ₹ 200 per transaction to unregistered customers are not required to issue invoice for every such transaction. They can issue one consolidated invoice at the end of each day for all transactions done during the day. However, they should issue the invoice where the customer so demands. Similarly, in order to keep compliance burden low for small taxpayers, GST law provides that taxpayers with annual turnover of up to ₹ 1.5 crore need not mention the HSN Code of the goods in the invoices.
- Registered persons are allowed to issue consolidated credit/debit notes in respect of multiple invoices issued in a financial year.
- Commissioners are now empowered to extend the time limit for return of inputs and capital goods sent on job work, up to a period of 1 year and 2 years respectively.
- Amount of pre-deposit payable for filing of appeal under the CGST Act, 2017 before the Appellate Authority and Appellate Tribunal is capped at ₹ 25 crore and ₹ 50 crore respectively.
- Traders will not be denied credits for taxes paid while sourcing goods that are eventually given away free under discount schemes such as *buy one, get one free*.

39

Sector-specific Concessions and Reliefs

39.1 Handicrafts

Handicrafts are items made by hand with the use of simple tools, generally artistic and/or traditional in nature, which are used for decorative purposes, including as gifts and souvenirs as well as for utility purposes.

39.1.1 Importance of Handicrafts: Handicrafts activity is predominantly carried out in the unorganized household sector. Handicrafts sector is identified as the largest sector of rural employment after agriculture. This sector also touches upon the lives of the most marginalized and has the potential to transform the economy of difficult areas like the North East, Jammu and Kashmir, and desert habitations. It produces a range of items from utility goods, to clothing and variety of lifestyle items.

Handicrafts sector has its roots in the rich traditional, historical and cultural diversity that distinguishes India from the rest of the world. The sector is particularly significant as it provides low-cost and green livelihood opportunities to lakhs of families, besides supplementing incomes in times of agrarian distress, checking migration and preserving the traditional economic relationship between different sections of the society.

39.1.2 Decisions Taken at the Twenty-first Meeting of the GST Council (September 9, 2017): The following decisions were taken with regard to handicrafts.

A. Exemption from Registration for Making Inter-State Supplies: Previously, any person making inter-State taxable supplies was not eligible for threshold exemption of ₹ 20 lakh (₹ 10 lakh in special category states except J&K) and was liable for registration. It was decided to allow an exemption from registration to persons making inter-State taxable supplies of handicraft goods up to aggregate turnover of ₹ 20 lakh as long as the person has a permanent account number (PAN) and the goods move under the cover of an e-way bill, irrespective of the value of the consignment.

B. Reduction in Rates on Handicraft Items: GST rate was reduced from 28 percent to 12 percent on the following items:

1. Statues, pedestals, high or low reliefs, crosses, figures of animals, bowls, vases, cups, cachou boxes, writing-sets, ashtrays, paper weights, artificial fruit and foliage, other ornamental goods essentially of stone.
2. Stones inlay work.
3. Worked ivory, bone, tortoise-shell, horn, antlers, coral, and other animal carving material, and articles of these materials (including articles obtained by moulding).
4. Pots, jars and similar articles used for conveyance and packing of goods of ceramic.
5. Cane furniture.

GST rate was reduced from 18 percent to 12 percent on the following items:

1. Glass statues.

2. Table and kitchenware of wood.
3. Carved wood products like boxes, inlay work cases, casks etc.
4. Bells, gongs, mirrors of base metal, metal bidriware etc.

GST rate was reduced from 18 percent to 5 percent on paper mache articles.

GST rate was reduced from 12 percent to 5 percent on grass, leaf and reed and fibre products including mats, pouches, wallets.

39.1.3 Another Round of Reduction in Rates on Handicraft Items: In its Twenty-eighth meeting held on July 21, 2018, the GST Council reduced GST rate from 18 percent to 12 percent on the following handicraft items:

1. Handbags including pouches, purses and jewellery boxes.
2. Wooden frames for paintings, photographs, mirrors etc.
3. Artware of cork.
4. Stone artware.
5. Ornamental framed mirrors.
6. Glass statues.
7. Glass artware.
8. Artware of iron.
9. Artware of brass, copper etc.
10. Aluminium artware.
11. Handicrafted lamps.

39.2 Textiles

GST rate structure on all goods in the textile value chain was deliberated upon in the Fifteenth Meeting of the GST Council held on June 3, 2017. Based on the pre-GST tax incidence, the Council recommended 18 percent rate on made-made filaments and yarns. Further, considering that there was no tax on made-made fabrics in the pre-GST regime, the Council recommended to fix GST rate of 5 percent on all fabrics including man-made fabrics.

As per the recommendations of the GST Council in its Twenty-first Meeting held on September 9, 2017, Khadi fabrics sold through certified outlets of Khadi and Village Industries Commission were exempted from GST to provide relief to MSMEs sector. Further, GST rate on saree falls was reduced from 12 percent to 5 percent.

After a series of rate reductions, the present textile rate structure is as under:

1. All yarns of cotton and other natural fibres	5 percent
2. Man-made fibres	18 percent
3. Man-made fibre yarn	12 percent
4. *Zari*	5 percent
5. Jute twine or ropes	5 percent
6. Products of coir	5 percent
7. Readymade garments	
• Sale value not exceeding ₹ 1,000 per piece	5 percent
• Sale value exceeding ₹ 1,000 per piece	12 percent

Part VIII
A Critical Review of GST

40

Challenges and Issues Facing GST

Implementation of GST is undoubtedly the most significant tax reform, unparalleled in the fiscal history of India. It signifies the spirit of co-operative federalism. It also reaffirms India's desire to play an effective role in global economy. GST is one indirect tax for the whole country which has made India one unified common market.

However, GST is a completely new and evolving tax. It is not something given finally and once for all. There are problems in its implementation.

40.1 Fraudulent Transactions

Tax evasion/fraud through fraudulent practices is common to all taxes.

The proponents of GST claim that evasion under it is difficult and minimal. The tax credit method ensures cross-checking of the records of taxpayers through invoices. Buyer firms insist on supplier firms to furnish invoices which help the former to claim tax credit. Since tax liability of a single taxpayer under GST is only a fraction of the total amount of tax, the incentive for evasion is relatively weak. Even a successful evasion would mean less revenue loss as compared to the one suffered under a system of turnover tax on gross value (excise duty or sales tax).

Despite the self-policing nature of GST, opportunities do exist under it for evasion and fraud. Unscrupulous elements may adopt the following methods to defraud tax authorities:

1. Use of fake invoices to claim tax credit. Unscrupulous elements create shell/fake companies and issue invoices on the basis of which ITC is claimed.
2. Tax credit claims on purchases for personal use.
3. Secret deals between suppliers and buyers as regards issuance of invoices.
4. Small businesses may not register for GST.
5. Suppliers may reduce their liability by exaggerating the proportion of supplies subject to lower tax slabs.
6. Suppliers who collect the tax may not remit the same to the government.
7. Suppliers may make false claims for refunds.

More specifically, fraudulent invoices are generated to claim ITC without depositing the actual GST amount with the Government. There are reports of inter-state fraudulent transactions based on invoices issued by fake companies to avail ITC.

Invoices are generated without actual movement of goods and suppliers down the line claim input tax credit based on such fake invoices. Money earned through these fake transactions is actually black money which is laundered by unscrupulous entities by creating a web of shell companies.

There are also reports of GST registration numbers being generated in names of dead persons using fake addresses.

CENVAT and VAT, during pre-GST era, also suffered from such malpractices.

Thus, GST is as susceptible to evasion and fraud as any other tax. An efficient tax machinery capable of cross-checking a large number of invoices through an elaborate computer system is a pre-requisite for the successful implementation of GST.

Fraudulent claim of input tax credit by suppliers based on fake GST invoices is contravention of Section 16 of the CGST Act, 2017.

GST fraud is an administrative problem which can be solved through a vigilant Directorate General of GST Intelligence (DGGI). [1]

To curb possibilities of GST evasion, GST Council in its Thirty-fifth Meeting held on June 21, 2019, decided to introduce e-invoicing in a phased manner for business-to business (B2B) transactions. Phase I is proposed to be voluntary and will be rolled out in January 2020. E-invoicing would help tax authorities in combating the menace of tax evasion. In the same meeting, the Council made it mandatory for multiplexes to shift to an electronic ticketing system. Registered multiplexes shall be required to issue a tax invoice electronically. E-tickets issued by them shall be deemed to be tax invoices. This move was aimed at curbing possible tax evasion.

40.2 Need for Strong IT Infrastructure

During the pre-GST era, the Centre and State indirect tax administrations worked under different laws, regulations, procedures and formats and consequently their IT systems worked as independent sites. Integrating them for GST implementation is a formidable challenge since it would involve integrating the entire indirect tax ecosystem of the country to the same level of IT maturity with uniform formats and interfaces for taxpayers and other external stakeholders. Besides, GST being a destination-based tax, the inter-state trade of goods and services would need a robust settlement mechanism amongst the Centre and the States. This is possible only when there is a strong IT infrastructure and service backbone which enables to capture, process and exchange information amongst the stakeholders.

The number of taxpayers is likely to go up significantly in the future. Central Board of Indirect Taxes and Customs (CBIC) would need to prepare for meeting the implementation challenges, which are quite formidable. Capacity building, particularly in the field of accountancy and information technology for the departmental officers has to be taken up in a big way.

GST requires a very high level of compliance. The age of hand-written ledgers, account books, balance sheets and manual record-keeping is gone. Everything will now be online and need to be updated regularly. A robust and fail-proof information technology (IT) framework is an essential pre-requisite for the success of the GST, given the large volume of transactions involved.

40.3 Public Outreach and Knowledge Sharing

It is expected that a momentous reform like GST is popularized and familiarized to trade and industry which are the vital stakeholders in successful implementation of this reform. Massive public outreach and knowledge sharing programmes are being conducted by various formations of CBIC. GST is not merely a tax reform. It is also a reform that will revolutionize the way business is conducted in India.

Besides, sensitising industry and public through information dissemination such as release of legislative documents and conducting outreach programmes and media interactions with the tax authorities are also critical. Furthermore, tax laws need to be simplified to avoid definitional issues and defray administrative costs.

To exploit the benefits of GST fully, it needs to be ensured that tax compliance costs are low and tax credits are available seamlessly across tax jurisdictions. Apart from uniform tax rates, this will also require harmonisation of procedures for levy, assessment, appropriation and even audit, between the States and the Centre, as well as amongst the States themselves.

40.4 Progressivity of GST

GST is an indirect tax. Like any other indirect tax, it is a hidden tax, lacking equity attribute. Indirect taxes do not allow considerations for the personal circumstances of taxpayers as do direct taxes. Indirect taxes are borne in relation to the consumption expenditure which constitutes a higher percentage of income for lower income groups than for persons in higher income brackets. Hence, indirect taxes are regressive by nature, meaning thereby that the poor pay more, as a percentage of their income, than the rich.

Degree of progressivity (or regressivity) of indirect taxes depends on the following factors: (a) selection of commodities for taxation and (b) the rate of tax on them. It is, therefore, always desirable that luxuries and comforts are chosen for heavy taxation with necessities of life either exempted or moderately taxed. However, in poor countries the demand for luxury items is limited apart from being price elastic. Conversely, the demand for necessities is vast and price inelastic, obliging tax authorities to extend the tax net to daily needs. This has a tendency to fuel inflation.

Analysis of rate structure of GST on goods reveals that many essential goods of mass consumption are either exempt from GST or bear a low rate which is affordable for the general public. Contrarily, demerit and ultra-luxury goods are subject to the highest rate of 28 percent plus compensation cess. It cannot be denied that GST Council has made efforts to improve progressivity (or reduce regressivity) of GST after its roll out from July 1, 2017.

40.5 Dispute Resolution Mechanism

Tax disputes often arise due to differences in the interpretation of the taxation law by the tax imposing authority and the taxpayers. Hence, all efforts should be made to simplify tax laws to avoid ambiguity and ensuring effective and timely settlement through a dispute resolution mechanism. It is a pre-requisite for the overall efficiency of tax administration and a conductive business environment. Under GST, multiple parties such as the Centre, States, and taxpayers are involved and the possibility of such disputes arising cannot be ignored. Disagreement may arise at several levels—between the Centre and States, among the States, and between taxpayers and tax authorities.

Article 279A of the Constitution empowers the GST Council to decide about the modalities of dispute resolution. Transparency in rules and procedures, easy availability of information, cooperation among the relevant parties, and guidance by tax authorities in filing returns may go a long way in minimising cases of disputes. This would minimise recourse to dispute settlement procedures.

Government receives representations from trade bodies, trade unions, associations and NGOs for tax reliefs and simpler procedures. These are considered and appropriate decisions are taken. In the case of GST, the country has a unique institutional mechanism with constitutional force, namely the GST Council. Even after the introduction of GST from July 1, 2017, the Council has met several times and successfully sorted out problems coming in the way of smooth functioning of GST.

40.6 Fiscal Autonomy of States

There are some sporadic voices criticizing GST for encroaching upon fiscal autonomy of States. The question of encroachment of financial/fiscal autonomy arises when one entity tries to impose its will or decisions on the other entity. In the context of India's federal structure, it can mean attempts by the Central Government to make inroads into subjects reserved for State Governments.

As regards GST, all decisions are taken by the GST Council—a constitutional body—which is a joint forum of the Centre and the States. Apart from the Centre, all the 29 regular States and 2 Union Territories with legislature (Delhi and Puducherry) find representation on it.

In all the 35 meetings of the Council held so far, decisions have been taken either unanimously or through consensus. Thus, when the States themselves are deciding for themselves then where is the question of financial autonomy being encroached upon.

In the Sixteenth Meeting of the Council held on June 11, 2017, all the States decided to roll out GST from July 1, 2017. GST Council is a unique example of co-operative federalism and it is discharging its functions to the satisfaction all parties.

Moreover, tax devolution from the Centre is different from SGST collections. What percentage of Central tax collections would be allocated to the states is decided by the Finance Commission. How the States' share would be distributed among the states is also decided by the Finance Commission. One can say that states are dependent on the Centre for tax revenues.

However, states are equal partners with the Centre in levying GST. SGST is levied, collected and appropriated by the states. Business entities collect SGST and deposit it directly into the account of the state government. So where is the loss of power to collect revenue?

See also sections 32.5 and 32.6 of chapter 32 of this book.

To sum up, Indian GST is 21st century standard for VAT in federal systems. Implementation of GST has left behind an inefficient, complicated and fragmented indirect tax system. Switch over to GST has led to many problems—administrative and technical. However, such problems are endemic of any change of revolutionary proportions and no one should expect a foolproof system from day one. Many of the problems are transitory in nature. GST Council has successfully sorted out differences among the stakeholders and it is competent enough to deal with any future challenges.

GST is a historic and game-changing tax reform. Domestically, it will help improve governance, strengthen tax institutions, facilitate *make-in-India by making-one-India*, and impart buoyancy to the tax base.

Endnote

1. DGGI is the apex intelligence agency under Central Board of Indirect Taxes and Customs (CBIC). It is the enforcement arm of the CBIC that focuses on anti-evasion work of GST. For details, see section 25.2.5 (B) of chapter 25 of this book.

41

GST: An Incomplete Journey

GST journey is incomplete because excise duties on alcoholic liquors are outside its purview. Five petroleum products—petroleum crude, high speed diesel, petrol, natural gas and aviation turbine fuel—though constitutionally under GST, are not subject to GST because GST Council has not taken any decision in this regard. Centre continues to impose excise duties and the states continue to impose VAT on these petroleum products.

Tobacco and tobacco products are subject to GST as well as Central excise.

States levy duty on electricity but GST is applicable only to ancillary services related to electricity.

Furthermore, taxes on entertainment and amusements are levied by states, through local bodies, and are also subject to GST.

The above underlines the need for further unification and uniformity of indirect tax structure of the country under the umbrella of GST.

41.1 Alcoholic Liquors

Excise duty on alcoholic liquors by the states is a colonial legacy. It is the only tax which is outside the purview of GST.

Under Entry 51 of List II (State List) in the Seventh Schedule of the Constitution, the States are empowered to levy, "duties of excise on: (a) alcoholic liquors for human consumption; (b) opium, Indian hemp and other narcotic drugs and narcotics; but not including medicinal and toilet preparations containing alcohol or any substance included in sub-paragraph (b) of this entry". The revenues accrue to the states in the form of licence duties from the vendors as well as the tax, which can be specific or ad valorem. Excise duties (on liquors and other narcotics) are an important source of States' own tax revenues.

It is noteworthy that while in Western countries the main objective of duties on intoxicants is revenue collection, in India the overriding consideration in imposing these duties is to discourage consumption of intoxicants as a matter of public policy. Since demand for alcoholic beverages is generally price-inelastic, this tax provides a case for keeping high tax rates for controlling the level of consumption. In fact, high tax rates yield both high revenues and greater control on consumption.

Some states have adopted the policy of prohibition (Gujarat and Bihar). However, it has resulted in export of the tax base to the neighbouring states. Bihar was declared a dry state on April 5, 2017. Media reports suggest that illegal alcohol is being smuggled in Bihar from neighbouring states (Uttar Pradesh, West Bengal and Jharkhand). As a result, revenue from excise on liquor in these states has shown an upward trend at the cost of Bihar. It goes to the credit of Bihar Chief Minister Shri Nitish Kumar who has preferred alcoholic-free environment in his state to revenue earning. Undoubtedly, liquor consumption impacts the society negatively.

GST represents national policy regarding the taxation of various goods and services. Then why there is no national policy on consumption and taxation of liquor? A national policy on taxation of alcoholic consumption is possible only when this *sin* commodity is brought under the purview of GST. This will also be in line with the true spirit of *one-nation, one-tax*.

See also section 15.2 of chapter 15 of this book.

41.2 Petroleum Products

By virtue of Article 279A (5) of the Constitution, the following five petroleum products are part of the GST regime: (a) petroleum crude, (b) high speed diesel, (c) motor spirit (commonly known as petrol), (d) natural gas and (e) aviation turbine fuel. However, the date on which GST would be levied on these petroleum products is yet to be decided by the Goods and Services Tax Council (GST Council), the constitutionally established joint forum of the Centre and the States. GST on petroleum products is a constitutional obligation.

Thus, the levy of GST on the five petroleum products would continue to hang in balance till notified at a future date on the recommendations of the GST Council. It is noteworthy that two other petroleum products (domestic LPG and PDS kerosene) are already subject to GST under the 5 percent rate category.

In the absence of GST on the said five petroleum items, the Centre continues to levy excise duty on them. Likewise, the States are levying sales tax/VAT on them. While the rate of excise duty has uniform applicability throughout India, the rate of sales tax/VAT differs from state to state because each state has its own legislation for the purpose. This is the reason why prices of the five petroleum items (mainly petrol and diesel) vary in different states.

What are the implications of inter-state variations in the prices of petrol and diesel?

Firstly, it leads to uneconomic diversion of trade. Consumers living close to inter-state borders are tempted to get their fuel tanks filled in the state where prices are lower. Apparently, they will go to the neighbouring state when the saving (in terms of lower prices) is more than the cost of a to and fro trip to the lower price state. Through this exercise an individual may save a few rupees, but the two-way unnecessary commute does entail a national loss which can be avoided if petrol/diesel prices are uniform across states. [1]

Uneconomic diversion of trade due to tax differentials is not a new phenomenon. During the pre-GST era, it was not uncommon for residents of one state to make purchases of consumer durables in other states because the sales tax (later on VAT) rates differed and therefore the market prices. A case in point was the purchase of motor cars. Haryana was a favourite destination for the residents of Delhi to buy cars because the rate of VAT on the product was lower as compared to Delhi. This is why some Delhi residents own cars with Haryana number plates. Purchase of truck chassis in Daman (a Union Territory levying a low rate of 3 percent VAT) by residents of a far-flung Jammu and Kashmir was another popular example in tax annals.

Similarly, rate differentials caused flight of capital and enterprise from high to low tax rate States thereby distorting natural selection of production centres based on geographical advantages. This led to unnecessary transportation of raw materials and finished goods and hence cost escalations. Such misallocation of resources undermined economic efficiency and thereby retarded developmental efforts.

After the introduction of GST from July 1, 2017, there is no incentive for residents of one state to make purchases in other states because GST rates on goods and services are uniform through out the country.

The second problem relates to the total tax burden on petroleum products. As things stand, there are many components of the price of a petroleum product (say petrol) as sold at the filling station. Chief among these components is the import price of crude oil which is subject to variations depending on international events. A rise in crude oil price in the international market adversely affects India because the commodity in question is a major item of the country's imports. Higher landing cost of crude oil is reflected in the price of petrol.

Under this scenario, one option to give relief to consumers is to reduce the total tax burden on petrol (excise duty by the Centre and VAT by the States). Recent experience shows that the Centre looks up to the States to reduce VAT while the States expect the Centre to do the needful. In this *war of expectations*, the users of petrol continue to suffer. Unreasonable increase in the price of petrol and diesel can have deleterious effects on the economy. The entire transportation sector is dislocated and disrupted. Input costs go up, causing chain reaction on the prices of finished products.

If petroleum products are brought under the purview of GST, a national policy can be worked out, under the aegis of the GST Council, as regards the total tax burden on different petroleum products. In other words, the rate of GST on the five petroleum products can be determined. What should be this rate?

GST Council has generally followed the principle of *revenue neutrality* in its earlier decisions on rate fixation for various goods and services. Revenue neutrality implies that the revenue from the new tax (in this case GST) should be almost the same as from the tax subsumed under GST. It is for the experts to work out the new rates for the purpose.

Suppose there is a shortfall in tax revenue under the new system. This loss of revenue would be shared equally by the Centre and the States because GST revenue (CGST + SGST) is shared between them in the ratio of 50:50. It means the Centre and the States sink and swim together as regards GST revenue.

The possibility of reduction in revenue may be a cause for worry on part of the Centre but States are adequately protected against such eventuality. There is a constitutional guarantee to the States that in no case would they suffer revenue loss on account of implementation of GST. In this connection, section 18 of the Constitution (One Hundred and First Amendment) Act, 2016 reads, "Parliament shall, by law, on the recommendation of the Goods and Services Tax Council, provide for compensation to the States for loss of revenue arising on account of implementation of the goods and services tax for a period of five years".

Pursuant to the stated constitutional provision, Parliament passed the Goods and Services Tax (Compensation to States), Act, 2017 which provides for compensation to the States for loss of revenue arising from implementation of GST. Not only this, Section 3 of the Act also provides for 14 percent annual growth in revenue from the tax subsumed under GST.

Section 8 of the Act provides for the levy and collection of cess—over the peak rate (28 percent)—on *paan masala*, tobacco, coal, aerated waters, and motor cars to create a fund for compensating States. The cess is to continue for a period of five years "or for such period as may be prescribed on the recommendations of the Council". It means States can continue to be compensated even after the expiry of the five years period if the GST Council so recommends.

In view of the above safeguards, there is no reason for any State to ask for delays in levying GST on petroleum products. The apprehension of some States that their resource position would be adversely affected is misplaced.

Incidentally, compensation to States under GST is not the first instance of its kind. In the early years of 2000s, when the Central Government was encouraging States to switch from sales tax to VAT, it did provide incentives in the form of compensation to States in case any of them suffered loss in the transitional years of such switch over.

Critics might argue that GST is yet to stabilize and more time is needed before it is imposed on petroleum products. It is true that the introduction of GST from July 1, 2017 created many problems, particularly for small business entities. However, these problems have largely been addressed and resolved by the GST Council in its various meetings held after the introduction of GST. GST has successfully transited from turbulence to tranquillity in its more than 2 years existence.

Moreover, GST is a continuing and evolving process. GST Council has come to symbolize the true spirit of co-operative federalism in India. Apart from the Centre, all the 29 regular States and the 2 Union Territories with legislatures (Delhi and Puducherry) find representation on it. In all the 35 meetings of the Council held so far—18 meetings before and 17 after the roll out of GST—decisions have been taken either unanimously or through consensus, i.e. no occasion has arisen so far that required voting to decide any matter. The decision to levy GST on petroleum products should also be taken keeping national interest in mind over any other consideration.

See also section 15.3 of chapter 15 of this book.

41.3 Tobacco and Tobacco Products

The most effective way to reduce tobacco use is to raise the price of tobacco and tobacco products through tax increases. Higher prices discourage youth from initiating cigarette smoking and encourage current smokers to quit.

Tobacco and tobacco products are subject to highest rate of GST (28 percent). In addition, they are also subject to GST compensation cess.

Centre is also continuing to levy excise duty on tobacco and tobacco products. This is so because Entry 84 of Union List (List I) of the Seventh Schedule of the Constitution was amended by section 17 of the Constitution (One Hundred and First Amendment) Act, 2016 in the following manner.

Earlier, Entry 84 comprised duties of excise on tobacco and other goods manufactured or produced in India except alcoholic liquors for human consumption etc. After the amendment, it comprises duties of excise on the following goods manufactured or produced in India, namely: (a) petroleum crude; (b) high speed diesel; (c) motor spirit (commonly known as petrol); (d) natural gas; (e) aviation turbine fuel; and (f) tobacco and tobacco products.

GST as well as Central excise on tobacco has created complications for the tobacco industry. Rationalization of tobacco taxation in the country is called for.

For more clarity, see Entry 84 in Table 10.1 of chapter 10 of this book.

41.4 Electricity Duty

Under Entry 53 of List II (State List) in the Seventh Schedule of the Constitution, electricity duty is charged to consumers along with the electricity consumption rates. The rates are meant for the providers of electricity (electricity boards) while the electricity duty is meant for the state treasury. Electricity duty is defined as per policy laid down by the Central Government (Ministry of Power) in Tariff Policy.

There is no constitutional bar on levy of GST on electricity. However, transmission or distribution of electricity by an electricity transmission or distribution utility is exempt service under GST. [2] Only ancillary services rendered by electricity distribution companies (DISCOMs) are taxable. [3] The following services are taxable under GST at the rate of 18 percent.

1. Application fee for releasing connection of electricity.
2. Rental charges against metering equipment.
3. Testing fee for meters/transformers, capacitors etc.
4. Labour charges from customers for shifting of meters or shifting of service lines.
5. Charges for duplicate bill.

Bringing electricity under GST would make this sector more competitive.

41.5 Taxes on Entertainments and Amusements

As per Entry 62 of List II (State List) in the Seventh Schedule (read with Article 246) of the Constitution of India, State Governments have jurisdiction over "taxes on entertainments and amusements to the extent levied and collected by a *panchayat* or a municipality or a regional council or a district council." It is noteworthy that taxes on luxuries, including taxes on entertainment, amusements, betting and gambling levied by State Governments were subsumed under GST.

See Entry 62 in Table 10.2 of chapter 10 of this book.

Thus, State Governments, through their local bodies, levy taxes on entertainments and amusements. GST is also leviable on these services.

From January 25, 2018, admission tickets to circus, dance, theatrical performances (including drama or dance, award functions, pageants, concerts, musical performances, recognised sporting events and planetarium) up to ₹500 per person were exempted from GST. Again, GST on tickets to amusement parks, including theme parks, water parks and merry-go-rounds, was reduced from 28 percent to 18 percent with effect from January 25, 2018.

Above measures were taken to promote social wellness, cultural and sports events in the country. However, for the success of these measures it is necessary that municipalities and panchayats do not increase the local taxes on entertainments and amusements and help keep the tax burden low. However, the fact is that State Governments are always nudging their local bodies to increase revenues through taxation of these services.

Endnotes

1. Taking note of the uneconomic diversion of trade, 5 States—Haryana, Punjab, Delhi, Himachal Pradesh and Uttar Pradesh—and the Union Territory of Chandigarh agreed on September 25, 2018 to move towards uniform fuel prices and a committee of officers was set up for this purpose. The objective of the initiative was to discourage consumers in one state to buy petrol/diesel in the neighbouring state due to different VAT rates and hence different fuel prices.
2. As per the notification No. 12/2017 (Central Rates) dated June 28, 2017.
3. As per the Circular No. 34/8/2018-GST dated March 1, 2018.

Bibliography

Ahmad, E. and N. Stern (1991), "Theory and Practice of Tax Reforms in Developing Countries", Cambridge University Press.

Ahmad, E. and N. Stern (1984), "The Theory of Tax Reform and Indian Indirect Taxes", *Journal of Public Economics*, Volume 25, pp. 259-298.

Aronson, Richard (1985), "Public Finance", New York: McGraw-Hill Book Company.

Bagchi, Amaresh et al. (1994), "Reform of Domestic Trade Taxes in India: Issues and Options", New Delhi: National Institute of Public Finance and Policy.

Barrand, Peter (1991), "The Treatment of Non-Profit Bodies and Government Entities under the New Zealand GST", *International VAT Monitor*, January.

Bird, Richard and Oliver Oldman (ed.) (1967), "Readings on Taxation in Developing Countries", Baltimore: The Johns Hopkins Press.

Bird, Richard (1970), "Taxation and Development", Harvard University Press.

Bird, Richard and P. Gendron (1998), "Dual VATs and Cross-border Trade, Two Problems and One Solution", *International Tax and Public Finance*, 5(3).

Canada Department of Finance (1987), "Federal Sales Tax Reform", Government of Canada.

Chakraborty, Pinaki and Manish Gupta (2016), "Evolving Centre-State Financial Relations", *Economic and Political Weekly*, Volume L1, Number 16.

Cutt, James (1969), "Taxation and Economic Development in India", New Delhi: Vikas Publications.

Empowered Committee of State Finance Ministers (2008), "A Model and Roadmap for Goods and Services Tax in India", New Delhi.

—(2009), "First Discussion Paper on Goods and Services Tax in India", New Delhi, November 10.

—Model GST Law, June 2016.

Gobin, Roy T. (1980), "An Analysis of the System of Sales Taxation in Caribbean Market", *Public Finance*, Volume XXXV, Number 2, pp. 272-273.

Government of India (1953-54), "Report of the Taxation Enquiry Commission", (Chairman: John Matthai), Volumes I, II and III.

—(1963), "Report of the Central Excise Reorganisation Committee" (Chairman: A.K. Chanda).

—(1964), "Report of the Committee on Sales Tax" (Chairman: R.G. Saraiya).

—(1968), "Final Report on Rationalisation and Simplification of Tax Structure" (Chairman: S. Bhoothalingam).

—(1973), "Report of the Central Excise (Self-Removal Procedure) Review Committee" (Chairman: B. Venkatappiah).

—(1977), "Report of the Indirect Taxation Enquiry Committee" (Chairman: L.K. Jha). Part I.

——(1978), "Report of the Indirect Taxation Enquiry Committee" (Chairman: L.K. Jha), Part II, January.

——(1980), "Report of the Expert Committee on Tax Measures to Promote Employment" (Chairman: V.M. Dandekar).

——(1983), "Report of the Expert Committee on Replacement of Sales Tax by Additional Excise Duty" (Chairman: Kamlapati Tripathi), January.

——(1985), "Long Term Fiscal Policy", December.

——(1985), "Report of the Technical Study Group on Central Excise Tariff" (Chairman: J. Datta), Part I.

——(1988), "Report of the Commission on Centre-State Relations" (Chairman: R.S. Sarkaria), Part I.

——(1991), "Interim Report of the Tax Reforms Committee" (Chairman: Raja Chelliah), December.

——(1992), "Final Report of the Tax Reforms Committee" (Chairman: Raja Chelliah), Part I.

——(2002), "Report of the Task Force on Indirect Taxes" (Chairman: Vijay Kelkar), December.

——(2003), Ministry of Finance, "Report on Implementation of the Fiscal Responsibility and Budget Management Act, 2003" (Chairman: Vijay Kelkar).

——(2005), "White Paper on State-Level Value Added Tax" (Chairman: Asim Kumar Dasgupta).

——(2012), Ministry of Finance, "White Paper on Black Money", May.

——(2015), Ministry of Finance, "Report on the Revenue Neutral Rate and Structure of Rates for the Goods and Services Tax (GST), December 4" (Chairman: Arvind Subramanian).

——(2016), "The Constitution (One Hundred and First Amendment) Act", September.

——(2017), "GST: Concept and Status", Central Board of Excise and Customs (CBEC), May 1, 2019.

——Ministry of Finance, Budget Papers (various years).

——Ministry of Finance, Economic Survey (various issues).

——Reports of Finance Commissions.

——Ministry of Law and Justice, "Constitution of India" (As on July 31, 2018).

James, Simon and Christopher Nobes (1978), "The Economics of Taxation", Oxford: Philip Allen.

Keen, Michael (2015), "Targeting an Indirect Tax Design", Inequality and Fiscal Policy, International Monetary Fund.

Kuo, C.Y., Tom McGirr and Saya Poddar (1988), "Measuring the Non-neutralities of Sales and Excise Taxes in Canada", *Canadian Tax Journal*, Volume 38.

Leemput, E.V. and E.A. Wiencek (2017), "The Effect of the GST on Indian Growth", International Finance Discussion Paper, March.

Mahler, Walter (1970), "Sales and Excise Taxation in India", New Delhi: Orient Longman Ltd.

Makin, A.J. and R. Arora (2012), "Fiscal Sustainability in India at State Level", *Public Finance and Management*, Volume 12, Number 4, October.

McLure, Charles (2000), "Implementing Sub-national VATs on Internal Trade: The Compensating VAT (CVAT)", *International Trade and Public Finance*, Volume 7.

Millar, Rebecca (2007), "Cross-border Services: A Survey of the Issues", in Krever, Richard and David White (eds.), 'GST in Retrospect and Prospect', New Zealand: Brookers Ltd.

Musgrave, Richard and Peggy Musgrave (1989), "Public Finance in Theory and Practice", New York: McGraw-Hill Book Company.

National Council of Applied Economic Research (2009), "Moving to Goods and Services Tax in India: Impact on India's Growth and International Trade", Prepared for the Thirteenth Finance Commission Government of India, Working Paper Number. 103, December.

OECD (2004), "Report on the Application of Consumption Taxes to the Trade in International Services and Intangibles", Centre for Tax Policy and Administration, OECD.

Palil, Mohd. Rizal and Mohd. Adha Ibrahim (2011), "The Impacts of Goods and Services Tax (GST) on Middle Income Earners in Malaysia", *World Review of Business Research*, Volume 1, Number 3, July.

Panagariya Arvind, Pinaki Chakraborty and M. Govinda Rao (2015), "Growth and Development of States in India", New York: Oxford University Press.

Peacock, Alan and Francesco Forte (eds.) (1981), "The Political Economy of Taxation", Oxford: Basil Blackwell.

Poddar, S. and M. English (1997), "Taxation of Financial Services under a Value-added Tax: Applying the Cash-flow Method", *National Tax Journal*, pp. 89-111.

Poddar, Satya (1990), "Options for s VAT at the State Level", in M. Gillis, C.S. Shoup and G. Sicat (eds.), 'Value Added Taxation in Developing Countries', Washington D.C.: World Bank.

—(003), "Consumption Taxes: The Role of the Value Added Tax", in Patrick Honohan (ed.), 'Taxation of Financial Intermediation: Theory and Practice in Emerging Economies', World Bank and the Oxford University Press.

—(2007), "VAT on Financial Services: Searching for a Workable Compromise", in Krever, Richard and David White (eds.), 'GST in Retrospect and Prospect', New Zealand: Brookers Ltd.

Poddar, Satya and Amaresh Bagchi (2007), "Revenue-neutral Rate for GST", *The Economic Times*, November 15.

Poddar, Satya and Nancy Harley (1989), "Problems in Moving from a Flawed to a Neutral and Broad-based Consumption Tax", *Australian Tax Forum*, Volume 6, Number 3.

Poddar, Satya, and Eric Hutton (2001), "Zero-Rating of Inter-State Sales under a Sub-national VAT: A New Approach", paper presented at the National Tax Association, 94th Annual Conference on Taxation, Baltimore, November 8-10.

Pomeranz, Dina (2013), "No Taxation without Information: Deterrence and Self-Enforcement in the Value Added Tax", Harvard University and NBER.

Prest, A.R. (1970), "Public Finance in Theory and Practice", London: Weidenfeld and Nicolson.

Rangarajan, C. and D.K. Srivastava (2011), "Federalism and Fiscal Transfers in India", New Delhi: Oxford University Press.

Rao, Kavita (2014), "Revenue Implications of GST and Estimation of Revenue Neutral Rate: Estimates for 2011-12", New Delhi: National Institute of Public Finance and Policy.

Rao, M. Govinda (2001), "Report of the Expert Group on Taxation of Services", Government of India, March.

Rao, K. (2008), "Goods and Services Tax for India", NIPFP Working Paper Number 57, November.

Rao, M.G. and N. Singh (2005), "The Political Economy of Federalism in India", New Delhi: Oxford University Press.

Reserve Bank of India, *Report on Currency and Finance* (various years).

—(2015), "State Finances: A Study of Budgets of 2014-15", May.

Sandford, C.T. et al. (1981), "Costs and Benefits of VAT", London: Heinemann Educational Books.

Shakdher, S.L. (1979), "The Budget and the Parliament", New Delhi: National Publishing House.

World Bank (2015), "Fiscal Policy for Equitable Growth", India Development Report.

Zhou, L.Z., J. Tam and J. Heng-Contaxis (2013), "The Introduction of Goods and Services Tax in Malaysia: A Policy Analysis", CPSS Policy Paper Series, October 22.

Websites

Ministry of Finance

Ministry of Micro, Small and Medium Enterprises

Ministry of Law and Justice

Central Board of Indirect Taxes and Customs (CBIC)

Goods and Services Tax Council (GST Council)

Reserve Bank of India

NITI Aayog

Index